The Ancient World

D1416082

The Ancient World

HELEN HOWE
ROBERT T. HOWE

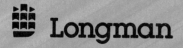

Longman

Authors:
Helen Howe
teacher of Ancient and Medieval History and of
Latin at Walnut Hills High School, Cincinnati, Ohio
Robert Howe
Professor Emeritus, University of Cincinnati

Executive Editor   **Lyn McLean**
Production Director   **Ed Castillo**
Developmental Editor   **Anne Jensen**
Project Designer   **Gayle Jaeger**
Photo Researcher   **Katherine Rangoon**
Art Studio   **J & R Art Services, Inc.**

ISBN 0-582-36761-1

Longman
95 Church St.
White Plains, New York 10601

Associated Companies:
Longman Group Ltd., London
Longman Cheshire Pty., Melbourne
Longman Paul Pty., Auckland
Copp Clark Pitman, Toronto
Pitman Publishing Inc., New York

Copyright © 1992 by Longman. All rights reserved.
No part of this publication may be reproduced, stored
in a retrieval system, or transmitted in any form or by
an means, electronic, mechanical, photocopying,
recording, or otherwise, without prior permission
of the publisher.

Supplementary Materials:
Teacher's Handbook
Worksheet Masters

4 5 6 7 8 9 10-DO-9594939291

Contributing Editor:
Dean Moore
Supervisor of Social Studies
Cincinnati Public Schools

Consultants:
Mildred Alpern
History Teacher
Spring Valley Senior High School, New York

Wentworth Clarke
Professor of Social Science Education
University of Central Florida at Orlando

William R. Dunnagan
Social Studies Teacher
Klein Independent School District, Texas

Roy Erickson
Program Specialist for Social Studies
San Juan School District, California

Jean Hutt
Social Studies Department Chairperson
Saline Area Schools, Michigan

Mary Lauranne Lifka
Professor of History
College of Saint Teresa
Winona, Minnesota

Roy R. Pellicano
Professor of Education, Social Studies Teacher
Brooklyn, New York

Denny Schillings
Western Civilization Teacher
Homewood-Flossmoor High School, Illinois

William White
Past Coordinator of Social Sciences
Jefferson County Public Schools, Colorado

Special thanks to:
Grace and Roy Pellicano
authors of chapters on India, China, Japan, Africa, and Middle America
Samuel Jenike
author of the Prologue and Prehistory chapters

v

Contents

Maps

Acknowledgments/Credits

BIBLIOGRAPHY
The following editions of classical works have been cited in the text, except where otherwise noted.
Aristophanes. *Aristophanes.* Translated by Patric Dickinson. Oxford University Press, 1970.
Arrian. *The Anabasis of Alexander.* Translated by J.G. Lloyd. Cambridge University Press, 1981.
Caesar. *Caesar's War Commentaries.* Edited and translated by John Warrington. Everyman. New York: E. P. Dutton. London: J. M. Dent, 1953.
Demosthenes. *Demosthenes.* Translated by J.A. Vince. London: William Heinemann Ltd. New York: G. P. Putnam's Sons, 1930.
Hadas, Moses. *A History of Rome from its Origins to 529 A.D. as told by Roman Historians.* Gloucester, Mass.: Peter Smith, 1976.
Hesiod. *Hesiod.* Translated by Richmond Lattimore. University of Michigan Press, 1959.
Howe, George and Gustave Adolphus Harrer, *eds. and trans. Greek Literature in Translation.* New York and London: Harper & Row, 1924.
Livy. *Livy.* Translated by B.O. Foster. Cambridge: Harvard University Press. London: William Heinemann Ltd., 1919.
The Oxford Book of Greek Verse in Translation. Edited by T.F. Higham and C.M. Bowra. Oxford: Oxford University Press, 1938.
Plutarch. *Lives of the Noble Grecians and Romans.* Translated by John Dryden and revised by Arthur Hugh Clough. The Modern Library. (No date.)
Thucydides. *The Peloponnesian War.* The unabridged Crawley translation. The Modern Library, 1934.

SOURCES OF CHAPTER-OPENING QUOTES
Page 22: Havelock Ellis, *Impression and Comments,* Series 1, p. 105. *Page 44:* Herodotus II, 35. *Page 66:* Bertrand Russell, *Analysis of Mind.* Quoted in *Great Treasury of Western Thought,* ed. Mortimer J. Adler and Charles VanDorn (New York: R.R. Bowker, 1977), p. 493. *Page 80:* Genesis 12: 1-3. *Page 91:* Homer, *The Odyssey* XIX, 171-8, trans. Richmond Lattimore. *Page 174:* Tom B. Jones, *Ancient Civilizations* (Chicago: Rand McNally, 1960), p. 283. *Page 199:* Virgil, *The Aeneid* VI, 851-3, trans. Allen Mandlebaum (Berkeley: University of California Press, 1971). *Page 223:* Cicero, Letter to Atticus, trans. Moses Hadas. *Page 243:* G.G. Byron, *Childe Harold's Pilgrimage,* Canto III, stanza 145.

BLACK-AND-WHITE PHOTOS
The publisher gratefully acknowledges the contributions of the agencies, institutions and photographers listed below.
Note: The following abbreviations have been used for frequently cited sources:
Art Resource Art Resource, Inc., New York City;
Barnaby's Barnaby's Picture Library, London;
Bettmann Bettmann Archive, New York City; **Frost** Frost Publishing Group, New York City; **Hirmer** Hirmer Fotoarchiv, Munich; **Mansell** Mansell Collection, London; **Metropolitan Museum of Art** Metropolitan Museum of Art, New York City.

Unit Openers **p. 20,** Statue of Osiris, Brooklyn Museum; **p. 114,** Statue of Augustus, Art Resource

The photographs on pages 73 and 78, by J.B. Pritchard, were originally published in James B. Pritchard, *The Ancient Near East in Pictures Relating to the Old Testament*, 2nd ed., copyright 1969 by Princeton University Press. They are reprinted here with permission of Princeton University Press.

The drawing of cone mosaics on page 23 originally appeared in *Ur of the Chaldees* by P.R.S. Moorey (1982), a revised and updated edition of Sir Leonard Woolley's *Excavations at Ur*. It is reprinted with permission of The Herbert Press, London, and Cornell University Press.

Prehistory   15, Art Resource
Chapter 1   32, Bettmann; **26, 29, 38,** British Museum; **41,** Mansell; **25,** Oriental Institute, University of Chicago: **30,** Service Photographique de la Réunion des Musées Nationaux, Paris; **40,** Staatliche Museum, Berlin; **35,** University Museum, University of Pennsylvania
Chapter 2   51, Barnaby's; **56** *(left and right)*, **57, 58, 59,** Bettmann; **63** *(bottom)*, British Museum; **48, 55** *(left)*, Metropolitan Museum of Art; **51** *(top)*, Museum of Fine Arts, Boston; **45,** Popperfoto, London; **47, 49, 55** *(right)*, **60** (left), Roger Wood, London
Chapter 3   68, British Museum; **75,** Cincinnati Art Museum; **71** Hirmer; **74,** Oriental Institute, University of Chicago
Chapter 4   82 *(top)* **87, 88,** Bettmann; **82** *(bottom)*, British Museum
Chapter 5   99 (top), Bettmann; **93** *(top)*, British Museum; **94, 95, 96** *(left and right)*, **98,** Hirmer; **93** *(bottom)*, Museum of Fine Arts, Boston; **101** *(bottom)*, Oriental Institute, University of Chicago
India   107 *(right)*, Air India Slide Library; **108,** Cleveland Museum of Art; **109,** Government of India Tourist Office; **106,** Museum of Fine Arts, Boston; **107** *(left)*, Nelson-Atkins Museum of Art.
Chapter 6   126, Art Resource; **118, 124** *(top)*, **132, 134,** Bettmann; **127,** British Museum; **119** *(left and right)*, **125,** Hirmer; **124** *(bottom)*, Popperfoto, London; **136,** Wadsworth Atheneum Museum, Hartford, Connecticut

Chapter 7   154, 155 *(top right)*, Art Resource; **156,** Barnaby's; **157** *(left)*, **163,** Bettmann; **158, 159, 160, British Museum; 152,** Allan Cash, London; **155** *(bottom left)*, Fogg Art Museum, Harvard University; **157** *(right)*, Hirmer; **151** *(top)*, Frederic Lewis, New York City; **146,** Library of Congress; **153** *(left and right)*, Mansell; **165,** Royal Ontario Museum, Toronto
Chapter 8   176, 181, 191, 195 *(right)*, Bettmann; **194** *(left)*, Hirmer; **184,** Frederic Lewis; **186,** Library of Congress; **178,** Magnum Photos, New York City; **193, 195** *(left)*, Metropolitan Museum of Art
Chapter 9   200, 204, Art Resource; **201** *(right)*, **213,** Bettmann; **201** *(left)*, British Museum; **211** *(left)*, Allan Cash, London; **203** *(bottom)*, Fabri Bompiani
Chapter 10   233, 240, Alinari/Art Resource; **239** *(right)*, Barnaby's; **229, 232, 236, 241,** Bettmann; **237,** British Museum; **241,** Giraudon/Art Resource
Chapter 11   249 *(right)*, **253** *(left)*, Alinari/Art Resource; **246,** Ashmolean Museum, Oxford; **249** *(left)*, **250, 252, 256,** Bettmann; **255,** Foto Marburg/Art Resource; **253** *(right)*, Metropolitan Museum of Art
China   261 *(right)*, Freer Gallery of Art, Washington, D.C.; **263, 266,** Museum of Fine Arts, Boston; **265,** Nelson-Atkins Museum of Art, Kansas City, Missouri; **261** *(left)*, C.V. Starr East Asian Library, Columbia University; **264,** Xinhua New Agency

COLOR PHOTOS
Cover photo: Throne of King Tut. **Lee Boltin,** Croton-on-Hudson, N.Y.
Art Resource. Golden sarcophagus of King Tut (p.2); Staircase reliefs at Persepolis (p.3); Kamares ware (p.5); Athenian vase design—Ajax and Achilles (p.5); Athenian vase design—Helen and Priam (p.5); Villa of Mysteries fresco (p.7).
British Museum. Ram in thicket/photographer Michael Holford (p.1); Assyrian hunting scene (p.1); Funeral mound at Marathon (p.4).
C.M. Dixon, Canterbury, England. Golden mask of an Aegean king (p.5).
A.F. Kersting, London. Ruins of Parthenon (p.4).
Frederick Lewis, New York City. Funeral mask of King Tut (p.2); Ruins of palace at Persepolis (p.3).
National Gallery of Art, Washington, D.C. Painting by Giovanni Paolo Pannini of Pantheon in Rome (p.8).

Glossary

anthropology the study of mankind, usually through the examination and comparison of human cultures, institutions, customs, myths, etc.

anthropomorphic having human characteristics. An animal or god is described as *anthropomorphic* if people believe it has the appearance, emotions, or other traits of a human being.

archaeology the study of ancient peoples through excavation and analysis of artifacts and other physical evidence.

autocracy a government in which one person or group of people has absolute, unlimited authority over others; despotism.

cynicism the attitude and beliefs of Diogenes (412–323 B.C.) and his followers; especially contempt for established values and social customs.

diaspora the scattered settlements of the Jews after the Babylonian exile.

dynasty a succession of rulers from the same family.

Epicurianism the doctrine formulated by Epicurus (342–271 B.C.), emphasizing the achievement of pleasure and tranquillity through avoidance of pain.

geocentric centering upon the earth. In a *geocentric* world scheme, the heavenly bodies are thought to revolve around the earth.

hegemony dominance or control. A nation is said to have *hegemony* over another if its leadership is unquestioned.

heliocentric centering upon the sun. In a *heliocentric* world scheme, the planetary bodies revolve around the sun.

hubris excessive pride or arrogance. The ancient Greeks believed that people displaying such an attitude were tempting Fate and would be punished for their presumption.

indigenous native to or preexisting in a particular region.

matriarchal ruled by or dominated by women.

necropolis a "city of the dead" or cemetery.

nemesis retribution or punishment. Also, the agent of such punishment.

oligarchy a government controlled by a small group of people.

patriarchal ruled by or dominated by men.

proscription condemnation. In ancient Rome, the names of people to be killed or banished were publicly posted.

satrap governor of a province or region (*satrapy*) of the Persian Empire.

scepticism the doctrine originated by Pyrrho of Elis (360–270 B.C.), who believed that nothing can be known with certainty.

steppe a grassy plain with few trees. Applies to regions of eastern Europe and Asia.

Stoicism the doctrine originated by Zeno (335–261 B.C.), stating that man must learn to live in accordance with natural laws that govern the universe rather than relying upon his own laws and morals.

tell a mound representing the successive habitation of a site by several different communities.

theocracy a government ruled by a priest or priests who are considered to be the representative(s) of gods.

timocracy a government in which political power is directly related to the amount of property a person has.

tyranny In ancient Greece, the government of a ruler who has seized power by force. Also, a cruel or oppressive regime.

vassal a person or state subject to a higher authority. In the Middle Ages, a person who received protection and rights of land tenancy in return for homage and allegiance.

The Ancient World

● *"History is bunk."*
HENRY FORD

Prologue

These three words of the American industrialist, Henry Ford, are perhaps the most popularly known definition of history. In fact, Henry Ford actually said, "History is more or less bunk." Is there a difference? Let us apply one of the techniques of the historian, and examine the context of the remark.

The statement was made in 1916, one year before the United States entered the first World War. Ford was giving an interview to a reporter from the Chicago *Tribune*, Charles Wheeler, to express his views on disarmament and pacifism. Ford was an ardent pacifist, and opposed the possible entrance of the United States into the war.

Wheeler had just given an example from history to demonstrate how Britain's military preparedness and the strength of its navy prevented Napoleon from crossing the English Channel and invading the British Isles. Henry Ford's response was:

● ● ● *What do I care about Napoleon. It means nothing to me. History is more or less bunk. We want to live in the present and the only history that is worth a tinker's damn is the history we make today. The men who are responsible for the present war in Europe knew all about history. Yet they brought on the worst war in the world's history.*[1]

What other historiographical methods can we apply to Ford's statement? First, we might ask the question, "Is it true that all the major European leaders knew all about history?" There is no evidence for this in Ford's statement. This raises other questions: Was Ford an expert on history? Did the timing of the interview affect Ford's reply?

Given Henry Ford's pacifistic sentiments and commitment to disarmament, perhaps Wheeler's question received a response that was emotional rather than rational. The same question asked at another time might have evoked a different answer. In addition, Ford, one of the great captains of industry, lived in an era when there was great optimism about the future of the United States. Many Americans had little interest in looking backwards.

From his other actions, we know that Ford's attitude toward history was ambivalent. Years later he established a museum in

---

[1] John B. Rae, ed., *Henry Ford: Great Lives Observed* (Prentice-Hall, 1969), pp. 53-4.

1

Greenfield Village, near Dearborn, Michigan. It is a recreation of artifacts of American life from the 18th century through the early part of the 20th century. It contains a large collection of American tools, agricultural implements, decorative arts, transportation and communication artifacts.

When asked why he had invested so much money in the project, Ford replied that he "wanted to preserve what was the contribution of plain men who never got into history."[2] Ironically, it was the widespread use of the automobile, Ford's contribution to culture, that did much to change the earlier way of life that Ford now sought to preserve.

Moreover, Ford, in an area adjacent to Greenfield Village, set aside land for houses, workshops, and other structures that were significant in American history. At great cost, these were removed from their original locations and transported to Michigan. The area contains the courthouse where Abraham Lincoln practiced law as a circuit rider, the laboratories of Thomas Edison, and birthplaces or homes of such famous Americans as the Wright brothers, Robert Frost, and Noah Webster. So, in spite of his statement, Ford had some sense of the importance of history and the necessity of preserving the past.

WHAT IS HISTORY? From the example of Henry Ford, it is clear that there is some confusion as to just what the discipline of history is and what its value is. Just what comes to mind when one asks, "What is history?" One of the clearest and simplest definitions of history is that by the American historian Carl Becker: "History is the memory of things said and done."

The historical memory is composed of many types of evidence. There are written records and artifacts that provide clues for the historian. By its nature this evidence is fragmentary. For some civilizations and periods, there is more evidence available than there is on others. Because it is impossible to know the complete picture at any given time in the past, much of history, particularly early history, is speculative.

Just imagine if the only evidence of modern American life were some scattered ruins of buildings. How could these be used to put together an explanation of American society? Yet this is the detective job necessary for historians who study early societies.

Written records would seem a better historical source than ruins or other archaeological evidence. However, these too can be misleading. If a historian of a thousand years from now had the full text of the United States Constitution, would it be possible to reconstruct what the American political system was like? The answer, of course, is no.

Even where there are extensive written materials available, the historian has a task of interpretation. For the names and dates of events are only the raw materials of history. It is the job of the historian to link together in a meaningful way what we know about the past. The historian's interpretations and re-creations, rather than the data, are what make up what we call history. Because of the historian's role as interpreter, history is an ever-changing field—for the same data will be viewed and evaluated differently by different people. Such factors as the selection of facts, the significance ascribed to them, and the climate of the times in which the historian is writing will affect his or her work.

This does not have to discourage us unduly. When we watch the most recent "history" on the television nightly news, we accept the fact that we are receiving only a minute fraction of the events that have happened that day. We are getting the "news" that seems important to whomever has prepared the news program. A description of every event that happened that day would

[2]Michael Kammen, ed., *The Past Before Us: Contemporary Historical Writing in the United States* (Ithaca: Cornell University Press, 1980), p. 24.

not only be impossibly long, but also not digestible. The same is true with history.

In order to make history intelligible, historians choose the items that they believe are significant from the data they have. No one could absorb history from the time of Sumerian civilization to the present if the material were not broken up into understandable periods. For European history, the traditional divisions of classical, medieval, and modern history are instructive for what they say about the study of history.

Obviously all history was originally experienced as contemporary events. No people actually thought of themselves as living in the classical period; they were living in their present. Labels such as these are given to the period by future generations. In addition they are not value-free labels. The implication of the term Classical Age, for example, is that the period was one of lasting achievement.

The term *medieval*, or *Middle Ages*, on the other hand, implies something that occurred between two periods of greater historical importance. During early modern times, when the medieval achievement was not clear to many, this term was used in a derogatory sense. People looked back with admiration to the Greeks and Romans, and felt that it was only with the period of the Renaissance (following the Middle Ages) that Europeans matched the achievements of their classical forebears. The Middle Ages was viewed merely as the long period in between. Today no historian would agree with that value judgment, but the name has stuck.

Moreover, out of the chaos of events, the historian must fashion order. To do this, he or she looks for patterns of continuity and discontinuity. For some periods of history, certain characteristics that fit the accepted pattern will be stressed; in other periods, alternate characteristics are emphasized.

Perhaps the most important influence on the shaping of history is that each historian

by necessity brings to the study of the past the values and questions of his or her own time. This can be useful in that it enables the past to shed light on the present. Indeed many historians believe that this is the primary usefulness of the study of history. Henry T. Buckle, a 19th-century historian, claimed, "There will always be a connection between the way in which men contemplate the past and the way in which they contemplate the present."

However, other historians feel the past should be appreciated for itself. According to this view, the past should be captured as much as possible in its own terms, without attempting to impose modern viewpoints on it. Even if the relevance to the present is slight, there are benefits in understanding earlier societies and the experiences of the people who lived in them.

The degree of accuracy possible is also a topic of debate. Perhaps the Greek historian Herodotus spoke most honestly to this point: "My business is to record what people say. But I am by no means bound to believe it— and that may be taken to apply to this book as a whole."

INTERDISCIPLINARY APPROACHES

In recent years many historians have expanded the definition of history by using data and discoveries from other fields of knowledge. The social sciences—particularly anthropology, archaeology, and social psychology—have been utilized to draw historical conclusions. Psychoanalytic insights have been applied to important historical personages such as Martin Luther and Adolf Hitler. The field of social psychology has been used to explain the rise of totalitarianism, and also to explain the increase in warlike sentiments during certain periods.

The discoveries of modern archaeologists have revolutionized ancient history. New findings have forced historians to reconsider many of their previous descriptions of an-

The walls of Troy. Heinrich Schliemann never saw these city walls, for he excavated another part of the site. They were discovered by later teams of archaeologists.

cient societies. For example, until Heinrich Schliemann discovered the site of ancient Troy at Hissarlik in 1868, the *Iliad* of Homer was considered to be a work of considerable literary merit, but not an historical text. Later, the site was carefully analyzed by Carl Blegen and a team of archaeologists from the University of Cincinnati, who worked at Hissarlik from 1932 to 1938. They verified that the Troy described in the Homeric epic was at level VIIa.

There is convincing evidence that Troy VIIa was destroyed by human hand. The archaeologists found that the city was burned, and other findings suggest that few, if any, inhabitants survived this fire. Human bones have been found near houses and in doorways, and one skeleton was discovered outside the walls in a position that suggested that it was left to lie where it fell. Two bronze blades of late Mycenaean origin have been found lying in the streets. Between levels VIIa and VII there is a thin layer of dust, suggesting that the city was completely abandoned for several years after the attack.

These discoveries showed that Homer's work had historical accuracy. His descriptions of social customs, weapons, methods of fighting, and so forth, often conform more closely to the archaeological evidence than to the time when Homer was reputed to have lived. The verification of Homer's work led to a major overhaul of our historical understanding of pre-classical Greece.

The methods developed for the social sciences, such as the use of statistics and other types of analysis, have been useful to the historian. So have the findings of social sciences. Historians now draw on both the techniques and knowledge of many fields to study the past.

DIFFERING APPROACHES

It was only in the 19th century that history was established as an individual discipline and profession. Previously history was a branch of literature, whose practitioners might be propagandists or those who sacrificed accuracy for literary effect. There was no professional tradition of historical standards.

No country was more important in the birth of modern historical writing than Germany. It was there that history was tied to the growing studies in philology, the history of language. The man who was to become the leading figure in German historical studies was Leopold von Ranke. In his view, no one who could not read the language of the culture should write about it. He believed that only primary sources—evidence, written and otherwise, that dates from the time being studied—should be consulted by an historian, since things written afterwards could not be proved to be accurate.

Von Ranke's ideal was history that only conveyed "what actually happened." Today we know that this is an impossible goal. But von Ranke's recognition of the importance of primary sources has remained to this day as an important part of historical studies.

Another approach to history has been that of the great systematizers. These historians, such as Karl Marx and Arnold Toynbee, believed that they found laws of history that were relevant to all civilizations. Marx believed that the core element of history was the struggle between the various classes of society. Toynbee saw civilizations as following a cycle almost like that of an individual human. In Toynbee's view, each civilization had a developing period, a period of ripeness, and then a decay. A similar idea was expressed by Oswald Spengler, who posited that the West was in a period of decline. Spengler's thesis of the decline of the West was influenced by the disillusionment with western civilization that was an important intellectual current in the years following World War I.

Most historians no longer believe that there are any such grand unifying principles relevant to all civilizations. This mode of historical interpretation is definitely not in favor today.

The professionalization of history in the 19th century led to an increasing specialization among historians. Much of traditional history had primarily concerned itself with political, military, and diplomatic affairs. It made great use of official records and materials. With the specialization of the field, economic history, cultural history, and social history emerged as distinct areas of study and thought. The British historian George Trevelyan offered a definition of one of the new fields: "Social history might be defined negatively as the history of a people with the politics left out."

As historians have benefited from knowledge in other fields, new historical specializations have emerged. Demographics, or population studies, have provided a new way of looking at the past. Geography has been increasingly used in combination with history to find insights into the causes of historical currents. Cliometrics approaches history from the perspective of statistical evidence. (The term combines the name of the muse of history, Clio, with *metrics*, or measurement.) These are just a few of the new fields that are expected to yield new historical insights.

A much-discussed question for historical thinking is whether the historian should be partisan. Some feel that the historian should make every attempt to be a neutral observer. This was the position of von Ranke. But others have claimed that neutrality, or complete objectivity, is neither a realistic possibility nor the responsibility of the historian. In this view, the historian should be open about his or her position on particular issues. The question of integrity for the historian lies not with partisanship but rather in maintaining the integrity of sources and in attempting to get as full a picture as possible.

The question of whether people or events make history has been a point of controversy among historians. It is sometimes called the "great man vs. historical forces" dispute. In the 19th century, Thomas Carlyle was an important proponent of the "great man" theory. Today it is somewhat discredited, and there is more interest in the conditions that lead to change rather than just the biographies and influence of great historical figures.

One of the most exciting developments in today's new approaches to history is the increasing realization that many people have been left out of the history written in the past. Traditional histories stressed the powerful individuals and the great public events. This was natural, as there is more definite information available on political and military leaders. But today there is a realization that there was always more to history than what happened at the top of society.

Historians are now trying to reconstruct what was life for the ordinary people of the day. Their study begins with records of births and deaths, tax records, and other statistical information. These can give information on life expectancy and the effects of weather and climate on agriculture, as well as other facets of a civilization. Through these techniques it is hoped that more can be gleaned about overall conditions of an era. The historian today does not find it necessary to write in terms of individuals, but rather considers the way groups of people were influenced by long-term trends and economic conditions.

One aspect of this new approach explores the role of women and the position of the family in different societies and times. This emphasis was partly the result of the women's movement. There has been criticism that the only references to women in traditional histories concerned exceptional women who were rulers or able to excel in a man's world. Some people argue that women's role in the past has been a distinct one, separate from that of men, and that efforts to explore it will yield significant historical insights:

● ● ● *It is not surprising that most women feel that their sex does not have an interesting or significant past. However, like minority groups, women cannot afford to lack a consciousness of a collective identity, one which necessarily involves a shared awareness of the past. Without this, a social group suffers from a kind of collective amnesia, which makes it vulnerable to the impositions of dubious stereotypes, as well as limiting prejudices about what is right and proper for it to do or not to do.*[3]

To get a truer picture of the recent past, many historians have made extensive use of the technique of recording oral histories. This allows the voices of ordinary people to be part of the record for historians of the future. Oral history has been used very effectively to document the civil rights movement, the Great Depression in the United States, and the experience of Holocaust survivors.

Moreover, historians today are willing to use literature and myths to deepen their understanding of a period or people. There is a feeling among today's historians that all information is grist for the historical mill. The search for undiscovered historical documents is a growth industry in the profession today. There is also a growing understanding that popular culture is a fertile field for study. Sports, amusements, and popular art forms all have a history, and they tell us something about the society in which they thrived. From this you can see the truth of the Carl Becker dictum: "Everyman is a historian." You already know some pieces of history even if it is only about the recent past.

WHY STUDY HISTORY? The study of history is important for all citizens because knowledge about the past is essential for an understanding of the present. For our own history, a knowledge of how and why our political and social institutions were created deepens our understanding of how they work today and what they mean to the society in which we live.

Similarly, knowledge of European and world history deepens our understanding of our culture, and of the shrinking world in which we live. The achievements of classical Greece and Rome remain relevant today. More than 2300 years ago, Aristotle wrote, "Poverty is the parent of revolution and crime." Philosophers since then have not been able to improve on his observation. Thinkers of the past dealt with questions that people still ask, and we benefit from learning of the answers they found.

Much of the culture of the United States has antecedents in Europe. Thus the study of European history can lead to a greater appreciation of western art and music, which are surely some of the great joys of civilized people. Similarly, learning about European political institutions can increase our understanding of the American political system that sprang from them.

[3]Sheila R. Johansson, "Herstory as History: A New Field or Another Fad?", in Bernice A. Carroll, ed., *Liberating Women's History* (Illinois University Press, 1976), p. 427.

The study of history enables the student to see how the world came to be what it is today. Because we live in a world in which little-known nations suddenly take on a significant role—as the recent examples of Vietnam, Iran, Afghanistan, and Libya illustrate—it is important to understand the culture and history that have shaped the present. The importance of promoting a mutual understanding between the various peoples of the world has never been as important as it is today. The first step in understanding other people is in comprehending their history.

Furthermore, though history does not repeat itself, the study of past events teaches useful lessons because some characteristics of human nature remain the same. The study of history, if creatively used, can lead to a better understanding of interactions between people or the likely consequences of actions.

Knowing history enhances understanding of current events, because many problems have antecedents in the past. Being knowledgeable means that one can make more intelligent judgments about a situation. One is less likely to be swayed by people who oversimplify causes and solutions. Historical understanding makes it easier to form one's own opinions.

Looking at civilizations that are separated from ours by different cultural practices and time is also a refreshing intellectual experience. The history of different cultures is a vast reservoir of possibilities as to how things might be done. Knowledge of other cultures forces an intelligent person to confront his or her own ideas and see that perhaps there are other ways of life that might be as satisfactory as their own. The discovery of affinities with different times and places is a pleasurable and exciting intellectual experience. In addition, the discovery of alternatives helps one see more of the complexities in one's own situation.

Finally, studying history can be fun. Current movies and popular fiction—particu-larly in the broad genre called "science fiction"—often present imagined cultures. The popular movie sequence *Star Wars* begins with this message on the screen: "A long time ago, in a galaxy far, far away . . ." Substitute "place" for "galaxy," and you begin the study of history. The stories of real people in different times and places can be just as thrilling as any fiction.

Although the various cultures and times we study each have their own flavor, human nature is not so different wherever one looks. History is filled with figures who are villainous, outrageous, and infamous. Edward Gibbon, the English historian, described history as "little more than the crimes, follies and misfortunes of mankind." History is also filled with the good and the ordinary. The range of people we learn about run the gamut of human experience and imagination.

The American historian Frederick Jackson Turner summarized the appeal of history this way:

• • • *History has been a romance and a tragedy. In it we read the brilliant annals of the few. The intrigues of courts, knightly valor, palaces and pyramids, the loves of ladies, the songs of minstrels, and the chants from cathedrals pass like a pageant, or linger like a strain of music as we turn the pages. But history has its tragedy as well, which tells of the degraded tillers of the soil, toiling that others might dream, the slavery that rendered possible the 'glory that was Greece,' the serfdom into which decayed the 'grandeur that was Rome'—these as well demanded their annals.*[4]

The study of history has the same joys as good literature. It is an attempt to capture the feeling of what is human, what endures. Discovering the past helps one to discover the present.

---

[4]Leften S. Stavrianos, ed., *Readings in World History* (Boston: Allyn and Bacon, 1964), pp. 784-5.

● *As we turned to leave, I noticed something lying on the ground partway up the slope. That's a bit of hominid arm, I said. We stood up and began to see other bits of bone on the slope: a couple of vertebrae, part of a pelvis—all of them hominid. . . . Could they be parts of a single, extremely primitive skeleton? No such skeleton had ever been found anywhere. In that 110 degree heat we began jumping up and down. . . .*

There was a tape recorder in the camp, and a tape of the Beatles song "Lucy in the Sky With Diamonds" went belting out into the night sky. . . . At some point during that unforgettable evening—I no longer remember when—the new fossil picked up the name of Lucy.

DONALD JOHANSON

Prehistory

The dramatic discovery of "Lucy" by Donald Johanson in 1974 is just one more piece in the unfinished mosaic of human prehistory. Prehistory is what happened before the beginning of recorded human history. The time-span of prehistory is much longer than that of the history of civilization.

In a universe which has an estimated age of 20 billion years, our little part of it, Earth, is barely 4.5 billion years old. Life on Earth began in the seas in the form of one-celled algae and bacteria about 3.5 billion years ago. For over three billion years, life was confined to the sea, and then, about 400 million years ago, some form of life crept onto the land. A long period of development ensued, during which reptiles—including dinosaurs—birds, insects, and mammals began to populate the earth.

Something like 60 million years ago, the first primate appeared. Primates are the order of mammals that include lemurs and bush babies, more developed forms such as monkeys and apes, and the most highly developed form of all: human beings.

You would not recognize that first primate, called a prosimian, as a close relative. Human-like primates did not appear until about 50-55 million years later, about 5-10 million years B.C.

The first creature that scientists classify in the genus *Homo*—true "human"—does not show up in the fossil record until about 2 million years ago. That was a creature called *Homo habilis*, distinguished from earlier creatures because of its larger brain, habit of walking upright, and ability to make tools.

Homo habilis' relatively large brain was not as large as yours. A creature with a larger brain, *Homo sapiens* (intelligent human), entered the world around 200,000 years ago. One type of *Homo sapiens*, called Neanderthal Man, who appeared in Europe about 100,000 years ago, hunted in groups, built fires, and had many of the characteristics of modern humans.

But scientists classify modern humans with an extra "sapiens" after their species name. By about 40,000 years ago, a type of creature had appeared, whose body and brain were the same as those of people today. These creatures made tools that were more highly developed than those of earlier human types; they made marks on bones that were apparently attempts to record the phases of the moon; and, as we shall see, they drew pictures on the walls of caves. This at last was *Homo sapiens sapiens*. Even then, *Homo sapiens sapiens* existed for at least 35,000 years before "history" began with the first real civilizations, some 5000 years ago. Thus, a time line showing the age of the earth would be 14 miles long if the era of civilized human beings were only one inch long.

Since the ancient ancestors of today's people left no written records, no tales or songs, how do we know anything at all about them, or about the creatures that lived even longer ago? The answer begins with fossils. Some fossils are the bones of ancient creatures which have turned to stone by reacting with the soil or lava in which they fell. A footprint of an animal left in soil that hardened is also a fossil record. So are the tiny impressions left in stone by shells, feathers, plants, or even by one-celled animals billions of years ago.

Fossils were noticed and speculated on by the ancient Greeks, and probably by earlier people. The Greeks recognized them as animal remains. From about the middle of the 16th century A.D., people have tried to use fossil remains to discover what ancient animals looked like. When it was discovered that some reconstructed fossils formed animals that no longer existed, people puzzled over why they had died out.

Two schools of thought developed. One group, called the diluvialists, relied on the story of the flood in the Biblical book of Genesis. According to diluvialists, the fossils were remains of animals who had somehow missed Noah's ark. Diluvialists held that God had created all species just as they were today, including his highest creation, human beings. Diluvialists were supported by the calculations of James Ussher, Archbishop of Armagh in the 17th century, who believed that the Creation took place in 4004 B.C. on the 23rd day of October at 9:00 a.m.

The other school, called the fluvialists, saw the physical world as part of an ongoing process set in motion by the Creator. They were quite willing to believe that some of God's creations had ceased to exist long ago, and saw no conflict between their beliefs and the Book of Genesis.

In 1830, Charles Lyell published his *Principles of Geology*, in which he supplied strong proof that the world was much older than Ussher had thought. The diluvialists suffered another blow with the discovery of Windmill Cave along the English coast in 1858. This cave contained the bones of mammoths and other extinct animals. In another stratum of the cave, below the level of the bones of extinct animals, were found stone tools obviously made and used by human beings. In one of those unusual coincidences in history, the findings from Windmill Cave, proving that humans lived longer ago than some extinct animal forms, were read before the Royal Society in London the same year that Charles Darwin published his *On the Origin of Species*.

Darwin's work offered evidence that animals changed their form over a long period of time in an evolutionary process that he called "natural selection." What was most startling about Darwin's theory—alarming, to some—was the implication that human beings themselves had evolved from some other form of life. Immediately, the popular press distorted Darwin's work by spreading the idea that apes and monkeys—clearly similar in shape to humans—were, according to Darwin, human ancestors.

THE SEARCH FOR HUMAN ANCESTORS In 1856, the skull of what appeared to be a human was found in the Neander valley in Germany. Neanderthal Man (*Homo sapiens neanderthalensis*), as he was called, had a "brute-like" appearance which included a receding forehead, thick brow-ridges, a pronounced jaw, bowed legs, and arms that almost dangled to the ground. It is estimated that most Neanderthals lived in Europe and the Middle East between 100,000 and 40,000 years ago. In the popular consciousness, Neanderthals became the archetype of the primitive "cave men." During the 1950s, it was discovered that the original reconstruction of Neanderthal Man was based on a skeletal specimen that was distorted due to a bad case of arthritis. Considerable disagreement still exists as to how different Neanderthals looked from present-day people. Some argue that if a Neanderthal dressed in a three-piece suit sat down on a bus, he might draw only a few nervous glances.

The next important discovery in human prehistory came in 1868 in western France. Here, another kind of ancient skull was discovered. It was named "Cro-Magnon," after the rock shelter in which it was found. Cro-Magnon had a pronounced forehead and a small jaw, typical of modern-day humans. Today, scientists recognize Cro-Magnons as the first examples of *Homo sapiens sapiens*, the species we belong to, but at the time of its discovery the Cro-Magnon was only one more piece in a growing puzzle.

More pieces were found in other parts of the world. A Dutchman, Eugene Dubois, uncovered the cranium of a human ancestor in Java in 1891. He named his find *Pithecanthropus erectus* (erect-walking ape-man). Dubois' discovery became popularly known as Java Man. The scientific world did not take Dubois' work seriously. As a consequence, Dubois locked his fossilized bones in a safe and refused to allow anyone to see them for years. Now, we know that he had found evidence of a creature classified as *Homo erectus*.

The discovery of Peking Man (*Sinanthropus pekininsus*) in the mid-1920s is one of the more unusual stories of anthropological detective work. Dr. Davidson Black, on the staff of the Peking Union Medical College in China, came across some ancient human teeth in an apothecary shop. Dr. Black was told that the teeth originally were found in caves just above the small town of Choukoutien in northern China. At the bottom of a trench in one of the caves, Dr. Black uncovered the skullcap of a prehistoric ancestor of the modern-day Chinese. The site also yielded the first confirmation of primitive people's use of fire. More evidence was unearthed, suggesting that Peking Man may have practiced cannibalism.

The original fossilized bones of *Sinanthropus pekininsus* disappeared under bizarre circumstances in 1937. Because of China's war with Japan it was decided to move the fossils out of harm's way. They were entrusted to a contingent of American marines, who were to take them by train to the coast. While en route, the fossils disappeared, never to be seen since. However, from photographs and notes, scientists have identified them as another example of *Homo erectus*.

Until the middle of the 20th century, scientists were unable to clearly classify the types of humans and their ancestors. The belief that Darwin's theory implied a human descent from apes sent some on a search for the "missing link," a supposed connection between humans and apes. Others pointed out, correctly, that in Darwinian theory a superior characteristic (such as a larger brain) would give those individuals that possessed it a survival advantage over those that did not; thus, in a developing species, the superior individuals would gradually supplant those without the key characteristic. The most compelling proof that humans did not "descend" from apes is the fact that apes are still a thriving species.

However, the "missing link" idea gained currency with the discovery of a creature called Piltdown Man in 1912. The cranium was large enough to be human, but the jaw appeared ape-like. Found in southern England, Piltdown Man was long accepted as a legitimate part of the record of human fossil history. Only in the 1950s was it discovered that Piltdown Man was a hoax—the cranium was in fact that of a human, fitted together with the jaw of an orangutan, and passed off as the complete skull of one creature.

Because of the scientific community's preoccupation with Piltdown Man, it overlooked the significance of a discovery by Raymond Dart in a limestone cave in South Africa in 1925. Dart had found the skull of an infant "man-ape" which he called "Taung child." But later researchers would see Dart's discovery as the beginning of a new era in the search for the physical origins of the human race.

The person most responsible for redirecting the hunt for early humans by focusing on east Africa was Louis Leakey. Dr. Leakey was born in Kenya, where his mother and father served as missionaries. While still in his teens he went to England to attend Cambridge University. After suffering an injury while playing rugby, Leakey decided to recuperate by joining an expedition to Tanganyika (today Tanzania) sponsored by the British Museum. The purpose of the trip was to collect fossilized dinosaur bones. The training and experience acquired on this expedition initiated Leakey into his life's work—the search for human origins in the fossilized records of prehistoric Africa. After a brief return to England to complete his degree in anthropology, Leakey returned to Africa to start his search. That quest would continue to the end of his life in 1972, and his son Richard carries it on today.

Virtually no one in 1926 believed that human beings might have originated in Africa. Neanderthal, Cro-Magnon, and other examples of early human-like remains had been discovered in Europe and Asia. The only "find" in Africa was Raymond Dart's Taung child, and it was thought to be more ape than human.

Leakey devoted most of his efforts to surveying Olduvai gorge in present-day Tanzania. For the next 30 years, Leakey searched for the remains of early hominids, or human-like creatures, with very little to show for his efforts. Only his will and the conviction that he was right sustained him. Some very primitive tools were found, but nothing of the hands that made the tools. Mary Leakey, Louis' wife, shared in the excitement of the hunt as she became her husband's equal in field experience and knowledge.

It was Mary Leakey who found the first physical remains of a hominid in Olduvai gorge, on July 17, 1959. While working on her own, Mary Leakey spotted some bones protruding from the soil. Further investigation revealed that they were two large molar teeth. They clearly belonged to a hominid, but not one of the genus *Homo*. "Dear boy," as the Leakeys called their find, is estimated to be 1.75 million years old. It has since been categorized as *Australopithecus Boisei*. Other species of the *Australopithecus* genus (called australopithecines) had been found earlier in Africa, though the Leakeys' specimen was a larger creature.

Two years later the Leakeys uncovered a creature whose brain size led them to declare it was a member of the genus *Homo*. Because it was a tool-user, they gave it the species name *habilis*, meaning "skillful." Not all scientists agreed with this classification; some argue that the Leakeys' *Homo habilis* is another type of *Australopithecus*.

In 1976 at Laetoli, near Olduvai gorge, Mary Leakey discovered footprints of three hominids. Three and a half million years ago, these early hominids walked upright across a carpet of wet ash, leaving impressions that have been preserved to the present day.

These footprints may have been made by the same species of hominids discovered by Donald Johanson at Hadar. "Lucy" walked upright and had some other clearly human physical characteristics, and yet she had several australopithecine characteristics, including a smaller brain than true humans. What is unique about "Lucy" is that 40 percent of her skeleton was recovered, making her the most complete early hominid ever found. In 1975 Johanson unearthed at Hadar what has been named "the First Family," parts of approximately 13 individuals from about the same time period as "Lucy." This additional evidence suggests that "Lucy" and her kind are not another species of *Homo*, but rather other examples of *Australopithecus*.

If the Latin terminology in the foregoing discussion seems confusing to you, don't feel as if you are alone. Anthropologists themselves are hardly in agreement about what conclusions to draw from their discoveries. It is difficult to assign neat categories of genus and species from the fragmentary remains that are available. Furthermore, as indicated by the disagreement over the Leakeys' *Homo habilis*, it is not always possible to tell exactly what makes a human (the *Homo* genus). Three characteristics have been suggested as identifying factors: brain size, pelvic shape (indicating the ability to walk upright), and type of teeth (non-humans, in general, were plant eaters, while true humans widened their diet to include flesh).

Humans and apes may have shared a common ancestor. At some point, the line that led to human beings diverged from the line that led to apes. An ancient creature known as *Ramapithecus* is a possible candidate for the title of first hominid. Known only from a few teeth and jaw fragments, *Ramapithecus* is thought to have existed throughout Asia, Africa, and Europe between 14 million and 9 million years ago.

Around 3.5 million years ago the earliest forms of *Australopithecus* appeared in Africa. They share certain characteristics with both human and ape. Their brains are about the same size as those of apes, but smaller than those of humans. At least six species of *Australopithecus* have been identified. *Homo habilis*, the Leakeys' discovery, lived in Africa between two million and one million years ago. For a time, it coexisted with australopithecines in eastern Africa.

HUMAN EVOLUTION

Examples of the first true human, *Homo erectus*, are found in Africa, China, and Indonesia. This creature appeared about 1.6 million years ago. It habitually walked upright, and made shelters and sophisticated tools. Its brain was larger than that of *Australopithecus*. It is probably in the direct line of human ancestors, evolving into the species *Homo sapiens* about 200,000 years ago.

The earliest form of *Homo sapiens* began to appear, possibly in Africa, about 200,000 years ago. The best known example is Neanderthal Man, which emerged around 125,000 years ago. The Neanderthalers were replaced by the Cro-Magnons who appeared in western Europe about 35,000 years ago. They are the first examples of *Homo sapiens sapiens*.

This accounting of human evolutionary history is far from complete. There are many gaps, differences of opinion, and possible reinterpretations as new information is unearthed. It is still a question as to what happened between eight million years ago and four million years later when the first australopithecines emerged. Richard Leakey and Donald Johanson disagree over the placement of "Lucy," "the First Family," and the hominids who made the footsteps at Laetoli. Did *Homo sapiens sapiens* evolve directly from Neanderthals, or were the Neanderthalers a dead end in evolutionary history? All of these and many other issues still need to be resolved.

HOW DID HUMANS DEVELOP?

The record of prehistory that scientists chip from the earth not only gives evidence of humans' physical development, but also provides clues as to the intellectual and cultural development of humankind. Somewhere in the sedimentary deposits of east Africa is evidence about the impact of the environment on human evolution. Although a few of those secrets have been brought to the surface, there are many more yet to be uncovered.

Twenty million years ago, the earth was warmer than it is now. In today's temperate zones it was blanketed with rain forests. Eurasia and Africa were joined, allowing many animals to move easily from one continent to another. Changes in environment encouraged the development of new species. These creatures lived primarily in trees, and probably had the ability to pick up objects and carry them. Long before, early primates had nails instead of claws and an opposable thumb that permitted them to close one hand on an object. They were probably herbivores, with a diet including plants, seeds, and nuts. Like monkeys today, they probably had the ability to stand for short periods of time, but the usual method of walking was on four legs. As the earth cooled, and the tropical forests receded, they came down from the trees and began to inhabit the open grasslands.

The first hominid habitually to walk on two legs appeared between nine million years and four million years ago. This creature known as *Australopithecus* was a biped, though it walked hunched over and low to the ground.

There are a number of theories explaining bipedalism. One advantage was that by standing up in the tall grasslands, a hominid increased the range of its vision. It could spot potential predators, or its own quarry. For *Australopithecus* had widened its diet from vegetable matter to small animals. It was the first hominid to hunt other animals for food.

Standing upright gave *Australopithecus* another advantage—it freed its front feet, now hands, for other activities. Among these activities was the making of tools. The earliest tools that appear to have been shaped by hominids date from 2.5 million years ago. Between the time when it developed the ability to walk on two legs and the time these tools were made, *Australopithecus* learned that a stick or a hand-sized rock could be used as an aid. Your imagination can supply the circumstances: to fend off an enemy, to stun or kill a small animal.

The ability to make tools coincides with the growth in brain size that eventually carried *Australopithecus* onto the next evolutionary step. Previously, the best survival tactics were the ability to run fast or to climb a tree or otherwise avoid a predator with sharper teeth and claws. Hesitating to "think" about the danger was not a good survival tactic. With the discovery and use of tools, the brain itself became a key to survival. The expansion of the brain found in *Australopithecus* was the result.

CHARACTERISTICS OF EARLY HOMINIDS

The new role of humans as hunters has been the subject of much speculation. Some argue that the aggressiveness and violent nature of modern human beings are a result of their hunter ancestry. Louis Leakey, when coming across the crushed bones of an early hominid, liked to theorize that what lay before him in the ground was the residue of an ancient murder or other form of violent death.

However, studies of contemporary primitive cultures, such as the San in southern Africa, suggest that these societies tend to be non-aggressive and rather timid. An argument can be made that the aggressive behavior of "civilized" people today is a product of the pressures of civilization rather than an instinct inherited from our primitive forebears.

Another characteristic of early hominids was their habit of sharing food. Many higher animals share their food with a family group, but of all the primates only the direct ancestors of humans seem to have been willing to portion out food to all members of the group—young and old, weak and strong. This too seems to have been a survival characteristic, for greater brain size meant that infant

13

humans required a longer time of growth and development before they could fend for themselves.

Instead of finding the key to human survival in the male's aggressiveness and hunting skills, there are many anthropologists today who prefer to concentrate on the female's role in the food-gathering and sharing process. In this new interpretation, the female plays a more central role in the survival of the species. In contemporary hunter-gatherer societies, such as the Efe pygmies in the rain forests of Zaire, the women who forage for plants and small animals furnish at least 60 percent of the total diet of the group.

It is not necessary to view Homo sapiens sapiens as the victor in the race for "the survival of the fittest." It is just as reasonable to explain the success of early hominids in terms of cooperation and food-sharing, rather than in terms of competition and conquest over the environment and other species.

THE PALEO-LITHIC AGE With the exception of the occasional fossilized physical remains of humans themselves, things made of stone have been the most obvious and enduring evidence of human beings' residence on earth. Archaeologists thus traditionally have called the period of time between the first toolmaking hominids and the beginning of metalworking cultures the "Stone Age." This covers a period from about 2,000,000 years ago to 5000 B.C.

The Stone Age is further divided into three periods, the longest of which is the Paleolithic (the Old Stone Age). It lasted till around 10,000 B.C. Besides making tools and weapons, the early humans who lived in this period had many other important accomplishments. They learned to control and use fire; they made artificial shelters from branches; and they began to use needles to sew animal skins together. In addition, they held ritual burials of their dead; in these ancient graves, archaeologists have sometimes found the remains of flowers. We may speculate that this is evidence of some form of belief in an afterlife. The oldest known written record dates from this period, between 30,000 and 40,000 years ago; it is a lunar calendar etched in bone, found in Europe.

Humans during the Paleolithic Era were nomadic, roaming in search of food. When their diet began to include meat, they hunted in groups. Organized hunts for elephants and mammoths took place in Europe. Recent archaeological work suggests that individuals in hunter-gatherer societies had a more varied diet than was previously thought.

DEVELOPMENT OF COMMUNICATION SKILLS
As Homo sapiens began to cluster into larger groups and share more activities, there developed a greater need for an organized form of communication. With the development of language, human activities could be coordinated more effectively. Plans could be laid out before the hunt, and inventions or new knowledge could be passed on to future generations. How and when humans developed the ability to communicate through symbolic means is mostly conjecture, although there are some interesting hypotheses.

An area in the frontal part of the brain, known as "Broca's area," coordinates tongue, throat, and mouth muscles, thus enabling us to speak. A barely discernible imprint of the brain left on the inside of a fossilized cranium helps us to determine the degree to which those sections of the brain associated with speech were developed in early hominids. Broca's area is identifiable in the australopithecines, and it becomes increasingly more distinct as Homo erectus evolves into Homo sapiens. This suggests the possibility that early hominids had already started to develop rudimentary communication skills.

Prehistoric stone tools are another source of information that could shed some light on the development of language. Until about 40,000 years ago, tools did not seem to have

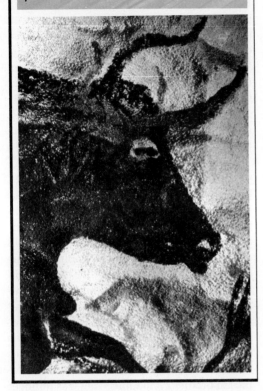

A detail of a bull painting from the caves of Lascaux in France. The Lascaux caves contain some of the most artistic works created by prehistoric man.

context, tonal level, and body movements. Maybe sounds within the context of "gestures" were a first step in the communication process of early humans. Clearly, the need for cooperation in the gathering and sharing of food, and the growing complexity of social relationships required a sophisticated form of communication.

Prehistoric art is another form of expression and communication used by early humans. The symbolism found in some examples of prehistoric art, such as zigzag markings and integrated color patterns, goes back as far as 250,000 years, and suggests that this form of expression could have been the end product of a fully developed language. There are two basic types of prehistoric art—"portable art" and "stationary art."

Portable art is art that can be readily picked up, easily moved, and looked at "in the round." Often it takes the shape of sculpted statuettes known as "Venuses." These are female figures, intentionally exaggerated and disproportionate in shape. Why they were carved in that way is not known, although it is assumed that it has some connection with prehistoric people's preoccupation with the concept of fertility. Another representative form of portable art is etching on tools and other personal items. Some examples of this art are quite old. An engraved ox-rib, discovered in France in 1969, is thought to be 300,000 years old.

The stationary art form includes the most impressive examples of prehistoric art. Paintings on the walls of caves became a form of expression about 30,000 years ago, and were created during the next 20,000 years.

In 1868, in northern Spain near a place called Altamira, a gentleman farmer, Don Marcellino de Sautola, learned that a hunter had discovered the entrance to a cave on his land. Being an amateur archaeologist, Don Marcellino explored the cave and found nothing but a few bones. It was not until 11 years later, in 1879, that Sautola's daughter,

any standardized form, although there were different types of implements serving a variety of functions. With the advent of *Homo sapiens sapiens*, standardization of tools within a culture becomes commonplace. This means that the maker of the tool has a preconceived idea of what the tool should look like, and could communicate his idea to others within his culture.

The "gesture" theory of language development suggests that there is more to symbolic communication than merely stringing a series of words together in some organized fashion. Meaning in a spoken language also requires an understanding of such things as

Maria, entered the cave and happened to look up at the ceiling to discover colored images of animals that appeared almost alive in the flickering light.

At Lascaux in southern France, in 1940, four teenagers decided to explore a hole left by an uprooted tree. As local rumor had it, at the bottom of the hole was a subterranean passage that led to a nearby castle. The four boys discovered a narrow entranceway at the bottom of the pit, but it did not lead to a medieval castle. Instead, they found themselves in the presence of a series of cave paintings of exquisite beauty. Other cave paintings have been discovered since, particularly in North Africa, but none have surpassed the beauty of those of Altamira and Lascaux.

Most of the depictions on the walls are of large meat-bearing animals—bison, mammoths, horses, cattle, and reindeer. The animals are painted only in profile, usually slightly distorted, and tending to be fat. There are few birds, no reptiles, and virtually no plants or scenery. Rarely—except on cave walls in North Africa—does one find any portrayals of humans, and when they do appear they are usually in the form of "stick-like" figures.

Most cave paintings were in a remarkable state of preservation when they were discovered because of the constant and cool temperatures. However, the thousands of people who have visited the underground chambers since have helped to dry and crack the paints, and contributed to the growth of bacteria and mold on the walls. Lascaux, in the last few years, has been closed to the public.

The tools and techniques used by prehistoric cave artists make their achievements all the more impressive. Most of the colors came from ground mineral oxides such as iron manganese and red ochre. The paints were mixed with water and some fatty substances, with a consistency of a heavy liquid or paste.

The artist applied the paint with a variety of instruments including fingers, wads of plant material, hair, shredded ends of sticks, or by blowing the powdered paint through a hollow tube onto a wetted surface. How difficult it must have been to paint on the uneven surface of a cave wall or ceiling, in cramped quarters, with the only illumination being the flickering light from an animal-grease candle. And yet the figures of the animals are so life-like that in a cave setting the shadowy outlines of 20,000-year-old buffaloes and bulls seem to be moving toward the person who has entered their sanctuary.

There have been a number of theories proposed over the years to attempt to explain the motives of prehistoric artists. The Abbé Breuil, for years the foremost authority on prehistoric art, believed the paintings to be a form of sympathetic magic. The artist would portray an exceptionally fat bison in the hope or belief that the hunters of the tribe would locate the living representation of the painting on their next hunt. One argument that raises doubts about Breuil's thesis is the minimal number of reindeer represented in the cave paintings. From archaeological sources we know that one of the most important staples in prehistoric people's diet was reindeer meat. Some scholars see the pictures as a memorial of a particularly successful hunt.

Other scientists see the caves at Altamira as a gathering point for various tribal groups who lived in the general area. Periodically, perhaps at the end of each season, they would meet to share ideas, swap stories, and possibly arrange marriages. The paintings are usually deep within the caves in hard-to-reach places. The lack of cultural debris and minimal evidence of food consumption indicate that these sites were not used for permanent habitations.

It is not necessary to accept only one motivation for the cave paintings, nor do the reasons have to be utilitarian. Art for art's sake should not be discounted as one possibility. Scholars now believe that prehistoric people had sufficient leisure time to pursue something as creative and demanding as art. Usually, the paintings are found in the most inaccessible part of the cave—on a ceiling, or in a corner area well 'above the floor. If the artists did not take some pride in their work, and if they were not concerned about the results of their efforts having some degree of permanence, they would have painted on the floors, and only on the flattest and most readily available surfaces. Whatever the reasons for this early and creative form of communication, it remains one of the most magnificent and impressive representations of prehistoric culture.

THE NEOLITHIC REVOLUTION The last part of the Paleolithic Age coincided with what is called the last Ice Age. Earth's climate cooled noticeably, and glaciers formed, moving southward into what are today the northern temperate zones. With the freezing of a much greater part of the oceans, land bridges were formed between the continents. People who had moved into areas now threatened by cold, migrated into more southerly climates. But around 10,000 B.C., the climate of earth warmed up again.

During a brief transition period around 10,000 B.C. called the Mesolithic Era (Middle Stone Age), archaeologists find evidence of European people using a bow and arrow; in Japan the first pottery appears.

Then followed the remarkable Neolithic Era (New Stone Age). Though lasting a brief 5000 years, its developments in human skills gave rise to what can now be seen as the first real civilizations.

AGRICULTURE AND THE DOMESTICATION OF ANIMALS

The domestication of animals and the beginning of agriculture meant that people no longer needed to roam in search of food; organized agriculture produced a permanent surplus in food that allowed humans to turn their now fully-developed brains to other uses than merely providing bare subsistence. Tied to the crops they had planted, human beings began to settle in permanent locations. The first towns sprang up.

Archaeological evidence shows clearly what happened, and where. In the Middle East, people planted wheat and barley and tended these crops with the knowledge that they would reap the harvest at the end of the growing season. This took place around 8000 B.C. About 3000 to 4000 years later, agriculture was independently invented in other parts of the world—North China, Mexico (where corn, or maize, was the crop), and Peru (where it was potatoes). From these early centers, agriculture spread throughout the world.

Along with the planting of crops came the domestication of animals. Sheep, with their docile nature, were probably the first animals tended and bred by people for food. At around the same time, archaeologists find the bones of dogs appearing around human settlements. It seems possible that there was a connection, and that people first kept dogs for the same purposes as sheepherders do today. Not long afterward, around 6000 B.C., people began keeping cattle as well. The domestication of animals, along with the discovery of agriculture, make up what has been called the Neolithic Revolution.

Traditionally, it has been thought that the domestication of animals began less than 9000 years ago. New evidence, and old evidence looked at in different ways, suggests that our ancestors might have started domesticating animals as far back as 30,000 years ago. For instance, several cave paintings of horses have been found with a tell-tale line across the muzzle, indicating a harness. A stone-carved head of a horse, approximately 15,000 years old, was located recently in southern France. Carved across the head and the muzzle are lines that strongly suggest a harness made of rope. Horses that have been domesticated and broken for riding have a dental malformation known as "crib-biting." When horses are tied up, they will chew on anything hard, such as a fence post. The result is a wearing down of the incisor teeth in a unique and discernible way. The same kind of wear pattern has been found on the fossilized teeth of horse as far back as 30,000 years ago.

If we can push animal domestication back 30,000 years instead of the 5000 to 8000 years as was traditionally believed, then the Neolithic Revolution loses some of its revolutionary character. However, the transition from food-gathering to food-producing is still revolutionary in terms of the changes it brought about.

THE TRANSFORMATION OF PRIMITIVE SOCIETIES

With the ability to grow their own food and store the surplus through the invention of pottery, people could stay in one area and construct permanent dwelling places. A permanent food supply resulted in a Neolithic population explosion. Agricultural needs stimulated the invention of new tools and techniques, and pottery itself became not only utilitarian, but the inspiration for art.

With the accumulation of a surplus food supply, some people were freed from the need to hunt or gather food. These people began to specialize in certain skills, such as the making of pottery. It was not long before potters began to decorate their work, and shape it in new ways. Human ingenuity had found another outlet.

Some farmers were more successful than others, and social and economic classes began to emerge within the society. As society became more complex, there was a greater need to transmit and store information. The invention of writing soon followed, and with it came civilization.

This description of the results of the development of agriculture does not explain why it came about. The archaeologist V. Gor-

don Childe argued in the 1940s that agriculture came about as the result of a drought that occurred at the end of the last Ice Age. In search of shrinking supplies of water, in Childe's theory, all living things began to cluster around sources such as rivers and lakes. Childe believed that humans' close proximity to different animals and plants resulted in human exploitation of them, and their eventual domestication. Unfortunately, no evidence has ever been found of a prolonged drought at the time and in the area Childe was discussing.

The archaeologist Robert Braidwood in the 1960s saw the development of agriculture as almost inevitable once people had acquired the technological sophistication and cultural adaptability to make it possible. He argued that humans are receptive to change and, when given the opportunity, they tend to experiment.

Barbara Bender recently proposed another theory, based on the complex nature of certain social systems. Hunter-gatherer tribes, she argues, began to make contact with each other on a regular basis, and they started to trade or share goods. This, in turn, led to a need for surplus amounts of food in order to retain one's social standing. With this kind of social pressure, the domestication of plants and animals became a real possibility.

How the change to agriculture came about is an altogether different question. At Abu Hureya, an archaeological site in the northern Euphrates river valley, evidence was uncovered in the 1970s that suggests a possible solution. With a slowly warming temperature, plant life began to spread onto the prairie lands. The wild wheat and wild barley became so dense and so easy to harvest that there was no need to migrate in search of food. Hunter-gatherers could settle permanently in one spot and build a village. Once a town was built, and a means of storing food was found, and trade routes were established, it would not have taken much additional ingenuity to find ways to cultivate certain plants and domesticate certain animals.

In light of the growing archaeological evidence and the emergence of new interpretations, it is not surprising that the frontiers of farming have been pushed back to almost 17,000 B.C. A farming community of that period has been uncovered in western Egypt at Wadi Kabbaniya. The Biblical town of Jericho in the Holy Land has been the subject of archaeological excavations for a number of years. Recent research indicates that the community of Jericho is at least 10,500 years old. In order for one of the last steps in human progress to civilization to be taken, it was only necessary for towns to grow into cities.

Our knowledge of prehistory is far from complete. We are just beginning to learn to ask the right questions. The full story of human prehistory will be determined by present and future generations of anthropologists and archaeologists.

Ancient Civilizations

● Many the wonders but nothing walks stranger than man.
This thing crosses the sea in the winter's storm,
making his path through the roaring waves.
And she, the greatest of gods, the earth—
ageless she is, and unwearied—he wears her away
as the ploughs go up and down from year to year
and his mules turn up the soil....
He controls with his craft the beasts of the open air,
walkers on hills. The horse with his shaggy mane
he holds and harnesses, yoked about the neck,
and the strong bull of the mountains.

Language, and thought like the wind
and the feelings that make the town,
he has taught himself, and shelter against the cold,
refuge from rain. He can always help himself.
He faces no future helpless. There's only death
that he cannot find an escape from.

SOPHOCLES

● Soldiers! Think that from the summit of these pyramids 40 centuries are looking down upon you.

NAPOLEON

● And it came to pass at the end of the 430 years, even the selfsame day it came to pass, that all
the hosts of the Lord went out from the land of Egypt.
It is a night to be much observed unto the Lord for bringing them out from the land of Egypt:
this is that night of the Lord to be observed of all the children of Israel in their generations.
And the Lord said unto Moses and Aaron, This is the ordinance of the passover: There shall no
stranger eat thereof.

EXODUS 12:41

● By the rivers of Babylon, there we sat down, yea, we wept, when we remembered Zion.
We hanged our harps upon the willows in the midst thereof.
For there they that carried us away captive required of us a song; and they that wasted us
required of us mirth, saying, Sing us one of the songs of Zion.
How shall we sing the Lord's song in a strange land?
If I forget thee, O Jerusalem, let my right hand forget her cunning.

PSALM 137

● *There is nothing so fragile as civilization and no high civilization has long withstood the manifold risks it is exposed to.*
HAVELOCK ELLIS

Civilization of the Tigris-Euphrates Valley

Scholars are undecided as to whether civilization as we know it first began in Egypt or in the Tigris-Euphrates valley of present Iraq. This valley has had many names over the years: the ancient Greeks called it Mesopotamia, meaning "The Land between the Rivers." Some Biblical scholars believe that it was the site of the Plain of Shinar or the Garden of Eden.

EARLIEST CULTURES The oldest known settlements in the Land between the Rivers were made by people called the *Ubaidians* (**u-BAD-ians**). This name was derived from the Tell el-Ubaid, a site near the ancient Sumerian city of Ur. Scholars believe that the Ubaidians probably migrated from the highlands of Iran, to the east of the Tigris River, about 5000 B.C., and that they were the first people to occupy the marshlands of southern Mesopotamia.

The excavations of the site uncovered the remains of a village of mud-brick houses having staircases to the roofs, ovens still containing shells of freshwater fish, slings made from deer antlers, pottery decorated with geometric and animal designs, and a few weapons and tools made of copper. Archae-ologists believe that the inhabitants probably cultivated wheat and barley with the help of a simple irrigation system. Small clay figurines found in the ruins may have represented deities.

A second settlement existed at Uruk from about 3500 to 3100 B.C., succeeding that of the Ubaid people. At this site, archaeologists found several large buildings constructed on a high terrace with a stepped altar at one end. As Leonard Cottrell, a British journalist and writer, described these buildings, each included:

● ● ● *examples of what is now recognized as the characteristic architectural decoration of the Uruk period. This consisted of thousands of little cones of baked clay roughly the shape of a rifle cartridge. The tips of these were painted in various colors and the cones driven into the mud-brick wall, forming a charming mosaic pattern. Originally, these cones may have been invented to strengthen the buildings, but later they were developed as an architectural adornment.*[1]

---

[1]Leonard Cottrell, *The Quest for Sumer* (New York: G. P. Putnam's, 1965), p. 84.

Decorative cone mosaics adorned the walls and pillars of buildings discovered at Uruk.

Excavations at Jemdet Nasr have uncovered remains of still another group of people who, like the Uruk people, probably migrated from the area now known as Iran. Between 3100 and 2900 B.C., these people made pottery with a characteristic latticework design and created figurines of cut stone.

SUMER   Between 3500 and 3000 B.C., a people known as the *Sumerians* developed the first great civilization in the Tigris-Euphrates valley of which we have extensive knowledge.

CLIMATE AND NATURAL RESOURCES

The climate of ancient Sumer was similar to that of modern Iraq. The summers were extremely hot and rainfall was scanty. The rivers overflowed their banks each spring because of snow melting at their sources in the mountains, but this flooding was rather unpredictable and often violent. When the people learned to build reservoirs and irrigation systems, they were able to avoid disaster and became very successful in agriculture. Arnold Toynbee suggested that the Sumerian civilization evolved to meet the challenges of living in the "jungle-swamp" created by the Tigris and Euphrates rivers.

Since Sumer had no good stone or timber for building, the people adapted the materials at hand to their purposes. To build small homes, they bundled reeds together to form columns. Each bundle was tied securely for a length of several feet, but the tops were left untied. The bottoms were then set into shallow holes in the ground in two parallel rows, and the tops were bent and tied together to form arches. Crosspieces of bundled reeds were lashed into place and the framework was roofed over with reed mats.

For more elaborate structures, the Sumerians used bricks made of clay, and they soon learned to bake and glaze the bricks to make a more durable material. Although baked clay was not an ideal material for large structures, they found that they could greatly increase the height and width of their buildings by creating arches in the walls and adding support columns. Clay was also used to make pottery, and archaeologists have determined that the Sumerians utilized potter's wheels to mass produce their pots and plates.

The first Sumerians used reeds to construct their homes. This method of construction is still utilized today in some villages of the Tigris river valley.

The Sumerians relied upon clay for so many purposes that when Hecataeus, the 5th-century Greek geographer, visited Mesopotamia, he was moved to say, "The civilization of Mesopotamia is built upon clay." He also speculated that the people must have had 360 uses for a date-palm tree, which was the only species of tree that grew along the river banks. The fruit of these trees provided nutritious food, while vinegar, thread, fuel, and fodder for animals were derived from the leaves and trunk.

The Sumerians early invented a method to write their language (see text on *Writing* below), and the observations they recorded tell us much about how they met the particular challenges of their environment.

Because there was very little rainfall in the Land between the Rivers, the people had to depend on the spring floods for the water they needed for agriculture and livestock. For the purpose of predicting when the floods would come, Sumerian astronomers observed and recorded the movements of the heavenly bodies. One result of these records was the invention of a calendar based on the lunar cycle of 28 days.

To channel and collect the flood waters, the officials of the ziggurats directed the engineering and building of a system of earth banks, canals, and underground reservoirs. During the long, dry summer months, the water was then distributed to the farmers' fields and the herders' grazing lands. Due to these cooperative efforts, the Sumerians were successful in averting flood disasters and in developing a thriving agriculture. Farmers grew wheat, barley, dates, and millet. Herdsmen raised pigs, goats, cattle, and sheep, from which they derived hides and wool for leather- and textile-making as well as food.

Although the favorable climate and the irrigation system allowed the Sumerians to develop a surplus of food and textiles, they

ANCIENT MESOPOTAMIA
In what modern countries is the Fertile Crescent located?

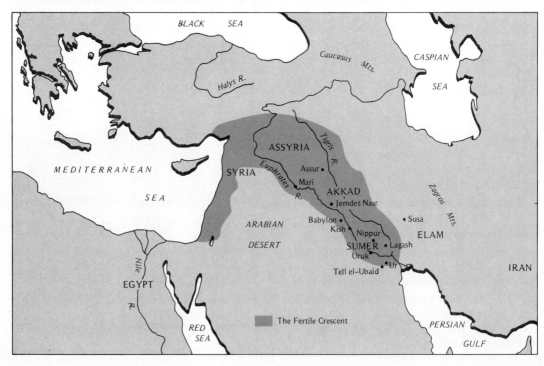

had very little stone or metal with which to manufacture tools and weapons. For the purpose of developing a trade for these items with their neighbors, the Sumerians built boats and domesticated donkeys for use as pack animals. Their tub-like rowboats plied the rivers and their donkey caravans crossed the Arabian Desert and the Zagros Mountains. They traded grain to their neighbors in Egypt and Nubia in return for copper, ivory, and gold. Their caravans traveled through the passes of the Zagros Mountains to secure semiprecious stones in Iran. From Anatolia and Armenia to the north, they obtained silver and tin.

From the artifacts uncovered by archaeologists, it is known that Sumerian craftsmen became very skillful in working with stone and metals. They learned how to fuse copper and tin to make *bronze*, an alloy that is much harder than either of these elements, and therefore more useful for weapons and tools.

By 3000 B.C. the plain of Sumer was dotted with small city-states such as Ur, Lagash, and Nippur. Each was an independent entity made up of the city and surrounding farmland, and was quite small by modern standards, having perhaps 12,000 to 36,000 inhabitants.

RELIGION

The most prominent feature of each Mesopotamian city was a temple dedicated to a

The skill of Sumerian craftsmen is demonstrated in the carving of these stone votive figures. The pupils of the enormous eyes once held semiprecious stones.

god who, it was believed, literally owned the city and the land around it. The Sumerians' gods were **anthropomorphic** in character—that is, they had the appearance and traits of human beings—and the temples were intended as residences for them.

The Sumerian temples still in existence resemble terraced pyramids and are called *ziggurats*. Each ziggurat was topped by a shrine which was thought to be the home of the god. The stairways that connected the various levels permitted the priests to ascend to the deities and the deities to descend to the people. The Sumerians believed that the gods controlled all aspects of their lives, including peace, health, the abundance of fish in the waters, the fertility of livestock, and even success in manufacturing bricks or tools.

As time passed, the people conceived of a whole pantheon of gods, and they created genealogies to keep track of the relationships and responsibilities of the various deities. Anu, the sky god, emerged as the ruler of all the gods. He was identified with the number 60. (The Sumerians' use of this number as their basic unit of mathematics, incidentally, is the origin of our 60-minute hour and 360-degree circle.) Enlil of Nippur, god of the wind, became the second most powerful god. He was represented by the number 50.

GOVERNMENT

Records on clay tablets indicate that the governments of the city-states were centralized from a very early time. The ruler of each city derived his authority from the fact that he was considered to be the representative of the god who owned the land. This form of government is known as a **theocracy**. As stewards of the god, the ruler and his officials allocated land to users, supervised the collection of grain, and directed the maintenance of the irrigation system. They lived and worked within a walled enclosure of the ziggurat and wielded enormous political and economic power over the lives of the ordinary people.

WRITING

The business activities of the ziggurat required the keeping of accurate records. The oldest examples of such records are baked clay tablets, dating to about 3000 B.C., which were affixed to sacks of grain to identify the type and amount of grain. Pictographs were scratched on flat tablets of wet clay, which were dried in the sun and then baked in an oven. In time, the Sumerian scribes began to use pieces of sharpened reeds, which they pressed into the wet clay to make wedge-shaped marks. This system of writing came to be called *cuneiform*, from the Latin word *cuneus*, meaning "wedge."

In order to express abstract ideas, the Sumerians transformed their pictographs into *ideograms*. For example, a picture of a pot would have originally represented a real pot, but later might have been transformed to represent "eating." A picture of a foot might have come to stand for the idea "to go." By combining two or more such ideograms, it

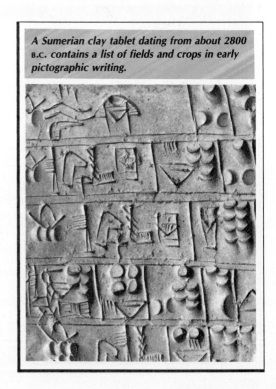

A Sumerian clay tablet dating from about 2800 B.C. contains a list of fields and crops in early pictographic writing.

became possible to create new, more complicated words without inventing new pictures or symbols. In time, the cuneiform symbols came to represent syllables, or phonograms. The Sumerians used several hundred pictograms and about one hundred phonograms, but neither they nor their successors in the Land between the Rivers developed an alphabet.

The Sumerians' invention of a system to represent sounds was adopted by successive cultures in the Land between the Rivers. The Akkadians, the Babylonians, and the Assyr-ians all utilized a cuneiform script to represent their own languages.

The translation of cuneiform tablets was made possible by the independent efforts of two men: Georg Friedrich Grotefend, a German schoolmaster, and Sir Henry Rawlinson, a British army officer. The keys to deciphering the tablets were provided by the inscriptions in three languages—Akkadian, Elamite, and Old Persian—which King Darius the Great had ordered carved on the *Behistun Rock* on a mountainside in Iran, about 520 B.C. In 1802, Grotefend concluded that a

Original Sumerian pictograph	Pictograph turned 90°	Cuneiform symbol, about 2500 BC	Assyrian cuneiform	Original or derived meaning
				BIRD
				FISH
				OX
				SUN DAY
				GRAIN
				TO STAND TO GO

single diagonal wedge mark had been used as a divider between words and found that the same set of symbols occurred repeatedly on successive lines: this led him to believe that these sets might represent the titles of Persian kings. In 1835, unaware of Grotefend's deductions, Rawlinson became interested in the inscriptions on the Behistun Rock. He also decided that the repetition of sets of symbols might be the titles of the Persian kings. He then fitted the names of Darius and Xerxes into the pattern "X, Great King, King of Kings, Son of Y." From this reading of the Old Persian script, Rawlinson was able to decipher the Akkadian cuneiform. The translation of the Old Persian script on the Behistun Rock led to the understanding of the cuneiform symbols. The translation of the cuneiform writing, in turn, made it possible for scholars to reconstruct the life of the people of ancient Sumer.

Those who mastered the art of cuneiform writing were held in high regard by the Sumerians. Boys selected for the scribal school studied for many years under strict discipline. One ancient tablet describes the difficulties experienced by a scribal student on a particular day:

• • • *When I awoke early in the morning, I faced my mother. I said to her: "Give me my lunch, I want to go to school. . . ." I went to school. The school monitor said to me, "Why are you late?" I was afraid, and with a pounding heart I entered before my teacher and made a respectful curtsy. . . .*
He who was in charge of drawing (said), "Why, when I was here, did you stand up?" (and) caned me. He who was in charge of the gate (said), "Why, when I was not here, did you go out?" (and) caned me. . . . He who was in charge of Sumerian (said), "You spoke . . ." and caned me. My teacher said, "Your hand is not good," (and) caned me.[2]

Literature. Most of the existing Sumerian clay tablets are legal documents such as deeds, receipts, and contracts. Some tablets contain words of wisdom of the type found in the Book of Proverbs in the Bible, while others are poems in praise of a god or king. Still others related myths of creation that parallel those found in the Book of Genesis. The story of Noah, for example, is similar to the Sumerian epic of Utnapishtun, who survived a great deluge by building an ark that floated on flood waters for six days and six nights. Although there are many differences between the two stories, this passage from Utnapishtun's reminiscences will sound familiar to anyone who has read the story of Noah:

• • • *I looked for land in vain, but fourteen leagues distant there appeared a mountain, and there the boat grounded; on the mountain of Nisir the boat held fast, she held fast and did not budge. One day she held, and a second day on the mountain of Nisir she held fast and did not budge. A third day, and a fourth day she held fast on the mountain and did not budge; a fifth day and a sixth·day she held fast on the mountain. When the seventh day dawned I loosed a dove and let her go. She flew away, but finding no resting place she returned. Then I loosed a swallow, and she flew away but finding no resting place she returned. I loosed a raven, she saw that the waters retreated, she ate, she flew around, she cawed, but she did not come back. Then I threw everything open to the four winds, I made a sacrifice and poured a libation on the mountain top.*[3]

Still another Sumerian legend involved a man who found himself alone and ill for reasons that he could not understand. The questions raised about this man's suffering and the justice of the gods resemble the story of Job in the Bible:

---

[2]S. N. Kramer, *History Begins at Sumer* (New York: Doubleday & Co., 1959), p. 9.

[3]N. K. Sanders, *The Epic of Galgamesh* (Baltimore: Penguin Books, 1960), p. 111

My god, the day shines bright over the . . .
  land; for me the day is black.
Tears, lament, anguish, and depression are
  lodged within me.
Suffering overwhelms me like one chosen
  for nothing but tears.
Evil fate holds me in its hand, carries off
  my breath of life.
Malignant sickness bathes my body.[4]

ARCHAEOLOGICAL FINDINGS

Royal Cemetery of Ur. Some of the most beautiful artifacts of Sumer were found in the tombs built for King Abargi and Queen Shubad, who ruled the city of Ur about 3000 B.C. The tombs were found in 1922 by Sir Leonard Woolley, a British archaeologist. The exquisite objects in the tomb included beautiful bowls and cups of alabaster and soapstone carved in shallow relief, fluted gold vases, gaming boards inlaid with shells, a dagger with a filigree sheath, and a lyre with a golden bull's head.

Adjacent to the stone burial chambers of the king and queen, there was a sloping ramp on which lay the skeletons of attendants and soldiers, who had apparently given up their lives so that they could serve their rulers in the afterlife. Alongside several of these skeletons there were small gold cups from which, Woolley deduced, the attendants had drunk a potion which rendered them unconscious.

Royal Standard of Ur. One of Woolley's most important finds was the Royal Standard of Ur, made of two rectangular panels of wood, each 22 inches long by 11 inches wide, inlaid with shell and lapis lazuli. On one side of each panel were scenes of war, and on the other side, scenes of a banquet. As he reported:

• • • *The separate pieces of inlay have never been taken apart and replaced but remain in the position in which they were set by the original artist. . . . Taken as a whole, the standard is unusually authentic, and, considering how peculiarly liable to destruction it was, wonderfully perfect.*[5]

---

[4]Kramer, *History Begins at Sumer*, p. 117.

[5]Shirley Glubok, *Discovering the Royal Tombs at Ur* (London: Collier-Macmillan, 1969), p. 61.

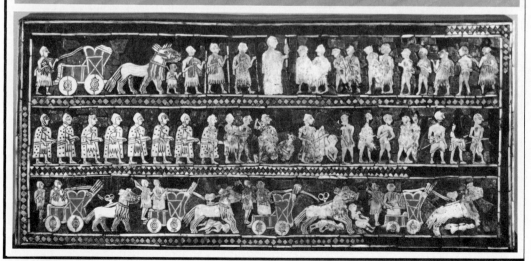

The pictures on the war side of the Royal Standard of Ur show soldiers bringing prisoners of war to their king. The four-wheel chariots on which some of them are riding are the oldest known evidence of the use of wheels.

THE DYNASTY OF SARGON

Although rivalries among the Sumerian kings had led to many infantry battles between the city-states prior to 2400 B.C., no ruler had managed to create an empire for any length of time. The first ruler to successfully unite the Land between the Rivers was Sargon I of Akkad, ruler of the kingdom to the north of Sumer. The dynasty he established in 2371 B.C. lasted for 200 years.

The city-states of Akkad were inhabited by Semitic people who had entered the valley from the west and had settled near the site of present-day Baghdad. They spoke their own language, but had many cultural and commercial ties with the Sumerians. Sargon began his career as a common citizen of Kish, one of the Akkadian city-states. By means that are unknown, he managed to usurp the rightful ruler of Kish and was accorded the title of king. After adopting the bronze weapons and infantry formations of the Sumerians, Sargon subdued the northern part of Mesopotamia and conquered the city-states of Sumer as far south as the Persian Gulf. He then led his army eastward into Elam and westward through Syria and the Lebanese mountains to the Mediterranean Sea. His kingdom finally extended along most of the Fertile Crescent and united all of this territory for the first time in history.

To conduct the business affairs of the new empire, Sargon and his officials adopted the cuneiform script of the Sumerians and used it to write their Semitic language. The conquered peoples were allowed to keep their ancient traditions and religions, as long as they paid tribute to Sargon and the Akkadians. Written records indicate that the Sumerians and other peoples of the empire willingly accepted Sargon's rule.

Sargon's most famous successor was his grandson Naramsin, who consolidated and possibly expanded the empire that his grandfather had built. Whereas his two predecessors had been called "king of Kish," Naramsin proclaimed himself "king of the four quarters of the earth." He commissioned the carving of a *stele*, or stone pillar, to depict his military victories. This *Stele of Victory*, as it came to be called, is the oldest surviving piece of Semitic artwork.

Naramsin's Stele of Victory depicts the king of Akkad as he celebrates a victory over his vanquished enemies.

THE THIRD DYNASTY OF UR

In 2200 B.C., the Gutians, a fierce, semibarbaric tribe from the Zagros Mountains, invaded Mesopotamia, destroyed several cities, and imposed a harsh rule over the valley. In 2112 B.C., Ur-Nammu, the governor of Ur, led a revolt against the Gutians and succeeded in driving them out

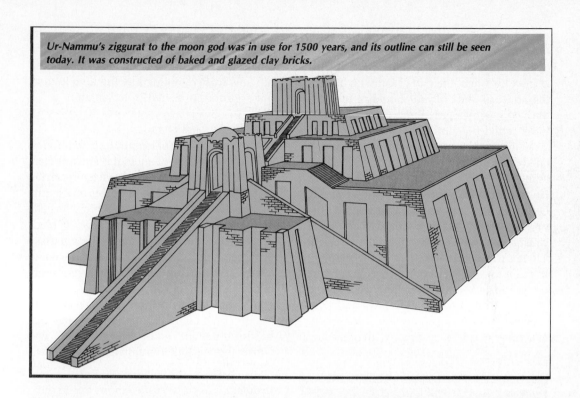

Ur-Nammu's ziggurat to the moon god was in use for 1500 years, and its outline can still be seen today. It was constructed of baked and glazed clay bricks.

of the area. The dynasty he established is known as the Third Dynasty of Ur, because he was the third monarch from Ur listed in a Sumerian list of kings. During his reign, the city-states of Sumer reached high levels of development and prosperity. Literature flourished, and temples were built and repaired. One ziggurat, dedicated to the moon god Nanna, was built in three levels to a total height of 80 feet, on a base 200 by 140 feet.

In the interest of promoting peace and civil order in his kingdom, Ur-Nammu published a code of laws. Only fragments of this oldest known law code have been found, but from these samples scholars have determined that monetary penalties were established for many common offenses.

After the death of Ur-Nammu, his kingdom continued to be ruled independently by three of his descendants. However, when the fifth, and last, king of the Third Dynasty came to the throne, he faced a famine and threats of invasion from the Elamites on the east and the Amorites (Semitic nomads) on the west. In 2004 B.C., Ur was besieged and destroyed by the Elamites. About 1850 B.C., the Amorites seized control of the valley and established their capital at Babylon.

While the Sumerians never again played an important role in history, their civilization was adopted the Akkadians, the Babylonians, and the Assyrians, who, as we will see, successively dominated the Land between the Rivers. The Sumerian language ceased to be used, but their cuneiform method of writing remained the standard form for thousands of years. And the rich heritage from Sumer continues to live today because of the legacy they left to succeeding peoples: laws to regulate human behavior, a method of recording history, and principles of metallurgy, architecture, and astronomy.

BABYLONIA Hammurabi was the sixth king of the Amorite Dynasty, and one of the most important rulers of ancient times. He united all of the city states of Mesopotamia under his rule, and, in time, his empire was as large as that of Sargon I. During his reign, the city of Babylon became the political and cultural center of the Middle East, and the Tigris-Euphrates valley came to be called *Babylonia*.

Hammurabi was a capable warrior and an effective ruler, but it is not as a conqueror or administrator that he is best known today. He is most famous for his code of laws. This code was one of the earliest attempts in history to ensure that men would accept decisions made by courts rather than seek to avenge wrongs on the spur of the moment. In order to establish a uniform system of justice throughout his kingdom, Hammurabi probably compiled existing laws and court judgments, and added new laws as necessary to achieve consistency. Finally, all of the laws

At the top of the stele that contains Hammurabi's code, the king is shown receiving the laws from Marduk, the god of justice. The Code is carved on the shaft of the stele.

were inscribed on several *stelae*, which were set up in various cities of the empire. Everyone was expected to obey these laws, and officials were appointed by the king to mete out appropriate penalties to violators.

THE CODE OF HAMMURABI

A copy of the *Code of Hammurabi* was found at Susa, the capital of ancient Elam. Scholars believe that this copy may have been carried off with other spoils of war during an Elamite raid on Babylon. The stele on which the code is inscribed is an eight-foot-tall block of black diorite, and the writings are in three parts: a prologue, the code itself, and an epilogue. In a carving at the top of the stele, Hammurabi is shown receiving the law from Marduk, the god associated with the sun and justice. In the prologue below, Hammurabi relates that he, the "devout, god-fearing prince," was chosen by Marduk to publish a code of laws:

● ● ● *to promote the welfare of the people, . . . to cause justice to prevail in the land, to destroy the wicked and the evil. That the strong might not oppress the weak and that widows and orphans might be protected from injustice.*[6]

The code itself consisted of 282 regulations affecting the social and economic affairs of the people. The epilogue, at the bottom of the stele, promised rewards to those who obeyed the laws and punishment to those who disobeyed.

Hammurabi's code is important to us today because it provides much insight into Babylonian society. Since agriculture was the most important occupation and the greatest source of wealth, many of the laws concern the cultivation of fields and the maintenance of irrigation systems:

● ● ● *53. If a seignior [a free or noble man] was too lazy to make (the dyke of) his field*

---

[6]J. B. Pritchard, *Ancient Near East Texts Relating to the Old Testament* (Princeton: Princeton University Press, 1955), p. 164.

strong, and a break has opened up in his dyke, and he has accordingly let the water ravage the farmland, the seignior in whose dyke the break was opened shall make good the grain that he let get destroyed.

54. If he be not able to make good the grain, they shall sell him and his goods, and the farmer whose grain the water has carried off shall divide the profits of the sale.[7]

A concept of strict accountability is evident in these examples: if the farmer was unable to pay for losses he had caused through carelessness, he could be sold into slavery to settle the account. This same principle also extended to people in other trades, such as building. A builder whose careless workmanship resulted in an accidental death was subject to the death penalty.

• • • 229. If a builder constructed a house for a seignior but did not make his work strong, with the result that the house which he built collapsed and so caused the death of the owner of the house, that builder shall be put to death.[8]

Other laws dealt with marriage and the relationships between men and women. By the standards of the time, certain "rights" of women were set forth. Husbands who abused their wives without cause had to pay a penalty in silver coin. And a wife was entitled to get her property back in a "no-fault" divorce.

• • • 138. If a seignior wishes to divorce his wife who did not bear him children, he shall give her money to the full amount of her marriage-price and he shall make good to her the dowry which she brought from her father's house, and then he may divorce her.[9]

The code reveals that there were three distinct strata in Babylonian society: the nobles, who were the priests of the temple and the officials of the palace; the commoners, who were the farmers, artisans, and merchants; and the slaves, who had either been purchased or taken as prisoners of war. While the nobles and commoners were held to a high level of accountability for the injuries they did each other, crimes against slaves were considered to be less serious. If a noble injured a slave, his penalty was much less severe than if he had injured another noble or a commoner. And the penalty he paid (usually in silver coin) was given to the slave's owner, not to the slave himself.

Some of the penalties involving death or mutilation seem harsh to us today, but they were probably intended to limit the cycle of violence that results from private vengeance. In general, the victims of crime, or their survivors, were prohibited from inflicting a greater injury than they had received. The following excerpts illustrate this principle:

• • • 196. If a seignior has destroyed the eye of a member of the aristocracy, they shall destroy his eye. . . .

197. If he has broken another seignior's bone, they shall break his bone. . . .

200. If a seignior has knocked out the tooth of a seignior of his own rank, they shall knock out his tooth. . . .

201. But if he has knocked out a commoner's tooth he shall pay one-third mina of silver.[10]

We do not know how often the penalties in Hammurabi's code were actually carried out, for only a few law court records have been found. However, the code itself had an important influence on the behavior of people long after the fall of Babylonia. In fact, the Law of Moses contains many similarities to it. While it was not the first law code in history, it was the most comprehensive of the ancient world until the Byzantine Emperor Justinian ordered the compilation of the Corpus Juris Civilis about 550 A.D.

[7]Pritchard, Ancient Near East Texts, p. 168.
[8]Ibid., p. 176.
[9]Ibid., p. 172.

[10]Ibid., p. 175.

After Hammurabi died in 1750 B.C., his kingdom began to decline almost immediately, for his successors were not capable of ruling such a large empire. Enemies began to attack Babylonia from both the east and the west. In 1595 B.C., for example, the Hittites of Anatolia (present-day Turkey) raided and plundered the land with the aid of weapons made of iron and war chariots drawn by horses. They left the valley so devastated that the Kassites, from the east, easily conquered the area in 1555 B.C.. We know very little about these Kassites except that they ruled the valley for almost 500 years, allowing the Babylonian city-states some independence. Literature, architecture, and other peaceful arts continued to flourish until the Kassites were displaced by the Assyrians.

ASSYRIA Semitic nomads called Assyrians established settlements to the northwest of Sumer and Akkad as early as 4000 B.C. Very little has been discovered concerning their earliest history in northern Mesopotamia, but it is known that they were ruled by the Mitanni tribes for several centuries and then established an independent kingdom around 1250 B.C. Their capital city, Assur, was named after and dedicated to the god of war, who was the chief god in their pantheon. After establishing their kingdom, the Assyrians resolved to build a mighty empire that could not be threatened by any outside force. Adopting the latest military technology of the Hittites and adding many innovations of their own, the Assyrians proceeded to fashion the most fiercely militaristic empire the Western world had ever known.

When the Hittite power in Anatolia collapsed about 1200 B.C., a situation of instability existed throughout the Middle East. For the next few centuries, the Assyrians' principal enemies were the Aramean tribes who were infiltrating the Mesopotamian valley and threatening their borders. For military campaigns against these tribes, the Assyrians usually assembled a large force of cavalry and chariot troops as well as infantry. The bows and arrows, slings and lances that they carried were of superior quality, for the Assyrians had learned the secret of making iron from the Hittites. The speed of their cavalry and two-wheel chariots—another invention of the Hittites—often enabled them to surprise and overwhelm their enemies. Once defeated, their enemies were not shown any mercy: some were beheaded, and many thousands of others were flayed or subjected to other tortures. The Assyrians eventually established their rule over all of Mesopotamia, and, on several occasions, they carried their campaigns as far west as the Mediterranean Sea, where they exacted tribute from the Syrians.

Assurnasirpal (884-859 B.C.) may have been the first Assyrian leader to resort to a policy of mass deportations as well as terror. Under his rule, conquered Aramean tribes from Syria were brought to the cities of Assyria and put to work in constructing palaces and monuments. One of the palaces they helped to build was so immense that 69,574 guests could be entertained at the dedication. In this palace and in other places throughout his realm, Assurnasirpal had inscriptions and paintings displayed which depicted the atrocities that he and his troops had committed against unarmed civilians as well as captured soldiers. His cruel policies—and his publicizing of them—soon made the very word "Assyrian" a synonym for terror.

During the reign of Tiglathpilesar III (745-727 B.C.), who is referred to as Pul or Pulu in the Bible, the Assyrians began to incorporate conquered territories into their empire. At its peak, the empire extended from the Mediterranean Sea through part of present day Iran. Roads were built and a postal service created to enable the Assyrians to administer this extensive region. Provincial governors were installed to administer the law, collect taxes, and conscript soldiers for the Assyrian army.

This winged bull once guarded a palace entrance at Assurnasirpal's capital city of Kalakh.

Some conquered areas, including Phoenicia and Israel (the northern kingdom of the Hebrews) became **vassal** states, meaning that their kings were permitted to keep their thrones as long as they paid tribute to the Assyrians. Troublesome rebels were punished quickly and harshly, and whole groups of people were deported from their homelands to other parts of the empire. For example, 30,000 Syrians were removed from their homes and resettled to the east, while 18,000 Arameans were forced to migrate to Syria. Assyrian colonists were often sent to live in the depopulated areas.

When Tiglathpilesar III died in 727 B.C., many subject people believed that the new Assyrian king would be too weak to control them. Revolts broke out in many parts of the empire. In 722 B.C., a man who used the name Sargon II seized the throne of Assyria. Some scholars believe that this man ordered the murder of the rightful heir and assumed the name of Sargon in order to be identified with the great Akkadian king who had ruled about 2500 B.C.

For three years, Sargon II laid siege to the city of Samaria, the capital of Israel, because Israel refused to pay tribute. When the inhabitants finally surrendered, Sargon ordered that 27,290 of them be deported. Because these people were no longer permitted to identify themselves as Israelites, they became known as the Lost Tribes of Israel. Assyrian colonists were then moved into Samaria, and their descendants, who intermarried with the Hebrews not sent into exile, came to be known as *Samaritans*.

When Sargon's son, Sennacherib, came to the throne of Assyria, he established his capital at Nineveh and was soon threatened by widespread revolts throughout his empire. Using the same methods as his predecessors, he quickly suppressed a revolt in Babylonia, then turned west toward Palestine and Phoenicia. The 19th-century poet Byron read the account of Sennacherib's attack on Judah in the Bible (2 Kings), and was moved to write:

*The Assyrian came down like the wolf
  on the fold,
And his cohorts were gleaming in purple
  and gold,
And the sheen of their spears were like
  stars on the sea
Where the blue wave rolls nightly on
  deep Galilee.* [11]

By 701 B.C., Sennacherib had crushed the Phoenicians, who were being aided by the Egyptians. Using heavy battering rams and siege ramps, he then captured 40 of the fortified cities of Judah. Over 200,000 Hebrews

---

[11] G. G. Byron, "The Destruction of Sennacherib."

were marched off into captivity. King Hezekiah was shut off "like a bird in a cage" in Jerusalem, the capital of Judah, surrounded by an overwhelming force of Assyrians. But he refused to surrender the city because the prophet Isaiah had assured him that the city could not be taken if the people would remain faithful to their god:

Thus says the Lord concerning the King
* of Assyria:*
He shall not enter this city nor shoot an
* arrow there,*
He shall not advance against it with shield
Nor cast up a siege ramp against it.
By the way on which he came he shall
* go back;*
This city he shall not enter.
This is the very word of the Lord.
I will shield this city to deliver it.
For my own sake and for the sake of my
* servant David.*[12]

Miraculously, Sennacherib abandoned his siege of Jerusalem and returned to Babylon. Scholars have not been able to explain this withdrawal of the Assyrian forces. Some suggest that an epidemic struck the soldiers, while others say that a rumor of revolt in Babylon forced Sennacherib to abandon his plans to take Jerusalem. Herodotus gave still another reason:

• • • *[A] number of field mice, pouring in among their enemies, devoured their quivers and their bows, the handles of their shields; so that on the next day, when they fled bereft of their arms, many of them fell.*[13]

In 681 B.C., Sennacherib was assassinated as the result of a palace conspiracy. When his son Esarhaddon came to the throne in Nineveh, he immediately made plans to avenge the murder of his father. The cruelty of Esarhaddon created great political unrest within Assyria and encouraged revolts throughout the empire. Nevertheless, he at-

tempted to expand the empire by invading Egypt in 671 B.C.. He captured the city of Memphis and imprisoned the pharaoh, but found that Egypt was too large and too far from Nineveh to be controlled effectively. Within a short time the Egyptians rose up in arms and expelled the Assyrian invaders.

Among his peaceful accomplishments, Esarhaddon rebuilt the city of Babylon, which his father had destroyed. He voluntarily retired in 668 B.C., turning the throne over to his son, Assurbanipal.

During the 42 years of Assurbanipal's reign, the Assyrian empire reached its greatest extent, stretching from the Nile valley to the Caucasus Mountains.

Unlike most other Assyrian kings, Assurbanipal was known for peaceful accomplishments as well as conquests. He created a great library of ancient Mesopotamian texts, and here is shown helping to rebuild the city of Babylon.

---

[12] 2 Kings 19:32-34.
[13] Herodotus II, 141.

THE OLD BABYLONIAN, ASSYRIAN, AND CHALDEAN EMPIRES
Why was Assurbanipal's empire so much larger than those of Hammurabi and the Chaldeans?

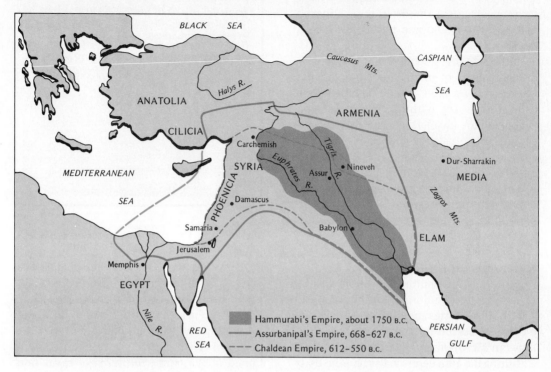

Hammurabi's Empire, about 1750 B.C.
Assurbanipal's Empire, 668–627 B.C.
Chaldean Empire, 612–550 B.C.

Using tribute collected from his vast empire, Assurbanipal made Nineveh the showplace of the ancient world. At his palace, he established a royal library where ancient manuscripts from Sumer and Akkad were collected and preserved. When the remains of this palace were excavated during the 19th century, archaeologists uncovered 22,000 clay tablets from the royal library, including hymns, dictionaries, grammars, treatises on astrology and medicine, lists of kings, chronicles of events, and myths about the creation of the world and a deluge that almost destroyed the world.

During the reign of Assurbanipal, the seeds of discord sprouted throughout the Assyrian empire. Nabopolassar, the governor of Babylon, encouraged other cities under Assyrian control to revolt. Unfortunately for Assyria, Assurbanipal's conquest of Elam had removed a buffer zone and had opened Assy-

ria's eastern borders to attack by the hostile Medes. In 612 B.C., the Chaldean people of Babylonia joined forces with the Medes of Persia to destroy Nineveh.

The prophet Nahum summed up the attitude of the victims of Assyria when he wrote:

Ah! blood stained city, steeped in deceit,
  full of pillage, never empty of prey!
Then all who see you shall shrink from
  you and say,
Where shall I look for anyone to
  comfort you? . . .
Your wounds cannot be assuaged, your
  injury is mortal;
all who have heard of your fate clap
  their hands in joy.
Are there any whom your ceaseless
  cruelty has not borne down?[14]

---

[14]Nahum 3:1, 7, 19.

To the present time, no nation has been so completely destroyed as was Assyria. Its three great cities, Dur-Sharrakin, Nineveh, and Assur, were burned to the ground and never rebuilt.

Although the downfall of Assyria was brought about by the Medes and the Persians, scholars have discovered that there were also events within Assyria that contributed to the invaders' success. Around 634 B.C., Assurbanipal had appointed one of his twin sons to be his successor. The other twin rebelled against his brother, and a bitter civil war ensued. The political divisions and economic disruptions caused by this war were probably an important factor in the Assyrians' defeat.

ARCHAEOLOGICAL FINDINGS

Prior to the 19th century, the Bible was the primary source of information about Assyria. The Biblical stories inspired several archaeologists to search for the ruins of Assyrian cities in Mesopotamia (present Iraq).

During the 19th century, Paul Emilie Botta, an agent in the French consulate at Mosul, Iraq, uncovered the ruins of the ancient city of Dur-Sharrakin and the palace that Sargon had built. The palace had 209 rooms and covered an area of 25 acres. Within the fortress-like walls were living quarters for the king and his servants, and treasuries and administrative offices. There were statues of awesome creatures, with human heads on bodies of winged lions or bulls, guarding the gates of the palace. The walls inside the palace were decorated with alabaster and limestone relief carvings depicting Sargon's military campaigns and royal lion hunts. The palace would certainly have impressed visitors with the power and majesty of the king of Assyria.

Another important discovery was made by Sir Henry Austen Layard in 1839. He excavated near present-day Mosul, and found the remains of ancient Nineveh. In particular, he found a 71-room palace built on a

A limestone relief found at Nineveh conveys the agony of a dying lioness. Assyrian palaces were decorated with many such artworks depicting the royal hunt.

terrace, and the remains of walls, with fortified gates, that once surrounded the palace. Layard estimated that these walls might have been eight miles in circumference and approximately 100 feet high. In 1852, Harmuz Rassam, a Turkish explorer, made additional excavations at Nineveh and uncovered the tablets of Assurbanipal's royal library, mentioned above, and sculptures of royal lion hunts. In these sculptures, the king was usually portrayed wearing the wings of an eagle, the horns of a bull, and the mane of a lion, symbolizing that he had the strength and ferocity of these wild animals.

THE ASSYRIAN CIVILIZATION

The Assyrians inherited many aspects of their civilization from earlier peoples and adapted ideas from their contemporaries, but they used this inheritance to create a very different type of society. Having learned from the Akkadians how to use cuneiform script to write their Semitic language, they used this valuable skill to administer their empire. The postal service that they created enabled the king to send written orders to the governors of his widespread empire and to receive information from them. The Assyrians also used writing to record the activities of the royal court: they were the first people to create a written chronicle of their kings.

From the Hittites, the Assyrians learned how to work with iron, and from the Mitanni tribes they learned how to breed and train horses. Their iron weapons and well-drilled cavalry and chariot troops made an important contribution to their war victories, for many of their opponents had only bronze weapons and infantry troops.

In government, too, the Assyrians made many important innovations in traditional practices. Although in theory the Assyrian kings ruled as representatives of the god Assur, in practice they did not derive their authority from this connection. Their monuments and palaces were not built in honor of the god, but for the use of the king. Religious leaders never became a political force in Assyria as they had in Sumer and Egypt.

One problem in the Assyrian system was that there were very likely to be disruptions and rebellions when a king died, since he was the source of all authority in govern- ment. To overcome this problem, each Assyrian king chose an *heir apparent* and made sure that this heir was recognized as such by the nobles and officials of the realm. Years later, the Persians and Romans adopted this and many other features of the Assyrians' imperial administration.

After the fall of Assyria in 612 B.C., the four most important powers in the Middle East were Egypt, Lydia, Chaldea, and Medea. The Egyptians, under the Saite dynasty (650-625 B.C.), enjoyed a period of prosperity and cultural renaissance. The Lydians, under King Croesus, were the chief power in Anatolia. The Chaldeans ruled Syria, Palestine, Phoenicia, and the Land between the Rivers, with Babylon, their capital, once again becoming the most important city in the Middle East. Farther east, the Medes took control of Persia in 550 B.C. Under the leadership of Cyrus the Great, they captured Babylon and established the *Persian Empire*, which dominated the Middle East for 200 years.

THE LAND BETWEEN THE RIVERS★

AKKAD	
2371-2316	**Sargon I**
2291-2255	**Naramsin**
2112-2004	**3RD DYNASTY OF UR**
2112-2094	**Ur-Nammu**
BABYLON	
1792-1750	**Hammurabi**
ASSYRIA	
884-859	**Assurnasirpal**
745-727	**Tiglathpilesar III**
722-705	**Sargon II**
705-681	**Sennacherib**
681-668	**Esarhaddon**
668-626	**Assurbanipal**
CHALDEA	
612-604	**Nabopolassar**
604-562	**Nebuchadnezzar**

★All dates are approximate years B.C.

CHALDEA Nabopolassar, who led the successful revolt against the Assyrians in 612 B.C., was proclaimed king of the Babylonians. The society he helped to build is called *Chaldea*, or *Neo-Babylonia*. He considered the kings of Syria and Phoenicia to be his vassals, and sent his son Nebuchadnezzar II to assert control over them. Meanwhile, Necho, pharaoh of Egypt, took advantage of the turmoil following the collapse of Assyria to become involved in Palestine and Syria. Necho marched northward into Syria and met Nebuchadnezzar at Carchemish, in 605 B.C. In the resulting battle, the Egyptians were defeated disastrously and retreated to Egypt.

When Nabopolassar died, in 604 B.C., Nebuchadnezzar returned to Babylon, claimed the throne, and became the most important ruler of the dynasty. The pharaoh again tried to stir up trouble by encouraging Jehoiakim, the king of Judah, to throw off the Chaldean yoke. In response to this threat, Nebuchadnezzar's army marched through Palestine and besieged Jerusalem in 597 B.C.. Jehoiakim was killed in battle, and his 18-year-old son, Jehoiachin, ascended the throne of Judah. Within three months the young king was forced to surrender, and Nebuchadnezzar confiscated the treasuries of both the palace and the temple. The king and his mother, together with almost 8000 Judeans, were marched off into captivity in Babylon.

A few years later, Egypt again stirred up revolt and again insisted that Judah join in the conspiracy against Chaldea. In 587 B.C., Nebuchadnezzar returned to Jerusalem and besieged the city. After 18 months, the starving people were forced to surrender. Zedekiah, whom Nebuchadnezzar had appointed as vassal king of Judah, was captured as he attempted to flee the city. His sons were executed before his eyes, and he was blinded and taken captive to Babylon. Thus the Jews began the "Babylonian Exile," which lasted until 538 B.C.

After the death of Nebuchadnezzar, in 562 B.C., several unpopular rulers came to the throne of Chaldea. One of these rulers, Nabonidus, antagonized the priests of Marduk, the god of justice, when he attempted to make the moon-god Sin the chief deity. While Nabonidus was absent from Babylon, in 539 B.C., his son Belshazzar governed the nation. The Book of Daniel tells the story of how the Chaldean monarchy was overthrown. As Belshazzar and his guests were feasting at a great banquet at the palace, Cyrus, the king of Persia, with help from the priests of Marduk, captured Babylon. Chaldea then became part of the vast Persian Empire.

ARCHAEOLOGICAL FINDINGS

While Nebuchadnezzar is best known today for destroying Jerusalem, he also made Babylon the most beautiful city in the ancient Middle East. In 1899, Robert Koldeway, a German archaeologist, excavated the site of Babylon and was eventually able to lay out the plan of the ancient city. The walls surrounding the city formed a square, and each wall was nine miles long. Outside the walls, there was a deep moat. For over 2000 years, scholars had assumed that Herodotus, writing in the 5th century B.C., had been exaggerating when he wrote the following description:

• • • on the top of the wall, at the edges, they built dwellings of one story, fronting each other, and they left a space between these dwellings sufficient for turning a chariot with four horses. In the circumference of the wall there were a hundred gates, all of brass. . . . This outer wall, then, is the chief defense, but another wall runs round within. . . .[15]

Archaeologists now know that this wall was actually 300 feet high and 80 feet thick, with 250 watchtowers and 100 bronze gates.

Herodotus also described a bridge, 400 feet long and supported on seven boat-shaped

---

[15]Herodotus I, 180-1.

The Ishtar gate of ancient Babylon was constructed with glazed and molded bricks.

piers, that crossed the Euphrates River and formed a part of Babylon's Procession Street. This street passed through the outer walls and bisected the city. On both sides of the street were sidewalks paved with small red stone slabs, and along the edge of every stone were carved the words, "I am Nebuchadnezzar, king of Babylon, who made this." At the south end of Procession Street was a double gate covered with brilliant blue glazed bricks and bas relief animal sculptures, dedicated to the goddess Ishtar. This gate can be seen today in the German Museum in East Berlin.

• • • *In the midst of this precinct is built a solid tower of one stade [517 feet] both in length and in breadth, and on this tower rose another, and another upon that, to the number of eight; and an ascent to these is outside, running spirally round all the towers. About the middle of the ascent there is a landing place and seats to rest on; . . . and in the uppermost tower stands a spacious temple, and in this temple is placed, handsomely furnished, a large couch, and by its side a table of gold. No statue has been erected within it, nor does any mortal pass the night there, except only a native woman, chosen by the gods out of the whole nation, as the Chaldeans, who are priests of this deity, say. These same priests assert, though I cannot credit what they say, that the god himself comes to the temple and reclines on the bed.*[16]

The temple Herodotus described is now believed to have been the inspiration for the Biblical story of the Tower of Babel (Genesis 11:4-9).

Nebuchadnezzar's great palace in Babylon was, he declared, "the admiration of all who saw it." The walls were decorated with colorful friezes made up of blue and yellow enameled bricks, and the throne room opened onto a vast courtyard. A palace garden was built for the queen in the form of an artificial mountain, to remind her of her mountain

The hanging gardens of Babylon, built by Nebuchadnezzar for his queen, were one of the Seven Wonders of the World.

birthplace. This garden had several terraces supported by huge man-made vaults. Amid the ruins of these vaults, archaeologists found a well, with a pump designed to provide a continuous flow of water for the garden. The *hanging garden*, as it came to be called, was one of the legendary Seven Wonders of the World.

The construction of Babylon required many thousands of bricks, and it is probable that these bricks were molded and fired by captives. The story of Shadrach, Meschach, and Abednego, in the Book of Daniel, probably originated from this activity.

THE CHALDEAN CIVILIZATION

The Chaldean culture was essentially a continuation of the older cultures in the Land between the Rivers. The greatest contributions they made were related to their studies of the heavens and their observations of the movements of the sun, the moon, and the planets. Indeed, they may be considered to have been the first astronomers because they

---

[16]Herodotus I, 181-2.

were able to forecast eclipses of the moon and identify the signs of the zodiac (12 constellations which are almost uniformly spaced around the celestial equator). Although the Babylonians continued to use a lunar calendar of 28-day months, Naburimannu, a priest, computed the length of a solar year. Kidinnu, another priest, determined the tilt of the axis of the earth and the precession of equinoxes.

The Chaldeans learned to distinguish the planets from the stars. They regarded the five planets closest to the earth (Venus, Mercury, Jupiter, Mars, and Saturn), together with the sun and the moon, to be manifestations of their major deities. Each of the deities was worshiped on a separate day, and this practice led to the concept of a seven-day week, which the Romans later adopted. The Chaldeans' work with lunar cycles strongly influenced Meton, a Greek astronomer of the 5th century B.C., who devised a workable calendar based on the Babylonian system. (In Meton's system, an extra month was added every few years to reconcile the lunar calendar with the solar year. His calendar was in error by only 5 days every 19 years.)

The Chaldeans developed the science of astronomy for a practical purpose: they believed that knowledge of celestial events would enable them to foretell the future. In addition to their work in astrology, the Babylonians became known in the ancient world for their expertise in several other forms of divination. They wrote detailed treatises, for instance, on the art of predicting the future through studying the liver of a sacrificial animal. Archaeologists have found models of livers which were probably used to train priests in this form of divination.

SUMMARY

The earliest major civilization developed in Sumer, which occupied the marshlands of the Tigris and Euphrates rivers. As early as 3500 B.C., under the leadership of their priest-kings, the Sumerians learned to work together to control the flooding of the two great rivers. Over the years, they invented cuneiform writing, a calendar, and a system of weights and measures. They also discovered the principles of metalworking and of the wheel and the arch.

The Sumerian civilization provided a foundation for the emerging cultures that overran the region in successive centuries. The Akkadians used the arts of the Sumerians to develop military skills, and adopted the Sumerian cuneiform to the writing of their own language. The Babylonians made a great contribution to legal philosophy in Hammurabi's code of laws. The Assyrians then conquered the land and established the greatest empire of the Western world up to that time. In the process, their name became synonymous with terror. The Chaldeans converted Babylon into a monumental city and contributed to human knowledge by observing the heavens and developing some principles of astronomy.

QUESTIONS

1 How did geography affect the development of civilization in Sumer? Why did this civilization affect the development of all the peoples who invaded and conquered the Tigris-Euphrates Valley?

2 Explain the meaning of the phrase "codification of law." What is the significance of a law code? What would life be like if there were no codes of law?

3 What does the law code of Hammurabi tell us about the way people lived when he was king?

4 Compare the flood story in the Bible with that found in the "Epic of Gilgamesh."

5 What modern laws are similar to those described in Hammurabi's law code?

BIBLIOGRAPHY

Which book would you use to learn more about the Behistun Rock?

CERAM, C. W. *Gods, Graves and Scholars.* New York: Knopf, 1967. *A popular book about the archeologists who have contributed to our understanding of the past; arranged by area rather than by chronology. Includes exciting human interest stories about the archeologists and emphasizes the significance of their findings.*

COTENAU, GEORGES. *Everyday Life in Babylonia and Assyria.* Chatham: Mackay, 1954. *Discusses the history of the Tigris-Euphrates Valley between the rise of Sargon II of Assyria and the conquest of the Babylonians (Chaldeans) by the Persians; reviews thousands of clay tablets, which revealed how the kings, nobles and common people thought and lived; includes stories, legends, religious rituals, hymns, and scientific and mathematical treatises.*

2 *Egypt*

● *But concerning Egypt I will now speak at length, because nowhere are there so many marvelous things, nor in the whole world beside are there to be seen so many works of unspeakable greatness; therefore, I shall say the more concerning Egypt.*

HERODOTUS

The Nile valley was a second important cradle of civilization in the ancient world. Herodotus[1] described Egypt as a "gift of the Nile River," because in this almost rainless land, the Nile provides a ribbon of green bisecting hundreds of miles of scorched desert and barren hills.

Egypt has continued to fascinate travelers over the centuries. Visitors today can see the same river, the same desert, and the same ancient works that Herodotus described, varying from the towering Great Pyramid to the small treasures from the tomb of Tutankhamun.

THE NILE RIVER VALLEY The White Nile, which rises in Lake Victoria in equatorial Africa, and the Blue Nile, which has its origins in the highlands of Ethiopia, join at Khartoum, the capital of Sudan. Between the sites of present-day Khartoum and Aswan, six cataracts, or major "rapids," interfered with transportation on the river. (Some of these cataracts are now covered by Lake Nasser, created by the Aswan Dam in 1971.) From Aswan to Cairo, a distance of about 550 miles, the Nile is unobstructed and flows throughout the year. From a point north of Cairo to the Mediterranean Sea, the very large, fertile delta of the Nile provides many waterways and good agricultural land.

The distinctive landscape of Egypt provided the early Egyptians with natural defenses against invaders. The deserts to the east and west formed a vast ocean of sand, while the Mediterranean Sea formed a secure boundary to the north, and the cataracts discouraged Nubian raiders from the south. Because of this natural protection, the early Egyptians were undisturbed by invaders for many centuries and thus were able to develop a culture essentially free from outside influence.

The Nile River was a major factor in the development of the arts and sciences of civilization in Egypt. Since there was so little rainfall, the early people were forced to develop techniques for collecting and distributing waters from the annual flood. These techniques included the *shadoof*, a simple

---

[1]Herodotus was a Greek historian who traveled widely in the Middle East during the 5th century B.C. He is one of our most important sources of information concerning the cultures and events of the ancient world.

THE COURSE OF THE NILE
Look at a physical map of Africa to find the location of desert and mountains.

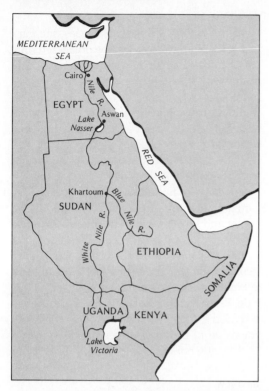

Nile. The stems of this plant could be pressed to make a form of paper, and the fibers could be twisted into rope. Copper and turquoise were available in the Sinai Peninsula, and gold was found in the desert to the east of Thebes. Limestone for many building purposes was available in Lower Egypt, and granite was quarried near the first cataract in Upper Egypt. Fine pottery clay was readily available; mixed with water and straw, this clay could be formed into bricks which were hardened by exposure to the sun.

When the Egyptians learned how to quarry and transport stone, this resource began to replace clay bricks as a building material for

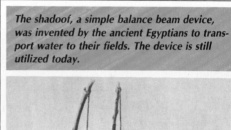

The shadoof, a simple balance beam device, was invented by the ancient Egyptians to transport water to their fields. The device is still utilized today.

balanced beam with a bucket at one end, which was used for lifting water out of the river into irrigation ditches.

The need to relocate property lines inundated by the flooding led the Egyptians to develop the science of geometry: in fact, the Greek word *geometry* means "land measure." The long stretch of unobstructed river from the first cataract to the sea provided easy transportation, and thus promoted communication and trade between the towns along its banks.

NATURAL RESOURCES
The banks of the Nile, and the deserts and hills around them, provided a variety of resources which the Egyptian people learned to exploit. The papyrus plant grew profusely along the banks and northern marshes of the

45

some dwellings and houses. They used what is called a post-and-lintel construction.[2] By contrast, the people of Mesopotamia had no such rock, but discovered that they could build larger structures by adding supports and creating arches with clay bricks.

EARLY CULTURES

Campsites of Paleolithic people, dating from the 5th or 4th millenium B.C., have been discovered in gravel terraces along the Nile, and in places that are now in the desert. Judging from the well-made stone implements and the animal bones found in these camps, the people killed and ate wild cattle, antelope, and sometimes a hippopotamus. Fish must have been an important source of food because many hooks made of ivory, shell, or bone have been found. As the climate changed and the region turned into desert, the people of Egypt were forced to migrate to sites along the Nile.

PREDYNASTIC EGYPT

By the end of the 4th millenium B.C., many of the characteristic features of Egyptian society had been developed. Irrigation was practiced, a system of writing had been devised, and the basic religious beliefs of later generations were established. Wealthy people were buried in houselike tombs called *mastabas*, which are similar to the great tombs of later times. In the mastabas, archaeologists have found jewelry and vases wrought from gold and copper, and linen woven from flax. The mastabas also contained many slate cosmetic palettes, indicating that early Egyptian women were applying the makeup that became characteristic in later times. In the paintings of the mastabas, the artistic conventions of later times are also apparent: the torsos of human figures are seen in full frontal view, while the faces, legs, and arms are seen in profile.

GOVERNMENT

Over the course of many centuries, the various tribes of Egypt came to be organized into small political districts called *nomes*. Each nome was ruled by a leader called a *nomarch*, who lived in the capital city of the nome, near the temple of the tribal god. The nomarch was the chief priest of the tribal god and was also in charge of supervising the irrigation system, collecting taxes, and leading the nome's military force.

In time, the nomes came to be loosely organized into the two distinct kingdoms of Upper and Lower Egypt. The ruler of the most important nome in each kingdom gradually gained **hegemony** over the other nomes and took the title of *pharaoh* [FARE-oh]. *Upper Egypt* extended through the higher ground of the Nile River valley, from Nubia to the delta, and used the falcon as its symbol. *Lower Egypt* consisted of the delta area and was symbolized by the cobra.

RELIGION

From the earliest times, the Egyptians' most revered god was Re, or Ra, the god of the sun. Whereas certain other deities were worshiped only locally, in the towns that contained their temples, Re was worshiped by all Egyptians and became the state god during the dynastic period. The sun god had many different manifestations, since separate cults in honor of him had developed throughout Egypt. Re-Atum, whose temple was in Heliopolis, represented the declining sun and was associated with the wisdom of an aged man. The sky god Horus, originally represented as a falcon on the horizon, also came to have associations with the sun god.

One of the central legends of Egypt concerned the god Osiris, who was thought to have been a pharaoh in prehistoric times. Osiris was killed by the wicked god Seth and then brought back to life through the efforts

---

[2]In this system of construction, many upright *posts*, or columns, are used to support horizontal *lintels*, or beams. The maximum spacing between the columns is determined by the strength of the materials used.

Osiris

Seth

Isis

Thoth

Anubis

of his wife, Isis. Osiris and Isis then conceived a son, Horus, who later took revenge upon Seth with the help of the benevolent god Thoth. The figures in this legend came to have important associations with the pharaohs of Egypt. Egyptians believed that their pharaoh, the son of Re, was also closely linked with the gods Osiris and Horus. In life, the pharaoh was associated with the living Horus, and in death he became joined to Osiris, the ancient pharaoh who had achieved life after death.

Most of the Egyptians' gods were *anthropomorphic* in character, even though they were frequently able to assume the strengths or capabilities of certain animals. In this respect they were very much like the gods of the Mesopotamians. However, several of the Egyptian gods were more animal than human in their conception. One of these animal gods was Anubis, the jackal who roamed the cemeteries and communicated with the dead. He was usually portrayed as a realistic-looking jackal, but occasionally was given the body of a man with a jackal's head.

Belief in a life after death remained fairly consistent throughout Egypt's history, although there were many contradictory ideas about the subject. From the earliest times, it was thought that dead people came to life again after they were buried, and for this reason their tombs were equipped with furniture, food, and other necessities of life. Later,

it was thought that the pharaoh, and perhaps certain nobles or members of his family, joined the sun god Re in his daily journey across the sky. To provide a vehicle for this solar journey, model boats were often included in the tomb furnishings. (There may have been some doubts about the solar journey, for the pharaohs' tombs continued to be furnished, as before, with the necessities of everyday life.)

During the period of the New Kingdom, the legend of Osiris provided the basis for an extremely imaginative conception of life after death. People began to think that Osiris' kingdom was beneath the western desert, and illustrated guides called Books of the Dead

The ancient Egyptians sometimes placed models of boats in tombs so that the souls of the deceased could travel. Two full-size boats were found near the pyramid of Cheops.

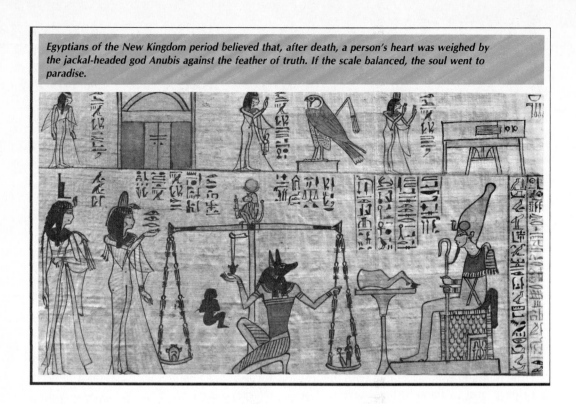

Egyptians of the New Kingdom period believed that, after death, a person's heart was weighed by the jackal-headed god Anubis against the feather of truth. If the scale balanced, the soul went to paradise.

were painted in tombs so that the deceased could find their way there. (Some guides showed both a land and a sea route to the underground kingdom.) Once the dead person had found the gates to the underworld, he confronted Osiris himself, who judged whether the person was worthy to enter. If the judgment was favorable and the person was admitted, people believed that life proceeded much as it had in the real world of Egypt. Many tombs contained small statues called *shabti* which the dead person could send out as substitutes if he or she were summoned to work in the fields.

THE DYNASTIES OF EGYPT Around 3100 B.C., a political union of Upper and Lower Egypt was achieved under the leadership of Narmer, who was a ruler of Upper Egypt. To symbolize the unification of the two kingdoms, Narmer wore a crown that combined features of the orig-

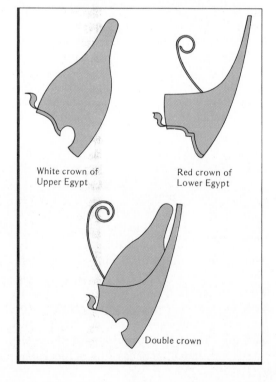

White crown of Upper Egypt

Red crown of Lower Egypt

Double crown

inal crowns of Upper Egypt (white, with a falcon symbol) and Lower Egypt (red, with a cobra symbol). Entwined stems of reed and papyrus plants were also used as a symbol of the combined kingdoms. To further symbolize the unification, Narmer built a new capital city, later called Memphis, at the meeting point of the Upper and Lower Kingdoms. The use of these symbols indicates how important the unification was to the people of the time, and it came to be equally important to succeeding generations. Later Egyptians considered the unification to be the beginning of their nation's history.

In 1898, archaeologists found the Slate Palette of Narmer, which became one of the most important sources of information about this early period. On one side of the palette, Narmer is shown walking in a procession while wearing the crown of Lower Egypt. On the other side, he is shown wearing the tall crown of Upper Egypt.

THE THREE KINGDOMS

According to Manetho, an Egyptian priest who lived in the 3rd century B.C., there had been 30 dynasties in the history of Egypt. Archaeologists have found a number of ancient inscriptions which support many of the listings in Manetho's chronology. In these inscriptions, years were often numbered in relation to an outstanding event in a pharaoh's reign, such as a major conquest, the erection of an important structure, or a tomb ritual. By comparing these inscriptions to the records left by the peoples of Mesopotamia, Syria-Palestine, Greece, and other areas, scholars have been able to establish many dates within reasonable limits. Modern Egyptologists now divide Manetho's dynasties into three major periods: the Old Kingdom, or Pyramid Age, covering the 3rd to 6th dynasties (2686-2160 B.C.); the Middle Kingdom, or Feudal Age, covering the 11th and 12th dynasties (2040-1786 B.C.); and the New Kingdom, or Empire, covering the 18th to 20th dynasties (1570-1075 B.C.).

Narmer's Slate Palette celebrates his victory over Lower Egypt, around 3100 B.C. This is the oldest surviving image of an historic person identified by name.

THE OLD KINGDOM

Nothing was more representative of the absolute power and imputed divinity of the pharaohs of the Old Kingdom than their pyramids. The inscriptions and statues in each pyramid complex tell us much of what we know about each pharaoh's reign. Zoser, in the third dynasty, was the first pharaoh to build a monumental structure to house his remains. The fact that he was able to marshall the immense work force needed to quarry and transport the stone for such a structure indicates that his administration was highly centralized and efficient.

Imhotep, Zoser's *vizier*, or chief official, is credited with being the architect and engineer of the Step Pyramid at Sakkara. The impressive stepped construction with its facade of limestone represented a great advance in the techniques of stoneworking and was considered a miraculous achievement at the time. Imhotep was regarded as a great philosopher and healer as well as an architect, and in time was even worshiped as a minor deity.

Because of his special relationship with the sun god Re, the pharaoh was believed to be immortal and to have the power to intervene with the gods on behalf of his people. His authority rested on *ma'at*, a concept that cannot be expressed in one English word. It related to continuity, eternity, harmony, goodness, and truth. As head of government, the pharaoh and his officials were in charge of administering the gods' law. In fact, there were no written laws, since the pharaoh and his appointed officials were considered to be in communication with the gods. Special altars were included within the complex of each pharaoh's tomb so that priests could pray to him for his continued guidance in the affairs of Egypt.

With the beginning of the fourth dynasty, around 2613 B.C., the building of great pyramids began in earnest. The biggest of these, located at Gizeh, is the Great Pyramid of Khufu. The name *Khufu* means "smasher of

Top: *Mastabas of the predynastic period resembled houses. The entrance to the underground burial chamber was filled with stones after the funeral.* Center: *Zoser's Step Pyramid was redesigned during construction to add two additional stages.* Bottom: *Chambers and passageways were cut into the Great Pyramid of Cheops after the interior was constructed.*

Pharaoh's chamber

Tomb

A photograph taken in the 1920s shows the Nile in flood, with the great pyramids of Cheops at right and that of his son Khafre (Chephren) at center.

foreheads,'' and this pharaoh was known as a particularly autocratic and difficult ruler. The ancient Greeks referred to him as *Cheops* [KEY-ops], and most people use this name today.

The pyramids at Gizeh, and particularly that of Cheops, so impressed the people of later times that they devised various explanations of their purpose. Some early Christians believed that they were granaries erected by the Jewish patriarch Joseph. Other people suggested that they were treasuries, or the palaces of kings, or astronomical observatories. The Great Pyramid is indeed an awe-inspiring structure. Herodotus reported that Cheops' pyramid, as originally built, was 481 feet high, and each side was 755 feet long. The average block of stone weighs 5000 pounds, and some of the granite blocks that were quarried at Aswan and brought to the site by boat weigh 30 tons. Each block was measured and cut so precisely that even today a knife blade cannot be slipped between two adjacent blocks.

Khafre (or Chephren), the son of Cheops, continued the tradition of pyramid-building at Gizeh, and also added an enormous sphinx to the mortuary grounds. He had his own features inscribed on the face of the sphinx, and thus commemorated his reign in this statue as well as in his pyramid. Like his father, Khafre was known as a difficult king.

The sphinx erected by Khafre still guards the royal tombs at Gizeh.

THE THREE KINGDOMS OF EGYPT★	
-3100	*Predynastic Period*
	OLD KINGDOM
2686-2613	*3rd dynasty*
	Zoser
2613-2494	*4th dynasty*
	Khufu (Cheops)
	Khafre (Chephren)
2494-2345	*5th dynasty*
2345-2160	*6th dynasty*
	Intermediate period
2160-2040	*7th-10th dynasties*
	MIDDLE KINGDOM
2040-1991	*11th dynasty*
2040-2010	*Mentohotep II*
1991-1786	*12th dynasty*
1991-1961	*Amenemhet I*
1961-1938	*Sesostris I*
	Intermediate Period
1786-1674	*13th dynasty*
1674-1570	*Hyksos rule*
	NEW KINGDOM
1570-1320	*18th dynasty*
1570-1546	*Ahmose I*
1504-1482	*Hatshepsut/Thutmose III*
1482-1450	*Thutmose III*
1417-1379	*Amenhotep III*
1379-1362	*Akhenaton*
1361-1352	*Tutankhamun*
1352-1348	*Ay*
1348-1320	*Horemheb*
1320-1200	*19th dynasty*
1320-1318	*Ramses I*
1318-1304	*Seti I*
1304-1237	*Ramses II*
1200-1075	*20th dynasty*
1198-1166	*Ramses III*

★All dates are approximate years B.C.

First Intermediate Period. Some of the Old Kingdom pharaohs became so preoccupied with the building of pyramids that they exhausted their treasuries and had to look to the nobles of the provincial districts for financial aid. In return for such aid, these nobles were given large tracts of land or important positions of authority in their districts, and eventually developed autonomous small kingdoms of their own. As the pharaoh's power declined, there was no longer any central authority to set irrigation policy or to administer justice. Periods of famine and social unrest began to occur, and many people enriched themselves at the expense of others. The following lament expresses the indignation of a person who had been used to a more stable social order:

● ● ● *The land spins like a potter's wheel; noble ladies are gleaners, and nobles are in the workhouse, but he who never slept on so much as a plank is now the owner of a bed; he who never wove for himself is the owner of fine linen.*[3]

Since the pharaohs no longer had the means to deal with these issues, the nation again broke into two separate kingdoms.

THE MIDDLE KINGDOM

The 11th Dynasty. After a long period of turmoil, the reunification of Egypt was achieved under the leadership of Mentohotep II, who founded the 11th dynasty. A new capital was established at Thebes, where the ancient temple of Amun, a god associated with life-giving qualities, was located. This god became the new national god under the name Amun-Re.

Mentohotep II was one of the first pharaohs to build his tomb in the Valley of the Kings and Queens, a range of hills to the west of Thebes. His reign and that of his succes-

[3]"Lament of Ipuwer," quoted in *Temples, Tombs and Hieroglyphs*, revised ed., by Barbara Mertz (New York: Dodd, Mead & Co., 1978), p. 99.

sors was also marked by the opening of trade relations between Egypt and the peoples of Syria and Palestine.

The 12th Dynasty. About 1991 B.C., the grandson of Mentohotep II was succeeded as pharaoh by his vizier, Amenemhet, who founded the 12th dynasty. Under Amenemhet I and his successors, Egypt enjoyed one of the most stable and prosperous periods of its history. Late in his reign, Amenemhet initiated a new policy of appointing a co-ruler in order to assure an uneventful succession to the throne. Thus, his son Sesostris ruled with him for the last 10 years of his life and succeeded him when he died. This policy of co-regency was later adopted by the pharaohs of the New Kingdom.

Under the pharaohs of the 12th dynasty, a number of new projects were carried out. To facilitate trade with the countries around the Mediterranean Sea, the Egyptians learned to build ocean-going ships, using wood from the renowned "cedars of Lebanon." They also built a canal, the Wadi Tumilat, to allow boats to pass from the Red Sea to the Mediterranean Sea. In order to develop trade with the peoples to the south, the pharaohs cut a canal into the first cataract so that boats could proceed past the falls and into Nubia. The marshes of Fayum, an area about 50 miles southwest of Memphis, were drained so that the region could become an agricultural center. In addition, the monumental city of Heliopolis was built to the northeast of Memphis.

The prosperity of Egypt under the 12th dynasty attracted a group of Asiatic peoples called the *Hyksos* to the area. These people—sometimes known as the Shepherd Kings—migrated from Palestine, Syria, and Phoenicia, and found work in Egypt as artisans in various trades. Eventually, they established a small kingdom at Avaris, in the delta region. They assimilated many aspects of Egyptian life into their own culture.

Although we do not know exactly how the Hyksos went about conquering Egypt, we

ANCIENT EGYPT
Why did Herodotus call Egypt "the gift of the Nile River"?

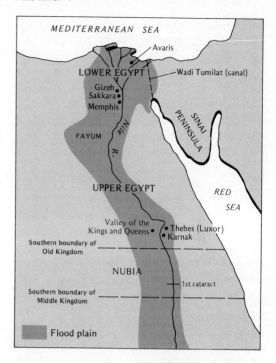

do know that their military equipment, including horse-driven chariots and a new, stronger type of bow, was superior to that of the Egyptians. In 1674 B.C., the Hyksos captured Memphis, and sometime after this date, a Hyksos ruler was crowned as pharaoh. An Egyptian pharaoh continued to rule at Thebes, under relaxed control of the Hyksos ruler. Although the Hyksos controlled Egypt, they did not interfere with the religion and customs of the Egyptians, but rather assimilated Egyptian customs into their own system.

After about a hundred years of fairly peaceful coexistence between the Egyptians and the Hyksos, quarrels began to break out between them. Because the Hyksos were allied with the Nubians to the south, the Egyptians felt that they were caught between two alien powers. The Egyptian pharaoh Kamose expressed his view of the situation:

. . . I sit associated with an Asiatic and a Negro. Each man has his slice of Egypt. . . . My wish is to smite the Asiatics.[4]

Kamose carried out his wish by launching a surprise attack on the Hyksos, using the military technology that they had introduced to Egypt. His campaign succeeded, but he was not able to drive the Hyksos out of their strongholds in the delta. Finally, his younger brother, Ahmose, succeeded in expelling the Hyksos, and became the founder of the 18th dynasty.

THE NEW KINGDOM

During the New Kingdom period (1570-1075 B.C.), Egypt developed into an imperial power and experienced one of the most glorious periods in its long existence. Whereas the pharaohs of the Middle Kingdom had fought only occasional battles in order to keep their trade routes open, the pharaohs of the 18th dynasty found it necessary to establish a permanent military presence in Syria and Palestine. The Egyptians' chief rivals for influence in the Middle East were the Hittites and the Mitanni, each of whom at times controlled the northern part of Mesopotamia and part of Syria. The Egyptians eventually used diplomacy as well as military campaigns to establish their sphere of influence in the area.

The 18th dynasty. When Ahmose I, the first pharaoh of the 18th dynasty, returned to Thebes after his successful campaign against the Hyksos, he brought with him a large army which had grown rich with the spoils of war. These troops became the nucleus of a permanent professional army. Under Ahmose and his immediate successors, the Egyptians annexed territory in Nubia and carried out a military campaign in Syria. They then realized that a literate bureaucracy was needed to administer the affairs of the expanding empire. To meet this need, they or-

dered the priests who ran temple scribal schools to train young prospective bureaucrats to read and write. The new emphasis on literacy eventually meant that many of the common people of Egypt had a chance to enter a career that had not been open to their parents.

The first rulers of the 18th dynasty made several other changes in the established order as well. To emphasize the separateness and divinity of the ruling family and to provide for a peaceful succession in the event there was no male heir, the pharaohs' daughters were each given the title "god's wife" in childhood. If a pharaoh had no male heirs, he could appoint a successor from outside the royal family; that person would then le-

SITES OF THE NEW KINGDOM PERIOD
Why did Egypt develop to the northeast rather than to the west, south, or east?

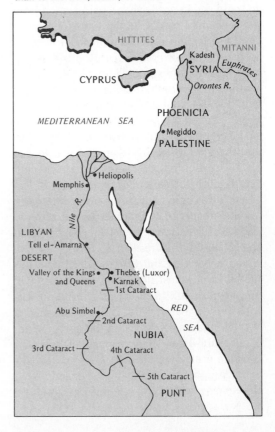

[4]J. B. Pritchard, *Ancient Near East Texts Relating to the Old Testament* (Princeton: Princeton University Press, 1955), pp. 232-4.

In this statue of Hatshepsut, the queen wears the regalia of a pharaoh but is definitely feminine in appearance. In other portraits, she sometimes wore a beard.

The funerary temple of Hatshepsut. The paintings within describe her peaceful accomplishments, such as the expedition to Punt and the construction of obelisks.

gitimize his claim to the throne in the eyes of the people by marrying a "god's wife."

In about 1504 B.C., the new succession procedure resulted in the reign of Hatshepsut, the first woman pharaoh. As a "god's wife," Hatshepsut had been married to the pharaoh Thutmose II. When he died, Hatshepsut's 10-year-old stepson, Thutmose III, became pharaoh in name. However, Hatshepsut seized the authority of the pharaoh and was herself crowned in a ceremony at Karnak. For the next 30 years, Hatshepsut was the dominant ruler, and Thutmose III served in a minor role.

Hatshepsut is known for several special achievements: she expanded the Egyptians' trade network to the south by organizing an expedition into the heart of Africa, to a region known as Punt (possibly modern Somalia). From Punt, the Egyptians were able to obtain valuable exotic products such as leopard skins, feathers, hardwoods, and myrrh, a valuable resin used to make fragrant oils. Hatshepsut also carried out several monumental building projects, including an enormous funerary temple for herself in the Valley of the Kings and Queens and several great obelisks for the temple of Amun in Thebes. In most respects, Hatshepsut seems to have operated just as a male pharaoh would. She probably commanded the expedition to Punt, and, in some portraits and statues, she was portrayed as a man. In several of these, she even wore the decorative long, narrow beard that the male pharaohs sometimes taped to their chins.

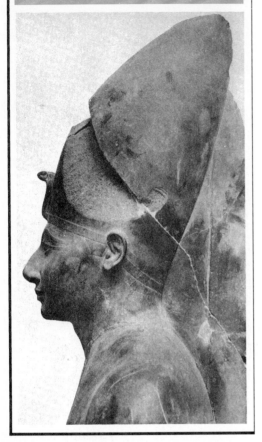

Thutmose III was one of the great military strategists of the ancient world. His conquests led to increased trade and commerce between Egypt and the rest of the Mediterranean world.

Babylonians, Assyrians, and Hittites all sent tribute to Egypt in recognition of Thutmose's conquests.

Thutmose waged a total of 17 military campaigns during his reign. At its peak, his empire extended from the fourth cataract of the Nile, in present-day Sudan, to the Euphrates River in modern Iraq. To administer his empire, Thutmose instituted a policy of bringing nobles from the conquered areas to Egypt, where they were educated and trained at the Egyptian court. Many of these people then returned to their homelands and governed them as loyal vassals of Egypt.

The tribute submitted by Thutmose's vassals greatly enriched the royal treasury and led to a period of great prosperity for Egypt. Trade with the peoples of Crete and the city-states around the Aegean Sea enabled the wealthy people of Egypt to import many new luxuries and to enjoy the art and culture of other civilizations.

The Amarna Period. The pattern of military conquest and domestic prosperity continued under Thutmose's successors, Amenhotep II, Thutmose IV, and Amenhotep III. Then, with the accession of Amen-

Statues of Amenhotep III, the father of Akhenaton, were called the Colossi of Memnon *by Greek travelers. They were a very popular tourist attraction in the ancient world.*

When Thutmose III ascended the throne after the death of Hatshepsut, he immediately faced a threat from the Mitanni tribes, who were gathering an army at Megiddo and possibly intended to march into Egypt. Thutmose quickly proceeded to Palestine with his army. As he drew near to the Mitanni forces, he decided to overrule his military commanders and make a very risky approach to Megiddo through a mountain pass. His tactics succeeded, and he was able to establish Egyptian domination over the entire area of Palestine and Syria. Although he was never able to subjugate the Mitanni completely, the

hotep IV, a strange interlude in the history of Egypt began to develop. Amenhotep IV had an eccentric personality and probably also suffered from a glandular disease which gave him an odd physical appearance. Egyptologists refer to his reign as the *Amarna* period, because the art and religious customs that he developed at Tell el-Amarna are quite different from those of any other pharaoh's reign.

Some of the origins of Amenhotep's radically "new" ideas were actually to be found in Egypt's ancient history. For many centuries, the priests of Heliopolis had been concerned about the adoption of Amun-Re as the state god. Whereas the pharaohs of the Old Kingdom had worshiped the sun god as Re-Atum, the pharaohs of the Middle and New Kingdoms worshiped him as Amun-Re. Although the two gods were almost identical, they were symbolized differently. The priests of Heliopolis believed that the true sun god could only be symbolized by the solar disk (the *aton*); the feathers and other insignia of Amun-Re were, they believed, a corruption. In the fifth year of his reign, Amenhotep IV became convinced that the priests of Heliopolis were correct. He then went a step further and proclaimed that the *only* true god was the Aton. To emphasize his proclamation, he built a new temple to Aton and suspended the worship of all other gods. In addition, he changed his name to Akhenaton [ak-NA-ton], meaning "the glory of Aton."

It is not known how much active opposition Akhenaton encountered in Thebes as he proceeded to carry out his ideas. Soon, however, he found it convenient to move to the site of present-day Tell el-Amarna, an area midway between Thebes and Memphis. Encouraged by his beautiful and influential wife Nefertiti, Akhenaton proceeded to build an open-air temple to Aton. Unlike the temples of Amun-Re and other gods, which had been filled with mysterious corridors and dark inner sanctuaries, the new temple of Aton

Akhenaton insisted that he be portrayed realistically. In some depictions, such as this one, Egyptian artists even emphasized his physical deformities.

was completely open to the light and air. Akhenaton encouraged his retainers and followers to share his uncomplicated life and religion, which he described as "living in truth." He commissioned artists to portray himself, Nefertiti, and their six daughters being blessed by the sun's rays and making offerings of flowers, and he insisted that the artists portray them as they really were, not in the stylized manner of previous times.

This bust of Nefertiti, Akhenaton's beautiful queen, is one of the best known works of Egyptian art.

While Akhenaton was busy introducing his new ideas, the political and business affairs of the empire were neglected. A library of tablets found at Tell el-Amarna includes a number of urgent messages to Akhenaton from his generals and vassals, all urging him to take one action or another. Very few of these messages were acted upon.

Return to Thebes. When Akhenaton died, his 10-year-old son-in-law, Tutankhaton, became pharaoh. Although Tutankhaton had been brought up in the Aton religion, pressure from the priests of Amun forced him to abandon these beliefs. He moved to Thebes and reinstated the worship of Amun-Re and other gods. He then changed his name from *Tut-ankh-aton* (meaning "living image of Aton") to *Tut-ankh-amun* (meaning "living image of Amun"). The real powers behind the throne during Tutankhamun's reign were

his vizier and his chief general, whose names were Horenheb and Ay.

Tutankhamun, popularly known as "King Tut" since 1922, was not an important pharaoh in the history of Egypt: he died at the age of about 19, before he could make his character known. But he became world famous when his undisturbed tomb was discovered by Howard Carter, a British explorer, in the Valley of the Kings and Queens.

After many months of searching, Carter happened to discover the buried entrance to the tomb of King Tut. After forcing his way in, Carter found four successive burial chambers filled with priceless objects of gold, alabaster, lapis lazuli, and other precious materials. This discovery led to a great popular and scientific interest in Egyptology. During the late 1970s, Egypt exhibited 50 pieces from the tomb in museums around the world.

Tutankhamun was succeeded as pharaoh by his vizier, Ay, and then by his general, Horenheb. Both of these rulers justified their reigns by marrying into the family of the 18th dynasty. Despite Horenheb's military background, Egypt's campaigns in Syria-Palestine did not resume until the accession of the 19th dynasty.

The 19th Dynasty. The 19th dynasty was founded by Ramses I, a long-time military colleague of Horenheb. Ramses' reign was fairly uneventful, and was overshadowed by that of his grandson, Ramses II. During his 67 years as pharaoh, Ramses II established himself as the most important ruler of this dynasty.

Unlike his predecessor Thutmose III, who left an accurate and matter-of-fact account of his achievements, Ramses II tended to embroider his military feats. He also inscribed his name on many monuments that had been built by earlier pharaohs. Because of these embellishments, early scholars, seeing Ramses' name everywhere, referred to him as "Ramses the Great." When later scholars succeeded in distinguishing Ramses' real achievements from the false ones, they found that he nevertheless still deserved his original nickname.

When Ramses II came to the throne in 1304 B.C., the growing Hittite empire in northern Syria posed a possible threat to Egypt's interests. In the fifth year of his reign, Ramses decided to challenge the Hittite kingdom in Syria. He led his army northward as far as the Orontes River and approached the town of Kadesh. Reportedly, Hittite spies then infiltrated the army and spread the false information that the Hittite troops were far to the north. Ramses was not prepared for battle when the Hittite troops made a surprise attack, and the Egyptians were driven out of the area. Nevertheless, Ramses had inscriptions carved in the temples of Egypt stating that he had defeated the Hittites.

Sixteen years after the battle at Kadesh, Ramses again led his army through Palestine and Syria, with the intention of confronting the Hittites. This time, the Hittite king was preoccupied with other problems, so he negotiated a treaty with the Egyptians. This treaty has been called the first nonaggression treaty in history. In it, the two kings agree not to make any further attacks upon each other, and to come to each other's aid if attacked by a third party. The northern part of Syria was allocated to the Hittites, and the southern part, with Palestine, was allocated to the Egyptians.

The treaty with the Hittites meant that the Egyptians no longer had to mount frequent military campaigns in order to protect their interests in Syria-Palestine. Ramses was now free to embark on one of the most massive building programs in Egypt's history.

Ramses II made Thebes the first monumental capital city of history. The already large temples at Luxor and Karnak were further enlarged to reflect the vast wealth of the pharaoh. The temple of Amun-Re, at Karnak, grew to be 1200 feet in length, and a sacred lake was built adjacent to it to supply holy water for religious rituals. A *hypostyle* hall (meaning "resting on pillars") was built as part of this temple. The walls and columns were inscribed with hieroglyphics glorifying the pharaoh and his accomplishments, and clerestory windows permitted light to penetrate throughout the hall so that these inscriptions could be read.

In addition to expanding the temples at Karnak and Luxor, Ramses II built a magnificent mortuary temple for himself on the west bank of the Nile opposite Thebes, a temple to Ptah at Memphis, and a gigantic temple at Abu Simbel in Nubia.

In this scene from a mural painting, Ramses II is shown leading his troops to battle. He devoted the first years of his reign to military conquest and the last 45 years to large-scale building projects.

The temple of Amun-Re at Karnak, built by Seti I and his son Ramses II, contains a hippo-style hall. Columns are almost 43 feet tall.

One of the four colossal statues of Ramses II that once guarded his temple at Abu Simbel. The temple now lies under Lake Nasser.

The temple at Abu Simbel was built by removing an estimated 365,000 tons of rock from the cliff. It was oriented in such a way that on two mornings each year, about 30 days before the spring equinox and 30 days after the autumnal equinox, the sun's rays would penetrate 200 feet into the temple to illuminate the interior statues. When construction was begun on the Aswan High Dam in 1964, it was known that this temple would be flooded by the reservoir. The United Nations then sponsored a project to carve the original temple out of the cliff and re-erect the excavated blocks of stone above the highest level of the reservoir. Visitors to the site today can see the outline of the temple as Ramses II created it, but about 200 feet above the site Ramses selected, while deep-water divers today can find a huge cave where the temple existed for more than 3000 years.

The 20th Dynasty. When Ramses III ascended the throne of Egypt, around 1198 B.C., the nation was confronted by a new and formidable enemy called the Sea Peoples. These mysterious people, probably of Indo-European stock, had plundered the Hittite king-

dom and were attempting to find homes along the southeastern coastline of the Mediterranean Sea, from Syria through the Egyptian delta. Ramses III proved to be a very competent military commander, and succeeded in driving the Sea Peoples away from the area after fighting two great battles. These victories were commemorated in an Egyptian temple inscription:

• • • *Now the northern countries [people] which were in their islands were quivering in their bodies. They penetrated the channels of the river mouths [the Nile delta]. They struggle for breath, their nostrils cease. His majesty is gone out like a whirlwind against them fighting on the battlefield like a runner, the dread of him and the terror have entered their bodies, they are capsized and overwhelmed where they are. Their heart is taken away and their soul is flown away, their weapons are scattered upon the sea. His arrow pierces whom he wishes, and the fugitive is a drowned man.*[5]

Unfortunately, Ramses' defensive battles against the Sea Peoples did not enrich his people, as earlier campaigns had done. During his rule, the royal treasury became impoverished, and the common people began to express dissatisfaction with their lot. On several occasions, the workers in the royal necropolis were not paid their rations of food on time. As a result, they refused to go to work, and thus carried out the first recorded labor strike in history.

The Final Years. After the brilliance of the 18th and 19th dynasties, Egyptian civilization suffered a period of decline. Nubian and Libyan mercenaries of the army settled in the Delta under the weak successors to Ramses III. A group of powerful priests gained dominance over the pharaohs and passed regulations which exempted all temples from taxation. The enormous cost of operating the temples, which employed two percent of the population and controlled 15 percent of the arable land, ruined the economy.

The conservatism of Egypt's **theocracy** discouraged the development of new ideas, such as the use of iron in place of bronze for tools and weapons. Thus, the Egyptians were surpassed in technology by other powers of the Middle East, and their attempts to undermine the Assyrian and Babylonian empires in Syria-Palestine were unsuccessful. In 525 B.C., Egypt was conquered by the Persians; in 322 B.C. by the Greeks and Macedonians; and in 30 B.C. by the Romans. When Queen Cleopatra committed suicide to avoid surrendering with Anthony's Romans in 30 B.C., Egypt ceased to be an influence in the Western world.

WRITING Even before the beginning of the Old Kingdom period, the Egyptians had developed a system of writing. Like the Mesopotamians, the Egyptians began by creating a group of *ideograms*, small pictures that represented various ideas and objects. These pictographs were often straightforward drawings of the objects or ideas they represented, but sometimes a well-known legend could be used as the basis for devising them. The following passage explains how a legend was used to create symbols for fractions:

● ● ● *The wicked god Seth plucked out the eye of Horus and tore it into bits. But the wise god Thoth stuck it back together again —as if it were just a cracked grain of barley. And so each part of the eye became a hieroglyphic sign for a fraction used in measuring out bushels of grain:* ◁ *for ½;* ○ *for ¼;* ⌒ *for ⅛;* ▷ *for 1/16;* ◁ *for 1/64. When the fraction symbols are put together, the marvelously restored "sound eye" looks like a composite of the symbols shown in this paragraph.* [6]

One of the disadvantages of the pictograph system is that the reader sometimes cannot tell exactly which word the writer had in mind, since some words have many synonyms. (For example, a hieroglyph might be devised for the concept of "area," but it would not be certain whether the writer meant to say "space," "distance," or "region.") To overcome this problem, symbols called *phonograms* were developed to indicate syllables or individual sounds. Since some phonograms were also ideograms, scribes indicated which meaning they intended by using a *determinative* symbol.

Even though the Egyptians very early developed an abbreviated, cursive script which could be written much more quickly than the pictorial symbols, they continued to use

[5]M. K. Sandars, *The Sea Peoples* (London: Thomas and Hudson, 1978), p. 124.

[6]*Ancient Egypt: Discovering Its Splendors*, ed. Jules B. Billard (Washington: The National Geographic Society, 1978), p. 155.

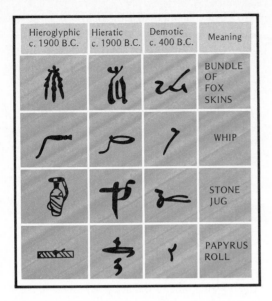

Hieroglyphic c. 1900 B.C.	Hieratic c. 1900 B.C.	Demotic c. 400 B.C.	Meaning
			BUNDLE OF FOX SKINS
			WHIP
			STONE JUG
			PAPYRUS ROLL

the original symbols for most of their formal writings. The old pictorial symbols were used for official inscriptions such as those carved on stelae or on temple walls. The cursive script, called *hieratic*, was used for less formal writings such as temple accounts, recipes, and poems. Around 700 B.C., an even more abbreviated script called *demotic* was developed. This was a type of shorthand and was often used by busy merchants and traders. Although the Phoenicians developed an alphabet around 1000 B.C., the Egyptians never adopted this more convenient system.

Many of the hieroglyphic inscriptions were chiseled on hard surfaces such as slate, granite, or limestone. However, the scribes also had the option of using paint brushes or sharpened reeds as writing implements, for the invention of papyrus paper occurred at least by 3000 B.C.[7]

When the Greeks first encountered the Egyptians' pictographs, they called them

[7]One of the oldest known papyrus documents dates to the Old Kingdom period, around 2500 B.C. It is a temple accounting, written in hieratic script. A blank role of papyrus from a tomb dated 3000 B.C. has also been found.

"sacred writings" (*hieroglyphics*), because they assumed the inscriptions had a religious purpose. Many of the hieroglyphics did in fact communicate messages to the gods or describe religious ceremonies, and the scribal schools were sponsored by the temples. However, an accomplished scribe in ancient Egypt might find a variety of careers open to him aside from the priesthood. Because of the pictorial nature of the Egyptian writing system, many scribes went on to become artists after mastering the approximately 700 hieroglyphic characters. Others became accountants, writers, and poets. And during the period of the New Kingdom, as literacy became increasingly important in government, scribes had the additional option of entering the pharaoh's civil service.

For many centuries, the writings of the ancient Egyptians were a complete mystery and a subject of much conjecture. Then, in 1798, Napoleon invaded Egypt, bringing with him a number of scholars who were interested in Egypt's history. When one of Napoleon's engineers discovered a large, flat slab of basalt with three sets of inscriptions, the French scholars recognized its importance. The slab, which came to be known as the Rosetta stone, contained Greek, hieroglyphic, and demotic translations of the same message. When the finding became known, a number of scholars throughout the world set to work to decipher the hieroglyphics.

A British scholar, Thomas Young, realized that some hieroglyphics represent individual sounds, much like alphabet letters. Soon afterwards, a French scholar, Jean-François Champollion, decided that the *cartouches* (oval outlines) he had seen in many inscriptions contained the names of Egyptian rulers. Champollion deciphered the hieroglyphics in several cartouches, and then used the Greek letters on the Rosetta stone to enlarge his vocabulary of hieroglyphics. In 1828, he announced that he had deciphered the entire message of the Rosetta stone. The message proved to be a proclamation

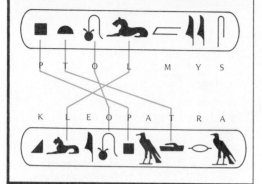

Jean-François Champollion realized that the cartouches he saw on obelisks and in tombs contained the names of rulers, and deciphered these letters.

P T O L M Y S

K L E O P A T R A

After deciphering several hieroglyphic signs through his work with cartouches, Champollion proceeded to translate the message of the Rosetta stone.

THE ROSETTA STONE

issued by Ptolemy V in 196 B.C., and with the basic vocabulary of signs that Champollion had deciphered, scholars were able to deduce the meanings of many more hiero-

glyphics. Eventually they could read almost all of the innumerable symbols on the walls of ancient monuments.

SCIENCE One of the most surprising achievements of the ancient Egyptians was their discovery that the solar year has 365 days. Whereas the Mesopotamians and other ancient peoples based their calendars on the moon's cycle, the Egyptians had discovered the solar cycle as early as 4000 B.C. They accomplished this feat by noting that the highest flood levels of the Nile occurred on the same day that the star Sirius aligned with the rising sun. By counting the days between the annual floodings (and the alignment of Sirius), they realized that the lunar calendar of 28-day months did not correspond to the Nile's year.

The Egyptians' "Nile Year" was divided into twelve 30-day months, with an added 5-day festival period. The Romans later adopted this calendar, and it continued in use for many centuries. (Later, the need to add a quarter day each year—a "leap year" every four years—was recognized.)

By 3000 B.C., the Egyptians had learned to make papyrus paper by crosshatching the fibers of the plant, then pressing them together to allow the natural gums to bond the materials. The invention of paper undoubtedly encouraged the communication of ideas and the growth of literature and other arts.

One of the most famous papyrus scrolls is the so-called Edwin Smith papyrus, named after the person who once owned it. Although many other manuscripts illustrate the Egyptians' interest in surgery and medicine, the Edwin Smith work is unique in its methods and exposition. Rather than just describing a "cure" for each disease discussed, the papyrus sets forth a detailed description of 48 cases of clinical surgery. It describes how to make a diagnosis in each case, and what course of treatment to follow. In a case of severe head injury, for instance, the physician is instructed to pick out the fragments

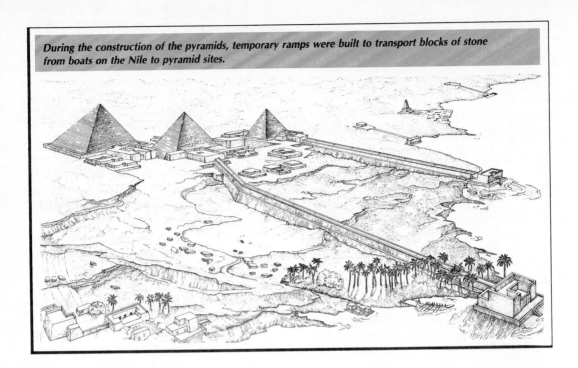

During the construction of the pyramids, temporary ramps were built to transport blocks of stone from boats on the Nile to pyramid sites.

of bone, feel the pulse, move the legs to check for paralysis, and watch for irregular movements in the face. The scholar J. H. Breasted believed that this papyrus was the work of Imhotep, the Old Kingdom vizier who built the first pyramid.

For many years, travelers and scholars speculated about the construction methods used to build the pyramids. Egyptologists now believe that the pyramids of the Old Kingdom were built by free peasants, paid by the pharaoh, and that most of the work was carried out during the months of the Nile's inundation—when the land was under water and could not be farmed. Large sledges were used to slide the gigantic blocks of stone over the wet ground to the site of a pyramid. To move the heavy blocks in a vertical direction, the Egyptian workers utilized a system of ramps and balanced levers. Of course, the construction of a pyramid also required careful measuring and an application of geometrical principles. The Egyptians had developed much knowledge in these areas through their measuring of the annual flood levels and surveying of property lines.

SUMMARY

Egypt is truly a marvelously mysterious land and culture. It has the world's longest continuous record of civilization, one that has been thoroughly researched by a great variety of scholars, and yet there are still many things we do not know about it.

Because the Egyptians' form of government was founded on their religious beliefs, the nation had a sense of purpose and a rare unanimity of opinion. Under a pharaoh who was just and capable, the people could achieve a high standard of living and enjoyed a sense of stability and continuity. However, the same system could lead to disaster if a pharaoh used his power for selfish purposes, or was too weak or indecisive to administer the nation effectively.

The Egyptians' art and culture exerted a fascination over many later peoples, and their concept of a life after death became very influential in the development of other civilizations.

While recent leaders of Egypt have worked hard to modernize life in this ancient land, Egyptians today practice some of the same ways of life that were developed during the 3000 years we have been discussing in this chapter.

QUESTIONS

1 Discuss the influence of geography and climate on the culture and history of Egypt.
2 Create pictographs to express several words or concepts.
3 Debate the issue: the need to control floods and to allocate irrigation waters to farmers led to the formation of centralized government in Egypt.
4 Look at some examples of Egyptian art. What are some of the principal artistic conventions? How do you explain the fact that Egyptian art changed so little over the centuries?
5 Most archaeological discoveries in Egypt and Mesopotamia reveal the way of life of the upper classes. Why? What should archaeologists look for in order to help us understand how the common people lived?
6 What did the Egyptians believe about their gods and their pharaoh? What changes did Akhenaton attempt to make? Why was his "revolution" a failure?

BIBLIOGRAPHY

Which books might tell when the tombs at Thebes were looted?

CASSON, LIONEL. *Ancient Egypt.* New York: Time, Inc., 1985. *A comprehensive, readable discussion of the ancient Egyptians by an eminent Egyptologist; includes a chronological chart of Egyptian technological developments and other events of interest to scholars; beautifully illustrated with color maps and photos.*

MERTZ, BARBARA. *Temples, Tombs, and Hieroglyphs: the Story of Egyptology.* New York: Coward-McCann, 1964. *Straightforward history of Egypt, from predynastic times to the New Kingdom; includes many inferences concerning the intellectual and cultural life of the Egyptians, based upon their inscriptions and artifacts.*

RUFFLE, JOHN. *The Egyptians: An Introduction to Egyptian Archaeology.* Cornell University Press, 1977. *A review of archaeological findings and what they reveal about the Egyptians' accomplishments in science, art, and writing.*

3

● *If we trace the Indo-European language back far enough, we arrive hypothetically (at any rate according to some authorities) at the stage where language consisted only of roots out of which subsequent words have grown. . . . The association of words with their meanings must have grown up by some natural process, though at present the nature of the process is unknown.*

BERTRAND RUSSELL

The Arrival of the Indo-Europeans

About 2500 B.C., waves of migrating tribes swept into the known centers of civilization in the Middle East. One group, the *Semites*, moved northward from the desert peninsula of Arabia and settled in the Fertile Crescent. Their descendants became the Babylonians, whom we studied in Chapter 1, and the Phoenicians, Arameans, and Hebrews, whom we shall study in Chapter 4. Another group moved southward from the **steppe** lands, or grassy plains, which lie between the Danube and Volga rivers, to the north of the Black and Caspian seas. Because the descendants of these latter people eventually settled in many places over the vast area stretching from India to Europe, scholars have named them *Indo-Europeans.*

The Indo-Europeans were probably forced to migrate from their homelands with their flocks and herds because of famine, climatic changes, or pressure from other tribes. In their search for pasture lands, these tribes roamed far and wide, and tended to lose contact with each other. Some of them eventually settled in western Europe, where their descendants became known as the Celts. Others moved into Italy, the Aegean area, and Anatolia (modern Turkey), where their descendants became known, respectively, as the Italic tribes, the Greeks, and the Hittites. The Indo-Europeans who settled farthest to the east split into two groups: one group entered northwestern India and destroyed several cities of the Indus River Valley about 1500 B.C. The other settled in Persia and gave their tribal name (Aryan) to the area now known as Iran.

The term *Indo-European* is also used to designate the family of languages derived from the original language of these migrants. The intruders interacted with so many different native peoples that each migrant tribe eventually developed individual cultural and linguistic characteristics. The most remarkable aspect of this interaction was the fact that the migrating people retained so many words of their original language. Linguists have found many similar words in Sanskrit (the language of ancient India), Greek, Latin, German, and English.

TRIBAL MIGRATIONS IN THE ANCIENT MIDDLE EAST, 2000-1700 B.C.
What climates were the Semites and Indo-Europeans accustomed to?

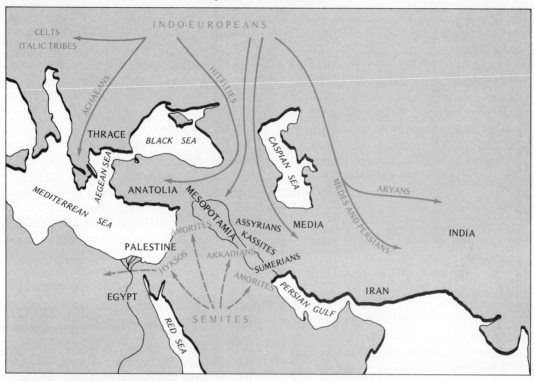

Greek	Latin	English	German	Sanskrit
treis	tres	three	drei	trayas
	vidua	widow	witwe	
		assemble	samm-eln	sam-adhi
bous	bos	bovid (cow)		
meli	mel	mellifluous	mil	
mater	mater	mother	mutter	matar

By studying the various Indo-European languages, linguists have been able to reconstruct, to some extent, the way of life of the people who spoke the original Indo-European language. The fact that no common root for *sea* or *ocean* has been found suggests that they may have lived far from large bodies of water. Because they had several words for *snow* and *ice*, they probably lived in a cold climate. They domesticated cattle, sheep, and horses, and probably stayed in one place long enough to plant and harvest wheat and barley. They worked with copper and bronze, and they were organized in a **patriarchal** society; that is, one ruled by men.

THE HITTITES The earliest known group of Indo-Europeans to migrate into Asia Minor arrived in Anatolia about 2500 B.C., and became the ancestors of the Hittites. These people established the third oldest civilization in the western regions of

Asia. While the civilizations of Egypt and of Mesopotamia were developing and prospering in broad, fertile river valleys, the Hittites settled in the rugged highlands of Anatolia, where the climate was difficult, with extremes of heat and cold, and fierce storms occurred frequently. They learned how to utilize the metals they found in the mountains and to farm in the sheltered valleys that are scattered through the high Anatolian plateau. Although they managed to develop a self-sufficient, well-organized society, the prosperous civilizations to the south eventually presented an attractive target for conquest.

In 2000 B.C., the valley of the Halys River (today known as the Kizil) and the surrounding highlands were settled by a little-known people called the Khatti. By about 1900 B.C., the Hittites had conquered the Khatti and established their capital at Hattusas, in a bend of the Halys River. Within a century, they controlled most of Anatolia.

The most powerful king of this early period was Mursilis I, who established a federation of 10 great city-states, each owing allegiance to him as the Great King. Around 1595 B.C., he led his army through the passes of the Taurus Mountains and conquered northern Syria. He then continued down the Euphrates River valley, captured Babylon, and, together with the Kassites from the mountains of western Persia, overthrew the kingdom that Hammurabi had built. After completing these conquests, he was called home to deal with a domestic crisis. Soon after his return to Hattusas, he was murdered as the result of a palace conspiracy.

At the royal court of the Hittites, the conspiracies and blood feuds that had led to Mursilis' death continued for almost a century, and the country fell into a state of anarchy. Finally, in about 1525 B.C., a noble named Telipinus seized the throne. He consolidated his authority by killing his rivals and married a princess of the royal family. He then published new, precise rules for the succession to the throne: if a king had no heir, the crown was to go to the noble of highest rank. This noble would then marry a daughter of the previous king in order to establish continuity of the royal line. Telipinus' rules accomplished the purpose of ensuring a fairly uneventful succession for several centuries.

THE HITTITE EMPIRE

For a long period after Telipinus' rule, the Hittites did not make any notable attempts to extend their borders. Then, in 1380 B.C., a period known as the Hittite empire began under the reign of Suppiluliumas. This Great King of the Hittites ruled for 40 years and proved to be the most capable military leader in the Middle East since Thutmose III of Egypt. After his military conquests had been achieved, Suppiluliumas took the trouble to

The Hittites built their chariots large enough to hold two or three men for added advantage in hand-to-hand combat.

Hittite warriors were renowned for their skill in battle. They carried iron-tipped lances, as shown here, swords, and battle axes.

successful show of force, almost all of Syria fell to the Hittites. Suppiluliumas appointed two of his sons to govern the conquered territory, and he himself returned to Anatolia.

Late in Suppiluliumas' reign, an incident occurred which illustrated the new international status he had achieved through his conquests. The young widow of Tutankhamun, the late pharaoh of Egypt, sent him a letter requesting that he send one of his sons to Egypt to marry her and become pharaoh. Suppiluliumas sent one of his sons, but the young man was murdered as soon as he entered the country, perhaps at the order of the Egyptian general Horemheb, who shortly afterward seized the throne. (Suppiluliumas was not able to avenge this murder, for he died shortly afterwards.)

Under the rule of Suppiluliumas' successors, the Hittite empire was not seriously threatened. Although the towns of Syria occasionally revolted, the appearance of the Hittite charioteers was sufficient to restore order. Then, with the accession of Seti I and his son Ramses II of Egypt, the Egyptians once again became interested in regaining their former territory.

The Egyptians and the Hittites fought at Kadesh in 1300 B.C. While both sides claimed victory, only the personal courage and skill of Ramses prevented a disastrous defeat for the Egyptians. The battle at Kadesh was the first military engagement of which we have a detailed contemporary account, thanks to Ramses' commemoration of it on a temple wall in Egypt.

Sixteen years later, Ramses realized that he could not dislodge the Hittites from Syria. At the same time, Hattusilis III, the Hittite king, was fearful of the growing power of the Assyrians and did not want to waste his resources in fighting the Egyptians. The two rulers agreed to a treaty of peace. This treaty survives in two fragmentary copies; one on a silver tablet in the temple of Ramses at Thebes, and the other on a clay tablet which was found at Hattusas, the Hittite capital.

set up a permanent administration for the new territories, and so was able to consolidate his rule over them.

By the 14th century B.C., the Hittites, like the Egyptians and the Mitanni, had adopted a new chariot design. The new chariot was lighter and faster than the old models, since it had two spoked wheels rather than four solid-wood wheels. The Hittites had also made another improvement: their chariots were built to hold three men, while the Egyptian chariots held only two. The extra man in the Hittite chariots provided a definite advantage in hand-to-hand combat, and the Hittite charioteers were renowned for their skill and discipline.

While Egypt was preoccupied with the religious revolution of Akhenaton, Suppiluliumas gradually brought his army south. In 1375 B.C., he crossed the Euphrates River and fought a battle with the Egyptian loyalists at Kadesh on the Orontes River. Due to this

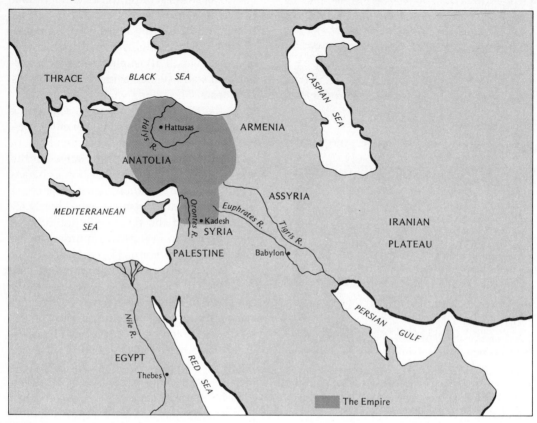

The following quotation has been translated from the Egyptian version, in which the Hittites were referred to as the *Kheta*.

••• *There shall be no hostilities between them, forever. The great chief of the Kheta shall not pass over into the land of Egypt, forever, to take anything therefrom. Ramses-Meriamon, the great ruler of Egypt, shall not pass over into the land (of Kheta, to take anything) therefrom, forever. . . .*

If another enemy come against the land of Ramses II, the great ruler of Egypt, and he shall send to the great chief of Kheta, saying: "Come with me as a reinforcement against him," the great chief of Kheta shall come, and the great chief of Kheta shall slay his enemy. But if it is not to be the desire of the great chief of Kheta to come, he shall send
his infantry and his chariotry, and shall slay the enemy.

Or if Ramses, the great ruler of Egypt, be provoked against his delinquent subjects, when they have committed some other fault against him, and he come to slay them, then the great chief of Kheta shall act with the lord of Egypt.[1]

In the two versions, each king claimed to have yielded to a plea for peace from the other. The two kings swore an oath to maintain the peace, to provide mutual assistance in time of danger, and to exchange fugitives. Although there had been earlier treaties among the nations of the ancient world, this

[1]J. H. Breasted, *Ancient Records of Egypt*, Vol. 3 (Chicago: University of Chicago Press, 1906), p. 45.

treaty has been called the first *nonaggression* treaty in recorded history. The agreement between the two kings was strengthened by Ramses' marriage to a Hittite princess 13 years later.

Around 1200 B.C., the Hittites, like the other civilizations of the Middle East, were confronted by a mass migration of peoples from the west and north. At the same time that Egypt was threatened by the Sea Peoples, the Hittites were overwhelmed by tribes known as the Phrygians. Unlike the Egyptians, the Hittites did not succeed in driving off the invaders. The Hittite civilization was completely supplanted by that of the Phrygians. Except for a few Biblical references to a group of Hittites who had settled in Palestine,[2] there

---

[2]One notable Biblical mention is the account of how King David sent *Uriah the Hittite* into the front lines of battle so that he could marry Uriah's beautiful wife, Bathsheeba (2 Samuel 11). Another mention occurs in Genesis 23:10, where it is related that Abraham purchased a burial place for his wife from *Ephron the Hittite*.

was no historical record of them until a site was uncovered early in the 20th century.

ARCHAEOLOGICAL FINDINGS

In 1906-7, the German archaeologist Hugo Winckler began to excavate the site of Hattusas (modern Boghazköi in Turkey). He uncovered impressive sculptures and the remains of a massive fortress. This city was built about 1650 B.C., and surrounded by stone walls almost 25 feet thick. The walls were pierced every 100 feet by double-towered gates, the best known of which is strikingly similar to the famous *Lion Gate* at Mycenae in Greece. The entrance to the palace of the kings was guarded by stone lions. On each side of the porch there was a square tower, so archaeologists called this palace the *House of Two Towers*. The walls of the palace were decorated with large slabs of stone carved in relief. In these reliefs, the chiefs and priests are shown participating in religious ceremonies. The people are depicted as short and heavily built, with prominent cheekbones,

The Hittites fortified their capital city of Hattusas with a 4-mile-long stone wall. The lions at this gate were carved from massive blocks of stone.

sloping foreheads, and recessed chins. Soldiers are armed with swords, spears, and bows. Women are wearing long veils.

LANGUAGE

At Hattusas, archaeologists found thousands of clay tablets inscribed with hieroglyphic symbols. They deduced that the Hittites had developed their own system of hieroglyphics to write their language, and later adopted the Egyptians' practice of decorating their buildings with inscriptions. In 1915, Bedrich Hrozný, a Czechoslovakian linguist, was studying a Hittite writing when he suddenly:

• • • *took a deep breath and, conscious of the boldness of his own thesis, dared to think: "If I am right about the interpretation of this line, there is going to be a scientific storm." But the sentence he was reading seemed clear and unambiguous. He had only one choice: to say what it was he saw—even if it overturned the views of all specialists in ancient history.*

The text which led Hrozný to this resolve was the sentence: nu ninda-an ezzatteni vâdor-ma ekutteni.

In this sentence there was only a single known word: ninda. *It could be deduced from the Sumerian ideogram that this word meant "bread."*

Hrozný said to himself: "A sentence in which the word bread is used may very well (though it need not necessarily, of course) contain the word eat." Since at this point the indications that Hittite might be an Indo-European language were already becoming overwhelming, he drew up a list of various Indo-European words for "eat." Was it possible that he was dealing here with a Hittite cognate? English "eat" was in Latin edo, *in Old High German. . . . As soon as Hrozný wrote down the Old High German word he knew that he was on the right track.* Ezzan *certainly bore a strong resemblance to the Hittite* ezzatteni.[3]

---

[3]Kurt W. Marek, *The Secret of the Hittites*, trans. by Richard and Clara Winston (New York: Knopf, 1958), pp. 82-3.

After much further study, Hrozný concluded that the Hittite language was of Indo-European origin. He supported this conclusion by pointing out that many suffixes of nouns and verbs, as well as many root words, were similar to those of other languages of Indo-European origin. While much progress has been made in understanding the Hittite writings, several major problems remain. A few scholars have refused to accept Hrozný's theory at all, because they cannot believe that any Indo-European language could have been written in cuneiform.

GOVERNMENT

The Hittites had a form of feudal society, much like the Assyrian society as it evolved. A group of nobles held important offices and large tracts of land, and in return for these benefits, they supplied the king with weapons, soldiers, and chariots for his campaigns. In the early period of the Hittite settlements in Anatolia, the Hittite nobles assembled to hear and pass judgments on legal cases, and possibly also elected the king. However, after Telipinus' rules of succession were published, around 1525 B.C., the assembly of nobles lost much of its importance in national affairs. After this period, the king of the Hittites gained supreme authority, comparable to that of the Mesopotamian and Egyptian monarchs. In fact, the Hittite kings were often referred to as "the Sun," and were believed to have a special relationship with the gods.

The wives and mothers of Hittite kings had more authority than did the women of other royal families in the ancient Middle East. They frequently participated in affairs of state and sometimes cosigned the official documents of the king.

THE LEGAL SYSTEM

Clay tablets found at Hattusas reveal that the Hittites had a well-developed legal system. Capital punishment was seldom used, and most criminals were called upon to compensate their victims for the damages they had caused by paying a fine. In contrast to the "eye for an eye" philosophy of Hammurabi's code, the Hittites' code emphasized compensation to the victims of a crime, and recognized the difference between accidental injuries and those that were committed purposefully.

THE ECONOMY

Because of the cold winters in the Anatolian steppe lands, the Hittites were not able to harvest two or three crops per year, as the Egyptians and Mesopotamians did. However, they were able to grow good crops of barley and wheat in their fertile river valleys, and they cultivated grapes on the hillsides. Agriculture was the mainstay of their economy.

Another primary source of wealth for the Hittites was iron. Their lands contained the only extensive source of iron ore in the Middle East, and they were the first people to learn to extract iron from this ore. Earlier peoples had learned that copper and tin were both rather soft and melted at relatively low temperatures. They had also discovered that when the melts were mixed, they produced the much harder and stronger material called bronze. The Hittites learned that they could extract metal from iron ore by creating a still hotter fire and by mixing limestone with the ore. When the liquid iron was poured into molds, it produced a relatively weak material which we call *cast iron*. The Hittites discovered that they could reheat this iron, beat it, and then cool it, producing a much more useful material, which we call *wrought iron*. The Hittites jealously guarded the secrets of working with iron, and once suggested to an Egyptian pharaoh that he could purchase iron from them for an equal weight of gold.

RELIGION

The gods of the Hittites were *anthropomorphic* in character, and were believed to have the same needs and shortcomings as human beings. Priests gave them daily offerings of food and clothing, and were not surprised if the gods did not respond to their prayers. The most important deity of the Hittites was Teshub, the god of weather. He was often shown with a thunderbolt in one hand and an axe in the other, with a bull close behind him. The concept of a sun god was adopted from the Egyptians, but this god never became a real part of the Hittites' pantheon. Rather, a Hittite sun goddess was assigned the role of Teshub's wife. Another important deity was Ishtar, the goddess of fertility, who was adopted from the Babylonians.

Teshub, the weather god, was the most important deity in the Hittites' pantheon. In this relief, he holds a 3-pronged bolt of lightning and a battle ax. Above him is the solar disk, an Egyptian symbol of divinity.

The shrines of the Hittites' gods were located in the small towns throughout Anatolia. One of the main duties of the king was to visit each small town during festival times and serve as chief priest for the special services.

The Hittites probably introduced the worship of Ishtar to the Lydians, who developed an important civilization in Asia Minor during the 8th century B.C. The Lydians, in turn, introduced Ishtar to the Greeks, who renamed her *Cybele*, meaning the Great Mother. The Hittites used the Egyptian art forms of the winged sun disk, relief sculpture, and hieroglyphics to decorate their buildings, and passed these practices on to the Lydians. The Lydians, in turn, had great influence on the Greeks.

THE PERSIANS

The descendants of the Aryans who settled on the Plateau of Iran came to be called the Medes and the Persians. These two tribes were first mentioned in the 9th century B.C. in the tribute lists of the Assyrian royal court. When Assyrian power began to disintegrate, the Medes, who were great warriors, were able to form a strong kingdom in northern Iran, with their capital at Ecbatana. They gradually extended their control over the Persians who lived in the southern part of Iran. In 612 B.C., the Medes, in alliance with the Babylonians, captured Nineveh and brought an end to the Assyrian empire.

The Persians originally migrated to the southwestern edge of the Iranian Plateau. This plateau, which extends from the eastern portion of Mesopotamia in the west to the Indus River valley in the east, and from the Caspian Sea in the north to the Arabian Sea in the south, is a high, bowl-shaped desert surrounded by mountain ranges. Although much of Iran is barren today, in ancient times herds could be pastured on the hillsides and bountiful crops of wheat, barley, grapes, and figs were grown in the valleys. The lower slopes of the mountains were then covered with for-

ests, and the land yielded such valuable minerals as iron, lead, turquoise, and lapis lazuli.

CYRUS THE GREAT

Cyrus II, known as Cyrus the Great, was the first important ruler of the *Achaemenid* dynasty, so called because the line was founded by a leader named Achaemenes.

In 559 B.C., Cyrus began to rule the Persians as a vassal of the Median empire. Although he married a daughter of the Median king, he soon began to organize a rebel coalition of Persians and other tribes, and eventually challenged the Medes in battle. By 550 B.C., the Median empire had fallen under the control of Cyrus and the Persians.

The sudden change of government between the Medes and Persians was a cause of concern for other countries in the area. Because Cyrus and the Babylonians were on friendly terms, Croesus, the fabulously wealthy king of Lydia, began to fear that he might be the next target of the new Persian empire-builder. Croesus consulted the oracle at Delphi, in Greece, for advice as to whether he should lead his army against Cyrus. According to Herodotus, the oracle told Croesus that if he attacked the Persians he would destroy a great empire. Croesus believed that this message supported his in-

Cyrus the Great was buried in a simple tomb at Pasargadae.

tentions, so he gathered his army for an attack. But in 546 B.C., Cyrus made a surprise move into Lydia, defeated Croesus, and captured Sardis, the capital city. Cyrus then annexed the Greek city-states of Ionia along the shores of the Aegean Sea.

In 540 B.C., Cyrus took advantage of an unpopular monarchy in Babylon to assert his presence there. The priests of Marduk (the Babylonian god of justice) and the captive Jews of Babylon were among the groups who welcomed his intervention. With hardly a struggle, Cyrus was recognized as king of the Babylonians and acquired all of the Chaldean empire, including the former Assyrian colonies of Syria, Phoenicia, and Palestine.

In 530 B.C., Cyrus was killed in battle while fighting Iranian tribes on the eastern boundary of his empire. He was buried at a simple tomb in Pasargadae. Alexander the Great found this tomb when he led his troops through the area 200 years later.

Cyrus had not only been a capable military leader, but he had shown excellent political skills as well. He courted the good will of potential subject peoples, and proved himself a wise and capable ruler once he had completed his conquests. Unlike the Assyrian and Babylonian conquerors, he spared the lives of his conquered enemies, and left their cities intact. He permitted the Jews, who had been enslaved in Babylon for 50 years, to return to Jerusalem and rebuild their temples. In just 20 years, he created a vast empire stretching from the Mediterranean Sea to the steppes of Asia, and from the Black and Caspian seas to the Arabian Sea.

Zoroastrianism. Traditionally, the Persians worshiped a pantheon of nature gods. They made animal sacrifices at altars on mountains and in other open-air sites, and believed that these sacrificial offerings could appease the gods who controlled the wind, sun, fire, and water. A special caste of people called *Magi* officiated at the ceremonies and were believed to have special powers to drive away evil spirits.

Around 600 B.C. or possibly earlier, a prophet named Zoroaster withdrew to a wilderness for a period of meditation, and then returned to society to teach a radically new religion. He denounced the practice of animal sacrifice and the worship of nature gods. Instead, he preached that there are just two forces in the world: the force of truth, goodness, and light, personified by the god Ahuramazda; and the force of evil, deceit, and darkness, personified by the evil god Ahriman. He stressed that each individual had to decide which power to serve, and that this decision would result in happiness or despair in the afterlife. Because the teachings of Zoroaster emphasized righteous *conduct* rather than religious rites or "magic," his theology is known as an *ethical* religion.

For Zoroaster, fire was the symbol of Ahuramazda and signified purification and truth. Thus, his followers built fire altars much as the traditional Magis had done. However, in the new religion, fire was used as a symbol and as a reminder of how people should conduct themselves; not to invoke magic or to show reverence for the forces of nature.

Zoroastrianism was opposed by the Magi and many other traditionalists in Persia, who maintained their old religion and supersti-

Although Zoroastrianism won many converts, the ancient gods of the Magi were not forgotten. One of these ancient gods was Mithras, who created the world by sacrificing a bull. He was still worshiped in Roman times.

tions for several centuries to come. However, the new religion was embraced by the Achaemenid dynasty and had a great impact upon all of the people they ruled. As one historian put it:

• • • *Zoroaster's teachings deeply affected the religious ideas, and tinctured the conduct of the Persians who ruled the civilized world. This fact alone sufficed to bring his ideas to the attention of the medley of peoples within the empire. Zoroastrianism was thus bound to influence other religious traditions, notably Judaism; and through Judaism it has played a far wider role in the world's history than would be suggested by the comparatively modest number of those who through subsequent ages have looked directly to Zoroaster as the founder of their faith.*[4]

Zoroastrianism had an important effect on later Judeo-Christian thinking because of its emphasis of a final judgment, immortality, and Satan.

Centuries later, when the Arabs invaded Iran in the 8th century A.D., many followers of Zoroastrianism took refuge in India, where their descendants came to be known as Parsis. It has been estimated that the Parsis who live today number about 100,000, and most of them reside in and around Bombay.

CAMBYSES

The death of Cyrus prompted civil unrest in Persia, perhaps due to a religious struggle between the Magi and the followers of Zoroaster. After ascending the throne, Cyrus' eldest son, Cambyses, killed his own brother, Smerdis, in order to prevent a possible threat to his rule. He then carried out his father's plan to conquer Egypt, and continued his campaign in Nubia.

In the seventh year of his reign, Cambyses was forced to abandon his military cam-

paigns after receiving news of a revolt in Persia. The revolt was led by a Magi who was impersonating the dead prince, Smerdis, and claiming to be the rightful king. Cambyses departed for Persia, but died enroute. The cause of his death remains a great mystery. Some historians believe that he died accidentally, others that he committed suicide.

DARIUS

By the late 6th century B.C., the support of the army had become critical to the success of any Persian monarch. The elite of the army were the 10,000 Mede and Persian troops, the so-called "Immortals," and thousands of additional troops were levied from the vast areas the Persians had conquered. In 522 B.C., Darius, a distant cousin of Cambyses, won the support of the army and was declared king. Because he had the loyalty of the troops, Darius was able to overcome the false Smerdis and consolidate his own reign within a year.

At the beginning of his reign, Darius took some time to establish administrative and judicial reforms throughout his empire. He divided his territories into 20 *satrapies* (administrative districts), each under the control of a *satrap* (governor) chosen from the royal family or from the nobility. The satrap collected taxes, administered justice, and raised levies for the army. Inspectors, the "eyes and ears" of the king, traveled throughout the realm and reported regularly to the king as to whether or not the satrapies were well-governed and prosperous. Laws were enforced uniformly throughout the empire by royal judges, whose personal conduct was closely watched. As long as the conquered people paid their tribute promptly, they were permitted a large degree of self-government and religious freedom.

Darius also enhanced the unity of his far-flung empire by improving transportation. He ordered that roads be built in order to promote trade throughout the empire and to enable his armies to move quickly in time of

[4]William H. McNeill, *The Rise of the West: A History of the Human Community* (Chicago: University of Chicago Press, 1963), p. 172.

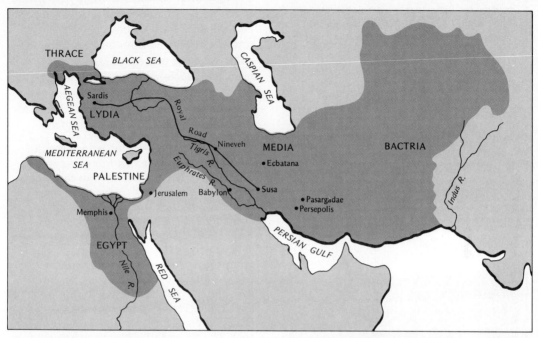

danger. The most famous of these roads was the *Royal Road* from Sardis, in Lydia, to Susa, in Persia, a distance of 1680 miles. Royal messengers, mounting fresh horses at stations spaced 14 miles apart along this road, could cover the distance in seven days, whereas ordinary travelers required almost three months to move the same distance. Military garrisons were stationed at strategic points throughout the empire so that the armies could respond quickly to threats of revolt or invasion.

Like the Sumerians before him, Darius established a standard system of weights and measures, and he issued gold coins (darics) which were accepted as the standard of exchange throughout the empire. He conscripted Greek, Phoenician, and Egyptian ships and sailors to form a navy, and sent an expedition to explore the possibility of a trade route from the mouth of the Indus River, in India, along the coast of the Arabian Sea and Red Sea to northern Egypt.

In 516 B.C., after Darius had consolidated his control over the Middle East, he crossed the Bosporus, the narrow waterway that connects the Black Sea and the Mediterranean and separates Europe from Asia at the site of present-day Istanbul. He conquered Thrace to gain access to its silver mines and to acquire a base from which to attack the Greeks, who controlled the trade routes from the Black Sea to the Aegean Sea.

In 490 B.C., Darius invaded Greece and was defeated by a united Greek army at the battle of Marathon. The Persians then spent several years making extensive preparations for another invasion of Greece, but these plans were interrupted by Darius' death in 486 B.C. (The wars which Darius and his son Xerxes fought against the Greeks are covered in detail in Chapter 6.)

Inscriptions. In the first year of his reign, Darius had had an inscription carved on a mountainside in Behistun, 500 feet above the road that connected Persia to Babylon. In it,

Darius' inscription on the face of a mountain at Behistun, Iran, contained a message translated into the Old Persian, Babylonian, and Elamite languages. It enabled scholars to decipher Babylonian cuneiform symbols.

Art and Architecture. Although the Persians made their own distinctive contribution to civilization in the areas of government and religion, most of their art and architecture was borrowed from other cultures. This *eclecticism*, or process of selecting elements from diverse sources and styles, is best illustrated in the remains of their great palaces at Susa and Persepolis. Darius himself described the palace at Susa as follows:

• • • *The decoration of this palace which I built at Susa was fetched from far away. . . . The bricks were molded and baked in the sun by the Babylonians. The cedar beams were brought from a mountain called Lebanon. . . . The wood called yaka was brought from Gandhara and Karmana. The gold was brought from Sardis and Bactria and wrought here. The magnificent stone called lapis lazuli and the cornelian were wrought here but were brought from Soghdiana. The precious turquoise was brought from Kharizmia and wrought on the spot. The silver and ebony were brought from Egypt. The decoration for the walls was brought from Ionia. The ivory wrought here, was transported from Kussa, Sind, and Arachosia. The stone columns, which were wrought here, were transported from Elam. The stone dressers were Ionians and Sards. The goldsmiths who wrought the gold were Medes and Egyptians. The men who worked the sun-baked bricks, they were Egyptians.[5]*

Darius selected *Persepolis* ("City of the Persians" to the Greeks) as the site for a new capital in 518 B.C. The palace at Persepolis was begun by Darius and completed by his successor, Xerxes, over several decades. The palace complex included royal apartments, rooms for the king's harem, treasuries, and an audience hall. It was constructed of sun-dried clay bricks, and erected on a man-made stone terrace which covered 33 acres. A monumental staircase was built from the natural ground level to the level of the palace.

he described how he had defeated the false Smerdis and restored law and order to his empire. In later inscriptions, he indicated that he was as proud of the fairness and efficiency of his rule as of his military exploits. Darius' effectiveness as a ruler was evident in the fact that he was able to administer an empire composed of many different people and cultures.

[5]*Ancient Civilizations*, ed. F. Clapham (New York: Warwick Press, 1978), p. 69.

SUMMARY

About 2500 B.C., waves of Indo-Europeans swept into the Middle East. Among their descendants were the Hittites, the first Western people to work with iron. Their introduction of iron, through trade and military conquest, to other peoples prior to 1200 B.C. led to the transition from what is known as the Bronze Age to the Iron Age. The Hittites also provided an important link between the civilization of the Middle East and that of the Aegean world.

The Persians created the first great Indo-European empire in history, and the people of the Middle East enjoyed 200 years of relative peace and prosperity under their rule. The religion founded by Zoroaster had great influence on Judaism and early Christianity, and survives even today among the small but influential community of Parsis in India. The Romans learned from the Persian example how to govern an empire of diverse peoples by granting certain rights to all citizens and creating an equitable system of justice.

QUESTIONS

1 How did the Hittites manage to establish and maintain hegemony over northern Syria-Palestine?
2 Why was the ability to make iron tools and weapons an important technological development?
3 Explain why Cyrus is referred to as "the Great."
4 What were the main features of the Zoroastrian religion, and in what ways might it have affected how the Persian kings ruled their empire?
5 Why is Darius considered to be one of the greatest administrators in history?

BIBLIOGRAPHY

Which book might describe the decoding of ancient languages?

LEHMANN, JOHANNES. *The Hittites: People of a Thousand Gods.* New York: Viking Press, 1977. *Presents the history of a vanished people whose power once rivaled that of the Egyptians and the Assyrians; provides illustrations of archaeological findings.*

PIOTROVSKY, BORIS. *The Ancient Civilization of Urartu.* New York: Cowles Book Co., 1969. *Author recounts his experiences on an archaeological "dig" in the 1930s; reconstructs the world of the Urartu, a major civilization which gave its name to Mount Ararat. Illustrated with splendid photographs of the sites and of museum artifacts.*

4

The Lord said to Abraham, "Leave your country, your kinsmen, and your father's house, and go to a country that I will show you. I will make you into a great nation, I will bless you and make your name so great that it shall be used in blessings: Those that bless you I will bless, those that curse you I will execrate. All the families of the earth will pray to be blessed as you are blessed."

Genesis 12: 1-3

The Eastern Mediterranean

At the beginning of the 12th century B.C., widespread migrations throughout the ancient world created such chaotic conditions that several powerful empires were destroyed, and many people were forced to move from their homelands. The Hittite civilization was overrun by migrating peoples called the Phrygians, and the Egyptians defended their borders against tribes they called the Sea Peoples.

The political vacuum created by the decline of the Hittite and Egyptian empires meant that several small groups of people were able to establish independent nations in the area of Syria and Palestine. Between 1200 and 600 B.C., the fates of these small nations inversely reflected the fortunes of the stronger nations around them. When the surrounding powers were strong, the small nations were dominated by them. When the surrounding powers were weak, the small nations enjoyed independence.

The portion of the eastern Mediterranean world we shall study in this chapter is presently occupied by the states of Israel, Lebanon, Syria, and Jordan. For simplicity, we shall call it Syria-Palestine. Overall, this area covers approximately 400 miles from north to south, and 200 miles from east to west. It extends from the northeastern shore of the Mediterranean Sea to the Egyptian delta in the southwest, and includes the northern portion of the Euphrates River. While the terrain is predominantly a mixture of mountain and desert, the entire western branch of the Fertile Crescent has been a land of agriculture and a corridor of travel for thousands of years, and frequently a battleground for competing great powers.

For many centuries, the available recorded history of this area was limited to Biblical accounts. During the 20th century, however, a great deal of knowledge has been gained through excavations. In fact, archaeology is considered to be a national pastime in Israel today, and exciting new discoveries are made every year.

THE PHOENICIANS In the northern part of Syria-Palestine, the snow-covered Lebanon Mountains are very close to the Mediterranean Sea, creating a narrow coastal strip which the Greeks called *Phoenicia*. The Phoenicians were related to the Canaanites, a mixture of Semitic and Hittite peoples who had given up nomadic ways

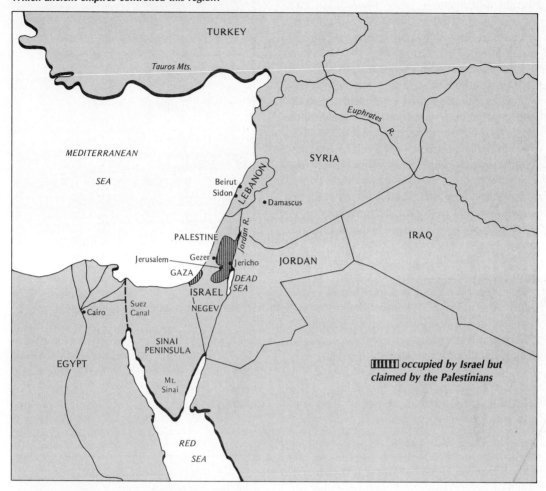

and adopted a blend of Egyptian and Babylonian cultures.

Much of our knowledge of the Phoenicians has come from the records of other people, which indicate that the Phoenician traders and sailors were known throughout the ancient world. In some of the Egyptian tombs there are paintings showing Phoenician ships, laden with cedar logs from Lebanon, tied up at Egyptian docks. These logs were used by the Egyptians to build masts for the boats they sailed on the Nile and on the Mediterranean. Temple inscriptions at Thebes-Karnak show Thutmose III boasting of using Phoenician harbors as bases for military campaigns against the people of Syria-Palestine. The Phoenicians were listed as vassals on tribute lists of Sargon I of Akkad, and of Hammurabi of Babylon. The great Hebrew king, Solomon, obtained artisans and lumber from the Phoenician ruler of Tyre (1 Kings 5:6), and the Persians confiscated Phoenician ships and sailors to create a Persian navy.

Phoenicia was made up of four small city-states: Beirut, Byblos, Tyre, and Sidon. Tyre was the most defensible of these coastal cities—it was strategically located on a small offshore island, with an excellent harbor, and strong fortifications. Each Phoenician city-state was ruled by a king, but in times of danger the city-states joined together for mutual defense.

Between 1200 and 900 B.C., following the decline of the powerful Egyptian and Hittite empires, the prosperity and influence of the Phoenician city-states was far out of proportion to the small area they occupied. Their fertile land produced wheat, olives, and figs. The Lebanon Mountains were thickly forested with the famous "cedars of Lebanon." Along the Mediterranean coast there were beds of murex—shellfish from which the people extracted a purple-red dye which they used to color cloth. The Greek word for this dye was *phoinix*, and thus the people who produced it became known as the Phoenicians. (Because this dye was difficult to produce, the cloth that was colored by it was one of the Phoenicians' more expensive products. It is for this reason that purple became the color associated with royalty.)

The narrowness of the coastal plain was probably one of the factors that led the Phoenicians to turn to the sea for their livelihood. As Herodotus said:

• • • *they migrated from that which was called the Red Sea to the Mediterranean, and having settled in the country which they now inhabit, forthwith applied themselves to distant voyages.*[1]

The Phoenicians became the first great navigators of the Western world. They manufactured bronze weapons and armor, gold, silver, and glass vessels, wine, inlaid furniture, carved ivory, woolen and phoinix dyed cloth, and traded these goods for the products of other people throughout the Mediterranean world. They charted sea routes and were the first to use the *Polaris* (north star) for navigation at night. The Greeks came to call this star the "Phoenician star."

[1]Herodotus I, 1.

Phoenician merchant ships were a common sight in ports throughout the Mediterranean world.

In their never-ending search for new markets and natural resources, they sailed through the Strait of Gibraltar, perhaps as far as Britain in the north. According to Herodotus, they also circumnavigated Africa, many centuries before the Portuguese explorers. They established colonies, primarily as trading

Colored glass objects were one of the Phoenicians' most popular exports.

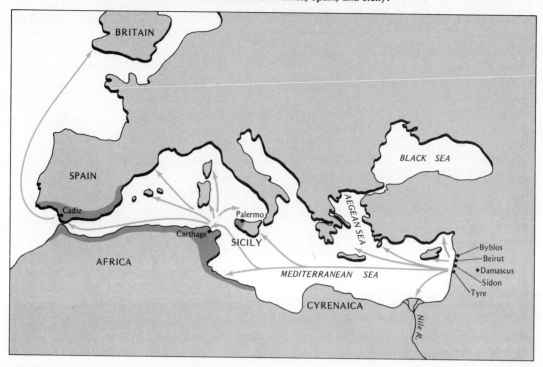

stations to exploit the raw materials of the local region, in various places along the shores of the Mediterranean. Many of these colonies developed into cities that still exist today, such as Cadiz in Spain and Palermo in Sicily.

Founded by merchants from Tyre in 814 B.C., Carthage, on the north coast of Africa in present Tunisia, was by far the most important of the Phoenician colonies. When the central power of Phoenicia waned during the 7th century B.C., Carthage was still powerful enough to hold the Mediterranean colonies in a strong maritime empire, stretching from Cyrenaica (on the north coast of Africa) on the east to Iberia (present Spain) in the west. During the 3rd century B.C., Carthage was the chief rival of Rome for control of the Mediterranean world.

In order to facilitate their trade, the Phoenicians abandoned the use of cuneiform writing on clay tablets, and developed a sim-

ple alphabet of 22 symbols, representing consonants adopted from Egyptian hieroglyphics. The Phoenician traders carried this concept of *alphabet* throughout their world of trade. The Greeks later modified the Phoenician alphabet by using as vowels those Phoenician consonants for which the Greeks had no equivalent sounds. A few centuries later, the Romans modified the alphabet of the Greeks and spread their version throughout the Western world.

Despite their innovations in navigation and trade, the Phoenicians did not have a distinctive culture of their own. Their art imitated the art of other peoples. Their religion, borrowed from early settlers in Syria-Palestine, was centered on the worship of the forces of nature, and marked by cruel rituals and human sacrifices. They believed that each city-state was owned by a deity (*Baal*) who would aid his people if they asked for his

The Phoenicians introduced the concept of an alphabet to their many trading partners. Most civilizations of the ancient Middle East eventually adopted this system of writing.

Early Phoenician	Early Hebrew	Later Phoenician	Early Greek	Early Etruscan	Roman
⟨glyph⟩	⟨glyph⟩	⟨glyph⟩	⟨glyph⟩	⟨glyph⟩	A
⟨glyph⟩	⟨glyph⟩	⟨glyph⟩	⟨glyph⟩	⟨glyph⟩	B
⟨glyph⟩	⟨glyph⟩	⟨glyph⟩	⟨glyph⟩	⟨glyph⟩	C
⟨glyph⟩	⟨glyph⟩	⟨glyph⟩	⟨glyph⟩	⟨glyph⟩	D
⟨glyph⟩	⟨glyph⟩	⟨glyph⟩	⟨glyph⟩	⟨glyph⟩	E
⟨glyph⟩	⟨glyph⟩	⟨glyph⟩	⟨glyph⟩	⟨glyph⟩	F

help, but demanded no ethical behavior on the part of the worshipers.

The Phoenicians spread the peaceful arts of weaving, glass-making, metallurgy, naval science, and the alphabet, from the Middle East to points throughout the Western world. Their independence came to an end in 854 B.C. when they were conquered by the Assyrians. During the 8th century B.C., their trade and colonization were greatly diminished because of competition from the Greeks. In 612 B.C. Phoenicia was overrun by Chaldea, and in 540 by the Persians. In 333 B.C. the city of Tyre fell to Alexander the Great. By 64 B.C. the remains of the original four Phoenician city-states had become part of the Roman province of Syria.

THE ARAMEANS

Like the Phoenicians, the Arameans were a Semitic people who gave up their nomadic ways to become farmers and traders. During the 12th century B.C. they gradually moved from the Arabian desert into Syria. They took over existing city-states and established new ones, the most important of which was Damascus, considered to be the oldest continuously inhabited city in the world today.

When the Hittite empire collapsed, about 1200 B.C., the Arameans were able to control the trade routes between Phoenicia, Egypt, and Mesopotamia. Their caravans carried ideas as well as wares. Their system of weights and measures came to be adopted throughout the Assyrian and Persian empires, and their Aramean language became the universal language of the Middle East. In Palestine, Aramaic replaced Hebrew as the spoken language, and was commonly used at the time of Jesus.

THE HEBREWS

The Semitic people who established the strongest monarchy in Syria-Palestine, and whose religion exerted the greatest influence on Western civilization, were the Hebrews. In fact, most of what we know about them is derived from their scriptures, which Christians call the *Old Testament*. These scriptures include books of law (*Torah*), history, prophecy, poetry, and wisdom. Like the Arameans, the Hebrews may have been nomads in the Arabian desert as early as 2000 B.C. According to tradition, Abraham, the forefather of the Hebrews, had a vision in which God instructed him to:

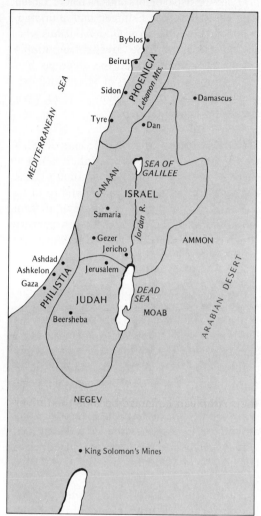

PALESTINE AND PHOENICIA, 900 B.C.
In what ways were Israel and Judah different?

• • • *leave your own country, your kinsmen and your father's house, and go to a country that I will show you. I will make you into a great nation. I will bless you and make your name so great that it will be used as a blessing.*[2]

The Torah relates that Abraham and his family left Ur in Sumer and traveled along the Fertile Crescent into southern Palestine. This migration may have occurred during the

20th or 19th century B.C. Because of a famine, Abraham's grandson Jacob (who came to be known as Israel) led the Hebrews to the northern edge of the Egyptian delta. For a time they prospered, but later (perhaps at the end of the 18th century B.C.) they were enslaved and forced to build storehouses for the pharaoh. A leader named Moses followed the commands of his God and led the Hebrew captives out of Egypt, across the Red Sea, and into the desert of Sinai.

The Torah also relates that Moses went up on Mount Sinai to receive from God what came to be called the Ten Commandments. These commandments became the foundation for the social order of the Hebrews. Moses also received the following instructions:

• • • *Speak thus to the house of Jacob, and tell this to the sons of Israel: You have seen with your own eyes what I did to Egypt, and how I carried you on eagle's wings and brought you here to me. If only you will now listen to me and keep my covenant, then out of all the peoples you shall become my special possession; for the whole earth is mine. You shall be my kingdom of priests, my holy nation. These are the words you shall speak to the Israelites.*[3]

The covenant with Yahweh, or Jehovah, as their God came to be known, bound the Israelites to worship and obey him to the exclusion of all other possible objects of faith. The concept that obedience to Yahweh would bring blessings, while disobedience would bring adversities, became a basic concept of their faith. Throughout the centuries since the time of Moses, the affirmation of the Jews (as the Israelites came to be called) has been:

• • • *Hear, O Israel, the Lord is our God, one Lord, and you must love the Lord your God with all your heart and soul and strength.*[4]

The Jews thus became the first practitioners of *ethical monotheism*, the worship of one

[2]Genesis 12: 1-2.

[3]Exodus 19: 3-6.

[4]Deuteronomy 6:4.

god, based on love between god and man and between man and man.

After many years of wandering in the wilderness of Sinai, the Hebrews entered the promised land of Palestine. There they displaced the Canaanites, a mixture of Semitic and Hittite peoples who had long ago given up nomadic ways and adopted elements of Egyptian and Babylonian cultures.

The Philistines. Before the Hebrews could fully occupy the land promised to them by Yahweh, they were confronted by the Philistines, who were called "Sea People" by the Egyptians. One of the Biblical prophets states that the Philistines had come from *Caphtor*, which may have been present Crete or Cyprus. He also indicates that the Hebrews intended to expell them:

Because the day is upon them when Philistia
will be despoiled,
And Tyre and Sidon to the last defender;
For the Lord will despoil the Philistines,
That remnant of the isle of Caphtor.[5]

Although the Philistines had failed in their attempts to invade Egypt, they had managed to gain control of the coastal area just north of Egypt's border by 1125 B.C. The region came to be known as Philistia, and it eventually contained five city-states: Ashkelon, Ashdad, Ekron, Gath, and Gaza. The Philistines' superior iron weapons and their well-disciplined military forces made it possible for them to keep the Hebrews well away from their coastal settlements.

The 12 Tribes. There were 12 tribes of Hebrews, each descended from, and named for, one of the sons of Jacob (who was also known as *Israel*). As they occupied the land of Palestine, they formed a confederacy, or religious league, in which the member tribes were bound together by the same religion, language, and laws. Each of 11 tribes was assigned a particular area of settlement, while the 12th tribe, the Levites, were named the

religious leaders of all the others. In times of crisis, the tribal elders chose a leader, called a judge, whom they believed had *charisma*, or special blessings from God. All tribes worshiped at the Ark of the Covenant, a portable shrine to Yahweh which the Hebrews had built under the direction of Moses and carried with them during their years of wandering through the Sinai.

THE KINGDOM OF ISRAEL
After many years of existence as a confederation of tribes, about 1000 B.C. the Hebrews united under the leadership of an outstanding young man named David to form the kingdom of Israel. Less than a century later, Israel split into two kingdoms: the northern one was called Israel and the southern one was called Judah.

DAVID

When the Israelites were unable to defeat the Philistines, their leaders demanded that Samuel, who was a judge at this time, appoint a king to lead them. Samuel tried to warn them of the evils that would befall the people under a monarch, but they persisted until Samuel appointed Saul to be their king, around 1020 B.C. Saul died in 1000 B.C. and was succeeded by David, who had achieved fame in several battles against the Philistines.

David's reign (1000-965 B.C.) soon became the model for all future rulers of the Israelites, for he confined the Philistines to the area known today as the Gaza Strip and united the 12 tribes into a single kingdom. Under his leadership, this new nation captured the Canaanite fortress at Jerusalem, converted it into a political capital, and made it the home of the Ark of the Covenant. Henceforth, the Jews referred to Jerusalem as *The City of David*.

SOLOMON

David was succeeded by his son Solomon (reigned 965-927 B.C.), who raised the nation

---

[5]Jeremiah 47:4.

Artists' reconstructions of the exterior (left) and interior of Solomon's Temple at Jerusalem. According to the account in the Book of Kings, Solomon conscripted 30,000 stonemasons and carpenters to build the Temple. The walls and floors as well as the altar were overlaid with gold.

to its pinnacle of prestige. Solomon acquired cedar logs and artisans from the Phoenician king of Tyre, and used them to build a great temple for Yahweh at Jerusalem and a palace for himself. He divided the kingdom into 12 administrative districts, each headed by a governor who was required to provide the court at Jerusalem with food for one month each year. He made trade alliances with the Egyptians and the Phoenicians, and sealed these by marrying princesses from each place.

Solomon built fortresses at strategic places throughout the realm. On the Red Sea, he constructed a fleet of ships which sailed to distant ports, including Ophir (which was probably in the vicinity of modern Yemen), to exchange copper, wheat, olive oil, and wool for products such as gold, silver, ivory, peacocks, and apes.

During the reign of Solomon, the Hebrews played their greatest role in the political and economic life of the Middle East. However, the oppressive taxes, conscripted labor, and loss of tribal independence led to dissension. When Solomon died, the 12 tribes split into two separate kingdoms.

Archaeological Findings. Yigael Yadin, the former director of the Institute of Archaeology at the Hebrew University in Jerusalem, was the major contributor to modern knowledge about ancient Palestine, and many of his excavations were of sites associated with King Solomon. The Bible mentions that Solomon conscripted forced labor to build a number of large constructions—a temple, a palace, the wall of Jerusalem, and the towns of Hazor, Megiddo, and Gezer—so Yadin decided to explore some of these sites.

Because the towns of Hazor, Megiddo, and Gezer had identical architectural features, Yadin decided that they had been built from the same set of plans. Each of the three towns was built on a *tell*, that is, a mound created by a sequence of towns built and destroyed on the same site over a period of many centuries. For example, Solomon's construction at Megiddo was on top of 18 earlier towns.

The outstanding engineering feat at both Hazor and Megiddo was the water supply system, an essential feature of every fortress designed to resist long sieges. In both cases, Solomon's new construction was between 50 and 100 feet above the original level of the ground; both had springs at the original ground level. In both cases, large square shafts were dug with flights of steps descending down to the level of the springs. From these points, tunnels were dug from the bottom of the steps toward the springs, and from the springs toward the bottom of the steps. These tunnels were high enough that women could walk through them carrying jars full of water on their heads. In his book describing the exploration of Hazor, Dr. Yadin writes:

••• In 732 B.C. Hazor fell to Tiglath-pilesar III and was destroyed. The Bible (2 Kings 15:29) describes this tragedy very laconically: "In the days of Pekah king of Israel, Tiglath-pilesar king of Assyria came and captured . . . Hazor; and he carried the people captive to Assyria." It is only through the archeological excavations that we now know the meaning of the words "came and captured." Tiglath-pilesar razed to the very ground the city of Hazor, once a key stronghold of the northern Kingdom of Israel. The sight we encountered in area B is worse than any I can remember in archeological excavations. The entire area was covered by a layer of ashes one metre thick and still black! Everything in sight was broken and scattered on the floors of the houses. We could visualize the Assyrian soldiers roaming about the houses, looting whatever they could and destroying the rest. The fire was so violent that even the stones were black, and numerous charred beams and pieces of burned plaster from the ceilings were strewn all over. The eastern side of the citadel, from which the fort had been attacked, was destroyed so thoroughly that in some places only the foundations below the floor level were visible. Here again we had visual evidence of the methods of destruction so vividly described by the Bible: "Rase it, rase it! Down to its foundations!" (Psalms 137:7.)[6]

6Yigael Yadin, Hazor (New York: Random House, 1975), pp. 175-6.

THE TWO KINGDOMS

After Solomon's death, the 10 northern tribes asked Solomon's oldest son and legal successor, Rheoboam, to ease their burdens. When he refused to do so, these tribes, under the leadership of Jeroboam, another son of Solomon, established a separate kingdom which they called Israel, with a capital at Samaria. The two tribes in the south remained loyal to Rheoboam and formed the kingdom of Judah. The southern kingdom had few natural resources and its only large town was Jerusalem, the religious center for the entire 12 tribes. The people of the south remained true to the worship of Yahweh. The northern kingdom had several times as many people as the southern and was fertile and prosperous. The people of the north frequently forgot about Yahweh and turned to the worship of the Canaanite Baal.

After about 850 B.C., the fate of Israel and Judah was determined by the succession of nations that controlled the Land between the

After the Babylonian exile of the 6th century B.C., the torah served as a guide to faith for widely scattered Jewish communities.

Rivers. In 722 B.C., Samaria was captured by Assyria and many of the people were marched to that land. In 587 B.C., Jerusalem was destroyed by the Chaldeans and the people were marched off to Babylon. From this point on, the Hebrews were commonly referred to as Judeans or Jews. During the period of the exile, the bonds of kinship among the Jews were strengthened, and a community created which stressed tradition, law, and ritual. After Cyrus conquered Babylonia in 540 B.C., he permitted the Jews to return to their homeland. The Persians helped to finance the reconstruction of the temple at Jerusalem, and returned temple objects that had been taken by Nebuchadnezzar II.

The Prophets. Between the 8th and 6th centuries B.C., the religion of the Jews, which came to be called *Judaism*, was shaped by the teachings of a succession of prophets whom the Hebrews believed spoke for Yahweh. In their teachings, these prophets denounced the sins of the people and warned them repeatedly that they faced the punishment of God for their transgressions. But they also preached a message of hope—that Yahweh was just and merciful and ready to forgive those who repented.

Amos was the first of a group of prophets whose messages were put into written form. He spoke out against the social and economic injustices of his time, denouncing wealthy merchants who exploited the poor and the hypocrisy of self-righteous people. Amos rebuked his listeners by crying out that Yahweh had told him to say:

••• *I hate, I spurn your pilgrim-feasts; I will not delight in your sacred ceremonies. When you present your sacrifices and offerings I will not accept them, nor look on the buffaloes of your shared offerings. Spare me the sound of your songs; I cannot endure the music of your lutes. Let justice roll down like a river and righteousness like an ever flowing stream.[7]*

---

[7]Amos 5: 21-24.

Several of the prophets taught that catastrophic events were a punishment for the people's sins. Jeremiah, in the 7th century, saw Assyria and Chaldea as the "rod of God's anger," used to chasten the sinful people. He preached that Yahweh would proclaim a new covenant with the Jews if each individual would make religion a matter of the heart and conscience. Jeremiah also proclaimed that the nation should be prepared to receive a *Messiah*, or God-appointed leader, who would save Israel from political bondage. Later, some people considered these and other teachings to have been predictions about Jesus.

Sacred Literature. The three most important items of sacred Jewish literature are the *Torah*, the *Mishnah*, and the *Talmud*. In 450 B.C., while the Persians still controlled Palestine, the scrolls of the Torah, or law, were written to systematize and preserve earlier writings and teachings. Several centuries later the Torah was incorporated into the Bible of the Christians as the first five books of the Old Testament.

Subsequent to 450 B.C., each generation of Jewish *rabbis*, or teachers, attempted to interpret these religious laws in ways relevant to their followers. Originally these interpretations, or *traditions of the elders*, as they came to be called, were passed along orally, but in time they became so extensive that memorization was very difficult. In 200 B.C., a group of very learned rabbis compiled the many interpretations into a scroll which they called the Mishnah (repetition). Many copies of the Mishnah were prepared and sent to Jewish communities everywhere to provide a uniform interpretation of the Torah and a common bond among the dispersed Jews.

About 500 A.D., all of the known laws and interpretations that evolved after preparation of the Mishnah were gathered together by another group of distinguished rabbis into the Talmud (instructions). Throughout the long centuries of *diaspora* (persecution and dispersion), the Torah and Talmud have provided Jews everywhere with a common bond.

SUMMARY

Between 1200 and 900 B.C. several small nations played important roles in the Middle East. The Phoenicians were a great seafaring people who carried the arts of civilization to all points on the coastlines of the Mediterranean Sea. The Arameans specialized in overland trade. Their language—Aramaic—and their system of weights and measures were used throughout the region for several centuries. The Hebrews had the most influence on other civilizations. Their concept of ethical monotheism had important consequences in the development of many other cultures.

QUESTIONS

1 In what ways have Biblical accounts of the Assyrians and Chaldeans been substantiated by archaeology and modern research?
2 How did the three small kingdoms of the Hebrews, Arameans, and Phoenicians manage to survive in the Fertile Crescent?
3 Research the circumstances under which the Dead Sea Scrolls were discovered. Why do modern Biblical scholars believe that this is one of the greatest archaeological discoveries ever made? In what ways has it changed our interpretation of the Bible?
4 Why are the ancient Phoenicians and Arameans called the "carriers of civilization"?
5 Explain the origin of the terms "Hebrew," "Israelite," and "Jew."
6 Jerusalem is a holy city to the Jews, Christians, and Moslems. How does this fact affect the political situation in Israel today?

BIBLIOGRAPHY

Which books might tell what event is celebrated during Passover?

KENYON, KATHLEEN. *Royal Cities of the Old Testament.* New York: Schocken Books, 1971. *The author, a renowned archaeologist, relates the evidence revealed by excavations to Biblical accounts of Solomon's royal cities: Jerusalem, Hazor, Megiddo, Gezer, and Samaria.*

MAGNUSSON, MAGNUS. *Archaeology of the Bible.* New York: Simon & Schuster, 1977. *Presents new interpretations of the religion, history, and literature of Biblical times, based on recent excavations in Israel, Jordan, Syria, and Iraq; illustrated with informative maps, drawings, and photographs.*

MOSCATI, SABATINO. *The World of the Phoenicians.* New York: Praeger, 1965. *Analyzes the civilization of the Phoenicians, emphasizing little known facts about the culture; traces the influence of the Phoenicians' culture through their Mediterranean settlements.*

SEIDMAN, HILLEL. *The Glory of the Jewish Holidays.* New York: Shengold Publishers, 1980. *Reveals the spirit of Judaism as it is reflected in the festivals and holy days; recalls the reasons for the establishment of these days and the laws and customs associated with them. Includes photographs of the art and literature associated with each festival.*

5

One of the great islands of the world
in midsea, in the winedark sea, is Krete:
spacious and rich and populous, with ninety
cities and a mingling of tongues. . . .
Here lived King Minos whom Zeus received
every ninth year in private council. . . .

HOMER

The Aegean Civilization

The *Iliad* and the *Odyssey* by the great Greek poet Homer inspired archaeologists to find out whether the people and places in these epics actually existed.[1] Excavations made since the middle of the 19th century have uncovered remains of a brilliant Bronze Age civilization which flourished around the Aegean Sea from about 2000 to 1100 B.C.

The three major centers of the Aegean civilization were: the *Trojan*, named for Troy, the most important ancient city on the western coast of Asia Minor; the *Minoan*, named for a legendary King Minos, who ruled Knossos on the island of Crete; and the *Mycenaean*, named for Mycenae, the largest settlement of the time on the mainland of Greece. This Aegean world was close enough to both Egypt and the Middle East to exchange goods, settlers, and ideas, but isolated enough to develop a distinctive culture of its own.

[1]The *Iliad* describes a war between the Greeks and the Trojans that may have taken place at the beginning of the 12th century B.C., four centuries before Homer's lifetime. The *Odyssey* relates the adventures of the Mycenaean leader Odysseus on his voyage home after the war.

THE ARCHAEOLOGISTS Because scholars have not yet deciphered the language of the Aegean world, most of our knowledge of this area has come from the material remains uncovered by archaeologists since the middle of the 19th century. The first important archaeologist to go into this area was Heinrich Schliemann (1822-1890). When he was a small boy in Germany, his father read to him the *Iliad* and the *Odyssey* of Homer. Fascinated by these tales, young Heinrich dreamed of searching for the places described in these poems. After he became a very successful businessman, he decided to use his wealth to fulfill his childhood dreams. In 1870, using the *Iliad* and the *Odyssey* as his guidebooks, Schliemann began to dig at a place currently named Hissarlik, in Turkey, because he believed that this site most closely resembled Homer's description of the location of Troy. He found the remains of not just one level of development, but of several levels. In the second oldest level he uncovered, Schliemann found a store of objects made of gold. He promptly called these objects *The Treasure of Priam*, because he assumed that they had belonged to Priam, the king of Troy dur-

ing the Trojan War. Later, it was found that this level actually dated to about 2200 B.C., or about 1000 years before the date traditionally given for the Trojan War. Many later scholars concluded that the city described by Homer had been destroyed by fire and was to be found on a higher level.

After his successful explorations at Troy, Schliemann's search for his heroes led him to Mycenae, in the Peloponnesus, which Homer said was the city of Agamemnon, the leader of the Achaeans in their attack on Troy. Here Schliemann found gold ornaments and bronze weapons similar to those described by Homer. Still in pursuit of his childhood dreams, he bought land at Knossos, on the island of Crete, but died before he could begin to explore there.

Another 19th century archaeologist, Sir Arthur Evans, curator of the Ashmolean Museum at Oxford University in England, visited Greece in search of examples of early

Nothing is known for certain about the life of the great poet Homer, whose epics inspired the search for Troy. He may have lived in the 8th century B.C. (see Chapter 6). The oldest known portrait of the poet is the profile on the 4th-century coin shown at top. The bust below, from about 150 B.C., reflects the ancient tradition that Homer was blind.

Greek writing. In an antique shop in Athens he found two small stones inscribed with pictographs. Such stones were called "milk-stones" by the peasant women of Crete, who often wore them as charms to ensure that they could produce enough milk for their babies. Evans decided that these particular stones were inscribed with an early form of writing, and his search for the meaning of the pictographs led him to Knossos, where he spent the remainder of his life and his fortune excavating the sites of a civilization which he called *Minoan*.

THE MINOAN CIVILIZATION

Between 2000 and 1450 B.C., the island of Crete was the center of an advanced maritime civilization which dominated the islands of the Aegean Sea, the mainland of Greece, and the coastal areas of Asia Minor. We know little about the people who preceded this civilization, but there is evidence to suggest that the first inhabitants of Crete could have immigrated there from Anatolia between 4000 and 3000 B.C. It has also been suggested that the first Cretans might have been refugees from Libya, near the Egyptian delta. In either case, the earliest peoples had close ties with the Egyptians of the dynastic period (beginning about 3100 B.C.), for many Cretan artifacts have been found in Egyptian tombs of that era, and a number of Egyptian artifacts have been found in Crete.

Around 2000 B.C., mainland Greece was invaded by Indo-European tribes from the north. Although the islands were not directly affected by this invasion, archaeologists have noted that important changes were occurring in Crete at the same time. These developments included the construction of palaces, a wholly new style for pottery decoration, the use of the pottery wheel, and the invention of a method of writing. It is not known whether these changes in Crete occurred naturally or if they were introduced by new settlers. It is possible that some of the peoples of mainland Greece migrated to Crete to avoid the Indo-European invaders. Alternatively, new settlers may have arrived from Anatolia or Phoenicia.

One of the significant changes that occurred in Crete was the building of great palaces such as those at Knossos and Phaestos. In time, Knossos became the most important city in Crete, and, under the leadership of the legendary King Minos, it became the most important city in the Aegean world. Thucydides, a Greek historian of the 5th century B.C., used an ancient Greek tradition as his source in telling how King Minos made himself master of the seas.

••• *And the first person known to us by tradition as having established a navy is Minos. He made himself master of what is now called the Hellenic sea, and ruled over the Cyclades [a group of islands in the southern Aegean Sea], into most of which he sent his first colonies, . . . appointing his own sons as governors; and thus did his best to put down piracy in these waters, a necessary step to secure the revenues for his own use.[2]*

---

[2]Thucydides I, 1, 4.

As Thucydides indicates, the Minoans developed an extensive fleet of ships to protect their trade routes. In fact, their navy was so powerful that their government came to be called a *thalassocracy,* or "rule by the sea."

The wealth and power of King Minos were evident in the ruins of the palace at Knossos which were uncovered by Evans. Construction of the palace, which covered about six acres, was begun about 2000 B.C., but additions were made over several centuries. It consisted of brick and limestone buildings arranged around an open courtyard, 200 feet long by 100 feet wide. Broad stairways from this central courtyard led to the upper stories, and a maze of corridors connected the royal apartments, reception halls, administrative offices, workshops, and storerooms. The roofs were supported by columns that were tapered at the bottom.

The walls of the palace were decorated with frescoes, an art form in which artists apply colors to plaster before it hardens. Many of the decorations incorporated stylized horns of bulls. An elaborate sanitary system included running water and flush toilets, and

A stone chair found in the palace at Knossos may have been the throne of the fabled King Minos.

Immense clay jars called pithoi *were used to store food for the large number of people who lived in King Minos' palace.*

lightwells permitted daylight to illuminate interior rooms. An audience chamber contained a simple stone chair which may have been the throne of King Minos; if so, this is the oldest throne thus far discovered in Europe. In the basement rooms, archaeologists found lead-lined chests, which probably held royal treasures, and storage spaces containing immense *pithoi*, or clay jars, which may have held olive oil, wine, or grain. An outdoor theater, made of stone steps rising on a moderate slope, could accommodate up to 500 seated spectators: here the Minoans probably watched a variety of performances, including dancing, wrestling, and boxing.

After uncovering the remains of this palace, Arthur Evans reconstructed several portions of it as he conceived it to have looked, based on the remnants found. Steel girders and concrete slabs were erected to protect portions of the original buildings. Evans even engaged artists to recreate some of the frescoes, and these can still be seen today. These frescoes show men with red-hued skin and

women with white skin. The women appear to be participating with the men in festivals, dancing, and athletic events. In fact, all of the Minoan people are depicted as young, lively, and pleasure-loving. The discovery of a gaming board, similar to the kind used for backgammon, indicated that the Minoans also enjoyed less strenuous activities.

Homes of the common people, made of bricks and built on foundations of stone, surrounded the palace. These buildings were one or two stories high, had flat roofs, few windows, and were coated with stucco.

RELIGION

Since no temples or large cult statues have been found, scholars have determined that priests did not play as important a role in Minoan society as they did in Egypt or Mesopotamia. The Minoans believed that gods resided in trees, stones, and other natural objects. They worshiped these deities in sacred groves, in caves, and at shrines in their own homes. To avoid displeasing the gods when they were busy with other duties, they often placed *reverence statues* in the holy places to act as their representatives.

The most important Minoan deity seems to have been a Mother Goddess, similar to the fertility goddesses worshiped in many other places throughout the Middle East. She was usually depicted as holding a snake in each hand and with a bird perched on top of her head. The snake may have been a symbol of renewal, because snakes regularly slough off their old skins and promptly develop new ones. The dominance of the Mother Goddess in Cretan religion could have meant that women served as priestesses and held important positions in the society. Another important deity was a bull god, who may have symbolized male strength and creative energy.

The Greeks of the Classical period (5th and 4th centuries B.C.) believed that Zeus, their chief deity, often assumed the form of a bull and was born in a cave on Crete. Other

The Mother Goddess of Knossos holds a snake in each hand, perhaps symbolizing her powers of renewal.

crafted items. After 2000 B.C., they adopted the use of the potter's wheel and produced eggshell-thin pottery, called *Kamares* ware from the name of the cave in which it was first found.

In earliest times Cretan pottery had been decorated with simple geometric designs and painted in earth colors such as brown, rust, and black. After about 2000 B.C., the Kamares style pottery began to be decorated in a "light on dark" style, with white and other light colors applied over a dark background. The patterns of this later pottery were based on the shapes seen in plants, animals, and marine life, and were much more naturalistic than the earlier designs.

The Minoans also crafted fine gold and silver jewelry and made vases of soapstone, a soft, easily carved mineral, which they decorated with sculptures. Many of the objects that have been found have been quite small, even miniature, but all have been beautifully worked, and all of them were in great demand throughout the Aegean world.

The renowned skill of Minoan craftsmen can be seen in this pendant of embossed and filigreed gold. At the top, two wasps are arranged around a honeycomb.

Greek gods also show the influence of Minoan nature worship. Athena, for instance, was usually represented with an owl, and Aphrodite with a dove.

ECONOMY

The island of Crete was, and is, very mountainous, but the pleasant climate and the fertile volcanic soil which fills the small valleys provided abundant harvests of cereals, vegetables, flax, olives, and grapes.

Since they were skilled in seafaring, the Minoans developed an extensive maritime trade in these agricultural products and in

Around 2000 B.C., the Minoans began to develop a system of writing. They kept accounts of their wide-ranging trading activities on clay tablets, thousands of which have been found on Crete. While the earliest inscriptions were hieroglyphic, these soon evolved into an essentially syllabic script; that is, the signs represented syllables rather than single letters. Examples of this latter script, called *Linear A*, have been found at Phaestos and at Hagia Triada, but it has not yet been deciphered satisfactorily.

About 1600 B.C., Knossos, Phaestos, and most other settlements of Crete were showered by debris from a volcanic eruption on nearby Thera. After this disaster, the Cretans seem to have had about 150 years of peace and prosperity. But around 1450 B.C., the Minoan civilization came to a sudden and unexpected end. Most of the small villages and farms and all of the major towns in Crete were looted and destroyed by fire. Many scholars believe that invaders from the mainland of Greece, probably the Mycenaeans, were responsible for this destruction.

LEGENDS

For many centuries, scholars assumed that the adventures of the heroes of ancient Greek legends were fictional. But after Schliemann's explorations had demonstrated that the epics of Homer dealt with real places and people, they began to analyze other myths for possible references to actual events.

According to one of these myths, King Minos kept a Minotaur, a monstrous creature which was half man and half bull, in a labyrinth beneath his palace at Knossos. No one who entered the labyrinth was able to escape from being killed by the creature. Minos demanded that the Greeks of Athens, on the mainland of Greece, pay tribute to him by sending seven maidens and seven young men to be sacrificed to the Minotaur once every nine years.

The legend continues by relating that Theseus, the son of Aegeus, a legendary king of Athens, volunteered to try to put an end to payment of this tribute. As Theseus set sail for Crete, along with six other youths and seven maidens, he told his father that he would change the black sails on his boat to white ones for the journey home if he succeeded in killing the Minotaur.

When Theseus reached Knossos, Ariadne, the daughter of Minos, fell in love with him and offered to help him escape from the labyrinth. She gave him a sword and a ball of thread, and instructed him to tie one end of the thread to the door at the entrance of the labyrinth, then unwind the rest as he moved through the labyrinth. Theseus did as she advised, killed the Minotaur with the sword, and then followed the thread back to the entrance.

While sailing back to Athens after his exploit, Theseus forgot the agreement with his father and did not change the sails from black to white. When Aegeus saw the ship approaching, he thought that his son had perished in his struggle with the Minotaur. In his grief, he hurled himself from a cliff into the sea, thus giving his name to the Aegean Sea.

Some scholars believe that this legend may reflect an actual situation in which the Athenian Greeks paid tribute to the Minoans, or were forced to send a group of young nobles to Crete as hostages. The triumph of Theseus over the Minotaur was celebrated as late as the Hellenistic period (323-30 B.C.), when children played a game based on a maze of lines marked on a pavement, which they called a *labyrinth*.

Homer related another myth about King Minos of Crete. According to tradition, he said, King Minos was the son of a Phoenician princess. The god Zeus, disguised as a bull, abducted her from her native land and swam

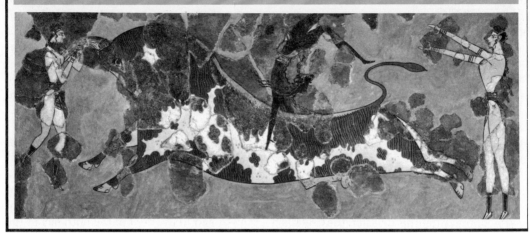

The Minoan sport of bull-vaulting required great daring and acrobatic skill. In this restored fresco, one acrobat somersaults over a bull's back while another grabs the bull's horns.

with her to his cave in Crete. There, Zeus fathered the child who later became known as King Minos. This myth raises the possibility that an actual Phoenician king could have journeyed to Crete and become the first King Minos.

Because there were so many colorful legends about King Minos, most scholars have concluded that the name *Minos* probably referred to a dynasty of kings, not to a single individual.

The Minoan sport of *bull vaulting* may also have had a mythic or religious basis. In this sport, acrobats (both men and women) would attempt to seize the horns of the charging beast and vault over its back in a somersault. The exact significance of this sport is not known.

THE MYCENAEANS

About 2000 B.C. or earlier, an Indo-European tribe known as the Achaeans invaded the peninsula of Greece. In time, they were able to overcome the earlier settlers and established several fortified strongholds, the most important of which were Pylos, Tiryns, and Mycenae—all in the region called the Peloponnesus. By 1600 B.C., the *Achaeans*, or *Mycenaeans*, as they are usually called, were sailing the Aegean Sea in their ships, first as pirates and later as traders. They became wealthy and powerful, and after Knossos was destroyed in 1450 B.C., the Mycenaeans became the most powerful group in the Aegean world.

The Mycenaeans adopted the art styles of the Minoans and took over the trading partnerships that the Minoans had developed throughout the ancient world, but their culture was very different. Whereas the Minoans' economy had been based on peaceful industries such as pottery-making, the Mycenaeans used their skills in warfare to gain and keep the territory they occupied. Archaeologists have found a vast array of bronze weapons in Mycenaean graves, which tend to support the portrait of Mycenaean warriors presented in the *Iliad* and the *Odyssey*. And while the Minoans had built their palaces without fortifications, secure in the protection of their navy and their good relations with their neighbors, the Mycenaeans built fortified citadels with walls so massive that the later Greeks believed that the stones had been put into place by a mythical race of giants called the *Cyclopes*.

A view of the citadel of Mycenae. The circle of shaft graves excavated by Sir Arthur Evans can be seen in the foreground, the plain of Argos in the background.

The Lion Gate is the principal entrance to the citadel of Mycenae, which was encircled with a massive Cyclopean wall. Unfortunately, the lions' heads have been lost.

GOVERNMENT

Archaeological findings and the writings of Homer indicate that the Mycenaeans retained many of their ancestral Indo-European customs. Tribal leaders established hereditary monarchies and ruled territories that were probably the size of city-states. Very often one king established his authority over a number of others, but none of the Mycenaean kings had the absolute powers of the Egyptian and Mesopotamian monarchs. Before making decisions, a king was expected to consult with an assembly of nobles. In the *Iliad*, Homer describes several of the assemblies that the Mycenaean king, Agamemnon, called in the course of the Trojan War. In these assemblies, Odysseus and other kings and nobles speak frankly to Agamemnon, and their advice is heeded. Although the position of the Mycenaean kings was hereditary, the continuation of their rule probably depended upon the quality of their leadership and the support of the nobles.

THE EPICS

In peacetime, the kings and nobles of Mycenaean Greece devoted much of their leisure time to athletic contests in order to keep themselves physically fit for battle. On cold evenings, they would gather around a glowing hearth in the great central hall of the king's palace to hear bards recite heroic tales about their exploits. These tales were passed down to succeeding generations over the course of several centuries. Around 750 B.C., according to tradition, the poet Homer recited the epic stories of the *Iliad* and the *Odyssey*, based upon an oral tradition at least four centuries old. Soon afterwards, the epics were finally written down.

Homer's epics reflect a society in which men are motivated to great deeds by the pursuit of honor. In the *Iliad*, Hector's speech to his infant son demonstrates a belief that courage and leadership in battle, not material possessions, will determine his son's place in society.

When he had kissed his child and swung him
high to dandle him, he said this prayer:
"O Zeus
and all immortals, may this child, my son,
*   become like me a prince among the*
*   Trojans.*
Let him be strong and brave and rule in
*   power at Ilion [Troy]; then someday*
*   men will say*
'This fellow is far better than his father!'
seeing him home from war, and in his arms
the bloodstained gear of some tall warrior
*   slain—making his mother proud."*[3]

The epics also depict other aspects of Mycenaean society. Families dutifully fulfill their obligations to the gods, and offer hospitality to all strangers, because it was believed that such guests might be gods in disguise.[4] In contrast to the cordiality shown to strangers,

however, there was no code of honor regarding enemies. While it was considered a sin to lie to a friend, it was admirable to deceive an enemy. In fact, craftiness and guile are the most outstanding characteristics of the hero Odysseus. Throughout the *Iliad* and the *Odyssey* he is spoken of admiringly as "wily Odysseus" and "Odysseus, master of stratagems."

Long after the Mycenaeans moved off the stage of history, their epics were recited for entertainment, for instruction in proper behavior, and as explanations of natural events. In the 4th century B.C., Plato complained that Homer's epics were still relied upon by the educators of his time.

ARCHAEOLOGICAL FINDINGS

Before 1500 B.C., the Mycenaeans buried their dead in what have come to be called "shaft graves." These graves were dug for family groups, and were arranged in a circle, perhaps 50 feet in diameter, with each grave marked by a sculptured limestone slab. Schliemann excavated one such circle containing the graves of a royal or noble family, and found a treasure of gold ornaments and bronze weapons inlaid with ivory and semiprecious stones. The faces of several of the skulls were covered by gold portrait masks, one of which Schliemann promptly decided was the *mask of Agamemnon*. Later scholars determined that the objects found by Schliemann were from a period almost 300 years before the dates traditionally given for the Trojan War (1194-1184 B.C.).

After 1500 B.C., the Mycenaeans built into hillsides large, circular, domed structures, up to 30 feet in diameter, called *tholoi* ("bee hive tombs"). The entrances were in the form of large trenches, with stone walls retaining the earth. Many artifacts which the wealthy might need in the afterlife were placed beside the bodies at the time of burial. The most famous *tholoi* at Mycenae are believed to be royal tombs. They are known as the Treasury of Atreus and the Tomb of Clytemnestra.

---

[3]*Iliad* VI, 474-87.
[4]The Greek word for "guest" (*Xenos*) is the same as the word for "stranger."

The chambers within the tholoi ("beehive tombs") at Mycenae had vaulted roofs.

THE TROJAN WAR

Troy was strategically located at the west end of the Hellespont, so that the rulers of Troy were able to control not only the water route from the Aegean to the Black Sea, but also the most direct land route between Europe and Asia. By the early 12th century B.C., the military and commercial ventures of the Mycenaeans had probably brought them into conflict with the Trojans.

Although the Trojan War was very likely fought for control of the Hellespont, the Mycenaeans and Greeks invented a much more romantic story of its origins. According to the *Iliad*, the cause of the conflict was the abduction of Helen, the wife of Menelaus, king of Sparta, and the most beautiful woman in the world. Paris, the son of the king of Troy, abducted Helen with the help of Aphrodite, the goddess of love. Aphrodite's action in helping Paris caused great dissension among the deities who resided on Mount Olympus. When the Mycenaeans went to war with Troy to rescue Helen, the gods quarreled among themselves about which side should be victorious, with many of the gods and goddesses intervening from time to time on behalf of their favorites.

The so-called Treasury of Atreus is the tomb of a Mycenaean royal family who lived about 1300 B.C. It is the largest of the tholoi at Mycenae and has an interior chamber nearly 50 feet high.

The Trojan War was one of the first wars fought in the ancient world in the region of the Hellespont, which today is called the Dardanelles. Subsequently, several other major battles were fought there, for the area had great strategic importance. In 495 B.C., the Persians seized the Hellespont in order to cut off the grain supplies that Athens received from the Black Sea area. Later in that century, the Spartans fought the Athenians on the shores of the Hellespont for the same reason: they wanted to stop the trade that Athens conducted with the Black Sea region. The area continued to be important throughout the centuries, for ships from the Black Sea must pass through the Dardanelles strait to reach the Mediterranean. During World War I, British Commonwealth troops fought a major battle at Gallipoli in an attempt to prevent the Germans from occupying this strategic area.

The second great epic of Homer, the *Odyssey*, tells of the adventures of Odysseus, who fought with the Mycenaeans in the Trojan War, but then had many adventures and suffered many hardships on his journey home to Ithaca, in western Greece.

THE END OF MYCENAEAN RULE

At the end of the 13th century B.C., many Mycenaean cities and palaces in the Peloponnesus were overrun by invaders from the north and destroyed by fire. It is not known for certain whether these invaders were the Dorians, an Indo-European tribe who settled in Greece around 1100 B.C., or another group.

Around 1100 B.C., the Dorians conquered the citadels of Mycenae, Pylos, and Tiryns. The surrounding countryside was abandoned, and the Mycenaeans who could not escape were enslaved. Many Mycenaeans fled to the islands of the Aegean Sea, and others settled in Athens, which was such a small village that the Dorians had ignored it. Other refugees founded settlements on the eastern coast of the Aegean Sea (the western coast of Asia Minor), a region known as *Ionia*. There they preserved and enhanced their customs and culture, and by the 9th century B.C. a brilliant civilization had evolved (see Chapter 7). Much of what later came to be called Greek philosophy, literature, science, and architecture actually had origins in Ionia. Ionian merchants traveled far and wide, creating trading settlements around the Mediterranean Sea. One such settlement was made at Massilia (modern Marseilles) on the south coast of present France, and from this point they traveled up the Rhone River far enough to encounter people from Cornwall, in present England.

The Dorians continued to migrate into Greece for several centuries. In the confusion that they created, earlier skills of writing, technology, and trade declined. The economy regressed to simple farming and animal husbandry. This period of Greek history, from 1100 to 700 B.C., is sometimes called the *Greek Dark Ages* or the *Archaic Age*. It is also known as the *Iron Age*, because iron tools and weapons increasingly replaced the bronze implements of the Mycenaeans.

SUMMARY

A brilliant Bronze Age civilization flourished around the Aegean Sea between 2000 and 1100 B.C. Remains of this civilization have been discovered at three distinct places: at Knossos on Crete, at Mycenae in the Peloponnesus, and at Troy in modern Turkey. The people of these cities developed an important and distinctive culture which was passed on to succeeding generations through their myths and epics.

The Minoan civilization ended abruptly about 1450 B.C., and leadership of the Aegean world passed to the Mycenaeans, or Achaeans, as Homer called them. The Mycenaeans then fought with the Trojans for control of the passageway to the Black Sea. About 1100 B.C., the Mycenaean civilization collapsed when the Dorians overran the peninsula of Greece.

QUESTIONS

1 What changes occurred in Minoan society around 2000 B.C.? What factors could have accounted for such changes?

2 In what ways did the early civilization of the Aegean world differ from that of Egypt? From that of the Land between the Rivers?

3 Compare examples of Minoan art with tomb paintings found in Egypt. What do these paintings tell us about the two societies?

4 How would the Minoan culture have been affected if the Mycenaeans had never learned seafaring skills?

5 Greek mythology explains that the Trojan War was brought about by Paris' abduction of Helen. What are more likely to have been the causes of this conflict?

BIBLIOGRAPHY

Which references might discuss the origin of the Minoans?

BLEGEN, CARL W. *Troy and the Trojans.* New York: Praeger, 1963. *An archaeologist who excavated Homer's Troy describes the various levels of the site; explains how the royal stronghold was destroyed and rebuilt several times and finally abandoned. Includes drawings of the plans of the various towns.*

COTTERELL, ARTHUR. *The Minoan World.* New York: Scribner's Sons, 1979. *Provides a comprehensive outline of what is known about the Minoans and their world; explores the problems associated with various theories of the origin of the Minoans.*

FINLEY, M.I. *Early Greece: The Bronze and Archaic Ages*, 2d ed. New York: Norton, 1982. *Reconstructs the preliterary age of Greece through examination of recent archaeological findings; traces the development of Greek institutions, providing an excellent background for the study of Classical Greece.*

"Minoans and Mycenaeans, Sea Kings of the Aegean." *National Geographic* 153, 2 (1978): 142-84. *Beautifully illustrated account of the Bronze Age civilization that developed on Crete and on the mainland.*

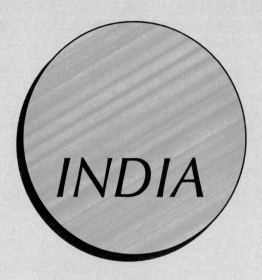

INDIA

3000–500 B.C.

To the east of Mesopotamia, in what is today Pakistan, a great civilization developed in the fertile Indus River valley. Like the early civilizations of the Tigris-Euphrates valley and the Nile valley that flourished about the same time, Indus valley civilization was built by people who established farming and herding communities.

Flanked on the west and northwest by the Hindu Kush Mountains and on the northeast by the Himalaya Mountains, the Indus valley civilization extended the length of the river and included the delta adjoining the Arabian Sea. Archaeological evidence suggests that trade took place between the peoples of the Indus valley and those of both Egypt and Mesopotamia. Trade goods were brought by boat through the Red Sea or Persian Gulf.

INDUS VALLEY CIVILIZATION

The origin of Indus valley civilization is largely unknown. It reached its height about 2500 B.C., began to decline about 1700 B.C., and collapsed about 1500 B.C. Archaeologists have excavated its two chief urban centers—Harappa and Mohenjo-daro. The carefully planned layout and rigorously uniform building materials found at these sites suggest that a strong, central authority exerted control over the people. Buildings were made of bricks dried in kilns, but the unusual feature of these bricks was that they conformed to a standard size over many centuries.

Harappa and Mohenjo-daro had well-planned sanitation systems that were superior to those in western Europe almost 4000 years later. Most homes had wells for water and drainage systems. Houses were built along wide streets that were laid on a grid pattern. The most important streets were oriented north-south; secondary streets ran east-west. Each city had large public baths that archaeologists hypothesize were used for religious as well as hygienic purposes.

At their height, Harappa and Mohenjo-daro may have had as many as 35,000 inhabitants and extended over six or seven square miles. They were the centers of an essentially agricultural region almost twice the size of the Old Kingdom of Egypt and almost four times the extent of Sumer and Akkad.

Very little is known about the political, social, and economic life of the Indus valley civilization. The cities were probably ruled by priest-kings who had the power to enforce the strict building standards that remained in use for a thousand years. The people, who were later called Dravidians, were polytheistic, and archaeological evi-

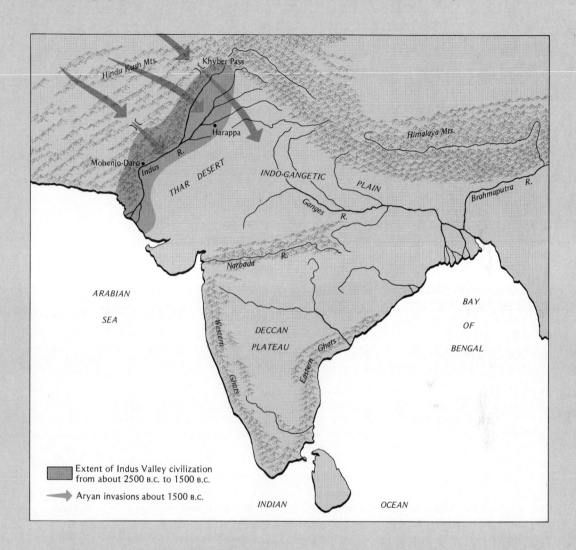

dence suggests that they worshiped a mother-goddess and a three-faced god. Stone seals with carved inscriptions indicate that the Dravidians had some kind of recordkeeping system, although these inscriptions have yet to be deciphered.

About 1700 B.C., the Indus valley civilization suffered a decline, as evidenced by low-ered building standards and other indications. The exact reasons for this decline are un-known. Recent excavations have suggested that mud and silt accumulations may have led to floods that severely damaged Mo-henjo-daro over several centuries and weak-ened its authority at a time when new groups of people with more advanced (iron) weap-ons and horsedrawn chariots swept into the region. By 1500 B.C. Indus valley civilization was replaced by a group of Indo-European invaders, known as the Aryans, who pushed through the Hindu Kush Mountains from what is today Iran.

Carved stone seals like this one were probably used by Mohenjo-daro merchants to stamp their possessions, and may also have had a religious meaning. On this seal, a bull stands near an incense burner.

ARYAN CONQUEST

Archaeologists believe that the Aryan conquest of India was part of a larger migration of Aryan people, some of whom pushed into Greece, Persia, and Italy. In India, the tall, light-skinned Aryans saw themselves as superior to the darker-skinned people they conquered, and they either enslaved the Dravidians or forced them to flee into other parts of India. Thus, unlike the early civilizations of Egypt and Sumer that greatly influenced later peoples, the Indus valley civilization was largely destroyed. It is only in the 20th century that archaeologists and historians have begun to explore its mysteries. They have slowly started to piece together evidence that this early Indian civilization did influence the Aryans, but the record is still incomplete.

The Aryans were only one of many invaders who pushed across the Hindu Kush Mountains into the northern plain in the course of India's long history. However, the Aryan influence on later Indian civilization was lasting and profound. The early Aryans were nomadic people loosely organized into tribes. After overwhelming the Indus valley civilization, they migrated eastward and eventually settled the entire region known as the indo-Gangetic plain. During this period from about 1500 B.C. to 1000 B.C., their chief enemies were the Dravidians, probably survivors of the Indus valley civilization, who were forced to retreat into southern India. Between about 1000 B.C. and 700 B.C., various Aryan tribes led by *rajahs*, or elected chiefs, fought for control of the Indo-Gangetic plain. Gradually, individual rajahs carved out small kingdoms across the northern plain.

ORIGINS OF HINDUISM

Very little material exists to reconstruct the early history of the Aryans, for these tribes had no method of writing their language until they developed Sanskrit about 700 B.C. Most of our knowledge about the early Aryans comes from the carefully guarded oral traditions that were handed down by the priests.

The earliest of these religious traditions are the *Vedas* (meaning "knowledge"), a collection of poems, religious writings, and hymns composed between about 1500 B.C. and 1000 B.C. The original Vedas were the *Rig Veda*, the *Sama Veda*, *Yajur Veda*, and *Atharva Veda*, and like the hymns and prayers of ancient Egypt, they offer our principal source of information about the people, their beliefs, and their daily lives. The *Rig Veda*, which is the oldest, includes 1028 hymns to various gods. Later writings, the *Upanishads*, are commentaries on the ideas expressed in the Vedas.

Together, the Vedas and Upanishads became part of the sacred literature of Hinduism, the religion that grew out of the beliefs of the Aryans, and the period from 1500 B.C. to 700 B.C. has been called the Vedic Age. Because Hinduism evolved slowly, it is said to be a religion without a founder. Within Hinduism, many ideas and inconsistencies coexist. However, the diversity and adaptability of this religion ensured its survival, and it is the oldest of the world's major religions.

Hindus believe in *brahma*, a single unifying force, but they worship many gods, each

Shiva the destroyer is one of the most important Hindu gods. Like other gods in the Hindu pantheon, Shiva is considered to be a manifestation of the supreme god, Brahman.

The elephant-headed god Ganesha, son of Shiva, is possibly the most popular divinity in the Hindu pantheon. His fat belly represents the prosperity he brings to his worshipers.

of whom is seen as a different aspect of brahma. By acting in accord with *dharma*, or universal moral laws, Hindus believe that an individual can attain the ultimate goal of existence—the reunifying of the individual soul with *atman*, the universal soul. Hindus believe that most people cannot achieve this reunion with atman in a single lifetime, and therefore that most souls pass through a series of rebirths. In each reincarnation, or rebirth, an individual has the opportunity to move closer to the ultimate goal.

While the Vedas provide valuable evidence about the development of Aryan religious beliefs, another series of oral traditions tell about the wars among rival Aryan kingdoms between about 1000 B.C. and 700 B.C. Two epic poems, the *Mahabharata* and the *Ramayana*, recount the struggles of this time. Like the Homeric epics, the *Iliad* and the *Odyssey*, these narratives mix fact and fan-

tasy. The *Mahabharata*, the longest poem ever composed, consists of 90,000 stanzas and describes the actions of gods and mortals.

The *Ramayana* relates the wanderings of the hero, Rama, who has been banished from his home by his father while Rama's faithful wife, Sita, awaits his return. The epic does more than tell a story, however. It also focuses on the ideals and virtues expected of both men and women. The religious themes woven into these two Aryan epics account for their importance as sacred Hindu literature.

ARYAN SOCIAL STRUCTURE

During the Vedic Age, the Aryans evolved a social structure that would eventually develop into the caste system of today's India. Among the early Aryans, there were three social classes: warriors, priests, and com-

An 18th-century illustration of an episode from the ancient Hindu epic, the Ramayana. *The* Ramayana *is an action-packed tale of love, abduction, and heroic rescue.*

moners, and it was possible to rise in society. By the end of the Vedic Age, however, the class system had become more rigid. A person's status was determined by birth, and priests replaced warriors as the highest order. Thus the Aryans were differentiated into four *castes*, or social groups based on birth: (1) Brahmans—priests and scholars; (2) Kshatriyas—rulers and warriors; (3) Vaisyas —craftworkers, merchants, and farmers; and (4) Sudras—unskilled workers and peasants tied to the land. Outside the caste system were the untouchables, completely without status. They included the Dravidians and those who had intermarried with them.

Over the centuries, the caste system became more complex as the four major castes were further divided into numerous sub-castes, and strict rules governed the behavior of people within each group. These rules applied to marriage, friendship, and work. The caste system became closely tied to Hindu concepts such as *karma*, the belief that all of a person's actions in this life determine his or her fate in the next life. By accepting this belief, Hindus acknowledged that their position in life was due to actions in their previous existence. They believed that they could acquire good karma only by obeying the social, religious, and moral laws of their caste.

RISE OF BUDDHISM

By the end of the Vedic Age, the Brahmans, or priestly caste, had acquired great power and influence in society because of their role as guardians of the sacred Hindu texts and their control of the rituals that enabled the soul to achieve oneness with atman. Their power did not go unchallenged, and various reformers sought to simplify the rituals by which the individual soul might achieve a higher level of understanding. Among the reformers was Siddhartha Gautama (563 B.C.–483 B.C.), a member of the Kshatriya caste, who was born to wealth and power. As a young man, Gautama became haunted by the suffering that he saw all around him, so he gave up a life of comfort and pleasure to seek understanding. After wandering for six years and searching for answers, he finally achieved enlightenment and became known as the *Buddha*, or the Enlightened One.

The Buddha taught the Four Noble Truths: (1) all life is suffering; (2) the cause of suffering is desire; (3) the only way to escape suffering is to end desire; (4) the way to end desire is to follow the Noble Eightfold Path that includes right belief, right thoughts, right conduct, right speech, right living, right ambition, right pleasures, and right effort. The goal of existence, the Buddha taught, was the attainment of *Nirvana*, the condition of emptiness.

This stupa, or burial mound, in central India is one of many such memorials that were raised to commemorate the death of the Buddha.

The Buddha set out to reform Hinduism, and his teachings reflected many Hindu beliefs. However, he did reject the increasingly rigid rules of the caste system and the domination of the Brahmans. After his death, his disciples spread his teachings, and these came to form the basis of a new religion, Buddhism. In India, Buddhism flourished for several centuries and was then merged back into Hinduism. But in the Far East, the message carried by Buddhist missionaries took root in China, Korea, Japan, and Southeast Asia. The impact of Buddhism on Asia parallels that of Christianity on Europe in the centuries after the death of Christ. Buddhist missionaries brought not only a system of religious beliefs and ethical values but also art, architecture, and literature.

INTRODUCTION TO THE DOCUMENTS

During the Vedic Age, the beliefs of the early Aryan invaders were gradually formulated into religious doctrine and dogma. In early Aryan society, war, drinking, chariot racing, and gambling featured as prominent activities. The chief Aryan god was Indra, a great warrior. Over the centuries, as Hinduism emerged, it incorporated a variety of beliefs and became intertwined with the increasingly rigid social structure. The *Rig Veda* describes the origins of the four castes and emphasizes that people of the lowest caste are to serve the three higher castes.

Of significance at the end of the Vedic Age is the emergence of Buddhism and its appeal to many Hindus. The Buddha was a skilled teacher who initiated a call for change and won many converts to his beliefs. Emerging at a time of political chaos, Buddhism offered an alternative to Hindu ideas with their emphasis on the caste system and the correct performance of prescribed behaviors. By contrast, Buddhist teachings focused on noble thoughts as a means to salvation and suggested that individuals held control over their destinies.

The following documents provide sources for analysis and comparison of developing religious traditions within the context of Indian civilization.

DOCUMENT 1   *THE HYMN OF CREATION*

This is one of the many hymns and prayers that make up the sacred Hindu text, the Rig Veda.

The Hymn of Creation

Then even nothingness was not, nor existence.
   There was no air then, nor the heavens beyond it.
What covered it? Where was it? In whose keeping?
   Was there then cosmic water, in depths unfathomed?

Then there were neither death nor immortality,
   nor was there then the torch of night and day.
The One breathed windlessly and self-sustaining.
   There was that One then, and there was no other.

At first there was only darkness wrapped in darkness.
   All this was only unillumined water.
That One which came to be, enclosed in nothing,
   arose at last, born of the power of heat.

In the beginning desire descended on it—
   that was the primal seed, born of the mind.
The sages who have searched their hearts with wisdom
   know that which is is kin to that which is not.

And they have stretched their cord across the void,
   and know what was above, and what below.
Seminal powers made fertile mighty forces.
   Below was strength, and over it was impulse.

But, after all, who knows, and who can say
   whence it all came, and how creation happened?
The gods themselves are later than creation,
   so who knows truly whence it has arisen?

Whence all creation had its origin,
   he, whether he fashioned it or whether he did not,
he, who surveys it all from highest heaven,
   he knows—or maybe even he does not know.

SOURCE: A. L. Basham, *The Wonder That Was India* (New York: Grove Press, 1954), pp. 247–48.

What questions was the poet who composed this hymn trying to answer? What clues to Hindu beliefs does this hymn provide?

DOCUMENT 2   BHAGAVAD GITA

The "Bhagavad Gita" (meaning "Song of God") is among the most popular Hindu literature. Composed sometime between the 5th and 2nd centuries B.C., it is a religious poem in which Krishna, a god who has taken mortal form, and a prince named Arjuna engage in a long dialogue against the background of an impending battle.

At the beginning of the poem, Arjuna is reluctant to go into battle against friends and relatives, but the Lord Krishna instructs him to follow his duty.

ARJUNA: But, Krishna, if you consider knowledge of Brahman superior to any sort of action, why are you telling me to do these terrible deeds?

Your statements seem to contradict each other. They confuse my mind. Tell me one definite way of reaching the highest good.

KRISHNA: I have already told you that, in this world, aspirants may find enlightenment by two different paths. For the contemplative is the path of knowledge: for the active is the path of selfless action.

Freedom from activity is never achieved by abstaining from action. Nobody can become perfect by merely ceasing to act. In fact, nobody can ever rest from his activity even for a moment. All are helplessly forced to act. . . .

Activity is better than inertia. Act, but with self-control. If you are lazy, you cannot even sustain your own body.

The world is imprisoned in its own activity, except when actions are performed as worship of God. Therefore you must perform every action sacramentally, and be free from all attachments to results.

In the beginning
The Lord of beings
Created all men,
To each his duty.
"Do this," He said,
"And you shall prosper. . . ."

But when a man has found delight and satisfaction and peace in the Atman, then he is no longer obliged to perform any kind of action. He has nothing to gain in this world by action, and nothing to lose by refraining from action. He is independent of everybody and everything. Do your duty, always; but without attachment. That is how a man reaches the ultimate Truth; by working without anxiety about results.

SOURCE: *The Song of God: Bhagavad-Gita,* trans. Swami Prabhavananda and Christopher Isherwood (New York: New American Library, 1944), pp. 44–47.

What ethical values does Krishna seek to teach Arjuna in their dialog? How can these values help the young prince achieve his dharma?

As Buddhism spread, it split into two sects: the Theravada sect, which was carried to Ceylon and Southeast Asia; and the Mahayana sect, which was carried into China, Korea, Tibet, and Japan. Despite differences over doctrine, both schools accepted the fundamental teaching of Buddhism: the Four Noble Truths and the Noble Eightfold Path. These teachings are contained in the "Sermon of the Turning of the Wheel of the Law."

Thus I have heard. Once the Master was at Banaras, at the deer park called Isipatana. There the Master addressed the five monks:

"There are two ends not to be served by a wanderer. What are those two? The pursuit of desires and of the pleasure which springs from desires, which is base, common, leading to rebirth, ignoble and unprofitable; and the pursuit of pain and hardship, which is grievous, ignoble and unprofitable. The Middle Way of the Tathagata avoids both these ends; it is enlightened, it brings clear vision, it makes for wisdom, and leads to peace, insight, full wisdom and Nirvana. What is this Middle Way? . . . It is the Noble Eightfold Path—Right Views, Right Resolve, Right Speech, Right Conduct, Right Livelihood, Right Effort, Right Recollection and Right Meditation. This is the Middle Way. . . .

"And this is the Noble Truth of Sorrow. Birth is sorrow, age is sorrow, disease is sorrow, death is sorrow, contact with the unpleasant is sorrow, separation from the pleasant is sorrow, every wish unfulfilled is sorrow—in short all the five components of individuality are sorrow.

"And this is the Noble Truth of the Arising of Sorrow. [It arises from] thirst, which leads to rebirth, which brings delight and passion, and seeks pleasure now here, now there—the thirst for sensual pleasure, the thirst for continued life, the thirst for power.

"And this is the Noble Truth of the Stopping of Sorrow. It is the complete stopping of that thirst, so that no passion remains, leaving it, being emancipated from it, being released from it, giving no place to it.

"And this is the Noble Truth of the Way which Leads to the Stopping of Sorrow. It is the Noble Eightfold Path—Right Views, Right Resolve, Right Speech, Right Conduct, Right Livelihood, Right Effort, Right Recollection and Right Meditation."

SOURCE: A. L. Basham, *The Wonder That Was India* (New York: Grove Press, 1954), pp. 268–69.

Compare the teachings of the Buddha in this excerpt to those of Hinduism in the excerpts from the Bhagavad-Gita.

INDIA		THE WEST	
3000	Rise of Indus valley civilization	3100	Narmer unites Upper and Lower Egypt; Sumerian city-states flourish in Mesopotamia
		2600	Pyramid of Khufu built
2500	Height of Indus valley civilization; Harappa and Mohenjo-daro flourish	2350	Akkad flourishes
		2000	Minoan civilization established on Crete; Mycenaeans invade mainland Greece
		1750	Hammurabi's law code in effect
1700	Indus valley civilization declines		
1500	Aryan invaders destroy Indus valley civilization; Vedic Age begins— development of Hinduism	1480– 1450	Thutmose III of Egypt conquers Syria-Palestine; Knossos destroyed
1400	Rig Veda composed		
		1375	Hittite invasions of Syria-Palestine
		1200	Hittite civilization overrun
		1100	Dorians conquer Greece; Mycenaean civilization collapses
1000– 700	Mahabharata and Ramayana composed	1000	David rules the kingdom of Israel
700	Sanskrit developed	750	Homer recites the Iliad and the Odyssey(?); Iron-Age Greeks begin to colonize the Mediterranean; Assyrians conquer Syria-Palestine
550	Siddhartha Gautama (the Buddha) attempts to reform Hinduism	550	Cyrus the Great creates Persian Empire

* All dates are approximate years B.C.

Rise of Classical Civilizations

- *The ideal state is that in which an injury done to the least of its citizens is an injury done to all.*

  SOLON

- *Our constitution...favors the many instead of the few; this is why it is called a democracy. If we look to the laws, they afford equal justice to all in their private differences....The freedom which we enjoy in our government extends also to our ordinary life. There, far from exercising a jealous surveillance over each other, we do not feel called upon to be angry with our neighbor for doing what he likes, or even to indulge in those injurious looks which cannot fail to be offensive, although they inflict no positive penalty. But all this ease in our private relations does not make us lawless as citizens.*

  PERICLES

- *Our Twelve Tables of law only carried the death penalty for a few crimes. Among these crimes was singing or composing a song that was derogatory to insulting to someone. This was a good law.*

  CICERO

- *Every man should be responsible to others, nor should any one be allowed to do just as he pleases; for where absolute freedom is allowed there is nothing to restrain the evil which is inherent in every man.*

  ARISTOTLE

- *If the people are sovereign in a state and the government is run according to their will, it is called liberty. But it is really license.*

  CICERO

- *The law speaks too softly to be heard amidst the din of arms.*

  GAIUS MARIUS

6

● *Under this monument lies Aeschylus the Athenian,*
Euphorion's son, who died in the wheatlands of Gela.
The grove of Marathon with its glories can speak of his
valor in battle.
The long-haired Persian remembers and can speak of it too.
AESCHYLUS

The Greek City-States

Around 1100 B.C., the Mycenaean civilization collapsed as Dorian tribes from the north invaded Greece. In the resulting confusion, some displaced Mycenaeans, or *Achaeans*, sought refuge along the northern shore of the Peloponnesus; in time, that area came to be known as Achaea. Others sought refuge in Attica, where they mixed with the original inhabitants of the area and eventually developed the great city-state of Athens. Still others migrated across the Aegean Sea to Ionia on the coast of Asia Minor.

The Dorian invaders claimed the fertile valleys of the southern Peloponnesus for their main settlements. In the valley of Laconia, they eventually developed the distinctive society that we know as *Sparta*.

The earliest societies of the Dorians in Greece followed the Indo-European pattern, and their political system was quite similar to that developed by the Mycenaeans. By the 7th century B.C., however, Sparta, Athens, and other city-states throughout Greece had evolved a variety of different political systems. This chapter will deal with the development of the Greek city-states and the spread of their culture throughout the Mediterranean world prior to the 5th century B.C.

GEOGRAPHY AND NATURAL RESOURCES

The geography of Greece is very different from that of Egypt and the Fertile Crescent. Greece is a mountainous peninsula bordered on the west by the Ionian Sea, on the south by the Mediterranean Sea, and on the east by the Aegean Sea. The few rivers are short, swift, shallow, and mainly seasonal—they are, therefore, unsuitable as inland transportation routes. Since the plains and valleys in which the early people settled were isolated from each other by the mountains, political unification was not possible for many years.

The peninsula is separated into two parts by the Gulf of Corinth, but the land masses are linked by the Isthmus of Corinth. The portion south of the Isthmus has been called the *Peloponnesus* for at least 3000 years, for the Mycenaeans who inhabited the area believed that they were descended from a legendary king named *Pelops*.

The mountains of Greece were once more wooded than they are today, providing timber for constructing buildings and ships and fuel for smelting metals. Unfortunately, the forests were not protected or replanted, and the denuded hills were subject to severe ero-

GREECE IN THE 8th CENTURY B.C.

Suggest a reason why Athens, Corinth, and Megara became more prosperous and influential than many other Greek city-states.

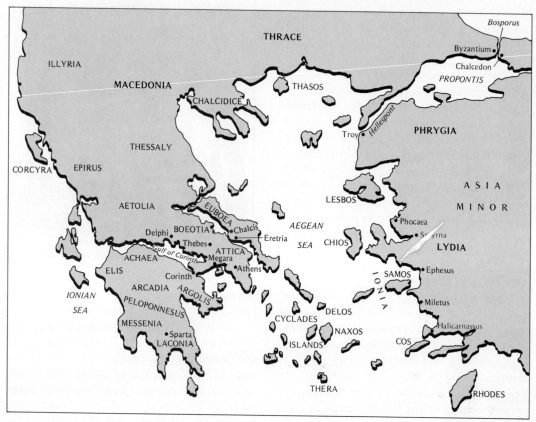

sion of the soil. Natural regrowth of the forests was prevented by the herds of goats which ate the tree shoots as they emerged.

The mountains contained few minerals, and those that were available were soon exhausted. While there was some copper, there was no tin available to make bronze, and the known deposits of gold, silver, and iron were small and widely scattered. The ancient people did have large deposits of clay suitable for making pottery. They also had marble and limestone in abundance for building and sculpture.

The moderate climate in the lowlands of Greece encouraged the Greeks to spend much of their leisure time outdoors. The steady summer winds, combined with the lack of inland transportation and the many offshore islands, encouraged them to become sailors. Through their seafaring ventures, they came into contact with the ancient civilizations of the Middle East.

In ancient times olives and grapes were very important crops, and they continue to be so today: unlike grain crops, grapes and olives can be grown successfully in hilly, rocky areas. The ancient people made wine from their grapes and pressed olive oil for use in cooking. Both of these products became important export items.

THE POLIS   Because inland transportation was so difficult in Greece, the inhabitants of each valley tended to develop

117

small, independent communities. Each city-state or *polis* included an *agora* (market place), and an *acropolis* (fortified citadel), which was usually built on a high, rocky place. The shrines of the gods were placed on the acropolis, and the people sought refuge there in times of danger.

In Mycenaean times, each city-state or group of city-states had been ruled by a tribal king who also served as military commander in times of war. Gradually, these monarchies began to lose much of their authority. Some of the city-states began to elect kings rather than accepting a hereditary monarchy, and council members, who were also elected, began to have more authority in making decisions. An assembly of the people, which had originally been convened to hear the rulings of the king and council, began to have the right to participate in certain decisions.

Since the population of each polis was quite small, all male citizens were expected to participate in the defense and government of the community. This process became the foundation for the Greek democracies that evolved during the 5th and 4th centuries B.C. Nevertheless, a relatively small number of people usually controlled the polis at any given time, and the question of representation was the subject of much debate throughout the centuries.

THE IRON AGE The Greeks of the 8th century B.C. believed that they were living in a period of decline which they called the *Iron Age*. In the mythical past, they believed, there had been a Golden Age, in which men and women lived like gods without care or trouble; a Silver Age, when a weaker generation of men antagonized the gods and lost many of the blessings their ancestors had enjoyed; a Bronze Age, in which a fierce, warlike people with superhuman strength roamed the earth and ended by destroying each other; and finally the Heroic Age of the Mycenaean and Trojan heroes. The Iron Age was considered to be the least

An episode from Homer's Odyssey: *the hero escapes from his enemies by hiding under a ram.*

happy of the five ages; a time when men and women had fewer heroic qualities, and were beset by anxieties and pain.[1]

The *Iliad* and the *Odyssey* of Homer preserved memories of the Heroic Age in which the legendary heroes Odysseus, Agamemnon, Achilles, and Hector had demonstrated their physical strength and grandeur of character on the battlefield of Troy. These epics became an important part of the education of young people during the Iron Age and for centuries to come, for people believed that they provided moral instruction as well as entertainment.

Homer was a native of Ionia, according to tradition, and Greeks of the 5th century thought that he had lived in the 8th century B.C. Although his epics concerned events that took place at the beginning of the 12th century, his narrative blended the traditions and customs of his own age with those of the ancient Bronze Age Minoan-Mycenaean civilization. For example, Homer's stories depict the Greek gods and goddesses that he and his contemporaries worshiped rather than

---

[1]Hesiod, *Works and Days*, lines 109-184.

An episode added to Homer's Iliad by a later writer: Achilles kills an Amazon warrior.

the nature deities of the Minoans and Mycenaeans. On the other hand, he describes the Mycenaean warriors as carrying bronze weapons and wearing helmets topped with boar tusks, equipment that was long outdated by his own time. Today, Homer is considered one of the most important sources of information about the Iron Age of Greece (1100-700 B.C.) as well as for the civilization of the Mycenaeans. Hesiod, a poet who may have been a contemporary of Homer, is another important source of information about this period.

EARLY RELIGION: THE GREEK PANTHEON

Through the writings of Homer and Hesiod, we have a very clear idea about what the Greeks of the Iron Age believed about their gods. The Greeks believed that their gods resided on Mount Olympus in northern Greece. These gods had supernatural powers and yet often showed human failings: they could be envious, proud, or overly impetuous. In Homer's epic stories, the gods helped certain heroes who were deserving, giving them added strength or wisdom to carry out their appointed tasks. However, they were not always consistent in their support—a hero might find, for instance, that his patron god or goddess had shifted loyalties in the midst of a battle.

Zeus, the father of the gods and lord of the sky, was considered to be the most pow-

erful god, and yet, on some occasions, he was the victim of plots conceived by the other deities. Zeus and Hera, his wife, were considered to be the patrons of married couples. Apollo was associated with the sun and provided inspiration for music and poetry. Athena was the special protector of Athens, and was looked to for special aid in times of war. Aphrodite was worshiped as goddess of love and beauty. She was known for her constant involvement in match-making schemes, which usually led to disaster for the human beings who became involved in them. Poseidon, whose symbol was a trident, a long three-pronged fork, was associated with the

The Muses provided inspiration for artists, writers, and orators. They were associated with measure and grace.

sea and was thought to be responsible for earthquakes and tides. Hermes, who wore winged sandals, served as messenger of the gods. He was associated with eloquence of speech, but also with lies and deceit. Demeter was the goddess of agriculture, and was associated with the fertility of the earth.

In addition to their pantheon of gods, the early Greeks also believed in the *Muses*, the *Fates*, and the *Furies*. The *Muses* were associated with the god Apollo and were originally three in number; they provided inspiration to artists, writers, and musicians. Eventually nine muses were named, including Terpsichore, the muse of choral dance and song; Clio, the muse of history; and Euterpe, the muse of lyric poetry. The six other muses provided inspiration to writers of epics, hymns, comedies, tragedies, and poetry, and to astronomers.

In very early times, the Greeks believed that there were three female deities called *Fates* who supervised, but did not control, the destinies of human beings. Later, the Greeks portrayed the Fates as three old women who spun the destinies of human beings like threads, with one drawing out the thread of life, another measuring it, and the third cutting it.

The *Furies* were believed to have been born from the spilled blood of Uranus, an ancient god who had been slain by his son, Cronus. They were considered to be fearsome beings who barked like dogs and had writhing snakes for hair. Their principal role was to enforce family law, and they were noted for avenging the murders of people who were killed by family members.

The Greeks traditionally believed that the souls of the dead were transported across an underground river to Hades, a mysterious shadowy afterworld. In the *Odyssey*, Homer portrays the inhabitants of this afterworld as dispirited beings who miss the light of day. For example, when Odysseus visits Hades, he encounters the soul or "shade" of Achilles and politely congratulates him upon his lot in the afterworld. Achilles responds that life is much to be preferred to death:

Let me hear no smooth talk
of death from you, Odysseus,
*   light of councils.*
Better, I say, to break sod as a farm hand
for some poor country man, on iron rations,
than lord it over all the exhausted dead.[2]

ECONOMY AND SOCIAL STRUCTURE

Although Odysseus and the other kings and lords that Homer described usually had a few servants or slaves, they actively participated in the work of their estates. In the *Odyssey*, Odysseus describes how he built his own house, and boasts that he can drive a plow as straight as anyone. His father, the old king Laertes, tends his own vineyard, and his wife, Penelope, weaves her own cloth. Homer's great noble families have a great emotional attachment to their homes and estates, and do not aspire to live differently by seizing the wealth of others. Although Odysseus becomes rich through spoils of war, he longs for the day when he can put aside his weapons and return to his farm in Ithaca. These vignettes very likely give us a truer picture of Homer's own time than of the society of the Mycenaeans.

Hesiod also emphasizes that the gods intended men to work hard on their estates rather than achieving wealth by other means.

It is from work that men grow rich and own
*   flocks and herds;*
by work, too, they become much better
*   friends of the immortals. . . .*
If any man by force of hands wins him
*   a great fortune,*
or steals it by the cleverness of his
*   tongue. . .*
lightly the gods wipe out that man, and
*   diminish the household*
of such a one, and his wealth stays with
*   him for only a short time.*[3]

---

[2]*Odyssey* XI, 481-4.

[3]Hesiod, *Works and Days*, lines 308-9, 321-2, 325-6.

SITES OF GREEK COLONIZATION
Why did the Phoenicians and Greeks select these sites for their colonies?

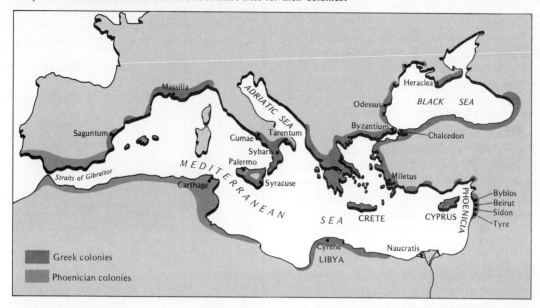

As indicated in the works of Homer and Hesiod, farming and raising livestock were the principal occupations of the Greeks during the Iron Age. The family-managed estates were almost totally self-sufficient, and were able to produce their own shoes and clothing as well as food and other necessities. The scholar H. D. F. Kitto speculated that there were only two specialized trades during this era in Greece: pottery-making and metalwork. He supported this theory with the observation that these were the only trades which had guardian deities to oversee them:

● ● ● *Of specialized trades we hear of only two, the trades of the smith and of the potter. . . . It is interesting to notice that these two are the only crafts which, in Greek, have divine exponents. . . . There is no god of shoemaking or farming or building. Obviously, these things everybody knows how to do, but it is very different with elaborate metal-work, or the making of an elegant piece of pottery.*[4]

[4]H. D. F. Kitto, *The Greeks*, revised ed. (New York: Penguin Books, 1957), pp. 40-41.

The family came to be the principal focus of the laws and traditions of Iron Age Greece, just as it was the basis of the economy. In Homer's world, family ties were sacred, and marital fidelity was considered to be highly important. The most admirable wife was one who conscientiously raised her children and ran an efficient household. Although a wife's status depended upon that of her husband, she was considered to be the social equal of her husband. In fact, women were held in much greater esteem during this era than in later periods of Greek history. Penelope, Odysseus' wife, is considered especially admirable because she remains faithful to Odysseus during his long absence and struggles to keep the family estate intact.

TRADING AND COLONIZATION
During the 8th century, many people found that their family farms could not support all of the people who depended upon them. As the population grew, trading and sea-faring increasingly became an attractive alternative to farming. Hesiod described the benefits of

this new livelihood, but emphasized the risks involved:

You will find it hard
*   to escape coming to grief. Yet still*
and even so, men in their shortsightedness
*   do undertake it;*
for acquisition means life to miserable
*   mortals;*
but it is an awful thing to die among the
*   waves.*[5]

There were undoubtedly those who shared the conservative attitudes of Hesiod, but many others discovered the benefits of earning their living through seafaring. The new products and ideas that these seafarers brought back made a permanent difference in the Greeks' culture and way of life. Through their contacts with the Phoenicians, they discovered that they could use an alphabet to write their language; thus, the art of writing, which had been lost since the Dorian invasion, was revived in the 8th century. They also found many areas throughout the Mediterranean world which could be colonized and which, in total, would provide thousands of acres of additional land for farming.

In searching for new lands for farming, the Greeks tended to select uninhabited coastal areas. The first settlements in Ionia had been possible because the Lydians and other inland peoples were not greatly interested in building ports or in farming the coastal plains. During the 8th century B.C., the Greeks found that a similar situation prevailed in a number of other areas along the southern coast of Europe, in southern Macedonia, around the Black Sea, and on the northern coast of Africa. Many of the colonies that the Greeks established in these areas became important cities.

A group of colonists from Megara, whose soil was so poor that it was said to "grow rocks," established the cities of Byzantium and Chalcedon on the two shores of the Bos-

---

[5]Hesiod, *Works and Days*, lines 684-6.

Around 750 B.C., the Greeks learned from the Phoenicians how to use an alphabet. Prior to this, the Greek language had not been written since the Dorian invasion of about 1100 B.C.

Early Greek (8th cent. B.C.)	Classical Greek (5th cent. B.C.)	Modern names of letters
Α	Α	ALPHA
Β	Β	BETA
Γ	Γ	GAMMA
Δ	Δ	DELTA
Ε	Ε	EPSILON
Ι	Ζ	ZETA
Β	Η	ETA
⊗	Θ	THETA
⌇	Ι	IOTA
Κ	Κ	KAPPA
Λ	Λ	LAMBDA
Μ	Μ	MU
Ν	Ν	NU
	Ξ	XI
Ο	Ο	OMICRON
Π	Π	PI
Ρ	Ρ	RHO
Σ	Σ	SIGMA
Χ	Τ	TAU
	Υ	UPSILON
	Φ	PHI
	Χ	KHI
	Ω	OMEGA

porus. Both cities grew prosperous by charging tolls for ships passing through the strait. Chalcidice was established on the northern shore of the Aegean Sea to provide homes for the land-poor farmers of Chalcis and Eretria in Euboea. Miletus, itself one of the first settlements of Ionia, participated in the colonization movement by establishing at least 80 settlements on the shores of the Black Sea. These settlements became so prosperous through the export of their wheat and fish that the Black Sea came to be known as the "hospitable sea" (*Euximus Pontus*). The people of Miletus also secured permission from the pharaoh of Egypt to establish a trading post in the delta, at Naukratis. At this trading center, Greek pottery, wine, and oil were exchanged for Egyptian wheat. Colonists from the island of Thera established a city called Cyrene on the northern coast of Libya. There, the coastal land was used to cultivate wheat, barley, and fruit, and to raise cattle and horses for export.

In Italy, the Greeks found that the Apennine Mountains on the eastern coast were a barrier to settlement. They were able to establish colonies on the western coast, however, because the Etruscan tribes had not yet begun to exert their influence in this area. Colonists from Euboea established the colony of Cumae on the western coast of Italy, and then set up a "new city" (Neapolis) just a few miles to the south. Today we know this second colony as Naples. Settlers from Achaea established Sybaris, which became so wealthy that its name became the source of our term *Sybarite*, meaning a person who lives in fantastic luxury. Sparta established one colony, named Tarentum, on the "instep" of the Italian peninsula. Altogether, so many Greek colonies were formed in southern Italy and Sicily that the region came to be called *Magna Graecia* (Great Greece).

When Corinth established its colony of Syracuse on the eastern coast of Sicily, the Phoenicians realized that this new city could become a threat to their own interests in the area. They therefore began to establish colonies on the western coast of Sicily, and did not allow the Greeks to settle near them. None of the Phoenician cities had a harbor as excellent as the one at Syracuse, however.

Massilia, the modern city of Marseilles, was founded by settlers from Phocaea, in Ionia. This colony became the center of Greek influence in ancient Gaul (present France). From Massilia, Greek traders moved up the Rhone valley far enough to meet traders from Cornwall, in England, who traveled down the Seine and Loire rivers. From these traders they were able to obtain rare commodities such as tin.

The colonizing movement produced important economic improvements in Greece. The settlements not only provided additional acreage for farming, but also opened up new markets and new sources of raw materials. A great colonizing city such as Corinth could provide unlimited job opportunities for ship builders, traders, and farmers in its home port and colonies. Even a city like Athens, which did not directly participate in the colonizing movement, benefited from the new opportunities opened up by trade. The Athenians developed several specialized industries to take advantage of the expanded markets. They were able to trade their pottery, textiles, and metalware for wheat and other foods which were difficult to cultivate in the rocky soil of Attica.

As they came into contact with other peoples and civilizations, the Greeks became more conscious of their own identity. They began to refer to themselves as Hellenes and to their native land as Hellas. They also began to use the descriptive term barbaroi ("jabberers") to describe certain foreign-language speakers. Thus, the term "barbarian" originally designated people whose language sounded inelegant or harsh to the Greeks. Within a few centuries, however, both the Greeks and the Romans used the term barbarian to deride any group of people who did not share their culture.

An artist's reconstruction of the Athenian harbor at Piraeus. The development of seafaring enabled the Athenians to import the grain they needed in exchange for such products as wine, olive oil, and pottery.

As manufacturing and trade grew in importance, the structure of Greek society began to reflect the changes brought about by these new ways of life. Land ownership continued to be the mark of nobility, but it was no longer the only measure of wealth and prestige. The influence of wealthy merchants and traders eventually led to important social and political changes. By the end of the Iron Age, the social structure of Greece was much less stable and predictable than it had been in Hesiod's time.

THE SPIRIT OF PANHELLENISM

The inhabitants of the Greek city-states referred to themselves as *Hellenes* and believed that they had descended from a common ancestor named *Hellen*, who was a grandson of Prometheus.[6] The spirit of pan-

An outstanding event of the Iron Age was the institution of athletic games at Olympia in the Peloponnesus. This is the athletes' entrance to the stadium.

---

[6]Prometheus was the ancient god who gave fire to mankind.

An Athenian relief shows athletes training for Olympic events: running, wrestling, and javelin throwing.

hellenism was reflected in a number of traditions and events. One of these was the institution of athletic competitions. The Panhellenic (all-Greek) Games were so important to the Greeks that a sacred truce was proclaimed in any war that might be underway at the time of a scheduled game, and all travelers to and from the games were given protection.

The most important of these games were the Olympic Games, which were held every four years at Olympia in honor of Zeus. Beginning in 776 B.C., the traditional date of the first Olympic Games, the Greeks dated all events by the *Olympiads*.

Only free Greek citizens could compete in these games, and each participant had to swear to abide by the rules. Later, some foreigners were granted citizenship so that they could participate. The athletes first competed in foot races. These were followed by the *Pentathlon*, a group of five contests involving discus throwing, spear throwing, running, jumping, and wrestling. The contestant who won three of these five events was declared the winner of the Pentathlon. Races of horse-drawn chariots were the next event, and the final event was boxing. The prize awarded to winners, a crown made from olive leaves, was regarded as the greatest honor a man could achieve. The victors of the games were commemorated in the sculptures and poems of famous artists.

Another common bond that united the ancient Greeks was the tradition of seeking advice from *oracles* which were thought to transmit prophecies from the gods to mortals. The oracle of Apollo at Delphi was the most famous. A supplicant wrote a question on a piece of lead and put it into a clay jar. A priest then read the question and listened for the answer of Zeus, which was uttered through the rustling of leaves in an oak tree. Three priestesses, known as "doves," interpreted the rustling and reported the response of Zeus to the supplicant.

Twelve city-states banded together in a religious league called the *Delphic Amphictyony* to protect the oracle and temple at Delphi. The oracle was renowned throughout the Greek world, and acquired great political importance. It was consulted by Greek colonists who wanted to find the best sites for new settlements, and its advice was also sought by such distinguished visitors as Alexander the Great and King Croesus of Lydia.

Several members of the Delphic Amphictyony set up individual treasury buildings near the temple of Apollo. This is the treasury building of the Athenians.

of events found the monarchy replaced by an *aristocracy*, or a government by a few; then a *timocracy*, a government in which participation is based on wealth. At this point, a *tyrant* who acted as champion of the common people and foe of the aristocracy often seized control. Finally, the tyrant might be expelled and a *democracy*, or government by the people, established.

Of all the Greek city-states, we have the most information about Athens and Sparta. Since both of these city-states were much larger than the average polis, there were certain problems involved in creating a government in which all members of the community were included. The Athenians' struggle for political equality led to the democracy of the 5th century B.C., for which Athens has been renowned throughout history. By contrast, the Spartans resisted any changes in their form of government. The Spartan government regulated every aspects of its citizens' lives, and applied stern military control to prevent the political evolutions which ultimately brought democracy to many city-states.

EVOLUTION OF GOVERNMENT

In the Greek language, the word *polis* refers to "the people" or "the community" as well as the actual city in which the people live. In ancient Greece, it was expected that each citizen would perform certain civic duties as a member of this community, and the *polis*, in turn, was responsible for educating its citizens and for teaching them its laws. Even after many of the city-states had grown into large areas with many thousands of citizens, people still retained the ideal of citizens being directly involved in government, and of a government concerned with every aspect of the lives of its citizens.

During the 7th century B.C., the various city-states began to follow different lines of political development. The typical sequence

ATHENIAN GOVERNMENT

In the earliest times, the government of Athens followed the pattern that had been established in Mycenaean societies prior to 1100 B.C. A hereditary monarch ruled the polis, and he was advised by a council of aristocrats who represented the most important tribes in the area. During the Iron Age, the civil, military, and religious duties of the monarch gradually came to be assumed by nine *archons*, who were chosen by an assembly of citizens from among the wealthiest and most influential families of Athens. By the 8th century B.C., the monarchy had disappeared completely, and its functions were taken over by the elected council of archons.

The nine archons were advised by a council of men who had formerly held office as archons. This group of advisers was called the Council of the *Areopagus* after the hill on which its meetings were held. The archons served in office for only one year, but then could continue to influence policy by joining the Council of the Areopagus.

During the 7th century, the outlying districts of Attica were incorporated into the polis of Athens, and the population of Athens itself became more diversified. While many Athenians had become wealthy through trading and colonization ventures, there was also a growing class of poorer citizens who came to resent the prosperity and expanding influence of the rich. Due to a combination of circumstances, these poorer people gradually lost their political rights, and Athenian society came to be polarized by social, economic, and political inequalities.

REPRESENTATION

Because the Assembly of Athens was responsible for electing the nine archons who ruled the polis, the question of who was entitled to belong to the Assembly was important. By 650 B.C., the Greeks had devised a new strategy of waging war, and this change came to have a bearing on the question of membership in the Assembly.

Because of the scarcity and high cost of horses, the use of chariots in battle became uneconomical. To replace the chariots, the Greeks adopted the *phalanx* method of fighting in which *hoplites*, or foot soldiers, equipped with spears, swords, and bronze armor, fought in close ranks. Thus, aristocratic heroes such as those Homer wrote about could no longer determine the outcome of a battle. Instead, those citizens who could afford to arm themselves in the new fashion became the mainstay of the army. These citizens continued to have the right to belong to the Assembly. However, the *thetes*, the class of poor, free farmers who could not afford weapons, were excluded from military service and consequently from the political process. The exclusion of the thetes meant that the government of Athens became a *timocracy* in which membership in the assembly depended upon property qualifications.

POLITICAL DEVELOPMENTS

Aristotle, the great Greek philosopher who lived during the 4th century B.C., is one of our most important sources of information concerning early political developments in Athens. Aristotle described 7th-century Athens as a city divided by bitter class antagonisms. The greed and political power of the oligarchs, or wealthy families, had led to this situation, he reported. Many of the small farmers and other common people of Attica had gradually fallen into debt to the oligarchs. Because they controlled the government of the polis, the oligarchs had been able to strengthen the rights of creditors. They had the right to seize the lands and property of the poor, and could even force debtors into slavery. As Aristotle concluded:

● ● ● *Thus the most grievous and bitter thing in the state of public affairs for the masses was their slavery; not but what they were discontented also about everything else, for they found themselves virtually without a share in anything.*[7]

The bronze helmets of hoplite soldiers protected the face as well as the head. A well-equipped hoplite also wore a bronze breastplate and leg shields (greaves).

[7]Aristotle, *The Constitution of Athens* II, 1.

The middle classes and the poor of Athens began to look to the government of the polis for a resolution of their grievances. Due to the efforts of several prominent Athenians, the government did succeed in averting a civil war and in asserting its authority against the interests of the powerful noble families. By the end of the 6th century B.C., the government was much more representative of all of the diverse groups who lived in the city and in the countryside of Attica.

Draco. In 621 B.C., the archons appointed an aristocrat named Draco to codify the laws of Athens. Only one of Draco's laws has been found, and it pertains to the case of involuntary homicide. From the content of his law, it is evident that his main concern was to put an end to private vendettas and blood feuds.

Draco's law stipulated that a court would convene to judge whether a murder had been committed intentionally or by accident. If the court decided that the murder was accidental, the family of the victim could agree to pardon the murderer. If the family did not agree with the court's verdict, however, the defendant would be banished from the area. Thus, the court played an important part in resolving a complex situation, while still allowing the victim's family a voice in deciding the affair.

It is not known for certain whether Draco concerned himself only with the subject of homicide, or if he also wrote other laws which were later destroyed. Later traditions, recorded several centuries after Draco's lifetime, indicated that Draco had written a complete code of laws. Reportedly, the laws were so severe that capital punishment was stipulated for even the most trivial offenses. Thus, Draco's name became the source of our adjective *draconian*, meaning "extremely severe or oppressive." Many modern scholars believe that these traditions concerning Draco may be inaccurate, for Solon did not mention such a state of affairs when he recounted his own achievements a few decades later.

Solon. Several years after Draco's term of office, Solon, a philosopher and poet who came from an aristocratic family, was appointed to deal with the problems of the Athenians. He was given unlimited authority to exact measures to benefit the polis, but it was understood that he would leave office once he had completed his task.

In poems written before he took office, Solon had expressed his deep distress over the divisions that had arisen among Athenians. He believed that the main cause of the trouble was the selfishness and greed of the wealthy and privileged classes. As he took office, around 594 B.C., he warned these people that their selfishness would, in the end, be self-destructive:

● ● ● *Confine your swelling thoughts within reasonable bounds. For we shall not comply with your present disposition, and you yourselves will not find it meet for your own interests.*[8]

Solon had no sympathy with the extremists who demanded redistribution of the land, and yet he clearly understood that reform was needed in order to alleviate the miserable plight of the masses. To correct the most pressing injustices, he proclaimed a policy of "shaking off the burdens," under which all debts of the small farmers were canceled. Enslavement for debt was forbidden, and those who had been enslaved were set free. Athenian citizens who had been sold abroad as slaves could, if they chose, return home to be set free.

Solon encouraged the development of industry and trade by several means. Since small, independent family farms were no longer practical in view of the cheap grain imported from the colonies, he encouraged farmers to find other trades or to use their land only for the crops that were best suited to it. To this end, he forbade the export of any farm product except olive oil. He re-

---

[8]Ibid., IV, 2.

quired each father to teach his sons a trade, and encouraged foreign artisans to come to Athens to teach new techniques and art forms. He granted citizenship to those skilled foreigners who promised to settle permanently in the city.

Solon instituted important political reforms to increase the number of citizens who could participate in government. He categorized citizens according to property qualifications, and set aside the special privileges of the nobility. The first of Solon's classes, the *pentecosiomediamni* ("500-bushel men") were those people who could produce the equivalent of 500 bushels of grain or an equal measure of wine or oil. The second and third classes were those people who were capable of producing 300 and 200 bushels, respectively. The fourth class, the thetes, were those who did not have property. Only men of the two highest classes were eligible to hold office as archons, but all citizens, including the thetes, could serve in the assembly. The shift from hereditary to property qualifications for the highest offices made it possible for those who had become wealthy through commerce and trade to participate more fully in the government. The inclusion of the poor people in the Assembly meant that their needs could no longer be ignored.

Solon's judicial reforms were also important. He codified the laws of the polis, except those dealing with homicide, to prevent favoritism and other abuses on the part of judges. (The laws pertaining to homicide, which had been codified by Draco, remained unchanged.) Law cases continued to be judged by the nine archons and by special courts of law. However, the most serious cases were judged by the assembly of all citizens. The Assembly became the court of final appeal for penalties of death, exile, or heavy fines which might be set by magistrates of the regular courts.

When Solon left office, he noted that his achievements had been made possible only because of the special authority he had been given. Without this authority, he said, the Athenians never would have reached a consensus on reform, for the privileged classes had a vested interest in keeping the lower classes enslaved.

● ● ● *These things I accomplished through arbitrary action, bringing force to the support of the dictates of justice, and I followed through to the end the course which I promised. . . . I drafted laws which show equal consideration for the upper and lower classes, and provide a fair administration of justice for every individual.*[9]

Solon realized that, if he had truly succeeded in being fair and impartial, no class within Athens would be entirely satisfied with the new state of affairs. He therefore left Athens to travel for a period of 10 years, and decreed that his laws should remain in effect for 100 years. His reforms made such a great contribution to the development of the Athenian democracy that he came to be regarded as one of the great sages of the ancient world.

THE TYRANTS

As the appointment of special administrators such as Draco and Solon suggests, there were times when the Athenians were not able to resolve their differences within the traditional government of the polis. During periods of crisis, many Athenians were willing to accept a strong central authority with the hope that order might be restored and their grievances resolved. During the 6th century B.C., this need led to the rise of *tyrants*,[10] men who were not elected by the people but had enough supporters that they were able to seize power.

Many of the tyrants who seized power in Athens and in other city-states were wise and able rulers who reduced the political

---

[9]Ibid., VII, 4.

[10]The word "tyrant" originally meant a person who seized political power illegally. Only later did it become a synonym for a cruel and oppressive ruler.

control of the aristocrats and paved the way for the institution of democracy. They often appeared to be champions of the poor and of the middle class, for by making economic concessions to these groups, the tyrants could count on their support to maintain their own political power. Successive tyrants fostered the development of art and literature, encouraged trade through the process of colonization, built temples, aqueducts, and harbors, and redistributed the lands of the aristocrats to the poor.

It is difficult to evaluate the period of tyranny in Greek history because later accounts were usually sympathetic to the aristocracy and disparaged the achievements of the tyrants. For example, in the 4th century B.C., Socrates expressed the opinion that the main goal of a tyrant was to remain in power:

• • • *At first, in the early days of his power, he is full of smiles, and he salutes every one whom he meets—he to be called a tyrant, who is making promises in public and also in private! liberating debtors, and distributing land to the people and his followers, and wanting to be so kind and good to every one! . . .*

But when he has disposed of foreign enemies by conquest or treaty, and there is nothing to fear from them, then he is always stirring up some war or other, in order that the people may require a leader.[11]

Although Aristotle approved of certain individual tyrants, he felt that, in general, "the evil practices of the last and worst form of democracy are all found in tyrannies." He indicated that tyrants were able to retain their offices because it was so difficult to overthrow them, not because they ruled with the consent of the people. The basis of a tyrant's power, he said, was:

• • • *1. The humiliation of his subjects; he knows that a mean-spirited man will not conspire against anybody: 2. the creation of*

mistrust among them; for a tyrant is not overthrown until men begin to have confidence in one another; and this is the reason why tyrants are at war with the good [people]; they are under the idea that their power is endangered by them, not only because they will not be ruled despotically, but also because they are loyal to one another, and to other men, and do not inform against one another, or against other men: 3. the tyrant desires that his subjects shall be incapable of action, for no one attempts what is impossible, and they will not attempt to overthrow a tyranny, if they are powerless.[12]

Pisistratus. Many Athenians were not satisfied with the reforms that Solon had made. The aristocrats, who had lost their exclusive rights, thought that Solon had gone too far in his reforms; the masses thought that he had not gone far enough. Although Solon had enacted important changes, he had not changed the basic form of government: there were still only nine archons, and this council was too small to represent all of the different interests in the city and the surrounding countryside. By 560 B.C., there was again great unrest in Athens as three groups struggled to control the government: the Plain party, consisting of the landed aristocracy; the Hill party, made up of the landless citizens and small farmers from the countryside outside of Athens; and the Shore party, representing the craftsmen and traders. In 546 B.C., Pisistratus, a leader of the Hill party, appeared in the marketplace, covered with blood, and asked for a bodyguard. Since he was a popular military hero, his request was granted. With the help of these guards, he seized the acropolis and established himself as a tyrant.

Pisistratus was an effective champion of the poor people of Athens. He exiled several important nobles, confiscated their estates, and divided the land among landless citizens. He used the revenues from a 10 percent tax imposed on the incomes of the wealthier

---

[11]Plato, *The Republic* VIII, 567.

[12]Aristotle, *Politics* V, 11.

classes to equip and stock these new farms. Public works projects were created to provide jobs for the unemployed. One such project was the construction of a large cistern near the headwaters of the Ilisus River and an aqueduct to convey the water to Athens.

New colonies were founded at strategic points along the important trade routes, including Segeum, on the coast of Asia Minor near the Hellespont, and Chersonesus, on the peninsula extending southwest from Thrace. New trading alliances were established with other Greek city-states, including Thessaly and Naxos. Pisistratus also developed a strong navy which came to be respected throughout the Aegean area.

In order to evoke civic pride among the Athenians, Pisistratus began the construction of the *Propylaea*, a monumental approach to the acropolis, and built or renovated several temples to the Olympian gods. He established the Panathenaic and Dionysiac Festivals to encourage the writing and public performance of epics and dramas, and consecrated the island of Delos as a religious center for all Greeks.

Aristotle evaluated Pisistratus' leadership in this way:

● ● ● *But most important of all the qualities mentioned was his popular and kindly attitude. For in every respect it was his principle to regulate everything in accordance with the laws without claiming a special privilege for himself. . . . For the majority both of the nobles and of the common people were in his favor. The former he won over through his friendly relationship with them, the latter through the help which he gave them in their private affairs; and he always proved fair to both of them.*[13]

John V. A. Fine, a modern historian, credits Pisistratus with maintaining a state that was free from factional strife:

● ● ● *One of Pisistratus' greatest services to Athens—if not the greatest—was that for a whole generation under his rule and that of his son Hippias, the country enjoyed almost complete freedom from factional strife. . . . As a tyrant he contributed greatly to the growth of a united state. . . . On the basis of the limited evidence, it seems clear that these were the ways in which he attempted to foster a spirit of unity among the Athenians: his conciliatory attitude to some prominent families and his suppression of those stubbornly resistant to his rule by exile or seizing their sons as hostages; his building program, which not only provided employment to many, but also must have increased the pride of Athenians in their city.*[14]

Pisistratus died in 527 B.C., and his son, Hippias, succeeded him as tyrant. Hippias' reign was an oppressive one, and he made a number of powerful enemies. He was overthrown by a faction of noble families aided by the Spartans.

THE 5TH-CENTURY DEMOCRACY

Once again the various factions struggled to gain control of the government, and in 508 B.C., Cleisthenes [KLICE-the-neez], a statesman with great popular support, came to power. He was determined to break down the sectional interests of the three major parties and to create a unified city-state in which all citizens could participate equally.

Cleisthenes. Cleisthenes recognized that the tribal and geographical factions that had developed among the Athenians would continue to prevent the creation of a unified state and an effective government for the polis. He therefore set up ten artificial "tribes," each including scattered precincts or *demes* from each of the three geographical areas: hill, shore, and plain. Each "tribe" thus contained a cross-section of interests and a mix-

---

[13]Aristotle, *The Constitution of Athens* XVI, 9.

[14]J. V. A. Fine, *The Ancient Greeks* (Harvard University Press, 1983), pp. 218-9.

ture of family loyalties. Since the territory of each tribe included a portion of Athens, the city became the focal point of the polis.

Every male of 18 years or older was required to register in the deme in which he lived. Membership in the deme became hereditary, and even if a person moved to another deme he retained his original registration. Although the Athenians would not accept Cleisthenes' suggestion that they change their surnames to the names of their demes, he did succeed in getting them to shift their basic allegiances from their clans or tribes to the polis.

The Boule. Cleisthenes made the Assembly of Athens the most important part of the government. To ensure that the Assembly could function effectively as a decision-making body, Cleisthenes created a committee called the *Boule* consisting of 50 men from each tribe. The Boule was responsible for preparing business for the assembly to vote upon, and its 500 members served for a term of one year. Within the Boule there were ten governing committees, each having 50 members, which rotated in office. Each committee had full-time responsibility for the Boule's business for one-tenth of the year, so that the Boule at any given time was represented by these 50 acting members.

The existence of the Boule ensured that the important business of the polis would be brought to the Assembly rather than to any other council. In order to prevent certain citizens from becoming too influential, the members of the Boule were chosen by lot rather than by election. Each day, an administrator was chosen, also by lot, from the members of the governing committee. This person was responsible for administering the government for that day.

The Assembly. All adult male Athenians over 18 years of age were eligible to vote in the Assembly. The members of this body discussed legislation submitted by the Boule, passed laws, voted on issues of war and peace, instituted taxes, and reviewed the accounts

Members of the Athenian Assembly wrote the names of those they wished to exile on these ostraka. Most of Athens' prominent citizens—including Miltiades and Themistocles, the historian Thucydides, and the philosopher Socrates—were impeached or exiled by the Assembly at some point in their careers.

of officials when their terms of office expired. In order to vote on any matter before the Assembly, a member had to be present from the beginning of the session and hear every speech dealing with the topic. A person could not speak before the Assembly if he was in debt to the state or if he had ever thrown his shield away during a battle.

Once a year, the Assembly met to discuss whether or not anyone posed a threat to the polis, and if so, whether that person should be exiled. To settle this question, each person qualified to vote picked up an *ostrokon*, a piece of broken pottery, from the ground and wrote the name of the person he thought should be *ostracized* (exiled). The votes were then carefully counted, and if a person received 6000 votes by this method, he was sent into exile for 10 years.

Courts of Law. The courts of law consisted of a committee of 6000 men chosen by

GOVERNMENT OF 5TH-CENTURY ATHENS

THE ASSEMBLY

Members:	All citizens of Athens.
	Requirements for citizenship: Either both parents Athenians, *or* awarded citizenship for distinguished service to state; 18 years of age or older; male.
Role:	Make all important decisions concerning foreign and domestic policy; appoint diplomats, *strategoi,* and other magistrates to carry out policy.

LAW COURT

Members:	6000 citizens chosen by lot from the Assembly to serve as jury pool. For important trials, several hundred citizens might serve on court.
Role:	Act as judge and jury for all major criminal and civil law cases of Athens and subject city-states.

THE BOULE

Members:	500 citizens, 50 men from each of the 10 tribes. Chosen by lot annually. Governing committee of 50 members serves in office for 1/10 year. Each day, an administrator for the committee is chosen by lot.
Role:	Prepare agenda for public discussion in the Assembly; prepare legislation to be debated by Assembly; administer policies enacted by the Assembly.

BOARD OF GENERALS

Members:	The 10 *strategoi,* or generals, are elected by the Assembly. In times of emergency, the office of supreme commander is rotated daily among the 10 *strategoi.*
Role:	Advise the Assembly on matters of war and peace; lead the army and navy on military campaigns.

lot from the Assembly. From these 6000, a jury was chosen by lot to hear each case.

Board of Generals. Each tribe was required to contribute a quota of men to the army, and to elect its own *strategos* (general). Unlike other magistrates, the generals could be re-elected for any number of terms. At first they served only as military leaders, but later, during times of crisis, they assumed control of finances and foreign affairs.

Cleisthenes' Legacy. Due to Cleisthenes' reforms, the opportunity to participate in the political process was open to all Athenian citizens. For the first time in history, common men had an opportunity to participate

in the political process. They could speak in the Assembly, elect their leaders, and even hold public office. The reforms that Cleisthenes implemented eliminated the old tribal loyalties and instead people began to think of themselves as Athenians. By 500 B.C., Athens was the most powerful and influential city-state in Greece.

Beginning about 450 B.C., the important decrees and decisions of the Assembly were carved on stone tablets and set up in a public place so that everyone could see them. This measure ensured that no one could tamper with the laws that had been enacted by the Assembly and the courts.

SPARTA During the Iron Age, the Dorian invaders from the north established villages in Laconia, a fertile valley in the Peloponnesus. In the 8th century B.C., Sparta, one of the most powerful and centrally located of these villages, established hegemony over the others.

The Spartans kept themselves separate from the original inhabitants of Laconia and did not grant them the privilege of citizenship. Those who chose to stay remained free, but had no political rights. The largest group within Spartan society consisted of the *helots*, peoples whom the Spartans had conquered in war and enslaved. These people had no personal freedom or political rights.

The early government of Sparta consisted of a monarchy, a council of aristocrats, and an assembly of weapon-bearing citizens. It was much like the governments that evolved in other city-states throughout Greece during the Iron Age. The Spartan government, however, traditionally had *two* kings instead of one, possibly to prevent one king from seizing too much power.

During the 8th century B.C., as city-states throughout Greece were solving their problems of over-population by establishing colonies, the Spartans decided upon a different solution. They established one colony, Tarentum, but gained most of the extra land that they needed by invading Messenia, their neighbor to the west. The combined territories of Laconia and Messenia were called *Lacedaemon*, and they were governed by the polis of Sparta.

In 640 B.C., the Messenians revolted against Spartan rule and continued to revolt for about 20 years. Because the Spartans were a minority in the state they had created, they had a great deal of difficulty in putting down the rebellions and in enforcing their rule. In addition, the common people of Sparta, who served as hoplites (foot soldiers), began to demand political reforms in return for their services. They wanted a greater voice in the government of Sparta, a removal of class distinctions among Spartans, and a redistribution of land. The Spartan leaders turned to the Constitution of Lycurgus for a solution to their internal problems.

The Constitution of Lycurgus. It is not known whether Lycurgus was a real or mythical person. Later generations of Spartans believed that he had been a real king and that he had created all of the laws and institutions of Sparta. The laws attributed to Lycurgus probably retained many of the ancient traditions of Sparta and added several important innovations. They were considered to be sacred, and represented an entire way of life as well as a political system.

The system of Lycurgus emphasized the equal treatment of each citizen under the law. The officials of the polis sternly regulated every aspect of the citizens' lives, but the powers of the government were carefully bal-

According to tradition, Lycurgus established Sparta's unique laws and institutions. Plato and Aristotle later expressed admiration for many aspects of his constitution.

anced so that no one person could usurp too much power.

In addition to the traditional monarchy, the council of elders, and the assembly, the laws of Lycurgus added a fourth agency of government: a council of five *ephors*. Under the system of Lycurgus, the authority of the monarchy, as before, was shared by two kings. The *Council of Elders*, or Senate, consisted of 28 citizens over the age of 60. It advised the kings, discussed matters that might be presented to the Assembly, and served as a court of law. The *Assembly* included all citizens over the age of 30. It had the powers of declaring war or making peace, of approving the choices of kings, and of electing the council members and the five *ephors*. The ephors exercised great power in Sparta. By the 6th century B.C., they had the authority to arrest a king and could recommend to the Assembly that he be put on trial. They were present at council meetings, and probably helped to prepare business for the Assembly to consider. They supervised the military training of young citizens, and they were in charge of public morals and of foreign affairs.

Spartan citizens were expected to devote themselves to the interests of the state, and every aspect of their lives was controlled so that they would do so. New babies were inspected by the Council of Elders, and babies considered to be too frail were left on a mountaintop to die of exposure. At the age of seven all boys were placed under the care of the state. Xenophon, a writer of the 4th century B.C., reported that the smallest offense was punished by whipping, and that food was rationed so stringently that the boys were forced to steal additional food in order to sustain themselves. Xenophon also reported:

• • • *Instead of softening the boys' feet with sandals he [Lycurgus] required them to harden their feet by going without shoes. He believed that if this habit were cultivated it would enable them to climb hills more easily and descend steep inclines with less danger, and that a youth who had accustomed himself to go barefoot would leap and jump and run more nimbly than a boy in sandals.*[15]

The Spartan young people were thoroughly indoctrinated in the ideology of the state. Most of their time was spent in physical exercises to make the boys excellent soldiers, and the girls good mothers who could produce strong, healthy children for the state. Little emphasis was placed on reading or writing. All luxuries and frivolity were forbidden, but dancing was encouraged, because the Spartans believed that dancing taught physical coordination.

Spartan men were forbidden to have any other career besides that of soldier: all other occupations were filled by non-citizens. Plutarch, a Greek historian of the 1st century A.D., described the effect that this law had on the lives of Spartan men:

• • • *Their discipline continued still after they were full-grown men. No one was allowed to live after his own fancy; but the city was a sort of camp, in which every man had his share of provisions and business set out, and looked upon himself not so much born to serve his own ends as the interest of his country.*[16]

Spartan men were permitted to marry at age 20, but all had to enter military training at that time. Married or not, the men were required to live in communal barracks until they reached the age of 30.

All Spartans were forbidden to travel abroad, and foreigners were not welcomed within Sparta for fear that they would corrupt the citizenry. All of the land was the property of the state, and each citizen was allotted the use of only enough land to support his family. Helots performed all of the

---

[15]Xenophon, "The Lacedaemonians." In *Scripta Minora* II, 3.

[16]Plutarch, *Lives*, Modern Library ed., p. 68.

This bronze figurine shows a Spartan warrior in battle dress, his long hair neatly combed and curled. The Spartans had so much confidence in their warriors that they never built defensive walls around their city.

work on the land so that the citizens could be available for military service.

The Spartans were constantly on guard against the possibility that the helots would revolt. Special secret police spied on them constantly, and each year one day was set aside to "wage war on the helots." On this day, a Spartan citizen could put to death any helot whom he disliked. In wartime, the helots served the Spartan soldiers but did not actually fight in battle.

The Peloponnesian League. Throughout their history, the Spartans were reluctant to send troops outside of the Peloponnesus for fear of a helot uprising or an attack from nearby city-states. In an effort to control the threat posed by Tegea, Argos, and other neighboring city-states, the Spartans formed the Peloponnesian League around 540 B.C. The purpose of the league was to unite all of the important city-states in the Peloponnesus. Each state was bound to Sparta by a separate 100-year treaty, during which time Sparta would provide military leadership for the League while the other members furnished troops.

The creation of the Peloponnesian League reduced the Spartans' fears about attacks from their neighbors, and was very effective in discouraging potential enemies because of the international reputation of Spartan soldiers. Herodotus reported the following conversation, in which the Persian king Xerxes learned of Sparta's military prowess:

••• *the Lacedaemonians [Spartans] in single combat are inferior to none, but together are the bravest of all men; for, though free, they are not absolutely free, for they have a master over them, the law, which they fear much more than your subjects do you. They do, accordingly, whatever it enjoins; and it ever enjoins the same thing, forbidding them to fly from battle before any number of men, but [commanding them] to remain in their ranks, and conquer or die.*[17]

[17]Herodotus VII, 104.

> *Several English words had their origins in Sparta: for example,* Spartan, *meaning "self-disciplined and austere";* laconic, *meaning "extremely concise of speech"; and* appellate, *meaning "having the power to hear appeals."*

Relations with Athens. In 500 B.C., Sparta and Athens were scarcely in the same world philosophically, although they were separated by less than 100 miles geographically. Sparta was closed to new ideas and foreign people, and dedicated to military self-preservation under a communal form of government. Athens sought out new ideas and people, and eventually developed the most nearly pure form of democracy that has ever existed. Although there was little possibility that these two leading city-states would give up their independence in order to form a unified nation, they did learn how to cooperate with each other under the threat of a foreign invasion.

THE PERSIAN WARS During the 5th century B.C., the Greek city-states united to defend themselves against a series of attacks by the Persians. The Persians had an untold wealth of men and materials, and were united under one rule. The Greek army, in contrast, was made up of troops from a number of independent city-states, and its generals were accountable to these small states rather than to one central authority.

The Greeks first became involved with the Persian Empire when Cyrus the Great, king of Persia, conquered the kingdom of Lydia in Asia Minor. The Ionian city-states, although they had their own independent governments, were considered to be part of Lydia and were incorporated into the Persian Empire. Under Darius the Great, the Ionians and the Lydians were placed under the control of a *satrap* (governor) who resided in Sardis. The satrap encouraged the development of tyrannies in the Ionian city-states, and permitted these local governments to function independently as long as they paid their taxes and provided military levies when required by Persia.

In 499 B.C., Aristogoras, the ambitious tyrant of Miletus, the most prosperous and cultured of the Greek colonies of Ionia, led a revolt against the Persians. Athens aided this uprising by sending 20 shiploads of soldiers. Eretria, on the island of Euboea, sent 5 shiploads. Sparta refused to participate when Cleomenes, one of its two kings, learned that the Persian capital at Susa was three months' march from the nearest seaport.

The Ionians and their allies advanced to Sardis, the headquarters of the satrap, and burned the city. Athens and Eretria then withdrew their forces. The Ionians continued the struggle, but collapsed when their navy, consisting of 353 ships, was defeated by the Persian navy, of almost double the strength, off the coast of Miletus.

In retaliation for this revolt, the Persians sacked and burned Miletus in 495 B.C., and deported the inhabitants to the Tigris-Euphrates valley, about 1000 miles away. Herodotus, who lived during this era and is our most important source of information on the Persian Wars, wrote:

> ● ● ● *the Athenians made it evident that they were excessively grieved at the capture of Miletus, both in many other ways, and more particularly when Phrynichus had composed a drama of the capture of Miletus, and presented it, the whole theater burst into tears, and fined him a thousand drachmas for renewing the memory of their domestic misfortunes; and they gave order that henceforth no one should act this drama.*[18]

In 492 B.C., Darius sent an army westward through Thrace and Macedonia to attack

---

[18]Ibid., VI, 21.

Persian empire
Darius' route by sea, 490 B.C.
Xerxes' routes by land and sea, 480 B.C.

THRACE

MACEDONIA

Mt. Athos

THESSALY

Thermopylae

EUBOEA

Chalcis
Eretria
Thebes
Plataea
Marathon
Eleusis
Megara
Athens
Corinth
Piraeus
SALAMIS
Saronic Gulf
Gulf of Corinth

Sparta

AEGEAN SEA

LESBOS

LYDIA

Sardis

IONIA

SAMOS
Mycale
Miletus

DELOS

NAXOS

Athens in retaliation for its support of the Ionians. As the troops marched along the coast, they were supplied by the Persian navy, but the fleet was wrecked in a storm off the promontory of Mount Athos. Because his army now lacked naval support and he did not wish to risk a battle, Darius sent envoys to various Greek city-states to demand tokens of submission in the form of earth and water. According to stories that were later told, the Athenians threw the Persian envoy into a pit and told him to dig his own earth; then the Spartans threw him into a well and told him to gather his own water. But although they were united in their determination to resist, Athens and Sparta could not agree upon a plan of action. Meanwhile, the Persians strengthened their control over the northern coast of the Aegean, and returned to their bases in Asia Minor.

In 490 B.C., Darius subdued the city-states of Euboea and landed on the plain of Marathon. From here, the Persians planned to lay seige to Athens and at the same time prevent the Spartans from coming to the city's aid. The Athenian *strategos* Miltiades, one of the greatest military geniuses of all time, had served as governor of Thrace and was familiar with Persian battle tactics. He understood what the Persians were attempting, and sent a message to the Spartans asking for aid. He then persuaded the Athenians and the Plataeans, who were allies, to seize the initiative immediately by marching 26 miles eastward to Marathon.

When the Greeks arrived at Marathon, the Persian cavalry troops were not present at the site; but neither were the Spartan allies, for they had been delayed by a religious observance. Miltiades decided to take advantage of the cavalry's absence and attacked the Persian troops at dawn rather than waiting for the Spartans. Herodotus described the battle as follows:

● ● ● *The battle of Marathon lasted a long time; and in the middle of the line, where the Persians themselves and the Sacae [their allies] were arrayed, the barbarians were victorious; in this part, then, the barbarians conquered, and having broken the line, pursued to the interior; but in both wings the Athenians and the Plataeans were victorious; and having gained the victory, they allowed the defeated portion of the barbarians to flee; and having united both wings, they fought with those who had broken their center, and the Athenians were victorious. They followed the Persians in their flight, cutting them to pieces, till, reaching the shore, they called for fire and attacked the ships.[19]*

[19]Ibid., VI, 113.

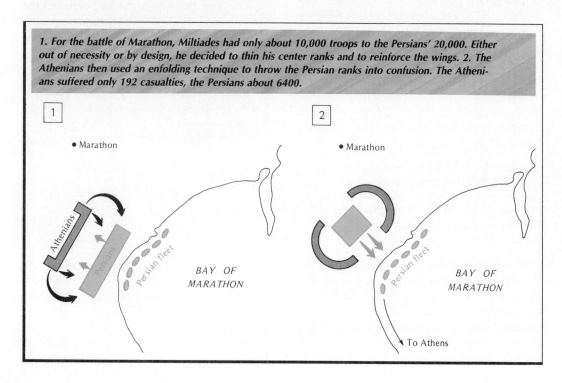

1. For the battle of Marathon, Miltiades had only about 10,000 troops to the Persians' 20,000. Either out of necessity or by design, he decided to thin his center ranks and to reinforce the wings. 2. The Athenians then used an enfolding technique to throw the Persian ranks into confusion. The Athenians suffered only 192 casualties, the Persians about 6400.

> *After the battle of Marathon, a runner was ordered to report the victory to the people of Athens. According to tradition, he ran the entire distance, managed to make his report, and then died from exhaustion. Today this athlete's feat is commemorated by marathon races in which runners compete over 26-mile-long routes.*

According to Herodotus, the Persians had lost 6400 men in the battle of Marathon, and the Athenians only 192. In spite of the Persians' heavy losses, Miltiades suspected that they would attempt to attack Athens from the sea. He led his army swiftly back to Athens. When the Persians found the Athenians waiting for their next attack, they abandoned their plans and returned to Asia Minor. The small city-state of Athens had, almost single-handedly, defeated the Persian empire.

The Athenians' victory at Marathon was an astonishing achievement, and the participants were long remembered: the dead were given a state burial and the survivors were honored throughout their lives. People continued to be impressed by the Athenians' feat for many centuries. Two thousand years after the battle, Lord Byron, a supporter of Greek independence from the Ottoman (Turkish) Empire, was moved to write:

*The mountains look on Marathon
And Marathon looks on the sea,
And musing there an hour alone
I dreamed that Greece might still be free;
For standing on the Persian's grave
I could not deem myself a slave.*[20]

Xerxes, the son of Darius, came to the throne of the Persian Empire in 485 B.C. His desire for revenge against the Greeks led him to make elaborate preparations for war against them. He planned a joint attack by land and sea, and made careful preparations for both campaigns. Supply depots were established along the line of march, and two pontoon bridges were constructed to cross the Hellespont. A canal was dug across the peninsula of Mount Athos in order to prevent the possibility of another disaster while sailing around the dangerous cape.

When news of these elaborate invasion plans reached the Greeks, they were undecided about how to defend themselves. The leader of Athens at this time was Themistocles. He was greatly concerned about the Persian threat, and, when a rich mine of silver was discovered near Athens, he persuaded his fellow citizens to finance the building of a navy rather than distribute the new wealth as a dividend among themselves. He also advised the Athenians to build a new harbor at Piraeus, which would be easier to fortify than the existing harbor, and to build two long walls from Piraeus to Athens to provide a safe passageway between the city and its port.

Although the Athenians had defeated the Persian army at Marathon without help from the Spartans, most of the Greek city-states

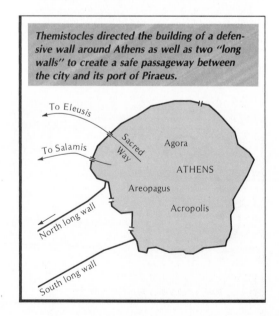

Themistocles directed the building of a defensive wall around Athens as well as two "long walls" to create a safe passageway between the city and its port of Piraeus.

---

[20]*Don Juan*, canto 3, stanza 83.

still regarded Sparta as the foremost military power in Greece. In 481 B.C., a league of Greek city-states was formed, and all members pledged to end their destructive quarrels for the duration of the Persian threat. Sparta was given command over the combined land forces and Athens command over the combined naval forces. After much discussion and with great reluctance, the two sets of leaders finally agreed to abandon a plan for making a major stand at Corinth, because this plan would have ceded all of northern and central Greece to the Persians. They decided instead to take their stand at Thermopylae, a pass on the Gulf of Euboea about 75 miles northwest of Athens.

In August of 480 B.C., the armies of Xerxes advanced across Asia Minor toward the Hellespont. Herodotus reported that the Persians had 2,641,610 men and 1207 warships, while the Athenians and their allies had 150,000 men and 700 to 800 vessels. Herodotus was probably exaggerating the Persian strength, but it was considerably greater than that of all the Greek allies combined. Herodotus also reported that when Xerxes reached the Hellespont, he had a pontoon bridge built to convey his troops across the water. The bridge was destroyed by a storm, and Xerxes, according to Herodotus, revealed his astonishing *hubris* (pride) by trying to punish nature for its insubordination:

• • • *When Xerxes heard of this [the destruction of the bridge], being exceedingly indignant, he commanded that the Hellespont should be stricken with 300 lashes of a scourge, and that a pair of fetters should be let down into the sea. I have moreover heard that with them he likewise sent branding instruments to brand the Hellespont. He certainly charged those who flogged the waters to utter these barbarous and impious words: "Thou bitter water! thy master inflicts this punishment upon thee, because thou hast injured him; and King Xerxes will cross over thee, whether thou wilt or not; it is with justice that no man*

sacrifices to thee, because thou art both a deceitful and briny river."[21]

Xerxes rebuilt his bridge and proceeded overland toward mainland Greece. As the Persians approached Thermopylae, a narrow mountain pass to the north of Delphi, King Leonidas of Sparta, with 300 of his own men and 6700 others, waited expectantly for reinforcements that had been promised as soon as the Olympic Games had ended. A Persian spy reported to Xerxes that the Spartans were exercising and combing their hair. Xerxes was puzzled by such behavior, and when he sought an explanation, he was told that:

• • • *These men have to fight with us for the pass, and are now preparing themselves to do so; for such is their custom, when they are going to hazard their lives, then they dress their heads; but be assured, if you conquer these men, and those that remain in Sparta, there is no other nation in the world that will dare to raise their hand against you, O king; for you are now to engage with the noblest kingdom and the city of all among the Greeks, and with the most valiant men.*[22]

About two weeks later, a Greek traitor agreed to lead a Persian force up a mountain path to a point behind the Greeks. Leonidas detected the movement of the Persians and called a council of war. It was agreed that some of the Greek troops should remain with Leonidas, while the remainder would move southward, perhaps to attack the Persians from the rear.

In the fierce fighting that ensued, Leonidas and many of his remaining troops were slain. Throughout history Thermopylae has been a symbol of heroic struggle against overwhelming odds. Herodotus described how these heroes were memorialized:

• • • *In honor of the slain, who were buried on the spot where they fell, and of those who*

---

[21]Herodotus VII, 35.

[22]Ibid., VI, 209.

died before they were dismissed by Leonidas and went away, the following inscription has been engraved over them: "Four thousand from Peloponnesus once fought on this spot with three hundred myriads [3,000,000 men]." This inscription was made for all; and for the Spartans in particular: "Stranger, go tell the Lacedaemonians that we lie here, obedient to their commands."[23]

Xerxes' army moved south through central Greece. The allies of Athens retreated to the Isthmus of Corinth, thereby abandoning all of northern Greece to the enemy. The Athenians sent messengers to the Delphic oracle to learn what course of action they should follow. The messengers were told:

● ● ● *wide-seeing Jupiter gives a wooden wall to the Triton-born goddess [Athena], to be alone impregnable, which shall preserve you and your children.*[24]

Some Athenians believed that the oracle was referring to a wall of wood on the Acropolis. But Themistocles persuaded the people that the oracle's use of the term "wooden walls" referred to the Athenian fleet. Hoping to defeat the Persians at sea, and thereby force them to leave Greece, he ordered the evacuation of all women and children to the nearby island of Salamis, and recruited all able-bodied men to take to the fighting ships. When Athens was abandoned, the Persians moved in and looted and burned the city.

The Greek city-states held a council of war, but argued among themselves. Corinth objected to the presence of Athenians at the council, arguing that they had no place there because their city had been destroyed. Most of the Greek allies wanted the combined navies to be close to where the armies were assembled near Corinth. But Themistocles urged that the fleet stay in the straits of Sal-

amis, the narrow channel of water above the island of Salamis. He went so far as to threaten to withdraw the Athenian navy from the alliance if the others did not follow his recommendation. Realizing that there was no hope of victory without the Athenian navy, the others acquiesced.

Themistocles then secretly sent a slave to Xerxes with a false rumor that the Greeks were in disagreement and planned to withdraw without a fight. As Themistocles had anticipated, the Persians then decided to send a fleet to the straits of Salamis to cut off the escaping armies.

The heavy Persian sailing ships could not maneuver in the narrow straits, and the lighter Athenian ships, which could be easily rowed and turned, inflicted heavy damage on them.[25] The last major action of the war took place at Mycale, where the Greeks attacked what remained of the Persian fleet that had been routed at Salamis.

After the naval defeat in the straits of Salamis, Xerxes withdrew his armies to the north to prepare for a new campaign in the spring. Again the Greeks disagreed about how to prepare for this new threat. In the spring of 479 B.C., the Persians marched south and reoccupied Athens. The Spartans, under Pausanias, attacked and drove the Persians about 40 miles northwest to Plataea. The Persian commander was killed, and the Persians were forced to flee. The remnant of this once great army faced disease and starvation as it retreated through northern Greece, and only a few troops finally returned to Persia.

The outcome of these 20 years of fighting was remarkable when one realizes that the Spartans were the only well-trained soldiers in all of Greece, and that the leaders of the various Greek city-states seldom could agree on a course of action. This great victory over the power of Persia imbued the Greeks with a great sense of self-confidence, and marked

---

[23]Ibid., VII, 228.
[24]Ibid., VII, 141.

[25]Two thousand years later, Sir Francis Drake used this same strategy to defeat the Spanish Armada.

the beginning of the brilliant era of civilization known as the Classical period.

Although they had been defeated in Greece, the Persians still had a great empire which controlled the city-states of Ionia. In order to forestall the possibility of another attack by the Persians, in 478 B.C. the Athenians persuaded 350 of the Greek city-states to form a defensive alliance, which came to be known as the Delian League. To seal this pact, the allies threw a lump of iron into the sea and pledged to support each other until the lump should rise to the surface. The league was named for the island of Delos, where the treasury was established and where meetings of the representatives took place. Athens determined the contribution, or tribute, each member should make, and these "tribute lists" were carved into marble slabs and set up in the agora at Athens.

In 454 B.C., the league's treasury was moved to Athens. By 450, the Persians had been driven from the Aegean, and the Athenian fleet patrolled the sea with ships financed by the league. Thereafter, Athens dominated the league completely, and would not permit members to secede from it. In time, the Delian League was transformed into the Athenian Empire, thereby creating frictions which ultimately led to the Peloponnesian War. Meanwhile, the Athenians developed ideas of art, government, philosophy, and science which continue to influence the thinking of the Western world.

SUMMARY

During the Iron Age of Greece (1100-700 B.C.), the governments of the city-states of Greece began to evolve from the system that had prevailed in Mycenaean times: monarchies were gradually replaced by elected councils and public assemblies. At the same time, the economy of Greece came to be based upon small, independent family farms rather than military ventures abroad.

During the 8th century B.C., when family farms could no longer support the growing population, the Greeks undertook colonization and trading ventures. These activities greatly expanded the economy and led to a more diversified society.

In the next century, various city-states began to experiment with different forms of government. Sparta, for example, adopted the laws of Lycurgus and resisted any change in this system. Athens, on the other hand, evolved into a democracy.

During the 5th century B.C., many of the city-states put aside their differences and combined forces to ward off several attempted invasions by the Persians. This success gave the Greeks a new self-confidence which led them into the brilliant era of achievement known as the Classical period.

QUESTIONS

1 Why is the study of the Homeric epics so important to historians who are seeking to understand the values and beliefs of Iron Age Greece?
2 Describe the political, legal, and economic reforms brought about by Draco, Solon, Pisistratus, and Cleisthenes. What impact did each have on the development of democracy?
3 Compare Athens to Sparta in terms of values and distribution of political power.
4 Read Plutarch's Lives of Lycurgus and Pericles. What can you learn from Plutarch about the societies in which these men lived?
5 Compare the ancient Olympic Games with the modern ones.
6 Why has the battle of Marathon been regarded as one of the most important battles in history?
7 Research one of the lesser-known Greek city-states, such as Corinth or Syracuse, and compare its political development with that of Athens or Sparta.

BIBLIOGRAPHY

Which books might discuss the leadership of Athens' democracy?

FINLEY, M. I. *The Ancient Greeks*. New York: Viking Press, 1963. *Discusses the culture and politics of the ancient Greeks from the Archaic, or Iron Age, through the 4th century. Includes such topics as the amateurism of office-holders in Athens' direct democracy; popular attitudes and morals.*

HUXLEY, G. L. *The Early Ionians*. New York: Humanities Press, 1968. *A comprehensive, scholarly history of the Ionian Greeks; their intellectual achievements and political history.*

LISTER, R. P. *The Travels of Herodotus*. London and New York: Gordon and Cremonesi, 1979. *Describes Herodotus' travels throughout the ancient world as he investigated the origins of ancient Greek legends and the culture of other civilizations; provides the same kind of detailed observations that have endeared Herodotus to generations of readers.*

> In short, I say that as a city we are the school of Hellas;
> while I doubt if the world can produce a man, who where he has
> only himself to depend upon, is equal to so many emergencies,
> and graced by so happy a versatility as the Athenian.
>
> PERICLES

Classical Greece

IONIA During the 7th and 6th centuries B.C., Ionia in Asia Minor was a center of Greek intellectual achievement. The wealth of the cities encouraged the pursuit of creative activities, and the adoption of the Phoenician alphabet facilitated the exchange of ideas. Many of the forms of learning that we enjoy today, such as literature, history, philosophy, and science, were initiated or perfected by the Ionian Greeks.

Sappho. Sappho of Lesbos was the first woman to gain fame from her writings. Her poems were often read to the accompaniment of a lyre (a small harp), so that the style came to be called *lyric* poetry. Her keen observations of nature, her vivid imagination, and her melodic cadences inspired Plato to call her the "Tenth Muse." Her poem *The Young Bride* reflects these qualities:

A Young Bride
(i)

Like the sweet apple which reddens on the
   topmost bough,
A-top on the topmost twig—which the
   pluckers forgot somehow—
Forgot it not, nay, but got it not, for
   none could get it till now.

(ii)

Like the wild hyacinth flower, which on
   the hills is found,
Which the passing feet of the shepherds
   for ever tear and wound,
Until the purple blossom is trodden into
   the ground.[1]

Hecataeus. The Ionians also created other forms of literature. Hecataeus of Miletus wrote a book of geography which described the world as he observed it during his travels, with the Mediterranean Sea as the center. He also wrote *genealogies* which traced all of the identifiable ancestors of certain noble families, and then named heroes or gods as the more distant ancestors.

Herodotus. Herodotus of Halicarnassus (484-425 B.C.) was the first Western writer to use the word *historia* ("inquiry"). He traveled widely throughout the Greek world, Egypt, and Mesopotamia, investigating legends about Greek history and gathering information on other cultures which he later

---

[1]T. F. Higham and C. M. Bowra, eds. *Oxford Book of Greek Verse in Translation* (Oxford University Press, 1938), p. 209.

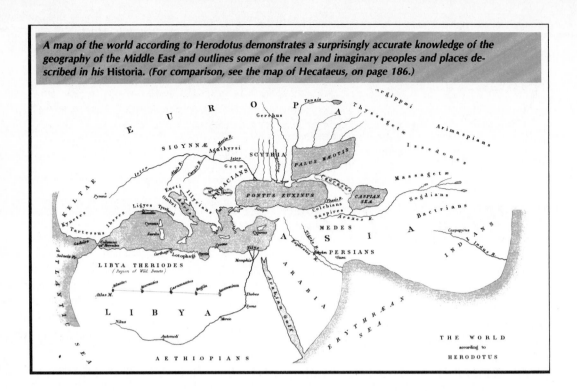

A map of the world according to Herodotus demonstrates a surprisingly accurate knowledge of the geography of the Middle East and outlines some of the real and imaginary peoples and places described in his Historia. (For comparison, see the map of Hecataeus, on page 186.)

consolidated into his great book. His writings are one of the most important sources of information that we have concerning the events and peoples of the ancient world.

In addition to his history of ancient times, Herodotus recounted the events of his own time, especially the ongoing conflict between the Greeks and the Persians. In the introduction to this important work, he said:

••• This is a publication of the researches of Herodotus of Halicarnassus, in order that the actions of men may not be effaced by time, nor the great and wonderous deeds displayed by both Greeks and barbarians deprived of renown; and among the rest, for what cause they waged war upon each other.[2]

In the first four of his books on the Persian-Greek conflict, Herodotus discussed the backgrounds of the two nations, and then traced the progress of the war. The events of the war, he believed, were directed by the gods. For example, he wrote that the defeat of Xerxes was brought about by his overwhelming pride (hubris), which had aroused the envy of the gods and led them to plot his destruction (nemesis) at the hands of the Greeks.

Over the centuries, scholars have known that Herodotus' fondness for a good story often led him to accept unreliable information. But as investigations of those ancient cultures have expanded in recent years, scholars have found his descriptions of places and events to be an invaluable resource. The historian Edith Hamilton evaluated Herodotus in this way:

••• Herodotus is a shining instance of the strong Greek bent to examine and prove or disprove. He had a passion for finding out. The task he set himself was nothing less than to find out all about everything in the world. He is always called the "father of history,"

[2]Herodotus I, 1.

but he was quite as much the father of geography, of archeology, of anthropology, of sociology, or whatever has to do with human beings and the places in which they live. The Greek contempt for foreigners—in Greek, barbarians—never touched him. He was passionately on Athens' side in her struggle against Persia, yet he admired and praised the Persians. He found them brave and chivalrous and truthful.[3]

THE EARLY PHILOSOPHERS

During the 6th century B.C., some Ionians were seeking to understand the world through introspection and analysis. Their investigations led them to be called *philosophers* ("lovers of wisdom"). They rejected the idea that the gods controlled the universe, and sought to discover instead the laws of *physis* (nature). Much of their philosophic thinking dealt with what we would call science. Today the science of energy and matter is known as *physics*.

Thales. The earliest known philosopher was Thales of Miletus (636-546 B.C.). After studying earlier Egyptian and Babylonian discoveries in astronomy and mathematics, he came to believe that the heavenly bodies were controlled by fixed laws. Like many later Greek philosophers, Thales believed that all things in nature derived from one basic element. He concluded that this element was water.

Thales was once ridiculed by his friends for his strange ideas. They taunted him, saying "If you are so smart, why aren't you rich?" Sometime later, his observations led him to believe that the olive crop would be exceptionally good that year, so he leased all of the oil presses he could find. Farmers with large olive crops were forced to come to him to have their crops processed, and he charged them very high fees for his services. He thus proved that he could become immensely

wealthy if he wanted to. Another story about him relates that he inadvertently fell into a well while gazing at a star.

Anaximenes and Anaximander. Thales' successor as the leading philosopher of the day was Anaximenes, who also lived in Miletus during the 6th century B.C. Anaximenes decided that the basic element of the universe was air, and that the rarefaction and condensation of air produced all forms in nature. One of his pupils, Anaximander (610-546 B.C.), concluded that the basic element was an undefined, formless, immortal substance, which he called "the Boundless." This substance contained elements of earth, air, fire, and water, and combined in different proportions to create everything in nature.

Heraclitus and Democritus. Heraclitus (540-475 B.C.) stated that the basic element of the universe was fire, and that all life went through a continual process of decay and regeneration. He is reported to have said, "Everything flows and nothing remains the same."

Democritus (460-370 B.C.) decided that the universe was made up of an infinite number of invisible and indivisible particles, which move about continuously and combine with other particles to create matter. His concept was close to modern ideas about the behavior of atoms.

Pythagoras. Pythagoras (582-500 B.C.) was born on the island of Samos. He believed that the underlying system of the universe could only be discovered by studying numbers, and that the sun, moon, and earth were round bodies which revolve around a central fire. He speculated that each celestial body produced a distinct tone. These tones were inaudible to the human ear, but corresponded to the notes of the musical scale. (This idea became the basis of the later concept of "the harmony of the spheres.")

The relationships between mathematics and music became an important part of the theories of Pythagoras and his followers. He analyzed the behavior of a lyre and discov-

[3]Hamilton, Edith, *The Greek Way* (New York & London: W. W. Norton, 1930), pp. 121-2.

ered that the vibrations of two strings, or wires, of the same material and diameter vary in inverse proportion to their lengths. The fact that harmonies in music—thirds, fifths, octaves, etc.—can be expressed in numbers reinforced Pythagoras' belief that numbers are the true expression of reality.

Hippocrates. Hippocrates (460-377 B.C.) founded a school of medicine on the island of Cos in 420 B.C. He rejected the belief that disease was caused by demons, and sought to find natural causes for various illnesses. He emphasized the value of careful observation and interpretation of patients' symptoms. He was the first to use such words as *crisis*, *acute*, and *chronic* to describe illnesses. His concept of "holistic healing," including hygiene, diet, and the curative powers of nature, is remarkably similar to the practices of many people today. The "Hippocratic Oath" he devised has served as an ethical guide for many generations of physicians.

The Ionian theorists were among the first people to pursue what is known as *disinterested* inquiry; that is, knowledge for its own sake rather than for a practical purpose; to understand nature, rather than to exploit it. While some of their ideas may seem fantastical, it must be remembered that their methods helped to create an atmosphere in which important discoveries could be made. Disregarding the evidence of their eyes, they theorized that the earth is round, not flat; and they searched for universal laws in nature rather than accepting its apparent diversity. Their work was later refined by Plato, Aristotle, and others, and became the foundation of modern science.

ATHENS After the Persian Wars ended, Athens emerged as the political and cultural center of the Greek world. The supremacy of Athens during the Classical period (479-323 B.C.) was largely due to the influence of Pericles, who was the most prominent politician in Athens between 461 and 429. Under his guidance, Athens' leadership of the Delian League became the basis for the creation of an empire. When Athens' hegemony over its empire was secure, Pericles encouraged his fellow citizens to use the tribute money they collected to underwrite the development of Greek culture. Due to his efforts, Athens became, in his words, the "school of Hellas." The Athenians' achievements in architecture, sculpture, drama, and philosophy are studied and emulated even today. Many scholars believe that the Classical period of Greece was the most fruitful period of development of thought in the history of the Western world.

PERICLES AND THE ATHENIAN EMPIRE

Pericles. Pericles' ancestry included two of the most distinguished families of Athens: his father was Xanthippus, the commander of the Athenian navy at Mycale in 479 B.C., and his mother was a niece of Cleisthenes, the statesman who reformed Athens' democracy. Like Solon, Pisistratus, and Cleisthenes, Pericles belonged to the aristocracy and yet encouraged the development of Athens' democracy.

Early in his political career, Pericles helped to strengthen the democratic system that Cleisthenes had instituted. To ensure that even the poorest citizens had an opportunity to serve in public office, Pericles initiated a policy of paying citizens for their time of service in the Boule and the law courts.

The Empire. In foreign affairs, Pericles became known as a strong advocate of Athens' supremacy in the Greek world. When the Persian Wars ended, in 479 B.C., Athens assumed the leadership of the Delian League, a confederation of Greek city-states (see Chapter 6). The purpose of the league was to avert any further threat of a Persian invasion, and the Athenian navy was the mainstay of the league's military force. Each member state contributed money (or ships) to the league, whose treasury was located on the island of Delos. Within a few years of its

Pericles—general, orator, and statesman of Athens—chose to be depicted with a war helmet in this portrait.

founding, however, several members of the Delian League tried to secede from it. These actions caused great concern to Pericles and other prominent Athenians, who strongly believed that Athens needed to maintain the league in order to survive.

Beginning in 465 B.C., the Athenians made it clear that membership in the league was no longer voluntary. They forcibly put down several attempted revolts of the allies, and moved the league's treasury from Delos to Athens. Athens also showed its imperialistic intentions through two other measures. The Assembly decreed that all of the league's members must use Athens' coinage as well as its system of weights and measures. In addition, the Assembly itself became a final court of appeal for every citizen within the league: all major law cases had to be reviewed by the Athenian court, which consisted of a committee within the Assembly.

In 443 B.C., an Athenian *strategos* (general) who had disapproved of Athens' imperial policies was ostracized, and Pericles was elected in his place. Pericles continued to uphold a stern policy toward Athens' allies. Each time that one of the city-states within the empire threatened to secede, Pericles argued that Athens must enforce its hegemony by sending troops to the scene of the trouble. As a citizen of the Athenian democracy, he had no more power than any other citizen to promote his policies. But because of his immense popularity and powers of persuasion, he was almost always able to convince a majority of the Assembly to follow the course he recommended. The historian Thucydides, who was a contemporary of Pericles, evaluated his leadership in this manner:

● ● ● *Pericles indeed, by his rank, ability, and known integrity, was enabled to exercise an independent control over the multitude—in short, to lead them instead of being led by them; for as he never sought power by improper means, he was never compelled to flatter them, but, on the contrary, enjoyed so high an estimation that he could afford to anger them by contradiction. Whenever he saw them unseasonably and insolently elated, he would with a word reduce them to alarm; on the other hand, if they fell victims to a panic, he could at once restore them to confidence. In short, what was nominally a democracy became in his hands government by the first citizen.*[4]

The Athenians used the money that they gathered in tribute to make Athens the center of culture in the Greek world. In return, the Athenian navy policed the seas, enabling all of the Greek city-states to develop a thriving trade. To ensure the loyalties of the league's members, Athens actively encouraged the installation of democracies. This type of po-

[4]Thucydides II, 7, 65.

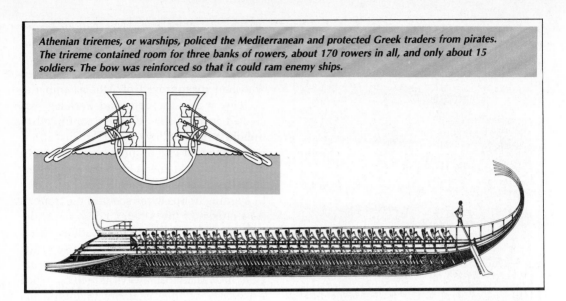

Athenian triremes, or warships, policed the Mediterranean and protected Greek traders from pirates. The trireme contained room for three banks of rowers, about 170 rowers in all, and only about 15 soldiers. The bow was reinforced so that it could ram enemy ships.

litical interference was the cause of most of the rebellions which broke out among the member city-states. For example, a revolt by the island of Samos, in 440 B.C., was led by wealthy oligarchs who did not want to see the spread of Athens' democracy.

The revenues from the empire enabled Pericles to administer the reconstruction of Athens, which had been destroyed by the Persians in 480 B.C. As architects rebuilt the public monuments of the city on an unprecedented scale, Athenian poets, philosophers, and artists also helped to make Athens the cultural and intellectual center of the Greek world. Within several decades, however, the firm imperialistic policies of Pericles led Athens into the devastating Peloponnesian War.

ARCHITECTURE

The most impressive remains in all of Greece are on the acropolis in Athens, the rocky citadel that rises approximately 200 feet above the plain on which most of the city is situated. Because the Persians had destroyed the earlier city, these magnificent buildings were entirely the product of the insight, vision, and persuasive powers of Pericles, who used the tribute money that Athens collected from

members of the Delian League to make Athens a symbol of power and wealth.

The Parthenon. By far the most beautiful building on the acropolis was the Parthenon, dedicated to Athena Parthenos, the patron deity of Athens. It was begun in 447 and completed in 438 B.C. The sides of the temple had a width-length proportion of four to nine, which is considered, even today, to be the most perfect proportion for appearance. The temple held a 40-foot-high statue of Athena by the sculptor Phidias, which was carved from wood and ivory, and covered with gold plates. Pausanias, a Greek traveler and writer of the 2nd century A.D., described this statue as follows:

● ● ● *On the middle of her helmet is placed a likeness of a sphinx . . . and on either side of the helmet are griffins in relief. . . . Athena stands erect with a tunic reaching to her feet, and on her breast, the head of Medusa is worked in ivory. She holds a statue of victory about 4 cubits [6 feet] high and in the other hand a spear; at her feet lies a shield and near the shield a serpent.*[5]

[5]*The Horizon Book of Ancient Greece* (New York: American Heritage Publishing Co., 1965), p. 214.

An artist's reconstruction of the 5th-century Athenian acropolis. The large building at the top of the hill is the Parthenon, which suffered great damage during an 18th-century battle.

Our only knowledge of this statue is from contemporary accounts, such as that of Pausanias, and from coins which depict it. During the 1st century A.D., it was carried off to Byzantium as a spoil of war and later destroyed by fire.

Phidias is also believed to have designed and supervised the many sculptures which adorned the exterior of the Parthenon. Above the two porticos were triangular gables or *pediments* containing sculptured scenes related to the cult of Athena. The eastern pediment depicted an array of gods witnessing the birth of Athena from the head of Zeus. On the western pediment, the rivalry between Athena and the sea-god Poseidon for possession of the city was shown. In addition to the pediment sculptures, there was a frieze, or band containing sculptures, just below the roof. The sculptures in the 525-foot-

A detail of the Parthenon frieze (west side) depicts two horsemen taking part in the Panathenaic Festival procession.

long frieze depicted a procession in the Panathenaic Festival, a celebration held every four years in honor of Athena.

The roof of the northern porch of the Erechtheum is supported by six caryatids, or maidens. Like the Parthenon, the Erechtheum was constructed of fine white marble.

The statues in the Parthenon's frieze and pediments were badly damaged over the centuries. Early in the 19th century, Lord Elgin, the British ambassador to Constantinople, obtained permission to remove many of these statues and to take them to the British Museum in London. The Elgin Marbles, as they are called, can still be seen at that museum.

The Erechtheum. The Erechtheum, which was built several decades after the Parthenon, is unusually interesting for two reasons: it was built on several levels to fit the terrain on the brow of the acropolis, and the columns which form the south portico are figures of *caryatids* (maidens) who appear to support the pediment on their heads.

SCULPTURE

The art form which has survived in greatest quantity from the Classical period of Greece is stone sculpture. Early stone statues, from the 7th century B.C., were very similar in appearance to the cult statues of ancient Egypt. The human figures were shown in a rigid frontal stance with hands clenched against the body and the left foot slightly forward. The fixed smiles and wig-like treatment of hair also resemble Egyptian techniques. Later statues were quite different from these models. They were free-standing, and the arms were separated from the body except at the wrists. Almost all of the earliest Greek statues represent either a *kouros* (young man) or a *koure*

(young woman). They may have been used as grave markers or as votive offerings to the gods.

After about 500 B.C., Greek sculpture became naturalistic, with human bodies standing in a relaxed position so that the weight seems to rest on one leg. The eyes of these statues seem to engage the viewer in direct gaze, and the earlier stylized smiles were changed to thoughtful expressions. The clothing is delicately draped to suggest the form of the body beneath. Throughout the 5th century B.C., sculptors strove to emphasize the divine qualities of man. Ironically, the statues of human beings, with their serene expressions and perfectly porportioned features, appear to be divine, while statues representing the gods often have more irregular, individualistic features.

The 5th Century B.C. The most important sculptors of the 5th century were Phidias, Polyclitus, and Myron. In addition to the statue of Athena and the other sculptures of the Parthenon, Phidias created a 60-foot statue of Zeus for a temple in Olympia.

Both Polyclitus and Myron were famous for their bronze figures of athletes. None of their original works survive, but several of them are known through Roman copies. Myron's "Discus Thrower" portrayed an athlete at the very moment when his body is poised to hurl a discus. It is said that his statue of a heifer was so realistic that when it was placed in a pasture, it deceived the cows who were grazing there.

The 4th Century B.C. The outstanding sculptors of the 4th century were Praxiteles, Scopas, and Lysippus. Two of Praxiteles' best known works were "Aphrodite of Cnidus" and "Hermes and Dionysus." The statue from Cnidus is known only through copies, but that of Hermes, now in a museum in Olympia, may be an original.

The style of Scopas was very different from that of Praxiteles. His figures were characterized by their vigor and intensity, in contrast to the grace and ease of Praxiteles'

Praxiteles' statue of Aphrodite created a great sensation in the Greek world when it was first unveiled. This is one of many Roman copies of the original.

images. In Scopas' work, staring eyes, dilated nostrils, and taut muscles were characteristic features.

Lysippus may have been the first sculptor to use casts of living models in his studio. His statues were free-standing so that they

Praxiteles may have created this statue of Hermes and Dionysius about 360 B.C. With his right arm, now lost, Hermes dangled some grapes in front of the infant Dionysius.

Lysippus was one of the most admired artists of his time. This sculpture shows an athlete scraping oil from his body with a tool known as a strigil.

The works of Scopas were known for their turbulence and emotion. This is a Roman copy of his portrait of Meleager, an angry young man who murdered his uncle and was in turn killed by his mother.

could be viewed from any angle. One of his works, of a young athlete scraping oil from his arm, is known to us through a copy. He also created idealistic portraits of Socrates and of Alexander the Great.

DRAMA

Greek drama had its origins in an annual religious festival in honor of Dionysus, the god of wine and immortality. In the earliest festivals, a chorus of men dressed as *satyrs*

The plays of Sophocles, Aeschylus, and Euripides were performed in theaters like this one throughout the Greek world. This is the theatre of the city of Ephesus in Ionia.

would sing *tragedoi* ("goat songs") as they danced about the altar. During the 6th century B.C., the tyrant Pisistratus enlarged the festival of Dionysus. Under his sponsorship, the festival lasted for three days, and four or five plays, written especially for the occasion, were presented each day. According to contemporary accounts, most of these plays were tragedies which centered upon ancient historical events or myths. None of these early works have survived to the present day.

Aeschylus, Sophocles, and Euripides, the great dramatists of the 5th century B.C., also chose ancient myths and legends as the basis for most of their dramas and tragedies. In fact, only one drama concerning a contemporary event has come down to us—namely, Aeschylus' play *The Persians* about the Persian Wars. But although these playwrights rarely dealt with topical themes directly, they often chose subjects which had clear parallels to contemporary events.

Like the philosophers of Ionia, the dramatists of 5th-century Athens believed that, in spite of the diversity and inconsistencies that could be seen in everyday life, there were universal laws of order. These moral laws were a mystery to mankind and could only be known after they had been violated. Thus, the action of the plays often centered upon a tragic hero who violated one of the hidden laws and, inevitably, had to suffer dire consequences—even if the transgression had been committed unknowingly or for a just cause. Edith Hamilton wrote that the dramatist Aeschylus, for instance:

● ● ● *knew life as only the greatest poets can know it; he perceived the mystery of suffering. Mankind he saw fast bound to*

The poet Aeschylus chose to be remembered, in his epitaph, for his early service at the battle of Marathon (see quote on page 116).

Aeschylus. Aeschylus, the "Father of Greek Tragedy," was born at Eleusis, in Attica, in 524 B.C. He fought in the battles of Marathon and Salamis during the Persian Wars, and died in Sicily in 456 B.C. He wrote more than 80 plays, but only 7 of them, including *The Persians*, have come down to us.

In his three plays known as the *Oresteian Trilogy*, Aeschylus addressed the conflict between tribal traditions of justice and the law of the Athenian state. The trilogy concerns the story of the legendary hero Agamemnon, who was murdered by his wife, Clytemnestra, when he returned home from the Trojan War. Aeschylus used the events and characters of this story to demonstrate how the early development of the Athenian polis contributed to justice and moral order.

In the play, Orestes, the son of Agamemnon, is encouraged by the god Apollo to avenge the murder of his father. This act was in accord with ancient tribal traditions, which dictated that a family must avenge the murder of one of its members. However, in kill-

calamity by the working of unknown powers committed to strange venture, companioned by disaster.[6]

The "unknown powers" responsible for mankind's tragedies were known as *Fate*, and were considered to be more powerful than any of the deities of the Greek pantheon. In the 5th-century dramas, the benevolent gods of Olympus often have the power to intervene in human affairs, but they, too, are subject to the laws of Fate.

Because the works of the Greek dramatists were concerned with Athenian traditions and values, performances were considered to be an important part of community life. Athenian citizens who could not afford the admission price were admitted as guests of the state.

[6]Hamilton, *The Greek Way*, p. 176.

This plate painting shows Clytemnestra killing the prophetess Cassandra, a scene from Aeschylus' Oresteian Trilogy.

A scene from Euripides' Hecuba: the soul of Achilles flies over a departing Greek ship, demanding that his death be avenged.

ing Clytemnestra, Orestes incurs the wrath of the Furies, the fierce female deities who enforce family law.

In the resolution of the play, the role of the emerging Athenian state becomes apparent. The goddess Athena convinces the Furies to put aside their anger and to abide by the decision of the court of Athens. Finally, even though the court's decision goes against them, the Furies are placated. They become known as the *Eumenides* ("The Kindly Ones"), and agree to uphold the authority of the state.

Sophocles. The second of the three great Greek tragedians was Sophocles (496-406 B.C.), who was born of noble parents and received the best education available. His friends included Pericles, Euripides (who will be considered next), and Herodotus. He served in public office on several occasions, and for 30 years received the first or second prize for the plays he wrote for the Festival of Dionysus. He wrote more than 100 plays, but only 7 are available to us today.

Sophocles believed that the inflexible moral laws of the universe made it impossible for a man to control his own destiny. But through the suffering which inevitably resulted from the imposition of these laws, man could gain wisdom and righteousness. His *Oedipus Rex*

tells the story of a man who unknowingly murdered his father and married his mother. The more he struggled against his fate, the more enmeshed he became. At last, he recognized what he had done and blinded himself in remorse. A few years after the play was written, Aristotle referred to *Oedipus Rex* in creating his definition of a "perfect tragedy":

● ● ● *A perfect tragedy should . . . imitate actions which excite pity and fear. . . . The change of fortunes presented must not be the spectacle of a virtuous man brought from prosperity to adversity, for this moves neither pity nor fear; it merely shocks us. Nor, again, that of a bad man passing from adversity to prosperity: for nothing can be more alien to the spirit of tragedy. . . . There remains, then, the character between these two extremes—that of a man who is not eminently good and just, yet whose misfortune is brought about not by vice or depravity, but by some error or frailty. He must be one who is highly renowned and prosperous, a personage like Oedipus.*[7]

Euripides. The third of the great tragedians was Euripides (484-406 B.C.), who also wrote approximately 100 plays, only 19 of which have survived. Euripides' plays usually concern passionate characters who commit rash actions which they later regret. In the plays, irrational passions are seen to be an essential part of humanity; they are an uncontrollable force which inevitably lead to tragedy.

Euripides' tragedies are thought to reflect the disillusionment and uncertainty that many Athenians felt during the years of the Peloponnesian War. In the *Trojan Women*, for instance, Euripides depicted a military action of the Trojan War. In the play, the Mycenaeans inflict terrible atrocities upon their defeated enemies at Troy, then are themselves destroyed by a shipwreck at sea.

---

[7]Aristotle, *Poetics* (trans. George Howe and Gustave Harrer), lines 25-43.

Euripides may have intended *The Trojan Women* as a warning to the Athenians concerning their heartless destruction of the city-state of Melos, an action that was carried out while Euripides was writing the play (416 B.C.). If so, his prophesy came true a short time later, for a large Athenian force then suffered a devastating defeat in Sicily.

In the play *Medea*, Euripides expressed great sympathy for the tragic, legendary heroine who had helped her husband, Jason, acquire the Golden Fleece and was then abandoned by him. As she struggled between her love for her children and her hatred for her faithless husband, she became distraught and murdered her sons. When Jason learned that Medea had killed the children, he sought revenge, but Medea appeared out of his reach above the palace roof, in a chariot drawn by dragons. This unusual scene allowed Euripides to end the play without pronouncing a judgment upon his heroine.

A terracotta mask worn by an actor in Athenian comedy. Actors also wore costumes that were padded to produce a grotesque effect.

In the staging of Euripides' play Medea, *the god and chariot of the final act were raised to the top of the set by a crane. This device for ending a play therefore came to be known as deus ex machina ("god from a machine"). For centuries to come, certain playwrights copied Euripides' strategy of introducing an extraneous character in the final scene of a play in order to resolve a complex situation.*

Euripides' plays won few prizes, but—perhaps because of their sensational content, and because the language was similar to everyday speech—they were immensely popular with audiences. His plays were staged more often than those of Aeschylus and Sophocles, and continued to be popular with later generations.

COMEDY

In contrast to the dramatists of the 5th century, the writers of comedies dealt almost exclusively with current events rather than with mythological themes. The greatest writer of comedies was Aristophanes (446-388 B.C.), who satirized well-known politicians, dramatists, and other public figures of Athens. Aristophanes was once impeached by the Assembly of Athens, but this experience did not temper his irreverent attitude.

Two of Aristophanes' favorite targets were Pericles and the demagogue Cleon, the politicians who promoted a warlike policy in the Assembly. He also satirized the endless litigation of court cases, and the beliefs and practices of the Sophists. He achieved comic effects through the use of grotesquely padded costumes, exaggerated facts, impossible situations, and coarse, but usually good natured humor. One of his most famous plays is *The Clouds*, in which he showed Socrates suspended in a basket in the heavens, dispensing his new philosophy.

159

PHILOSOPHY

The "new learning" that Aristophanes satirized in his comedies appeared in Athens during the last half of the 5th century. In Athens' democracy, a person had to be able to speak clearly and persuasively in order to achieve political power. Teachers who could offer such training gave exhibitions of their knowledge and skills, and offered to teach anyone willing to pay their fees. Young men from wealthy families enrolled in the classes of these *sophists* ("teachers of wisdom") to learn debating techniques and the art of *rhetoric* (public speaking).

The sophists were rather controversial figures because they demanded pay for their teachings, and this policy, as well as some of their teachings, conflicted with traditional concepts. In his comedy *The Clouds*, Aristophanes expressed the view that the sophists conveyed materialistic values to their students:

*But so you'll enter me amongst your
    scholars,
And tutor me like them to bilk my
    creditors,
Name your own price, and by the gods I
    swear
I'll pay you my last drachma.*[8]

Socrates. Socrates (469-399 B.C.) was one of a group of original thinkers who were wrongfully accused of being sophists. His method of thinking and teaching was actually quite different from that of the sophists: he did not claim to have answers, but instead asked questions of his students in order to explore their values and beliefs. Through his questions, he often forced his listeners to admit that their beliefs and opinions were not well-founded. The inscription "know thyself" in the temple of Apollo at Delphi was the theme of his teachings, for he believed that "the unexamined life is not

Socrates' teachings provided the foundation for Greek philosophy and inspired the schools of thought that came to be known as Scepticism, Stoicism, and Epicurianism.

worth living." He stressed that the conscience of an individual was a better guide to action than the laws of a government.

Socrates fulfilled his duties as an Athenian citizen according to his conscience and beliefs. He served as a soldier during a mil-

---

[8]Aristophanes, *The Clouds* (trans. Patric Dickinson), lines 248-51.

itary campaign in Thrace and later was remembered by his fellow soldiers for his heroism and his ability to withstand cold. In the Assembly, Socrates was known for his steadfast refusal to compromise. On one occasion, he became the leader of the government for a day when he was chosen by lot to serve as chairman of the Boule. The Assembly on that day was clamoring to impeach the ten *strategoi*, because the Athenian military forces had recently suffered a setback. Socrates, however, refused to present this business to the Assembly. Plato quoted his philosophy concerning his duty to himself and to the state as follows:

••• *Doing wrong, and disobeying the person who is better than myself, be it man or god, that I know is base and wicked. Therefore, never for the sake of evils which I know to be such, will I fear or flee from what for all I know may be good.*[9]

Socrates worked as an artisan and refused to take money from his students. Although he had many rich and powerful friends, he lived in poverty all his life, and was often criticized for his appearance and behavior. In 399 B.C., Socrates was impeached by the Assembly on charges of "corrupting the young" and "undermining religious beliefs." These charges may have had something to do with his association with Alcibiades, a former pupil who had disregarded his ethical teachings and had become a traitor to Athens.

After a trial, the Assembly voted to give Socrates the death penalty. Under Athenian law, he had the right to make a counterproposal suggesting a less severe penalty. Instead of proposing a true compromise, however, Socrates suggested that he be given a small fine. The Assembly then reconfirmed the death penalty. Socrates' friends urged him to flee the city, and offered to help him do so.

Socrates refused, however, and when the time came, he calmly took a potion of hemlock and continued to converse with his friends until the poison had acted.

Socrates left no writings, but after his death Plato made a record of several dialogs that Socrates had conducted with other citizens of Athens. These dialogs convey a vivid portrait of the personalities involved as well as of the great philosopher's teachings and method.

Plato. Plato (427-347 B.C.) was born of wealthy parents and received an excellent education. He originally intended to enter politics, but eventually became disenchanted with Athens' form of government: he described *democracy* as a tyranny of the common people. Around the time of Socrates' trial, Plato left Athens for a period of several years. In 388 B.C., he returned to Athens and established a school called the *Academy*, where he taught philosophy and science until his death at 81 years of age.

Plato taught that perfect truth, beauty, and wisdom existed only as ideas, and that every object was an imperfect reflection of the idea underlying it. For example, no one can draw a perfect circle freehand, but the idea of a perfect circle can be easily accepted.

His most important work was *The Republic*, in which he described an ideal state. The objective of such a state would be to ensure the welfare of all citizens, and to utilize the special talents and abilities of each class. The good of all could be achieved only when every citizen adhered to the four basic virtues of truth, wisdom, courage, and moderation. Each person could best attain these virtues by fulfilling the function in society for which he was best suited.

Plato decided that an ideal state could be established in a community of about 5000 people, with each citizen examined in infancy and placed in one of three categories: to serve as a worker producing the necessities of life; to be a soldier to guard the state; or to become a philosopher-king to rule the

---

[9]Plato, *Apology* (trans. George Howe and Gustave Harrer), lines 25-29.

state. To ensure that only the most capable would rule, he proposed that children who displayed virtue at an early age should be educated to govern. Insulated from all pleasures and luxuries, these future rulers would devote themselves to the study of philosophy so that, when they achieved enlightenment, the government of the state might be placed in their hands.

Plato was given an opportunity to put his theory into practice when the tyrant of Syracuse, Dionysius II, invited him to supervise the education of a group of children selected to be philosopher-kings. Unfortunately, the experiment failed. Later, Plato's educational theories were again tested—and achieved notable results—when his disciple Aristotle served as tutor to Alexander of Macedonia.

After Plato's death, his Academy continued in existence for almost 1000 years until the Byzantine emperor Justinian ordered that all pagan (non-Christian) schools of philosophy be closed.

Aristotle. Plato's best known pupil was Aristotle (384-322 B.C.). Aristotle was born in Macedonia, where his father was physician at the court of the Macedonian king, Philip II. At the age of 17, Aristotle enrolled at Plato's Academy in Athens, and he remained a disciple of Plato until Plato's death 20 years later. In 343 B.C., Aristotle accepted an offer to tutor the young prince of Macedonia, who later became known as Alexander the Great.

In 335 B.C. Aristotle returned to Athens to establish his own school, the Lyceum. Because he usually strolled along with his students as he taught, his school became known as the *peripatetic* ("walking") school.

While Aristotle was interested in logic, ethics, rhetoric, and political science—the conventional topics of philosophy—he was primarily interested in what we call biology. He came to believe that all natural phenomena are awesome, and even suggested that a spider is as divine as a star. He also taught that all organisms evolved from simpler to more complex forms. He collected over 500 specimens of flora and fauna, noted distinctions between them, classified them according to these distinctions, and arrived at general conclusions about what he observed. His inductive system of investigation is still the basis of the modern science of biology.

Aristotle agreed with his teacher, Plato, that the city-state was the best setting for a good life, and that an ideal state would help its citizens achieve a good life rather than mere existence. To better understand the nature of government, he wrote a work entitled *Politics* in which he analyzed the constitutions of 158 places, including Athens. Like Plato, he disapproved of democracy as a form of government, and advocated rule by philosopher-kings. He believed that justice would prevail only if all people practiced moderation so that no one group would have either too much or too little.

Aristotle's death marked the end of the great age of Greek philosophy, but his ideas have influenced Western thought ever since. In medieval Europe, his theories were so revered that scholars would ignore their personal observations if these seemed to contradict what Aristotle had written. The modern world is indebted to him for the scientific method he introduced, for his emphasis on balance between liberty and authority, for his insistence on the value of public education, and for the concept that government should help to provide a good life for all citizens.

ECONOMY AND SOCIAL STRUCTURE

Most areas of Greece were dependent upon foreign supplies of grain and other foods. In Boeotia and in the Peloponnesus, the soil was fertile enough to produce sufficient food for the local populations, but in the rest of Greece, and especially in the large urban areas, people depended upon imported foods. In fact, the very existence of Athens depended upon her ability to secure grain from the Black Sea area.

Most of the land of Attica was planted in orchards and vineyards. The olive oil and wine produced there were traded for grain and dried fish from the Black Sea area, timber and hides from Thrace, dates from Phoenicia, papyrus from Egypt, wool from Asia Minor, tin from Britain, and metals from Cyprus and Thrace.

Many citizens considered agriculture to be the most desirable way of life, but the aristocrats who owned the land often were more interested in manufacturing and commerce. The factories and shops owned by these wealthy investors were operated by slaves, poor free men, and resident aliens. The factories were very small, each one employing only a few people. The manufacturing operations were divided among several workers. For instance, in a pottery factory, one person prepared the clay, another molded vases, another prepared handles, and still another applied decorations. Such factories were usually located to the rear of the small shops in which the products were sold.

Slaves and Resident Aliens. About one-third of the population of Athens consisted of slaves who were acquired in raids or as prisoners of war. Many worked as domestic servants and as artisans, teachers, doctors, or scribes. Those slaves who received wages for their efforts were permitted to keep a portion of their earnings and, in time, could purchase their freedom. After they acquired their freedom, however, they had the status of aliens and did not enjoy the full rights of Athenian citizens.

Pericles encouraged foreigners to live and work in Athens, but citizenship in the polis was limited to Athenian men whose parents were Athenians. Resident aliens could not own land, but were required to pay taxes and to perform military service. Citizenship in Athens, as in most Greek city-states, was highly valued, and was granted to aliens only for meritorious service to the state.

Taxation. The Athenians early developed a unique form of taxation by which wealthy citizens were expected to subsidize public

Athenian pottery factories were usually located behind the shops that sold their wares. Vase painters seldom signed their work, but scholars have developed descriptive names to identify several individuals.

works through payments called *liturgies*. Although these *liturgies* were financial burdens, wealthy citizens competed with each other to see who could produce the best-trained chorus for a play or the best-equipped warship.

Expenditures by the state included wages for soldiers and sailors, payment to citizens for service on the Boule and in the courts, and expenses related to religious festivals. During the period of Athens' Empire, Athenian citizens paid few taxes to cover these expenditures, for tribute payments from the allies had created a booming economy. After the Peloponnesian War, a property tax was levied to compensate for the loss of tribute payments.

Family Life. In Athenian society, wealthy men had complete freedom and found pleasure in endless discussions of politics, exercise at the gymnasia, in drinking bouts, and in athletic contests. Men met at the agora to discuss public issues, to conduct business, and to listen to orators. Three sides of the agora were lined by colonnades to provide convenient places for such meetings.

Women, by contrast, were subject to their fathers before marriage, and to their husbands after marriage. Women of the upper classes were secluded in their homes and never participated in the entertainment of their husbands' guests. They left their homes only to attend a tragic drama, a funeral, or a wedding. They were excluded from all political rights. Outside their homes, men usually enjoyed the companionship of unmarried women who were knowledgeable about music, poetry, and dancing. Pericles, in his Funeral Oration, summed up the attitude of Athenian men to women as follows:

● ● ● *Great will be your glory in not falling short of your natural character; and greatest will be hers who is least talked of among men whether for good or for bad.*[10]

Some scholars believe that the importance of female characters in Greek dramas may indicate that women actually enjoyed more freedom and esteem than other writings seem to indicate.

Education. The purpose of education in ancient Athens was to produce citizens capable of serving the state. While there was no system of public education, most boys learned the fundamentals of literary knowledge. Poor boys were apprenticed to craftsmen, while the sons of wealthy citizens were enrolled in private schools. When a wealthy boy was eight years old, a *pedagogos* (slave) would accompany him to school and tutor him at home. Such boys studied reading, writing, and arithmetic, and learned to play a seven-string lyre. They practiced gymnastics, because the Greeks believed that physical fitness was as important as mental stimulation. They were required to memorize selections from the *Iliad* and the *Odyssey* of Homer, and the poems of Hesiod. At 18 years of age, each young man became eligible to vote, and enrolled in his *deme*. He took the oath of citizenship, vowing that:

● ● ● *I will not disgrace the sacred arms, nor will I desert my comrade in the ranks. I, alone or with many others, will defend the sacred and holy places. My fatherland I will transmit in no worse state but greater and better than I found it. I will obey those in authority, and I will observe wholeheartedly the laws now in force and whatever others the people may pass. And if anyone seeks to annul the laws or refuses to obey them, I will not heed him; but, alone or with many others, I will defend them. And I will honor the religion of my fathers.*[11]

Each young man was then required to complete two years of military service, and afterward continued his education by informal methods. Girls were rarely educated in

---

[10]Thucydides II, 6, 45.

[11]"The Ephebic Oath" in *Greek Literature in Translation*, trans. George Howe and Gustave Harrer (New York & London: Harper & Row, 1924), p. 586.

The agora of Athens was lined with colonnades where men could meet to discuss private business and public issues. The plan of the agora with its large open square was later copied by the Romans in the design of their Forum.

schools, but were taught by their mothers to manage a household and care for children.

Houses. The citizens of Athens were far more concerned about beautifying their city with impressive public buildings than about adorning their own homes. Their houses were constructed of sun-dried bricks and covered with stucco. They were usually two stories high with flat, tiled roofs. The side of the house facing the street was blank except for the door. A passageway led from the door to a small courtyard, which was surrounded by several rooms. There were openings in the interior walls to allow passage and to admit light, but no doors or windows as we know them. A limited amount of light was provided by oil-burning lamps, and water was obtained from the nearest public well. The houses were furnished with chests, couches, chairs, and tables, and were heated with portable braziers. Because the climate was mild, people spent most of their free time outdoors, in the public areas of the city.

THE PELOPON-NESIAN WAR The glory of Athens came to an end during the Peloponnesian War, which began in 431 and ended in 404 B.C. Due to the economic and psychological strains of the war, the moral and religious beliefs of the Classical Greeks were undermined, and social cohesiveness was lost. By the end of the war, all of the participants were so weakened that they became prey to a series of foreign invaders.

Thucydides. Our most important source of information for the events of the Peloponnesian War is the history written by Thucydides, an Athenian citizen who lived during this period and began his history of Greece at the point where Herodotus had left off.[12] In the first chapter of his book, Thucydides stated his belief that the Peloponnesian War

[12]Herodotus' history concluded with an account of the final battles against the Persians. His work was published in 430 B.C.

165

"would be a great war, and more worthy of relation than any that had preceded it."[13] To do honor to his subject, Thucydides took great care to evaluate the reliability of his sources and to let his readers know which statements were well founded and which could not be substantiated. He is known as the first *critical* historian.

Thucydides served as *strategos* in the battle of Amphipolis in 424 B.C. Due to the Athenians' defeat in that campaign, he was banished from Athens for a period of 20 years. He did not appeal this unjust sentence, but instead took the opportunity to travel and to gather information about the Peloponnesians' point of view in the struggle.

According to Thucydides' account, there were a number of incidents in the prewar years which caused tensions between the Peloponnesian League, led by Sparta, and the Delian League. Although each party honored the terms of a nonaggression treaty signed in 461 B.C., Athens committed a number of actions that violated the spirit of the agreement. In 435 B.C., Athens agreed to send military aid to the island of Corcyra, which was at war with Corinth. Since Corcyra did not belong to either the Peloponnesian League or the Delian League, this action did not violate the terms of the treaty. Nevertheless, the Corinthians deeply resented Athens' intervention in the war. At a meeting of the Peloponnesian League in 432 B.C., the Corinthians persuaded Sparta to prepare for a war against Athens.

Thucydides believed that although the immediate cause of the Peloponnesian War was the action of Corinth, the underlying cause was Sparta's fear of the growing power of Athens:

• • • *The real cause I consider to be the one which was formally most kept out of sight. The growth of the power of Athens, and the*

alarm which this inspired in Lacedaemon, made war inevitable. Still it is well to give the grounds alleged by either side, which led to the dissolution of the treaty and the breaking out of the war.[14]

In 431 B.C., the Spartans sent envoys to Athens with three separate ultimatums demanding that Athens avoid any interference in the affairs of the Peloponnesus. In the Assembly of Athens, Pericles argued that to give in to the Spartans' demands would only betray weakness and invite still more demands. He advised against any concessions, and urged his countrymen to prepare for war. He pointed out that the Spartans did not have any reserve of money with which to wage a war and did not have an experienced navy. Although the Spartan army was three times as strong as that of the Athenians, Pericles argued that internal divisions among the members of the Peloponnesian League would make their forces vulnerable.

The Peloponnesian War broke out in 431, when Spartan armies invaded Attica and plundered the countryside. Because Pericles thought it best to avoid a pitched battle, the Athenians gathered within the walls of the city while their navy engaged the enemy along the Peloponnesian coast.

During the second year of the war, in 430, a terrible plague swept over Athens, and one-third of the people within the walls died. Thucydides described the symptoms of the disease as follows:

• • • *There was no ostensible cause; but people in good health were all of a sudden attacked by violent heats in the head, and redness and inflammation in the eyes, the inward parts, such as the throat or tongue, becoming bloody and emitting an unnatural and fetid breath. These symptoms were followed by sneezing and hoarseness, after which the pain soon reached the chest, and produced a hard cough. When it fixed in the*

---

[13]Thucydides I, 1, 1.

[14]Ibid., I, 1, 24.

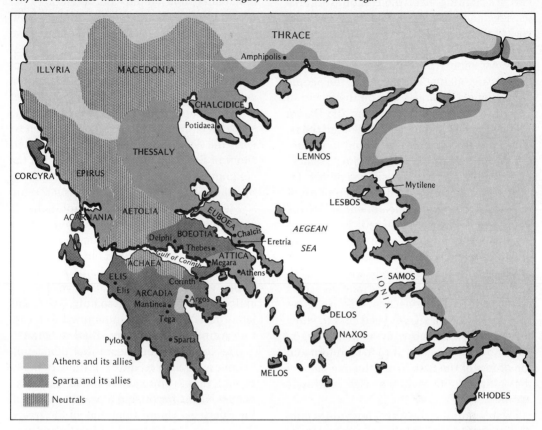

Athens and its allies	
Sparta and its allies	
Neutrals	

stomach, it upset it; and discharges of bile of every kind named by physicians ensued, accompanied by very great distress.[15]

Pericles died during the plague epidemic. The leadership of Athens then fell to Cleon, a demagogue[16] whose policies were much more belligerent and uncompromising than those of Pericles.

Cleon. According to Aristophanes, Cleon had a voice "like a mountain torrent," and had been a tanner before he entered public life. Aristophanes often invented occupations and parentages for the targets of his satire, but it is known from other sources that Cleon was a very persuasive speaker and that he had made his fortune in the leather business. In his play *Knights*, written during the Peloponnesian War, Aristophanes included this caricature of Cleon:

*Now at the beginning of last month,
He bought a new slave, a tanner,
Called Cle —, I mean Paphlageon —
The filthiest, most blatant, lowest-down
Liar of all time.*[17]

---

[15]Ibid., II, 7, 49.

[16]The term *demagogue* in ancient Greece denoted a politician who rose to power as a leader of the common people. A demagogue often achieved his ends by playing upon the emotions of a crowd.

---

[17]Aristophanes, *Knights* (trans. Patric Dickinson), lines 43-45.

As early as 431 B.C., Cleon had criticized Pericles, arguing that Athens should enforce its hegemony over its allies with more severity than Pericles recommended. After Pericles died, in 429 B.C., there was no speaker in the Assembly who could effectively counter Cleon's arguments. The next year, the people of Mytilene, the largest city on the island of Lesbos, voted to withdraw from the Delian League. The Athenian fleet blockaded the island until the people were forced to surrender. Cleon then prevailed upon the Assembly to order the harshest possible sentence for Athens' former ally: all of the men of Mytilene were to be put to death, and all of the women and children enslaved. The Assembly dispatched a ship to Mytilene to carry out the sentence. The next day, the people of Athens repented the harsh and indiscriminate measure they had passed, and met again to reconsider their decision. Cleon argued that it would be a sign of weakness to show pity, but the Assembly, by a small margin, voted to send a second ship to countermand the orders of the first. Thus, the massacre of the citizens of Mytilene was narrowly avoided.

At this point in the war, Thucydides concluded that the spirit that had made Athens the foremost city among the Greeks had begun to deteriorate:

● ● ● *Reckless audacity came to be considered the courage of a loyal ally; prudent hesitation, specious cowardice; moderation was held to be a cloak for unmanliness; ability to see all sides of a question inaptness to act on any. Frantic violence became the attribute of manliness; cautious plotting, a justifiable means of self-defence. The advocate of extreme measures was always trustworthy; his opponent a man to be suspected. To succeed in a plot was to have a shrewd head, to divine a plot still shrewder.*[18]

---

[18]Thucydides III, 5, 82.

At the outset of the war, Pericles had recommended that Athens not attempt to expand its empire while the war lasted. Cleon, however, wished to pursue a more aggressive policy. In 425 B.C., Cleon persuaded the Assembly to open a new front in the Peloponnesus, and he was elected general for a campaign to seize the city of Pylos. Together with the capable general Demosthenes, he succeeded in capturing the city. The next year, the Athenians tried to capture the territory of Boeotia, where they hoped that the common people would join them against the Spartans. This time they were unsuccessful.

Meanwhile, the city of Amphipolis in Chalcidice rebelled against Athenian rule. Thucydides led an army to the area in order to put down the rebellion, but the Spartans came to the aid of Amphipolis. The Athenian troops were defeated, and Thucydides was exiled by the Athenian assembly. Two years later, in 422 B.C., Cleon attempted to recapture Amphipolis and was killed in battle.

The loss of Cleon meant that other politicians were able to develop their policies. In 422 B.C., a popular Athenian politician named Nicias negotiated a peace treaty with the Spartans. Under the terms of the treaty, Pylos was to be returned to Sparta, and Amphipolis was to be returned to Athens. The Peace of Nicias, as the cessation of war came to be known, was a fragile truce and was soon threatened by the rise of aggressive pro-war politicians in both Sparta and Athens.

Alcibiades. Alcibiades belonged to an ancient Athenian noble family and also had family ties to one of the royal families of Sparta. He was known for his intellectual brilliance, personal charm, and unprincipled character. In the *Symposium*, Alcibiades gives this evaluation of his own character and of his relationship with Socrates, his long time friend and teacher:

● ● ● *Socrates is the only man in the world that can make me feel ashamed. Because there's no getting away from it, I know I ought to do the things he tells me to, and yet the moment I'm out of his sight I don't care what I do to keep in with the mob. So I dash off like a runaway slave, and keep out of his way as long as I can, and then next time I meet him I remember all that I had to admit the time before, and naturally I feel ashamed.*[19]

Due to his family connections and political gifts, Alcibiades became a prominent politician during the war. In the Assembly, he advocated that Athens ignore the treaty with Sparta and develop a strategy to overthrow the power of Sparta. In 420 B.C., Alcibiades persuaded Argos, Elis, Mantinea, and Tega, four cities of the Peloponnesus, to form an alliance with Athens.

In 418 B.C., the Spartans tested the alliance that Alcibiades had engineered by attacking Mantinea. They soundly defeated the allies, who did not receive sufficient support from Athens. The allies were bitter about the lack of support, and Sparta was bitter about the intrigue.

Having been defeated in their strategy to divide the Peloponnesus, the Athenians turned to the city-states of the Aegean. In 416, they demanded that the island of Melos, which had been neutral in the war, pay tribute to Athens. The people of Melos refused, and an Athenian force was sent to subdue the island. When they had captured Melos, the Athenians executed all men who were old enough to fight and enslaved the women and children. Thus, the policy that Cleon had advocated and that the Assembly had rejected for Mytilene in 427 was carried out against the people of Melos 11 years later.

In 415 B.C., the people of Segesta, in Sicily, appealed to Athens for protection against Selinus, another colony in Sicily. Alcibiades saw this appeal as an opportunity to achieve a great military triumph and to add the island of Sicily to Athens' empire. The Assembly of Athens agreed to this campaign, and three generals were appointed to lead the Athenian forces: Alcibiades himself; Lamachus, a competent military man with little political influence; and Nicias, who was opposed to the plan from the beginning. A force which represented a substantial part of Athens' military capability was gathered. It included 140 ships, 5100 hoplites, and about 130 archers, slingers, and lightly armed troops.

Shortly before the force was to leave Athens, the Athenians discovered that the statues of Hermes that guarded temples and homes throughout the city had been defaced. Since this was regarded as a bad omen, there was a thorough investigation. The culprits could not be identified, but several citizens remembered that Alcibiades had, in the past, parodied sacred rituals. His opponents demanded that charges be brought against him, but the Athenian force left before the Assembly had acted.

Several days after the Athenian force had sailed, the Assembly formally brought charges against Alcibiades, and a ship was dispatched to bring him back to Athens. Alcibiades, realizing that he had little chance to prove his innocence in a trial, escaped his escort and fled to Sparta. There, he provided the Spartan kings with valuable information and advice. He told them how they could defeat the Athenian forces in Sicily, and advised them to place a garrison in northern Attica to blockade the city of Athens.

In Sicily, the arrest of Alcibiades was a severe blow to the morale of the Athenian force, and was later blamed for the disaster that occurred there. The Athenians began to besiege the city of Syracuse, but soon began to suffer heavy losses as Spartan and Corinthian forces came to the aid of the Syracusans. Lamachus was killed in battle, and Nicias sent to Athens for reinforcements. The reinforcements arrived the next spring, led by the general Demosthenes. After sizing up the situation, Demosthenes saw that the Ath-

---

[19]Plato, *Symposium* (trans. Michael Joyce), 216.

enians were in a hopeless situation and advised that they withdraw. However, an eclipse of the moon convinced Nicias that the Athenian troops should stay and engage the enemy. During the following week, the Spartans and Syracusans blockaded the harbor and bottled up the Athenian fleet. In attempting to break through the blockade, the Athenians lost their entire fleet. The roads leading inland were also blocked to them. Thucydides described the final hours of the Athenian forces as they struggled to march inland toward their allies:

• • • [They fancied] that they should breathe more freely if once across the river, and driven on also by their exhaustion and craving for water. Once there they rushed in, and all order was at an end, each man wanting to cross first, and the attacks of the enemy making it difficult to cross at all; forced to huddle together, they fell against and trod down one another, some dying immediately upon the javelins, others getting entangled together and stumbling over the articles of baggage, without being able to rise again. Meanwhile the opposite bank, which was steep, was lined by the Syracusans, who showered missiles down upon the Athenians, most of them drinking greedily and heaped together in disorder in the hollow bed of the river. The Peloponnesians also came down and butchered them, especially those in the water, which was thus immediately spoiled, but which they went on drinking just the same, mud and all, bloody as it was, most even fighting to have it.[20]

Most of the Athenian troops, including Nicias and Demosthenes, perished.

The failure of the Sicilian expedition left Athens with many severe problems: most of its fleet had been lost, the treasury was depleted, its prestige among the Greek city-states was shattered, and the remaining subject allies were in revolt. Because the Spartans had taken Alcibiades' advice to place a garrison in Attica, Athenian farmers could not cultivate their lands, and the silver mines could not be operated.

After their victory over the Athenian navy in Sicily, the Spartans commandeered additional ships from their allies, and soon gained control of the western Mediterranean and of the Hellespont. Nevertheless, the Spartans did not have enough resources to destroy the remaining Athenian fleet, and they therefore approached the Persians for financial help. Meanwhile, Alcibiades had been forced to leave Sparta after it was reported that he had made improper advances to the wife of a Spartan king. He fled to Asia Minor, and attached himself to Tisaphernes, the Persian satrap at Sardis, who agreed to protect him from his enemies. Plutarch described how Alcibiades ingratiated himself with the Persian:

• • • This barbarian, not being himself sincere, but a lover of guile and wickedness, admired his address and wonderful subtlety. And, indeed, the charm of daily intercourse with him was more than any character could resist. . . . Even those who feared and envied him could not but take delight, and have a sort of kindness for him, when they saw him and were in his company.[21]

Since both the Spartans and the Persians were in favor of oligarchic governments, it appeared that the Persians would give aid to the Spartans. But Alcibiades was also negotiating with the Persians, on behalf of Athens, and finally won a promise of aid. Thus, through his influence with the Persians, Alcibiades succeeded in regaining a role in Athenian politics. Although he was still in exile in Asia Minor, he was then given command of an Athenian fleet. He proceeded to win several important victories for Athens, and finally destroyed the Spartan fleet in the Hellespont. The Athenians thus recovered control over this important area, and were

---

[20]Thucydides VII, 23, 84.

[21]Plutarch, *Lives*, Modern Library ed., p. 250.

again able to import grain from the Black Sea region.

In 407 B.C., Alcibiades decided that it was safe to return to Athens, for his naval victories had won him many new supporters, and the charges against him had been dropped. Plutarch described his homecoming as follows:

• • • *As soon as he was landed, the multitude who came out to meet him scarcely seemed so much as to see any of the other captains, but came in throngs about Alcibiades, and saluted him with loud acclamations. . . . They made reflections, that they could not have so unfortunately miscarried in Sicily, or been defeated in any of their other expectations, if they had left the management of their affairs . . . to Alcibiades.*[22]

Alcibiades was elected supreme commander of all the Athenian forces, but within a few months he lost several ships during a minor skirmish with the Spartans. The Assembly then voted to dismiss him from his command, and he fled again to Asia Minor.

In 405 B.C., the Spartan navy made a surprise attack on a large fleet of Athenian ships anchored in the Hellespont. As Alcibiades watched from a castle overlooking the Hellespont, the Athenian ships were destroyed. Because Athens' trade route to the Black Sea was now closed by the Spartans, it was evident that Athens would have to surrender eventually. All of its allies, except for the island of Samos, capitulated.

During the following year, the Athenians were starved into submission. By the terms of the peace treaty negotiated with Sparta in 404 B.C., Athens became a member of the Peloponnesian League, relinquishing its empire and most of its navy; the walls defending the city were torn down; and a government of 30 oligarchs was instituted. Many of the democrats of Athens took refuge in Boeotia.

---

[22]Ibid., p. 257.

THE GREEK CITY-STATES: 404-323 B.C.

To the bitter surprise of everyone, the end of the 27-year Peloponnesian War did not bring peace to the Greek city-states; instead, the 4th century B.C. was marked by constant warfare between them. Sparta did not have enough resources or capable leaders to maintain its empire without Persian support. Athens and Thebes each managed to create short-lived empires, but were unable to achieve unity among the city-states for a sustained period. Finally, the growing empire of Macedonia put an end to Greek independence.

In Athens, the oligarchy that had been instituted by the Spartans soon became a reign of terror, as the 30 oligarchs removed the laws that had been displayed in the agora and murdered more than a thousand of their political opponents. The democrats of Athens secretly negotiated with Thebes for aid. With the help of the Thebans, they were able to overthrow the oligarchy only eight months after it had been imposed, in 404 B.C. Meanwhile, the Spartans installed oligarchies in most of the Aegean city-states, and tried to create enthusiasm for their rule by organizing an expedition against the Persians. But in 395 B.C., while the Spartans were fighting the Persian armies in Asia Minor, the city-states of Athens, Thebes, Corinth, and Argos banded together and began to threaten Sparta's hegemony in the Peloponnesus. Faced with this threat, the Spartans again turned to the Persians for aid. In 386 B.C., a treaty known as the "King's Peace" was finally concluded. By the terms of the peace, the Persian king claimed the Greek city-states of Ionia for his own empire and pledged to support Sparta's hegemony over mainland Greece.

The peace established by the Persians was soon threatened by capable leaders in Thebes and Athens, who were determined to overthrow Spartan hegemony in Greece. In Thebes, the leaders Pelopidas and Epaminondas quietly worked for eight years to create an alliance of Boeotian city-states and to

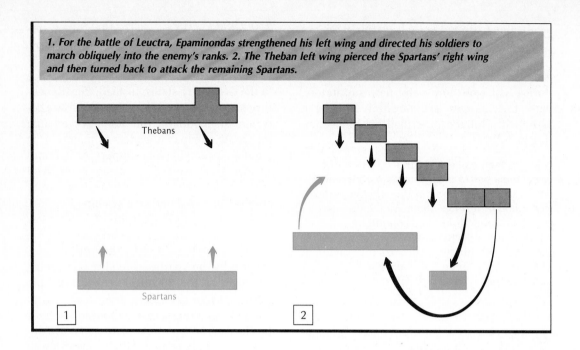

1. For the battle of Leuctra, Epaminondas strengthened his left wing and directed his soldiers to march obliquely into the enemy's ranks. 2. The Theban left wing pierced the Spartans' right wing and then turned back to attack the remaining Spartans.

modernize the Theban army. In 371 B.C., a Spartan army of 10,000 hoplites invaded Boeotia and was surprised by the Thebans at Leuctra. In defeating the Spartans, the Theban army, under the leadership of Epaminondas, used a new tactic called the "oblique phalanx" in which soldiers penetrated the enemy's ranks at an angle. With the victory at Leuctra, Thebes was recognized as the most powerful city-state in Greece. The Athenians also benefited, as city-states from the Peloponnesian League rushed to join the new Athenian Confederation. Under the leadership of Iphicrates, the Athenian army and navy were strengthened and began to assert Athens' influence throughout the Aegean.

The Theban army invaded the Peloponnesus and liberated the territory of Messenia, formerly subject to Sparta, in 369 B.C. The Thebans then challenged the Athenian naval power in the Aegean, and forced Thessaly and Macedonia to ally themselves with Thebes. Athens, however, was unwilling to submit to the domination of Thebes, and organized a new coalition of city-states to oppose the Thebans. In 362 B.C. the Theban army led by Epaminondas met the combined armies of Athens, Sparta, and northern Arcadia at Mantinea in the Peloponnesus. Just as it seemed that the Theban army was about to win the battle, Epaminondas was killed and the Thebans withdrew.

As he lay dying, Epaminondas urged the Thebans to make peace with their fellow Greeks. A treaty was concluded later and was effective for several years, but only because the city-states were too exhausted to fight another prolonged war. Athens continued its attempts to build and maintain an empire through force, and the Thebans engaged in various plots to undermine Athens' plans. Between 354 and 338 B.C., Philip II, king of Macedonia, took advantage of the chronic quarrels among the city-states to advance his own plans (Chapter 8). In 338, the Athenians and Thebans finally united to oppose him, but Philip defeated the Greek army at Chaeronea, and realized his ambition to impose Macedonian rule upon all of Greece.

SUMMARY

After its military successes in the Persian Wars, Athens became the center of influence in Greece. Under Pericles' leadership, the Athenians' achievements in art and architecture, philosophy, and government made Athens the "school of Hellas," and inspired many important developments in both Western and Eastern cultures.

Athens was not able to maintain its hegemony in the Greek world for a sustained period, however. Conflicts between Athens and Sparta led to the outbreak of the Peloponnesian War, which so weakened all of the Greek city-states that Philip of Macedonia was able to impose his rule over the area in 338 B.C.

QUESTIONS

1 What were the most important contributions of the early Greek scientists? Why did the Greeks consider science and philosophy to be one and the same discipline?

2 Choose one structure, artifact, or literary work and explain how it symbolizes the Athenians' concept of mankind in the 5th century.

3 Summarize briefly the plots of Aeschylus' Oresteia, Sophocles' Oedipus the King, and Euripides' Medea. Give reasons for the apparent timelessness of these plays.

4 Compare Herodotus and Thucydides in terms of their philosophies about history and their historiography. Why is Herodotus called the "father of history" and Thucydides the "first scientific historian"?

5 Describe the similarities and differences between a demagogue and a tyrant in ancient Athens. How did each one achieve and retain political power?

6 Read a sample of Socrates' dialog in the Phaedo, The Republic, Book 1, or another of Plato's works. Why do you think that Socrates had—in Alcibiades' words—an "extraordinary effect" upon his listeners?

BIBLIOGRAPHY

Which books might discuss the Spartans' foreign policies?

HAMILTON, CHARLES D. *Sparta's Bitter Victories: Politics and Diplomacy in the Corinthian War.* Ithaca: Cornell University Press, 1978. *Covers the period of Spartan supremacy from the end of the Peloponnesian War in 404 B.C. to the King's Peace of 386; analyzes the political situation in each city-state and the impact of the war upon their economies and social structures.*

H. D. F. KITTO. *The Greeks,* revised ed. New York: Penguin Books, 1957. *A comprehensive, readable discourse on the ancient Greeks; their political systems, ways of life, and unique contributions to Western civilization.*

YONAH, MICHAEL AVI and ISRAEL SHATZMAN. *Illustrated Encyclopedia of the Classical World.* New York: Harper & Row, 1975. *A concise and reliable guide to every aspect of Greek and Roman life and thought; subjects include classical terms, institutions, literature, religion, and society. Beautifully illustrated.*

● There are three Alexanders; the legendary Alexander, the historical Alexander, and the real Alexander. The first was born in men's minds soon after the death of the last, and he still lives in the East as Iskander. He has been many things: a saint and a devil, a defender of civilization and a barbarian, a perfect knight and a worthless debauchee. The historical Alexander is dead, but he is frequently revived in the pages of histories and biographies that fashion him in the image that each particular age admires; in one age he may be "greater than Napoleon," and in another he may be the man who first dreamed of "one world." The real Alexander died in Babylon about the thirteenth of June, 323 B.C. We know little of what he was like. The real Alexander is gone forever.

TOM B. JONES

Alexander and the Hellenistic Era

The failure of the Greek city-states to create a unified nation led to the conquest of Greece by Philip of Macedonia in 338 B.C.. But Philip was assassinated two years later, just as he was about to realize his plan to lead a united Greek-Macedonian army into Persia. He was succeeded by his son, Alexander (356-323 B.C.), who, during his brief reign, established a kingdom which stretched from the Adriatic Sea to the Indus River.

Alexander's death in 323 B.C. ushered in the Hellenistic era. Greek ideas were spread throughout the ancient world and the Greeks, in turn, were affected by their contacts with Asia. Many new cities were established, and for more than a century, the Greeks enjoyed a period of cultural unity and of economic expansion and prosperity. After 200 B.C., however, the Hellenistic influence declined because of the expansion of the Roman Empire in the West and of the Parthian Empire in the East.

MACEDONIA Macedonia (also called Macedon) was a mountainous country extending from Thrace (present northeast Greece and European Turkey) on the east to Illyria on the west. The Greek states of Thessaly and Epirus bordered on the south. The Macedonians were known as rough, hardy peasants, accustomed to constant warfare with their Illyrian and Thracian neighbors. Their form of government was similar to that of the ancient Mycenaeans: a king was elected from a select group of noble families, and was advised by an assembly of weapon-bearing men who represented the various tribal factions in the mountains and countryside. Although the Macedonians were of the same ancestry as the Greeks, they spoke the Greek language with a dialect not easily understood by other Greek peoples, and were thus regarded as barbarians.

During the Peloponnesian War, the Greeks had considered Macedonia to be an important ally because of its valuable resources and strategic location. Although the countryside was poor, the king's forests contained valuable shipbuilding timber. The area was also on the overland route used to transport grain to Greek cities from the Black Sea region. The Macedonians had not shown a partiality for either Athens or Sparta during the war, and had supported both cities at different times. By the end of the 5th century, however, the Macedonian kings began to take a real interest in Greek affairs. Archelaus, who ruled from 413 to 399 B.C., created a new capital city at Pella and invited some of the leading artists of Athens, including Euripides, to live and work there.

PHILIP

Under the leadership of Philip, who ruled Macedonia from 359 to 336 B.C., the process of Hellenization was greatly expanded. And, at the same time that Greek culture was developed and emulated, Philip encouraged his countrymen to respect their own traditions and to unite under his leadership to accomplish certain goals. Under his influence, the Macedonians came to think of themselves as citizens of a nation rather than of the particular localities in which they lived. For this reason, Macedonia is considered to have been the first nation established in Europe.

As a teenager, Philip had spent three years as a hostage of the Thebans. During his stay in Thebes, he gained an appreciation of Greek culture, learned many valuable lessons in military tactics, and, most importantly, gained an understanding of the weaknesses of the Greeks. It was probably during this time that he developed the ambitions that he later tried to fulfill as king of Macedonia: to raise the cultural level of his people; to unite the Greek city-states under his rule; and to lead a united Macedonian-Greek army against the mighty Persian Empire.

In 359, at the age of 23, Philip was appointed by the Macedonian army council to serve as regent for his young nephew. Philip immediately embarked on a program to Hellenize his country and to develop a professional army. He built urban centers modeled after Greek cities, and encouraged rural Macedonians to settle in them. He improved the road system, and began to train Macedonian peasants to fight in regiments.

In 356 B.C., Philip's wife, Olympias, gave birth to a son, Alexander. Soon afterwards, Philip declared himself king. He then invaded Thrace and seized an important gold mine there. With an assured income of 1000 talents a year from the mine, he was able to recruit and train a large army, including two cavalry units. One of these units, called the "King's Companions," was composed of 2000 noblemen trained to charge at high speed into enemy ranks. The other, more lightly armed, was trained to pursue fleeing enemy forces. Infantrymen were equipped with spears 14 feet long, and were trained to fight in an improved version of the phalanx system developed by the Thebans. Philip also built a navy, and developed siege machinery, such as movable towers and torsion catapults, for use in attacking fortified towns.

During his first year as king, Philip subdued Thessaly, and seized the city of Amphipolis in order to gain access to the Aegean Sea. His early achievements in mobilizing his countrymen and providing them with the benefits of an advanced civilization were later summarized by his son, Alexander, when he addressed a group of mutinous soldiers in 324 B.C.

● ● ● *Philip took you over when you were helpless vagabonds, mostly clothed in skins, feeding a few animals on the mountains and engaged in their defence in unsuccessful fighting with the Illyrians, Triballians and the neighboring Thracians. He gave you cloaks to wear instead of skins, he brought you down from the mountains to the plains; he made you a match in battle for the barbarians on your borders, so that you no longer trusted your safety to the strength of your positions so much as to your natural* courage. He made you city dwellers and established the order that comes from good laws and customs. It was due to him that you became masters and not slaves and subjects of those very barbarians who used previously to plunder your possessions and carry off your persons. He annexed the greater part of Thrace to Macedonia and, by capturing the best placed positions by the sea, he opened up the country to trade. . . .[1]

Conquest of Greece. Soon after Philip's conquest of Thrace, a religious war among the city-states of Greece gave Philip an opportunity to intervene in Greek affairs. The war had started when the city-state of Phocis seized the treasury of the religious sanctuary at Delphi. The Thebans prepared to avenge this outrage, and Philip's army soon came to their aid. In 353, Philip led his army through Thessaly, which he had annexed, and appeared at Thermopylae.

Philip's presence at Thermopylae created an excited reaction among the city-states of Greece. In Athens, two opposing parties arose to debate Athenian policy in front of the Assembly. The pro-Macedonian party of orators argued that Athens should maintain the peace and develop its economic interests. The anti-Macedonian party was led by the great orator Demosthenes (not to be confused with the Athenian general killed during the Peloponnesian War), who believed that Philip's ambitions were a threat to Athens' independence. Demosthenes was not a military strategist, but he became active on every other possible front in his efforts to defeat Philip's plans.

In 353, the anti-Macedonian party within Athens prevailed. The Athenians, with help from the Spartans, raised a force of 10,000 men and sent it to aid the Phocians. The arrival of this force convinced Philip to postpone his plans for conquest, and he withdrew without giving battle.

The orator Demosthenes devoted his life to an unequal battle against Philip of Macedonia. The original of this statue once stood in the marketplace of Athens.

Philip next turned his attention to the Chalcidice region and the Hellespont. Demosthenes realized the danger that Philip posed to Athenian interests in this area and delivered the first of his series of "Philippics" (orations concerning Philip) in 351. Due to his efforts, the Athenians sent three expeditions to aid the city of Olynthus in the Chalcidice. Philip was able to overcome these forces, however, and by 348 he had incorporated the Chalcidice into his territory.

---

[1]Arrian, *Anabasis of Alexander* VII, 9, 2-3.

The defeat in the Chalcidice convinced the Athenians, even Demosthenes, that it was necessary to come to terms with Philip. Demosthenes and two leaders of the pro-Macedonian party traveled to Philip's court on a diplomatic mission. There, they hoped to negotiate an agreement that would recognize the status quo: Athens would accept the loss of Amphipolis and the Chalcidice if Philip would renounce any further conquests in Greece. While treating the diplomats with great courtesy and charm, Philip postponed the signing of such an agreement for several months. Meanwhile, he completed his conquest of Thrace and seized the sanctuary of Delphi from the Phocians. Finally, he agreed to sign a treaty with Athens.

Despite the treaty with Macedonia, and the dangers that any resistance to Philip now posed, Demosthenes continued his efforts to undermine Philip's plans. He delivered his third "Philippic" in 341 B.C., as Philip prepared to besiege the city of Byzantium. He urged the Assembly to aid Byzantium and to recognize that the treaty with Philip would never guarantee Athens' safety:

•••*Neither the Greek nor the barbarian world is big enough for this fellow's ambition. And we Greeks see and hear all this, and yet we do not send embassies to one another, and express our indignation. We are in such a miserable position, we have so entrenched ourselves in our different cities, that to this very day we can do nothing that our interest or duty demands; we cannot combine, we cannot take any common pledge of help or friendship; but we idly watch the growing power of this man, each bent . . . on profiting by the interval afforded by another's ruin, taking not a thought, making not an effort for the salvation of Greece. For that Philip, like the recurrence or attack of a fever or some other disease, is threatening even those who think themselves out of reach, of that not one of you is ignorant.*[2]

---

[2]Demosthenes, *Third Philippic* 27, 29.

Demosthenes' arguments prevailed in the Assembly. To prepare for war against Philip, he personally supervised the modernization of Athens' naval forces and the creation of new treaties with the city-states of central Greece. As a result, Athenian forces successfully repelled Philip's attack of Byzantium. Almost immediately, however, Philip invaded the island of Euboea. He then sent envoys to Thebes in order to win the Thebans' assent to this invasion. Demosthenes realized what Philip was planning, and hurried to Thebes himself. There, he convinced the Thebans to stand with Athens against the Macedonians rather than signing a treaty with Philip.

The combined army of Thebes and Athens won two minor battles against Philip's forces in 339 B.C. In 338, however, Philip appeared with an even larger army and decisively defeated the allies at Chaeronea, in Boeotia. After Philip's victory, he garrisoned Thebes, but extended very favorable terms of peace to Athens because of his admiration for that city. Athens was forced to ally itself with Macedonia, but it was not garrisoned; its ports remained free, and it kept its navy.

The League of Corinth. After signing treaties with Thebes and Athens, Philip summoned all of the city-states of Greece to a convention at Corinth. In 337 B.C., the participating cities agreed to join a new general alliance, the League of Corinth. The member city-states were not required to pay tribute to Philip, and would remain independent. They agreed, however, to contribute troops to the league's army and navy and to accept Philip's direction of the league's affairs. The city-states also pledged that they would put aside their grievances against each other and renounce any further war against fellow Greeks. Thus, through the league, Philip succeeded in creating the framework for a unified Greek nation. Of all the city-states, only Sparta refused to participate.

The next year, Philip proposed to the League of Corinth that they undertake an expedition against the Persians, with the immediate goal of freeing the Ionic Greek cities from Persian rule. He sent a Macedonian army of 10,000 men to Asia Minor under the leadership of his capable general, Parmenio, and planned to join him with a Greek force soon after. But during the summer, as he was celebrating the wedding of his daughter, Philip was assassinated.

Philip's assassin was a Macedonian named Pausanias, but it is not known who, if anyone, encouraged him to commit the deed. The murder may have been planned by the Persians, who wanted to put an end to Philip's invasion of their territory. Alternatively, Philip's first wife, Olympias, may have been responsible. Because she was known to have a strong character and a fierce temper, some people believed that she had engineered the murder in order to assure the succession of her son, Alexander. The fact that she soon afterwards murdered Philip's second wife and infant son gave support to this belief.

Archaeological Findings. During the 1970s, Manolis Andronikas, a renowned Greek archaeologist, uncovered an ancient tomb at Vergina, in northern Greece. The tomb contained many treasures, and had been protected over the centuries by a large mound of earth which looked like a natural hill. One important finding was a pair of greaves (leg coverings), apparently fashioned for a man with one leg three centimeters shorter than the other. Andonikas also found a gold burial casket with a star engraved on the lid. Since, according to legend, one of Philip's legs was shorter than the other, and because stars were symbols of royalty in the ancient world, Andronikas decided that the remains within the casket were those of Philip of Macedonia.

ALEXANDER THE GREAT

Alexander, at the age of 20 years, succeeded his father, and became such a dramatic figure in the ancient world that he was called "Alexander the Great." For the details of Alexander's life and campaigns, our two most

At the age of 22, Alexander the Great set out to conquer the world at the head of a united Greek-Macedonian army. This portrait of Alexander may be based upon a contemporary statue by Lysippus.

important sources are Plutarch, who wrote essays on Alexander and other famous Greeks and Romans during the 1st century A.D., and Arrian, who wrote the *Anabasis* ("Campaign") *of Alexander* in the 2nd century A.D. Although no contemporary accounts of Alexander have come down to us, Plutarch and Arrian referred to eyewitness accounts that still existed during their lifetimes, including Alexander's own letters and the memoirs of two of his generals. Both Plutarch and Arrian describe the combination of shrewd calculation, reckless daring, and administrative skill which characterized Alexander's campaigns and enabled him to achieve his great victories.

Childhood. Alexander was born in Pella, Macedonia, in 356 B.C. Plutarch wrote that when Alexander was born, Philip received three messages:

> ●●● *that Parmenio [his general] had overthrown the Illyrians in a great battle, that his race horse had won the course at the Olympic Games, and that his wife had given birth to Alexander; with which being naturally well pleased, as an addition to his satisfaction, he was assured by the diviners that a son, whose birth was accompanied with three such successes, could not fail of being invincible.*[3]

When Alexander was 13 years old, Philip hired Aristotle, the Athenian philosopher, as tutor for his son. Aristotle instilled in his eager pupil a love for Greek art and poetry, and a lasting interest in Greek science and philosophy. Alexander is said to have remarked that he loved Aristotle more than his father, for while his father gave him life, Aristotle taught him how to live well. At other times, Alexander indicated that he wanted to be a man of action like his father. Plutarch reported that he once expressed anger after hearing about one of his father's conquests, remarking that his father would leave nothing for him to accomplish.

Campaign in Greece. Soon after he ascended the throne, Alexander traveled to Corinth to ensure that the League of Corinth would elect him commander-in-chief in place of his father. He then led his troops northward across the Danube River in order to subdue a revolt in Thrace (present Bulgaria and Rumania).

After subduing the Thracian revolt, Alexander marched west to deal with rebellious tribes in Illyria. While he was in Illyria, a group of Thebans circulated a rumor that he had been killed in battle, and the citizens of Thebes and Athens began to consider seceding from the League of Corinth. Alexander soon heard about this plot, and hurried to the scene, covering 300 miles in just

two weeks. The Thebans refused to surrender to Alexander, and he proceeded to overrun the city. After conquering the city, Alexander massacred the Thebans who had resisted his troops and sold the rest into slavery. The city was then razed, except for the temples and the house that had belonged to the poet Pindar. By these actions, Alexander demonstrated that he respected Greek culture but would tolerate no rebellion.

The Aetolians and Athenians, horrified by the events at Thebes, hastened to ask Alexander's pardon for their part in the revolt and to congratulate him upon his safe return from Illyria. After some hesitation, Alexander granted them what they asked and proceeded to work with them to organize a campaign against the Persians. According to Plutarch, Alexander later regretted his retribution against Thebes and, for the rest of his life, freely granted any favor asked of him by a Theban.

Voyage to the East. Before leaving Greece, Alexander stopped at Delphi to receive the oracle's advice concerning his plans to invade Persia. Plutarch reported that he soon received the prophecy he had hoped for:

> ●●● [H]appening to come on one of the forbidden days, when it was esteemed improper to give any answers from the oracle, he sent messengers to desire the priestess to do her office; and when she refused, on the plea of a law to the contrary, he went up himself, and began to draw her by force into the temple, until tired and overcome with his importunity, "My son," she said, "thou art invincible."[4]

The priestess's words came true in his brief lifetime.

In 334 B.C., Alexander set out for Persia with an army of more than 30,000 infantry troops and 5000 cavalry, recruited from Macedonia and the League of Corinth. His father's trusted advisor Parmenio was second in

---

[3]Plutarch, *Lives*, Modern Library ed., p. 803.

[4]Ibid., p. 810.

THE EMPIRE OF ALEXANDER THE GREAT AND HIS SUCCESSORS
Why did Alexander's empire split into three separate kingdoms after his death?

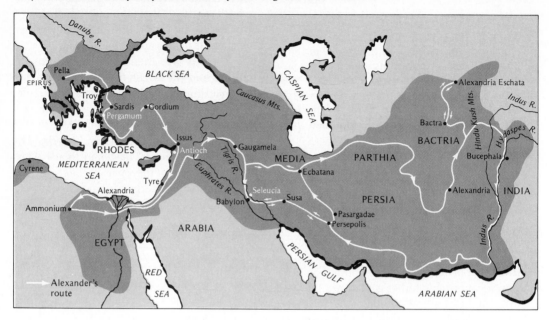

command, and another of his father's friends, Antipater, was left in charge of Macedonia and Greece. Traveling with the expedition were such practical specialists as engineers, carpenters, and seers—the former to build siege machinery and ships, and the latter to read the omens before each major battle. Alexander also took with him geographers, philosophers, and zoologists to record the strange new ideas and sights he expected to encounter on his travels.

Alexander's romantic ideas about his campaign were indicated by his choice of reading material: he carried with him a copy of the *Iliad*, personally annotated by Aristotle. And, upon arriving in Asia Minor, his first action was to visit the site of ancient Troy. There, he visited the tomb of his personal hero, Achilles, whom he looked upon as his ancestor, and offered sacrifices to Athena. According to Arrian's account, he then left his armor in Athena's temple and took in exchange a suit of armor which was said to date from the Trojan War period.

After a two-day march inland, Alexander and his troops reached the Granicus River, where they encountered the army of the Persian satrap for Asia Minor. In this first battle of the campaign, Alexander narrowly escaped death when a Persian commander struck him with a battle-axe. The axe split Alexander's helmet, but he survived the blow and his army routed the Persian soldiers. After the battle, Alexander honored the 25 Companions who had fallen in the first charge by having the famous sculptor Lysippus carve their statues. To honor the Greek forces, he sent battle trophies to Athens with the following inscription:

● ● ● *Alexander the son of Philip, and the Grecians, except the Lacedaemonians, won these from the barbarians who inhabit Asia.*[5]

After capturing Sardis, the most important Persian city in Asia Minor, Alexander

---

[5]Ibid., p. 812.

marched south along the coast, freeing Ephesus and the other Ionian Greek city-states from Persian rule. In each Greek city, he installed a government modeled on Athens' democracy in place of the oligarchies established by the Persians.

In 333 B.C. Alexander visited Gordium, the capital of the old Phrygian kingdom. On display in the city was the famous Gordian knot, securing a chariot said to belong to the legendary King Midas. According to legend, whoever could untie the intricate knot would be lord of all Asia. Alexander reportedly slashed the knot with his sword, thereby foreshadowing the fulfillment of the prophesy. Before moving on, he appointed one of his commanders as satrap of Phrygia.

Alexander then led his army southward through the Cilician Gates, a mountain pass so narrow that two loaded camels could not walk side by side, and moved into Syria. There, Alexander hoped to find Darius III, king of the Persians, and the main body of the Persian army. Darius, who was leading an army much larger than Alexander's, was also anxious for battle. Disregarding the advice of his generals, he advanced toward Cilicia rather than choosing a battle site and waiting for Alexander to appear. During the night, the two armies passed each other without realizing it. At the break of day, Alexander saw that Darius' army was scattered and disorganized as it negotiated the narrow mountain passes, so he arrayed his army and attacked the Persians near the town of Issus. The Persians, realizing that they were outmaneuvered and might be forced into the sea, beat a hasty retreat. Alexander actually captured Darius' family, but the king himself escaped.

After the battle of Issus, Alexander sent troops to Damascus to retrieve the baggage and treasures of the Persian army. He was greatly impressed by the vast wealth of articles his men brought back, but he kept for himself only a jeweled casket in which to carry his treasured copy of the *Iliad*. By this

A mosaic found in a Roman villa depicts the terrified Darius as he prepares to flee the battle at Issus.

act, Alexander perhaps intended to emphasize the contrast between himself and Darius, and to demonstrate his belief that a true king should be measured by his exploits, not by the luxuries he enjoyed.

Because Persia could not be truly conquered as long as its fleet continued to operate freely, Alexander's next goal was to seize the Phoenician ports where the Persian fleet was based. The towns of Sidon and Byblos surrendered without a battle and hailed Alexander as a liberator from Persian tyranny. The people of Tyre, however, decided to pursue a policy of neutrality, and announced that they would admit neither Persians nor Macedonians into their city. Arrian explained why the Tyrians could make this stand:

● ● ● *For the city was an island, protected on all sides by high walls, while any action at sea clearly favored the Tyrians in their present circumstances, because the Persians had command of the sea and the Tyrians themselves had numerous fleet. . . .*[6]

To overcome the city's advantages, Alexander's forces built a *mole*, or passageway of

---

[6]Arrian, *Anabasis of Alexander* II, 18, 2.

stones, through the water and constructed towers to defend the workers. When the mole was completed, Alexander's troops marched across it to storm the fortifications of Tyre, while supporting ships engaged the Tyrian navy. After seven months, Tyre surrendered, and the Persian fleet scattered because it no longer had a harbor.

During the siege of Tyre, Darius sent a messenger to Alexander with an offer of peace: Darius would yield all of the land west of the Euphrates River, 10,000 talents in gold, and his daughter in marriage. Parmenio urged the young king to accept, but Alexander refused the offer.

Alexander's army moved south along the Mediterranean coast, capturing Philistia (the present Gaza strip), and entering Egypt in 332 B.C. The Egyptians, who had been under Persian domination since 525 B.C., welcomed Alexander as a successor to their pharaohs. The city of Memphis, where the Persian satrap lived, surrendered without a battle. Alexander then founded the city of Alexandria, on the north end of the Nile delta. This city became the commercial and intellectual center of the Hellenistic world, and even today is one of the busiest ports in the Mediterranean region.

From his new city, Alexander made a perilous journey across the Libyan Desert to consult the oracle of Ammon. Plutarch observed that Alexander was well rewarded for his troubles when the high priest of Ammon addressed him:

• • • the priest, desirous as a piece of courtesy to address him in Greek, "O Paidion" [My Son], by a slip in pronunciation ended with the **s** instead of the **n**, and said "O Paidios" [Son of Zeus], which mistake Alexander was well enough pleased with. . . .[7]

Before leaving Egypt, Alexander appointed an Egyptian governor in place of the Persian satrap, and left troops to guard the country.

Campaign in the East. Alexander then led his army through the Fertile Crescent in pursuit of the Persians. In 331 B.C., at Gaugamela, he met the army of Darius. For this important battle, Darius had chosen a large, level field in order to obtain maximum advantage for his chariot troops. The chariots themselves were equipped with scythes on the wheels to cut through the Macedonian phalanx. Soon after the start of battle:

• • • the enemy launched their scythe-chariots in the direction of Alexander himself in order to disrupt his phalanx. But in this they failed badly, for as soon as they approached . . . they were met with a volley of javelins. They [Alexander's advance troops] also caught hold of the reins, pulled down the drivers, and surrounded the horses and cut them down. Some of the chariots did get through the ranks, but these [ranks] parted, as they had been told to do, where the chariots attacked, and the result was that the chariots were undamaged and those whom they attacked were unhurt.[8]

Soon afterwards, Darius gave up the battle and fled, pursued by Alexander and his Companions. But the Persian cavalry, not realizing that Darius had left, charged the left wing of Alexander's army. Alexander wheeled back to help his army, and encountered some retreating Persian troops. At this point, Arrian related, the fiercest fighting of all occurred, for the trapped Persian troops were now struggling for their lives. Sixty of the Companions fell, but Alexander's forces were finally victorious.

Darius fled on horseback across the mountains into Media. Alexander, meanwhile, proceeded to Babylon, where he was hailed as king. He permitted his weary troops to rest and celebrate for a month, and then marched toward Susa, the administrative capital of

---

[7]Plutarch, *Lives*, Modern Library ed., p. 821.

[8]Arrian, *Anabasis of Alexander* III, 13, 5-6.

For the battle of Gaugamela, Alexander utilized a modified version of the oblique phalanx. 1. The wings of the phalanx were turned in to form an "open rectangle" with movable ends, and cavalry troops were mixed with infantry. 2. The rapid Persian chariot and cavalry charges created gaps in the Persian ranks, and Alexander's forces were able to envelop those who did not retreat.

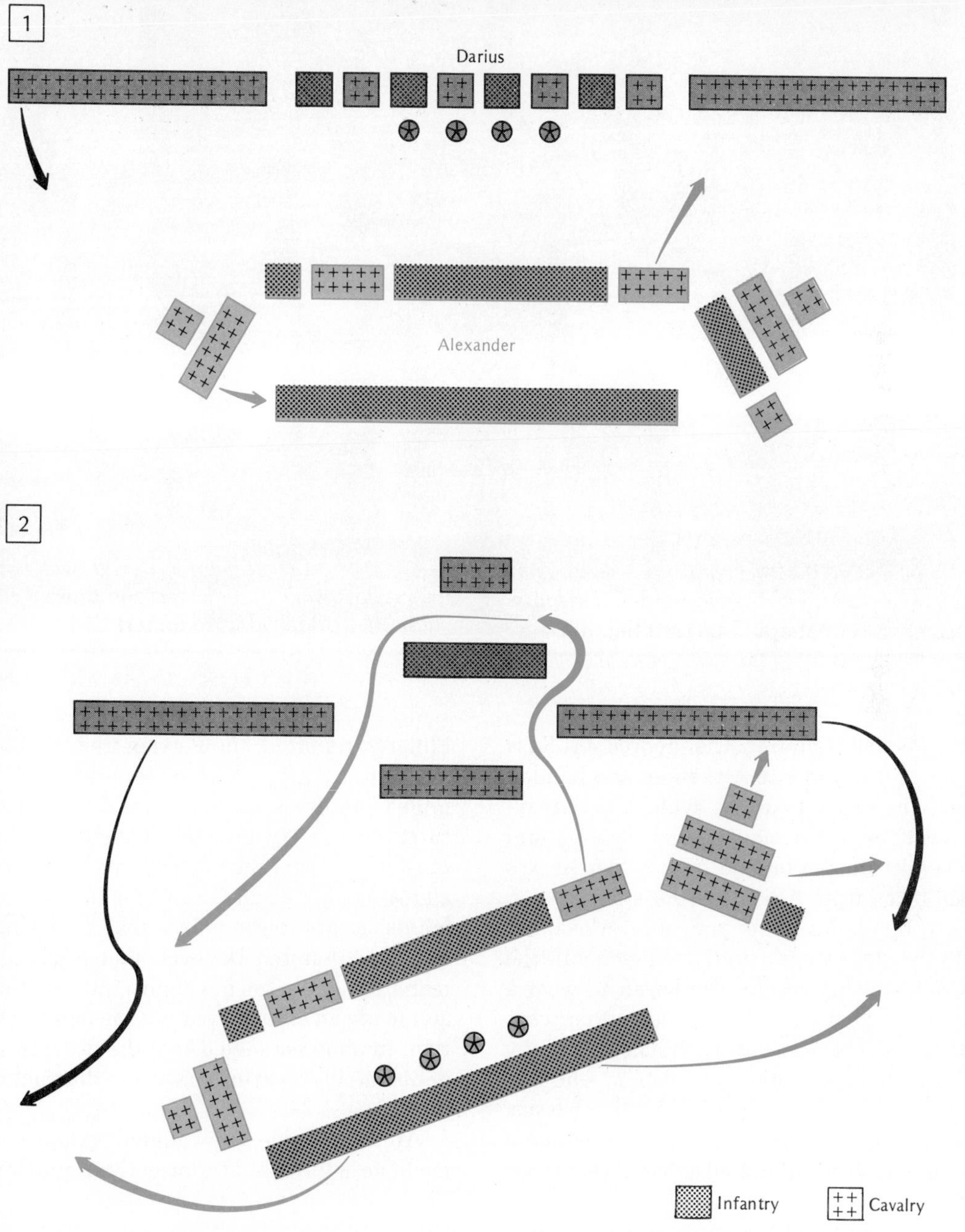

1

Darius

Alexander

2

Infantry   Cavalry

After the battle of Gaugamela, Alexander triumphantly entered Babylon. He later revisited the city to celebrate his victories in the Far East.

the Persian Empire. The people of Susa opened their gates to Alexander and handed over the city's treasury, which, Arrian reported, included 50,000 silver talents and several valuable bronze statues that Xerxes had taken from Athens in 480 B.C.

At this point in his campaign, Alexander began to take steps to unify and reconcile the peoples of his empire. He began to wear a modified Persian costume, and further demonstrated his respect for Persian culture by freeing Darius' mother and sisters, who had been his prisoners since the battle of Issus. Because the people of Susa had surrendered voluntarily, he appointed a Persian governor for the city.

Alexander and his army next proceeded to the Persian holy city of Persepolis where,

Plutarch reported, the Persian treasure they seized was "as much as ten thousand pair of mules and five thousand camels could well carry away."[9] An immense banquet was arranged and, after the participants had drunk a great deal, Alexander and his fellow celebrants set fire to the palace that Xerxes had lived in. Plutarch believed that Alexander regretted setting the fire almost immediately, and made an effort to put out the flames. Arrian, in contrast, stated that the fire was set deliberately, to avenge Xerxes' destruction of Athens.

At Pasargadae, Alexander stopped to meditate at the simple tomb of Cyrus the Great

---

[9]Plutarch, *Lives*, Modern Library ed., p. 828.

and to read that king's message to the world:

●●● *O man, whosoever thou art . . . I am Cyrus, the founder of the Persian empire; do not grudge me this little earth which covers my body.*[10]

Darius had now fled to Bactria, and Alexander pursued him, following the trail that later became part of the Silk Route between China and Arabia. But before Alexander could reach him, Darius was killed by Bessus, the satrap of Bactria. Plutarch described Alexander's reaction to finding Darius dead:

●●● *[H]e showed manifest tokens of sorrow, and taking off his own cloak, threw it upon the body to cover it. . . . Darius' body was laid in state and sent to his mother with pomp suitable to his quality.*[11]

Arrian reported that, some years later, Alexander ordered that Bessus be punished according to Persian tradition:

●●● *He then gave orders that his nose and the tips of his ears should be cut off, and that thus mutilated he should be taken to Ecbatana to suffer public execution before his own countrymen, the Medes and the Persians.*[12]

With Darius dead, the Persians considered Alexander to be the legitimate successor to the Persian throne. According to their customs and beliefs, the king was a living god, and they worshiped Alexander accordingly. Alexander did not discourage the cult that grew up around him. In 327 B.C., he married Roxane, the beautiful daughter of a Bactrian prince, an act which also indicated his intent to create a true union of Greek and Asian peoples under his rule.

Alexander's appointment of Persians to important positions in the army and government, his adoption of Persian manners and dress, and his claim of being a living god caused great resentment among his Macedonian and Greek troops. Eventually, the loyalty and steadfastness of the Macedonians began to disintegrate. Philotas, a friend of Alexander's since childhood, was found guilty of treason and was executed. His father, Parmenio, who probably had no part in the conspiracy, was also killed on Alexander's orders, for he was widely respected and could have posed a grave danger to Alexander if he had tried to avenge his son's death.

Two years after Philotas' treason had been revealed, Alexander again found himself in conflict with one of his oldest friends. Clitus, a chief officer of the Companions, was the victim of this second tragedy. One evening, after a long drinking bout, Clitus began to taunt a group of Companions who were flattering Alexander. When rebuked by Alexander, Clitus reminded him that he had saved his life at the battle of the Granicus River. Alexander's guards separated the two angry men by removing Clitus from the room, but he soon reappeared at the doorway, still yelling taunts:

●●● *Upon this, at last, Alexander, snatching a spear from one of the soldiers, met Clitus as he was coming forward . . . and ran him through the body. He fell at once with a cry and a groan. Upon which the king's anger immediately vanishing, he came perfectly to himself, and when he saw his friends about him all in a profound silence, he pulled the spear out of the dead body, and would have thrust it into his own throat, if the guards had not held his hands, and by main force carried him away into his chamber, where all that night and the next day he wept bitterly, till being quite spent with lamenting and exclaiming, he lay . . . speechless.*[13]

Expedition in India. In 326 B.C., Alexander set out to conquer India with a force of

---

[10]Ibid., p. 849.

[11]Ibid., p. 833.

[12]Arrian, *Anabasis of Alexander* IV, 7, 3.

---

[13]Plutarch, *Lives*, Modern Library ed., p. 838.

135,000 men. Before setting out, Alexander noticed that his soldiers were loaded down with a vast amount of booty, which would slow the army's progress. He set fire to his own superfluous baggage, and ordered his troops to do the same. The men enthusiastically complied with this order, Plutarch reported.

Alexander's army crossed the Hindu Kush ("Killer") Mountains, and then followed the Kabul River downstream to the Indus River, where a bridge of boats was built for the army to cross. He then continued eastward to the Hydaspes River, another tributary of the Indus, where he was confronted by Porus, the King of Punjab. Although Porus' war elephants made it necessary to revise his battle plan, Alexander and his troops were finally able to overcome the Indian forces. In recognition of Porus' valor, Alexander left him as governor of his own kingdom and of several other conquered cities. He also founded several cities in strategic locations and settled his veterans in them. Most of these cities were called *Alexandria*, but one was named after Alexander's beloved horse *Bucephalus*, who had died in India.

Alexander wanted to press further into India, to the limits of the known world, but his weary and homesick men threatened to mutiny. A spokesman presented their reasoning to Alexander:

• • • *Under your leadership, supported by those who set out with you from home, we have achieved very many great successes. But all the more because of that, I think it is right to set a limit to the tasks we undertake and the risks we run. You yourself see how many Macedonians and Greeks set out with you, and how few are left . . . but even they are not as vigorous as they were, and they are still more broken in spirit. All these long to see their parents, . . . to see their wives and children, to see their homeland, which they are eager to revisit, especially since they will be going back as great and rich men*

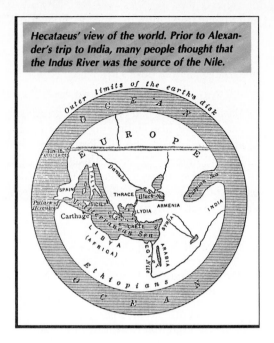

Hecataeus' view of the world. Prior to Alexander's trip to India, many people thought that the Indus River was the source of the Nile.

instead of insignificant and poor, with the treasures which they have gained for you.[14]

Return to Persia. Alexander sulked in his tent for three days, and then ordered his carpenters to build a fleet on the Indus River for the return to Persia. In following this river to a point near its mouth, he discovered that the Indus flowed into the sea and was not, as had been believed, the source of the Nile River. He then divided his men into three groups, assigning each a different route back to Susa. One army, led by Craterus, was to take a northern overland route; a second group, under the command of Nearchus, was to sail, via the Arabian Sea, to the Persian Gulf; and the third group, under Alexander's command, would march west across the Sind desert.

The route that Alexander himself took was so incredibly difficult that three-quarters of his troops perished. Nevertheless, the army overcame despair and struggled on through the desert sands, finally meeting the naval

[14]Arrian, *Anabasis of Alexander* V, 27, 5.

force led by Nearchus. Arrian described how the army dealt with one of the most difficult hardships, the lack of water:

... Some of the light infantry, who had gone off from the rest of the army in search of water, found a meager little trickle collected in a shallow gulley. They collected it up with difficulty and hurried to Alexander as if they were taking him a great gift. When they approached they poured the water into a helmet and offered it to the king. He accepted it and thanked those who brought it. But when he received it he poured it out on the ground for all to see. The whole army was so heartened by this act that you would have thought that the water which Alexander had poured away had provided a drink for every man.[15]

Nearchus, traveling the sea in improvised river boats, managed to collect many specimens of plants and animals from the desert coastland, which he eventually carried back to Greece for Aristotle to study. He also charted the sea route to India, making it possible for future sailors to open a trade route from West to East.

When Alexander heard about Nearchus' adventures, he immediately thought of making a voyage himself, planning to sail around the coasts of Arabia and Africa, then enter the Mediterranean through the Pillars of Hercules (Strait of Gibraltar). He was forced to postpone these plans, however, for a number of problems had arisen in his absence. Alexander spent several months straightening out these administrative problems and re-establishing his control over Persia and the Greek world.

Early in 324 B.C., Alexander presided over an extraordinary ceremony to celebrate the reunion of his three armies at Susa and to symbolize the union of the western and eastern halves of his empire. A mass wedding was performed, uniting 80 of Alexander's officers with Persian women. Alexander himself took Barsine, the daughter of Darius, as his second wife. In addition, nearly 10,000 Macedonians who had previously married Persian women were invited to the banquet with their wives and were rewarded with generous gifts.

Soon after the wedding ceremonies, Alexander made arrangements to release those veterans of his army who were too old or disabled for active service and to replace them with 30,000 young Persians, who would be trained to fight in the Macedonian phalanx system. This action caused great resentment among the Macedonian and Greek troops, and spokesmen from the army announced that all of the troops, as a gesture of pride, intended to join the disabled veterans in returning home. Alexander then addressed an eloquent speech to his troops, reminding them of all that he and Philip had achieved for them, and promising them that the returning veterans would be richly rewarded for their service. Finally, the troops relented and agreed to accept Alexander's decisions and the enhanced role of the Persians.

Last Days. Alexander traveled to Babylon to supervise the building of a Babylonian temple and to make plans to explore the Caspian Sea. There, at the age of 33, he was suddenly stricken by a fever and soon became too weak to leave his bed. Arrian described the events of his last hours:

... The soldiers were anxious to see him, some wanting to see him while he was still alive, others hearing a rumor that he was already dead and, I suppose, suspecting that his death was being concealed by his bodyguards. But most pushed their way in to see Alexander in grief and longing for their king. They say that he could not speak as the army filed past, but that he raised his hand, and with an effort raised his head and had a sign of recognition in the eyes for each man.[16]

---

[15]Ibid., VI, 26, 3.

[16]Ibid., VII, 12, 1.

THE HELLENISTIC ERA

Alexander's place in world history is based on far more than his military victories. He mapped previously uncharted territories, opened new trade routes, and stimulated the exchange of ideas between the West and the East. He promoted the fusion of two peoples, the Greeks and the Persians, by his own marriages and the marriages he encouraged his men to make. He founded at least 20 cities in the territories he had conquered, thereby supplying an opportunity for thousands of Greek colonists to settle in the East.

When Alexander's friends asked him, on his deathbed, to name a successor, he reportedly replied "To the strongest!" But no one person was capable of seizing and ruling the vast empire he had created. For 25 years, Alexander's generals battled among themselves for control of the empire. Finally, the empire split into three regional kingdoms, each ruled by one of Alexander's associates. Despite these destructive power struggles, Alexander's conquests produced an enduring legacy. One historian described his achievement in this way:

● ● ● *The body of Alexander's empire had disintegrated, but its soul survived, vigorous and as though arrayed in a new youthfulness. There was something touching, almost miraculous, about its resurgence. To what was this due? . . . To the fact that during the dark night which had descended upon the East, during all those years of rivalry and turmoil, the cities which Alexander had founded never ceased to shine like stars. Notwithstanding the breakdown of political ties, they had succeeded in preserving this inestimable benefit: the memory of their attachment to a common civilization.*[17]

PTOLEMY

Egypt, the richest and most powerful of Alexander's kingdoms, was seized by Ptolemy, whom Alexander had named governor of Egypt in 323 B.C. Ptolemy captured the embalmed body of Alexander, and then fought a fierce battle with three leading generals of Alexander's army to retain his possession. Ptolemy emerged victorious from this struggle, and by 305 B.C. he had eliminated all other claimants to the throne of Egypt. With Alexandria as his capital, he eventually assembled an empire which included Cyrenaica and Cyprus as well as the Syria-Palestine territory claimed by earlier Egyptian pharaohs. He and his descendants ruled Egypt until Cleopatra, the last of the Ptolemaic dynasty, committed suicide in 30 B.C. and Egypt became a Roman province.

Ptolemy and his successors encouraged Greeks to migrate to Egypt by granting them special privileges and appointing them to important positions in the government. Naukratis, Ptolemais, and the capital city of Alexandria soon became important centers of Greek culture.

Alexander's successors minted coinage in his name to encourage trade and commerce throughout his empire. On this coin, he is depicted with ram horns, a symbol of divinity.

---

[17]Jacques Benoist-Mechin, *Alexander the Great* (New York: Hawthorne Books, 1966), pp. 229-30.

Seleucus became governor of Babylon after Alexander's death, and eventually controlled most of the former empire of the Persians, a vast territory inhabited by many diverse peoples. In 303 B.C., he lost the easternmost provinces to an Indian emperor, Chandragupta Maurya, who established the Mauryan dynasty in India (322-232 B.C.).

In an attempt to unify the remaining peoples of his empire, Seleucus and his descendants (the *Seleucids*) encouraged the Persian tradition of emperor-worship. Seleucus himself was deified after his death, and his descendants were treated as gods during their lifetimes. As another strategy of unification, the Seleucids promoted the spread of Hellenistic culture by encouraging Greek colonists to settle in his territories and by sponsoring Greek theater and festivals. Like the Persians, the Seleucids appointed many native satraps to administer local areas, but also established two capital cities for their own administration—Seleucia, on the Tigris River, and Antioch, in Syria.

In spite of all of their efforts, the Seleucids were unable to control their vast empire. The Iranian peoples in the East— especially those who lived in rural areas— retained their own language and religion, and were not influenced by Greek culture. The Parthians gradually gained control of Media, Bactria, and Persia; most of the region east of the Tigris River. In Asia Minor, an independent kingdom arose around the city of Pergamum, which was considered to be one of the most beautiful cities in the world. Pergamum extended its control over all the Seleucid territory north of the Taurus Mountains, and remained independent until its childless king, Attalus III, bequeathed the kingdom to Rome in 133 B.C. By that time, the Seleucid kingdom consisted of little more than Syria.

ANTIGONUS

Antigonus had served Alexander as governor of Phyrgia in Asia Minor. After Alexander's death, he seized control of a vast territory in Asia and competed for control of Greece and Macedonia. In 315 B.C., he declared the Greek city-states to be autonomous and independent, and helped to establish a federation of island city-states.

At one point, Antigonus appeared to be in a position to control all of Alexander's empire, but he was defeated by Seleucus in 301 B.C. After his death, his descendants ruled Macedonia, and his eastern territories were incorporated into the Seleucid empire.

The Greek Federations. In keeping with their political traditions, most of the Greek city-states struggled to maintain their independence during the wars between Alexander's associates. After several decades, however, a number of them combined to form leagues for mutual defense.

The Achaean League, made up of 12 city-states in the northern Peloponnesus, was established in 280 B.C. It was governed by two bodies: an assembly in which the number of delegates from each city was based on population, and a federal council composed of one representative from each city-state. The council met twice a year to determine the general policies of the league. The assembly met annually to vote on questions of war and peace and to elect administrators.

Several city-states of central Greece formed the Aetolian League. This league was ruled by a popular assembly made up of all citizens of the member city-states. The assembly, which met biennially, proved to be too large to be effective. There was also a federal council in which the number of representatives from each city-state was based on the size of the military force that it furnished to the league. The member city-states remained independent in their internal affairs, but yielded control of external affairs to the league.

The Greek leagues were important historically because they represented the earliest instances of *federal* government, in which independent local governments yielded specific powers to a federation. Unfortunately, the leagues had limited effectiveness because Athens and Sparta, the two strongest city-states, refused to participate. Nevertheless, the concept of federalism was studied by the founders of the United States of America and influenced the framing of the Constitution.

THE HELLENISTIC ECONOMY

The Hellenistic era (323-30 B.C.) was a period of great economic prosperity in the Mediterranean world and the Middle East. In the interest of encouraging trade between the countries of Alexander's empire, the vast stores of gold and silver which the Persian kings had accumulated were minted into a standard coinage. Uniform systems of weights and measures were adopted, standard banking practices were established, and harbors and roads were improved.

Political barriers to trade were reduced, and a wide variety of products began to move freely between various lands. Sailors explored new routes and began to travel across open seas, navigating by the stars rather than staying within sight of land. The Hellenistic world obtained silver from Spain, tin from Britain, cattle and wine from Italy, ivory from the Sudan, and wheat and dried fish from southern Russia.

The Ptolemies improved the agriculture of Egypt by expanding the irrigation systems and by reclaiming marshlands in the Nile delta. Egyptians were encouraged to introduce new species of plants and to use iron tools. Farmers began to use fertilizer, to practice crop rotation, and to breed livestock selectively.

The Ptolemies also introduced a new system for collecting taxes: they contracted various individuals to collect taxes in exchange for a percentage of the money they collected. This system became the model for the "tax farming" which the Romans later practiced.

The Seleucid governments encouraged and protected overland trade, for this was the most important source of wealth for the region. Caravan routes connected Mesopotamia with Iran, Bactria, and India, and even extended to China after the 2nd century B.C. From ports in Asia Minor, ships carried parchment, silk, agricultural products, and manufactured goods throughout the Mediterranean region.

CITIES

Each of the cities Alexander established had a council and assembly similar to those traditional in Greek city-states, but each was administered by a royal governor. Each city was laid out on the Greek model with a market place, a gymnasium, a theater, a race track, and one or more temples and government buildings. Royal parks and gardens were adorned with statues and fountains.

Most Hellenistic cities had three levels of society, not including the population of slaves. Greek colonists formed the privileged class and served as officers in the army and officials in the government. The middle class was made up of tradesmen, bankers, craftsmen, physicians, and teachers.

The third class of free people was made up of the native peoples in the countryside who did not participate in the Hellenistic movement, but instead retained their own language, religion, and traditional way of life. They did not share in the growing prosperity, and the widening gap between the Hellenized middle classes and the poor led to social unrest. Many farmers did not own the land they tilled, and were forced to compete in marketing their crops against large estates worked by slaves. Impoverished farmers sometimes sought sanctuary in the temples while their elected leaders attempted to negotiate with the landowners. Artisans in the cities formed *collegia*, or trade associations, as a remedy against exploitation. They chose their own deities and looked after their mutual welfare.

The large population of slaves in the Hellenistic era had few recourses against unjust treatment. The Stoics taught that there was no such thing as a "natural" slave, and certain Hellenistic dramatists and artists portrayed the human suffering caused by slavery. But the Hellenistic economy was dependent upon slave labor, and most middle class people opposed any movement to free slaves or to improve their living conditions. Beginning in 135 B.C., large slave uprisings began to occur in Sicily, Athens, and elsewhere. These rebellions caused a great deal of panic and fear among the free peoples of the Hellenistic world until they were finally suppressed by Roman armies.

Alexandria. Alexandria, the capital of the Ptolemaic Empire, was the most important city of the Hellenistic world. It was located on a narrow strip of land on the Nile delta. The two major cross-streets, each 100 feet wide, were paved with squares of granite and illuminated at night by blazing torches. Alexandria had a waterway connection to the Red Sea, and was thus an important transshipment point for goods moving from the Mediterranean area to the East.

The lighthouse at Alexandria was considered to be one of the Seven Wonders of the World. Located on the island of Pharos, it could be reached by land via a mile-long causeway. The light generated by a fire was intensified with reflectors so that it could be seen 20 miles away. A *Museum* ("Temple of the Muses") established by the Ptolemies was the first institute to be founded and subsidized by a Western government for purposes of research and learning. Today we could call such an institution a university. About a hundred scholars were paid generous salaries to study botany, zoology, astronomy, and the graphic arts. Not everyone appreciated such learning, as demonstrated by this satiric verse:

Egypt had its mad recluses
Book bewildered anchorites,
In the hen coop of the Muses,
Keeping up their endless fights.[18]

The most important library of the ancient Western world was established at Alexandria by Ptolemy I. Modern scholars believe that the library held 700,000 papyrus scrolls by the 1st century B.C. At this library, scribes translated manuscripts into *koine*, a dialect of Greek which became the international language of the Hellenistic world. The librarians sought to preserve literary works by copying and translating them. Zenodotus, the chief librarian in 284 B.C., studied the extant manuscripts of the *Iliad* and the *Odyssey*, and prepared a standard version of the two epics. Callimachus, Zenodotus' successor, prepared the first catalog of the most important manuscripts in the library. This great library was destroyed in the 4th century A.D. (see Chapter 14).

The lighthouse that guided ships to the port of Alexandria was one of the Seven Wonders of the World.

[18]Tom B. Jones, *Ancient Civilizations* (Chicago: Rand McNally, 1960), p. 310.

Alexandria became a major center of Judaism. To meet the religious needs of those Jews who did not speak the Hebrew language, a group of scholars translated the Holy Books, which are known to Christians as the Old Testament, from Hebrew into *koine*. Today this translation is referred to as the *Septuagint* Bible because there were 70 translators.

Pergamum. The kingdom of Pergamum in Asia Minor prospered from its silver mines, its agriculture, and its textile and parchment industries. The capital city was renowned above all for its library of more than 200,000 volumes. A competition developed between the Ptolemies of Egypt and the Attalid dynasty of Pergamum to see who could develop the finest library. To prevent the Attalids from adding volumes to their library, the Ptolemies banned the export of papyrus to Pergamum. In response to this ban, the people of Pergamum began to process skins of sheep and goats to produce a writing material called *carta pergama*, which came to be known as parchment. This material had the advantage that both sides could be written on, and it was widely used for manuscripts until a process for making paper was invented during the Middle Ages.

Antioch. Seleucus named his second capital city after his father, a Macedonian named Antiochus. Antioch was located on the Orontes River, in Syria, and served as administrative center for the western portion of the Seleucid empire. The city prospered from manufacture of luxury goods and from the caravan trade, and continued to be important after the fall of the Seleucid dynasty. In 64 B.C., it was occupied by the Romans and became the capital of their province of Syria.

Rhodes. The island of Rhodes was situated near the southern coast of Asia Minor, and its capital city became the busiest commercial port in the Mediterranean. Its trading partners, which included Sicily, Egypt, and the countries of the Black Sea region and

Asia Minor, helped to establish Rhodes as an international banking center. The city also became renowned as a cultural center and for its school of philosophy. The "Colossus of Rhodes," a statue of the sun god, was one of the Seven Wonders of the World. This bronze statue, over 100 feet high, stood in Rhodes' harbor until it was destroyed by an earthquake in 227 A.D.

LITERATURE

During the Hellenistic era, more men and women could read and write than at any earlier time. The availability of papyrus and parchment for the manufacture of scrolls, and the fact that literary works were written in *koine* created great demand for written material. The potential patronage of monarchs and wealthy citizens encouraged would-be authors to settle in the major cities. But, for the most part, these authors tended to be critics and commentators on earlier writings rather than creators of new literature. Those who did create original works placed a great deal of emphasis on style and form. Many of their writings provided ideas for later Roman writers, who, in turn, influenced European writers many centuries afterwards.

Theocritus. One of the most famous poets of the 3rd century was Theocritus of Syracuse (315-250 B.C.) He wrote *idylls*, or short poems celebrating the joys of rural life, which appealed to the sophisticated urban readers of the Hellenistic world. His vivid descriptions and sincere expressions of feeling had great influence on later Roman poets.

Callimachus. Callimachus (310-240 B.C.), the librarian of Alexandria, disliked long epic poems, and advocated an *epigrammatic* style. He became known for short, carefully written poems that convey an emotional impact in very few words. One well-known example is *Heraclitus*, an epitaph he wrote in tribute to an old friend. In the first line, the poet concisely conveys his surprise and grief at hearing of his friend's death: "*They told me, Heraclitus, they told me you were dead.*"

Callimachus carried on a lifelong feud with the poet Apollonius, who wrote in the epic mode. To contrast his own style with that of Apollonius, Callimachus wrote the *Hecale*, describing a single episode in the life of Theseus. Only a few lines of this poem are known to us.

Apollonius of Rhodes. Callimachus' great rival originally lived in Alexandria, but moved to Rhodes as a result of his feud with Callimachus. Apollonius is best known for his *Argonautica*, a lengthy epic poem based on the story of Jason's search for the Golden Fleece.

Polybius. One of the most important historians of the Hellenistic era was Polybius (201-120 B.C.), whose father was president of the Achaean League. After the war between Rome and Macedonia (171-167), Polybius was taken to Rome as a hostage and became acquainted with many prominent Romans. After his return to Greece, in 150, he wrote a history of Rome to explain the successes of the Romans to his countrymen. His history, based on written sources, interviews with Roman leaders, and personal experiences, was a comprehensive account of the period from the second Punic War to the destruction of Corinth in 146 B.C. Unfortunately, only 5 volumes remain of Polybius' 40-volume work.

Menander. The most popular form of comedy during the Hellenistic era was that which originated in Athens. Menander (342-291 B.C.) was the outstanding writer of comedies for the Athenian stage. He amused his audiences by putting stock characters—lovelorn young men, bullying fathers, and clever slaves—in stock situations, frequently involving mistaken identities. In contrast to the "Old Comedy" of Aristophanes, the "New Comedy" of Menander dealt with family and social issues rather than political themes. Although many people did not share his irreverent view of authority figures and traditional beliefs, Menander's plays were staged—in modified form—throughout the Roman Empire.

ART

Artists, like writers, were drawn to the prosperous cities of the Hellenistic era, where monarchs commissioned public buildings and monuments, and wealthy merchants spent lavishly to adorn their homes. In contrast to the artists of the Classical age, Hellenistic artists tended to strive for realistic and dramatic effects in their sculpture and painting.

One important example of Hellenistic sculpture is the "Great Altar of Zeus" in Pergamum, which was completed in 180 B.C. to commemorate the victories of Attalus I over the Celtic Gauls. This altar was an open structure with colonnades on three sides and a grand staircase on the fourth side. A frieze on the base depicted the victory of the gods of Olympus over the giants, perhaps symbolizing the triumph of civilization over barbarism.

During the 3rd and 2nd centuries B.C., the kings of Pergamum erected a number of monuments to memorialize their victories over the invading Gauls. In the sculptures that are known to us, the Gauls are depicted as courageous and dignified opponents. "The Dying Warrior" shows a wounded Gaul who is supporting himself on one arm while his strength

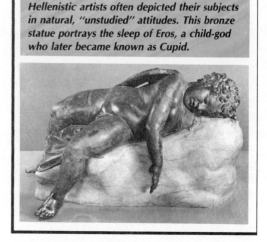

Hellenistic artists often depicted their subjects in natural, "unstudied" attitudes. This bronze statue portrays the sleep of Eros, a child-god who later became known as Cupid.

"The Gallic Chieftain." A brave Gaul kills himself and his wife to avoid surrendering to his enemies.

The statue known as the "Winged Victory of Samothrace" was erected about 190 B.C. to celebrate a Greek victory over Syria.

slowly ebbs away. "The Gallic Chieftain" depicts an officer who supports his dying wife while preparing to plunge his sword into his own chest.

Another world-renowned piece of sculpture from this era is the "Venus de Milo," whose appearance of serene dignity is suggestive of Praxiteles' work, but whose heavy drapery is typically Hellenistic in style. An equally fine work was the "Winged Victory of Samothrace," which depicted the goddess of victory alighting from the prow of a ship. Her clinging garment conveys a sense of the motion of wind and waves.

The "Old Market Woman" also exemplifies the realism and dramatic qualities of Hellenistic art. The strained facial expression and bent back of the old woman still evoke sympathy from the viewer.

PHILOSOPHY

During the Hellenistic era, uncertainties about existing political and social systems led to a renewal of interest in philosophy. As a result, the beliefs of Socrates, Plato, and Aristotle concerning the "good life" and the nature of truth were reevaluated and redefined, and four major schools of thought emerged. Each advocated a new way to achieve tranquillity and peace of mind.

Skepticism. The founder of skepticism was said to be Pyrrho of Elis, who lived from about 360 to 270 B.C. He denied the possibility of finding truth, arguing that everything is discerned through the senses, which are totally unreliable. In keeping with his belief that nothing can be stated with certainty, Pyrrho left no writings.

Cynicism. Diogenes taught that happiness

The artist who created "Old Market Woman" realistically portrayed the age and suffering of his subject. This approach is in marked contrast to the art of the Classical age, in which artists strove to present an ideal, dreamlike image of human beings.

that when Alexander the Great passed through Corinth, he sought out Diogenes and asked him, "What would you like me to do for you?" Diogenes, who was basking in the sun, had just one simple request: "Move aside. You're blocking my sun."

Diogenes mistrusted all social conventions and traditions, believing that they inspired falsehood and self-deception. He reportedly once walked through the streets of Corinth with a lighted lamp, seeking an honest man—or perhaps demonstrating that it would be difficult to find one.

Although Diogenes preferred to live without physical comforts himself, he deplored the existence of poverty, for he believed it produced a love of money. His followers continued his practice of criticizing the existing social order, and also imitated Di-

The "Laocoon" is one of the most famous Hellenistic sculptures. It portrays a mythical event of the Trojan War: Apollo has sent snakes to punish Laocoon, the priest of Troy, for warning his fellow citizens about the Trojan horse.

results from becoming self-sufficient, and that this state is achieved by limiting one's desires and needs. He actually attempted to live like a dog, using rags and a wooden barrel for clothing and shelter, and carrying on his private life in public view. In fact, the term *cynicism* was derived from the Greek word *kyon*, meaning "dog." Stories about Diogenes emphasized his efforts to live in the most "natural" state possible. For example, it was said that he once rolled in the snow clasping a marble statue in order to inure himself to the cold. Another story related ogenes' direct speech and rude manners. As a result, the term *cynic* came to refer to a person who has a contemptuous and critical attitude toward accepted beliefs and ways of life.

Epicureanism. One of the most popular schools of philosophy was founded by Epicurus (342-271 B.C.), who established a school in Athens in 306 B.C. He decided that pleasure is derived from the satisfaction of wants, and that pain results from the inability to satisfy them. Therefore, wise people will live in such a way that they have no wants that cannot be satisfied. The greatest obstacle to tranquillity of soul, he thought, was the fear of the gods and of death. Epicurus devised reassurances for people troubled by each of these fears. Humans have no reason to fear the gods, he said, because the latter have no interest in human affairs. And there is no reason to fear death, he maintained, because the soul would not survive the disintegration of the body's atoms.

Later followers of Epicurus corrupted his teachings to the point that today we refer to a person who is devoted to the pursuit of pleasure—especially the enjoyment of fancy foods—as an "epicure."

Stoicism. Zeno, the founder of Stoicism, was born on Cyprus in 335 B.C. Like Diogenes and Epicurus, he was greatly influenced by the teachings of Socrates and Plato, and used them as a starting point for his own thinking. Because Zeno taught in a building called the *Stoa Poikile* ("Painted Porch"), his teachings came to be called *stoicism*. He believed that the universe is governed by laws that guide all events to good, and that these laws are superior to the laws and customs of any human society. He taught that a wise person lives in harmony with these laws and recognizes that, since pain and misfortune are inescapable, all events should be borne with calm acceptance.

Zeno's followers later developed a theory that fire was the supreme power of the universe, that a spark of such fire resides in every individual, and that, because each person has a spark of divinity, all people are related as equals to all other human beings. The philosophy developed by the Stoics became very popular among Roman intellectuals during the period of the Roman Empire, and the concept of accepting all of the events of life as divine will later found its way into the theology of Christianity.

SCIENCE

During the 3rd century B.C., the observations that Babylonian astronomers had made over the course of several centuries were translated into Greek, and Greek scholars also became aware of the work of Egyptian and Babylonian mathematicians. The exchange of ideas between these cultures, as well as a widespread interest in new learning, led to great achievements in various fields of science during the Hellenistic era.

The Greeks used their knowledge of astronomy and mathematics to create incredibly accurate theories concerning the solar system and the laws of nature. They realized, for instance, that the earth is round, and that the planets revolve about the sun. However, the great theorists of the ancient world seldom put their discoveries to practical use. Because slave labor was cheap and plentiful, there was little incentive to invent labor saving tools. And the scientists tended to feel that practical applications were vulgar or demeaning. Even Archimedes, who became famous for his ingenious devices, was reportedly reluctant to allow his experimental machines to be utilized, for he did not want to be looked upon as a mere engineer.

Euclid. The most famous mathematician of the age was Euclid (365-300 B.C.), who is still known as the "father of scientific geometry." During the reign of Ptolemy I, Euclid opened a school in Egypt where he taught the theorems of plane and solid geometry. He blended original ideas with long established concepts in a book called *Elements of Geometry*, which remained a standard textbook until the 20th century. Ptolemy reportedly voiced the thoughts of many students by asking Euclid whether geometry might not be made easier to learn. Euclid replied, "There is no royal road."

Archimedes. One of the greatest scientists of ancient times was Archimedes (287-212 B.C.), who was born in Syracuse, Sicily, and studied at Alexandria. He developed new methods for measuring the surface area and volume of objects—the field now known as solid geometry—and was the first to compute the value of "pi," the ratio of the circumference of a circle to its diameter. He accidentally discovered the concept of "specific gravity" when he observed the displacement of water as he entered a bath. Legend has it that he became so excited about this discovery that he ran naked through the streets shouting "Eureka!" ("I have found it.").

Archimedes was interested in both theoretical and applied mechanics. He invented a planetarium to demonstrate the movements of heavenly bodies and to explain the phenomenon of eclipses. He studied the ratio of force and weight involved in moving heavy bodies with the assistance of pulleys and levers, and his knowledge of this subject led him to claim that he could move the earth if he had a long enough lever.

While living in Alexandria, Archimedes invented a water screw to raise water from the Nile River to irrigate the fields. The "Archimedian screw," as it came to be called, could also be used to pump water out of mines and from the holds of ships. When Rome besieged Syracuse in 215-212 B.C., the war machines designed by Archimedes helped to defend the city. One of the most famous of his "engines of war" was a group of concave mirrors arranged so as to focus the energy of the sun onto a very small spot. This device was used to set Roman ships afire before they could enter the harbor of Syracuse. One day, after Syracuse had fallen to the Romans, Archimedes told a Roman soldier not to interrupt him while he worked on a mathematical problem. The soldier took offense at this and killed him.

Aristarchus. Aristarchus of Samos (310-230 B.C.) proposed the heliocentric theory of the universe; that is, that the earth and other planets revolve around the sun. His theory was rejected by other prominent astronomers of the Hellenistic age, but it was finally confirmed many centuries later by Copernicus and Galileo.

Eratosthenes. Eratosthenes (276-195 B.C.), the chief librarian at Alexandria, was one of the most versatile thinkers of his age. He wrote manuscripts on mathematics, philosophy, grammar, and literary criticism, but is best known today for his contribution to geography. He was the first person to use grid lines to represent latitude and longitude on a map. He then used measurements of the sun's altitude on the horizon to calculate the circumference of the earth. Realizing that the sun would be directly overhead the city of Syrene in Egypt on the day of the summer solstice (June 21), Eratosthenes measured the angle of a shadow that the sun cast on the same day in Alexandria. Using an estimate of the distance between the two cities, he then used geometry to arrive at a surprisingly accurate calculation of the circumference of the earth.

Hipparchus. Hipparchus (165-125 B.C.) rejected the heliocentric theory of the planets, but used his knowledge of geometry and astronomy to develop many accurate observations. He refined the concept of latitude and longitude developed by Eratosthenes, and created the 360 divisions that are still used by cartographers today. He described the precession of equinoxes, and compiled a catalog of 1000 stars. His geocentric theory of the universe was supported by Ptolemy, who published a treatise on mathematical astronomy in the 2nd century A.D. The *Ptolemaic system* was universally accepted until the 16th century, when Copernicus proved, at least to his own satisfaction, that the sun is the center of our planetary system.

SUMMARY

During the 4th century B.C., the resources of the Greek city-states proved to be no match for the permanent, professional army and capable leadership of Philip II of Macedonia. Although Demosthenes, in Athens, succeeded in mobilizing the Greek city-states to fight the Macedonians, the fragile, temporary coalitions he created could not prevent Philip from conquering Greece. Philip succeeded in creating a united Macedonian-Greek empire, but was assassinated before he could fulfill his dream of conquering the Persian Empire.

Philip's dream of further conquests was realized by his son, Alexander, who came to be called "the Great." Alexander's empire became the basis for a vast colonization movement as thousands of Greeks and Macedonians settled in the cities that Alexander and his successors founded. The cultural exchanges and economic prosperity of the era following Alexander's death contributed to the artistic, literary, and scientific achievements of the Hellenistic era.

QUESTIONS

1 What effects did Philip II, Alexander the Great, and their successors achieve by developing cities? How did this policy of urbanization help them to promote Hellenistic civilization?

2 Why did Alexander become a model of the hero for many generations after his lifetime? How do you think his untimely death might have contributed to the mystique about him?

3 How was Alexander's conquest different from previous conquests? How might the world have been different if Alexander had lived longer?

4 How did the advocates of Cynicism, Stoicism, and Epicurianism define the good life?

5 What relation do you see between the government of the Aetolian and Achaean Leagues and that of the United States?

BIBLIOGRAPHY

Which reference might discuss Alexander's battle strategies?

FOX, ROBIN LANE. *The Search for Alexander.* New York: Little, Brown, 1980. *Traces the career of Alexander and evaluates the probable content of the memoirs written by Ptolemy and Nearchus, Alexander's boyhood friends and fellow adventurers. Lavishly illustrated with color photographs of the sites, landscapes, and artifacts associated with Alexander.*

"In the Footsteps of Alexander the Great." *National Geographic* 133, 1 (1968): 1-65. *The authors traveled 25,000 miles by jeep, by foot, and on horseback to trace the route of Alexander. They provide well-informed descriptions of the difficulties of the terrain and the physical hardships that Alexander and his men faced; excellent illustrations of the territories as they look today.*

9

Remember, Roman, these will be your arts: to teach the ways of peace to those you conquer, to spare the defeated peoples and tame the proud.

VIRGIL

Rome: City-State to Empire

The peninsula of Italy was invaded by Indo-European peoples about 2000 B.C. One of these tribes, the Latins, founded a settlement on the Tiber River which came to be called Rome. At the beginning of the 7th century B.C., a second wave of invaders descended into the area. These invaders were the Etruscans, a people whose culture and language still hold many mysteries for modern scholars. Within a century, the Etruscans established control over much of northern Italy and imposed their own government on the Romans.

In the year 509 B.C., according to tradition, the Romans threw off the yoke of their Etruscan overlords and established a republic. During the following years, the Romans refined the institutions of their republic in response to the need for a strong military establishment and to the demands of the common people. By 287 B.C., Rome had gained control of all of Italy, and had developed an effective system of governing conquered areas.

GEOGRAPHY AND NATURAL RESOURCES The best-known feature of the geography of Italy is its resemblance to a boot. The ranges of latitude and longitude are very nearly equal to those of California, but the area is only about two-thirds that of the state. Both Italy and California are quite mountainous, the Apennines forming a spine down the peninsula similar to the Sierra Nevada spine of California. The broad valley of the Po River, across the northern end of Italy, is a rich agricultural area, as is the Central Valley of California.

The best natural harbors on the Italian coasts were occupied by the Greeks by about 600 B.C. The Romans, therefore, tended to expand overland. To facilitate transportation inland, the Romans periodically dredged the seabed near the city of Ostia, at the mouth of the Tiber River, so that boats could pass from the Tyrrhenian Sea to Rome.

The minerals of Italy were an important resource in ancient times and continue to be utilized in the modern world. Italian marble, which is still used throughout the world for impressive structures, enabled emperors of the 1st century to create the monuments that symbolized Rome's imperial period. Tufa, an easily cut volcanic rock, was also utilized for building construction in Italy. Another important resource was clay, which was widely used for making bricks and pottery.

The climate and soil of Italy compared favorably to those of Greece. In ancient times, Italy had many forests and an abundance of wild animals, which the early inhabitants utilized for shipbuilding timber and food. When the forests were cleared, the fertile volcanic soil and mild climate proved to be highly suitable for growing grain as well as for cultivating grapevines and olive trees. The ancient Italians thus had two important resources—timber and grain—which were in short supply on the Greek peninsula.

THE ROMANS Historians have difficulty when they try to reconstruct the early history of Rome. The Greek colonists who settled in Magna Graecia (Chapter 6) did not consider the Romans to be worth writing about, and most of the physical facilities of the earliest city were destroyed by the Gauls in 390 B.C. Later Roman historians utilized oral traditions and written inscriptions that existed in their time to reconstruct the first few centuries of the city's history.

ORIGINS

The historians Livy and Dionysius, who lived in the 1st century B.C., are our most important sources of information concerning Rome's earliest history. Livy, who lived and worked in Rome, emphasized the dignity and virtue of the earliest Romans in his work *Ab Urbe Condita* ("From the Founding of the City"). Dionysius of Halicarnassus, a Greek writer, described the development of Roman civilization for the benefit of Greek readers. His *Roman Antiquities* draws many parallels between Greek and Roman civilization, and even suggests that the Romans' ancestors were Greek and Trojan heroes.

According to one ancient tradition, Rome was first founded by Aeneas, a hero of the Trojan War, and his followers, who conquered the native Latin tribes of the area and eventually intermarried with them. A second tradition recounted the founding of Rome

The story of Romulus and Remus was one of the central legends of Rome's early history. This statue of a wolf dates from the 5th century B.C.; the figures of the twins were added during the Renaissance.

as a city of Latins during the 8th century B.C. According to this story, Romulus and Remus, twins of royal birth, were nursed by a wolf and raised by a shepherd after their uncle abandoned them in the wilderness. Later, they discovered the secret of their royal birth and resolved to create a new city near the cottage where they had grown up. They fought a battle to decide who would be king of the new city, and Romulus finally emerged as the victor.

Archaeological Findings. Livy noted that the legends concerning Rome's beginnings could not be confirmed or denied by researchers of his own generation:

● ● ● *Events before Rome was born or thought of have come to us in old tales with more of the charm of poetry than of a sound historical record, and such traditions I propose neither to affirm nor refute.*[1]

Modern archaeologists, however, have found limited evidence for both legends of Rome's founding. They have discovered scattered traces of Bronze-Age navigators in Italy, making it possible to believe that Mycenaean adventurers explored and colonized the area. Also, post holes carved in the tufa rock of

[1]Livy I, Preface, 6.

the Palatine Hill in Rome have supplied important clues about the civilization that existed there in the 8th century B.C. Using the post holes as a guide, archaeologists have built round huts of wattle and mud to reconstruct the settlement that existed in Romulus' time.

RELIGION

The earliest Romans believed that there were spirits everywhere: in fire, water, stones, and trees; in the planting of seeds and the baking of bread. These spirits had no names and no specific shape, but people believed that they could help or hurt them. The spirits were at first worshiped by families in their own homes. Respect for the spirit of fire, for instance, was demonstrated by throwing salt into the hearth at mealtimes, and the spirit of the doorway was appeased by a special ceremony when a stranger entered. In time, these rituals became more public, and priests were appointed to build temples for the deities. As they established community cults,

After Jupiter, Mars was the most revered deity of the early Romans. In this portrait, the self-assured god poses on a war chariot.

Janus was one of the household spirits worshiped by the earliest Romans. With his two faces, he watchfully guarded all doorways and gates.

the priests assigned names to the ancient household spirits. The spirit of fire, for instance, became known as Vesta; the spirit of the doorway was named Janus; and the spirits that guarded cupboards were called the Penates. Other early deities were adopted from the Etruscans and Greeks, including Jupiter, the sky-god; Mars, the god of war; and Minerva, the goddess who protected cities.

According to tradition, Numa Pompilius, who succeeded Romulus as king of Rome, was responsible for creating the religious institutions of Rome. He reportedly appointed the first *Vestal Virgins*, the priestesses who maintained a temple of Vesta, and the *flamines*, or priests, who supervised the wor-

> *Several months in our modern calendar preserve the names of gods worshiped by the ancient Romans. January (Januarius) was sacred to Janus, the god of entrances and beginnings. March (Martius) was dedicated to a festival in honor of Mars, the god of war and agriculture. Juno, the wife of Jupiter, gave her name to June (Junius), the month considered most propitious for marriage.*

ship of Mars and Jupiter. Numa was also credited with reforming the Roman calendar so that special religious holidays could be named by date and observed by all.[2]

THE ETRUSCANS Rome began as a small village in a world not yet dominated by the Greek culture we have just studied. The village was, however, adjacent to the remarkable civilization of the Etruscans. We know much about the politics, philosophy, religion, and arts of the ancient Greeks, but very little about the Etruscans.

Ancient sources indicate that scattered groups of Etruscans had been present in Italy since prehistoric times. The first sizable group of Etruscans settled on the western coast of Italy about 700 B.C.. The territory they inhabited came to be known to the Latins as *Etruria*; today it is called Tuscany.

The Etruscans were accomplished metalworkers: they knew how to use the copper and tin that they found locally, and they refined iron ore obtained from the nearby island of Elba. They traded objects made from these metals with merchants from Egypt, Greece, Magna Graecia, and the Middle East for glass objects, textiles, and other items. In this process, they came in contact with the Greek and Phoenician civilizations.

---

[2]The reformed calendar had 12 months and corresponded to the solar year; the earlier calendar had been based on the moon's cycle of 10 months.

LANGUAGE

Because later Romans were not greatly interested in the Etruscans, their literary works were not translated or preserved. Most of the Etruscan writings that have come down to us are very short tomb inscriptions. The longest known Etruscan text, about 1300 words, was found on a linen cloth used to wrap a mummy in Egypt. Scholars have had little difficulty in deciphering these inscriptions, for the Etruscans used a 27-letter alphabet based on the Greek alphabet. But because the writings are limited in content and are quite brief, little can be discovered concerning the grammar and syntax of the language.

ORIGINS

Dionysius reported that there were two theories concerning the origin of the Etruscans: one theory was that they had migrated to Italy from Lydia, an ancient kingdom of Asia Minor; the other that they were **indigenous**, or native, to Italy. These two theories are still debated today.

Herodotus, who lived 400 years before Dionysius, reported that the Etruscans, or Tyrrhenians, as he called them, came from Lydia. Dionysius himself believed that the Etruscans were indigenous to Italy, arguing that their language was quite unlike that of the Lydians. Modern scholars tend to support Herodotus' opinion. Linguists studying the Etruscan and Lydian languages have found some similarities between the two. And in 1885, archaeologists discovered two funerary stelae with similar inscriptions; one on the island of Lemnos in the Aegean Sea, and the other in Tuscany. Many scholars now believe that the stelae were carved by the ancient Etruscans, indicating that the Etruscans used Lemnos as a supply point as they traveled from Lydia to Italy.

CULTURE

Like the Egyptians and Sumerians, the Etruscans spent much time and care in their preparation for life after death. Most of our

The tombs of this Etruscan necropolis are arranged like houses on a narrow street.

chaeologists have found sculptures, shields, pottery, and jewelry. Some of the tombs also contain frescoes that show fascinating glimpses of the everyday lives of these people, including scenes of chariot races, bull fights, dancing, and fishing. The pictures indicate that Etruscan women enjoyed equality and freedom, advantages enjoyed by few other women in ancient societies.

Between 650 and 600 B.C., a federation of Etruscan city-states moved south and conquered the plain of Latium, including the village of Rome. During the reign of the Etruscan monarchy in Rome (616-509 B.C.), the Etruscans made a lasting contribution to the city's institutions and government. Such distinctive features of later Roman life as gladitorial contests, chariot races, and symbols of *imperium*, or absolute authority, were inherited from the Etruscans. Through the Etruscans, the Romans also learned about certain aspects of Greek culture, including the use of an alphabet and the worship of anthropomorphic gods.

knowledge of the Etruscans has been derived from their *necropoleis* ("cities of the dead"), in which tombs were arranged like houses on small streets. Within these tombs, ar-

A gayly painted fresco in a 5th-century B.C. Etruscan tomb shows musicians marching to a banquet hall.

This painted statue of Apollo dates from the 6th century B.C. Apollo was one of many gods whom the Etruscans adopted from the Greeks.

THE FIRST KINGS OF ROME

Modern scholars have found evidence to support some of the ancient legends concerning the early kings of Rome, but they also have determined that these stories contain certain inaccuracies and exaggerations. For instance, all of the early Roman historians reported that the Etruscans were expelled from Rome in 509 B.C. Other evidence indicates, however, that the Etruscans actually ruled Rome for several years after this date. The Romans may have set the earlier date because they did not wish to credit the Etruscans with several large building projects completed after 509 B.C. But in spite of doubts concerning certain dates and details, modern scholars believe that the Roman historians were correct in stating that the central institutions and customs of later Rome were developed during the 140-year reign of Romulus and his three Latin-Sabine successors.

In ancient Rome, as in Greece, the basic unit of society was the tribe, a group of families who had a common ancestor. The Latin term for these related families was *gens*.

Romulus. According to tradition, Romulus organized the *gentes*[3] of Rome into larger groups called *curiae*. He established a total of 30 *curiae*, and decreed that they would meet in an assembly called the *Comitia Curiata*. Romulus is also credited with establishing the Senate, or "Council of Elders." This assembly consisted of 100 *patricians*, or nobles, who were summoned by the king to give their advice. Excluded from the *Comitia Curiata* and the Senate were the *plebeians* or *plebs*, a group of people who could not prove that they belonged to one of the recognized *gentes*. The plebs were also excluded from military duties, since army levies were contributed by the *curiae*.

In the system established by Romulus, the king served as war chief, high priest, and

---

[3]*Gentes* is the plural form of *gens*.

204

THE SEVEN LEGENDARY KINGS OF ANCIENT ROME	
753-717	Romulus (Latin)
717-673	Numa Pompilius (Sabine)
672-641	Tullus Hostilius (Latin)
641-616	Ancus Martius (Sabine)
616-579	Tarquinius Priscus (Etruscan)
579-535	Servius Tullius (Latin)
534-509	Tarquinius Superbus (Etruscan)

supreme judge. He had absolute powers while he lived, but could not designate his successor. The *Comitia Curiata* nominated a new king, and the Senate, after consulting soothsayers, confirmed or denied the nomination.

In addition to founding Rome as a city of Latins and establishing its laws and institutions, Romulus is credited with two other achievements. He reportedly united his own people with the Sabines, a neighboring tribe, by forcibly seizing the young women of the tribe and marrying them to his soldiers. He also established Rome's military domination over the surrounding countryside.

Numa Pompilius. The second of the legendary kings of Rome was known as a highly religious king. Later Romans believed that he established the religious institutions of Rome and revised the calendar (as mentioned above), assigning specific dates for religious festivals.

Tullus Hostilius. The third legendary king of Rome reportedly increased the population of his city through conquest. After destroying the nearby city of Alba Longa, he forced its citizens to move to Rome.

Ancus Martius. The last of the Latin-Sabine kings was credited with two peaceful achievements. He was reportedly the first king to think of dredging a harbor near Ostia, at the mouth of the Tiber River, and to build fortifications to protect commercial traffic on the river.

ETRUSCAN RULE

It is not known exactly how the Etruscans seized control of Rome. One tradition related that Tarquinius Priscus, the first Etruscan king, entered Rome in a cart to show his peaceful intentions. Little by little, he then gathered enough supporters to seize the throne.

The Etruscan monarchs of Rome, known as the Tarquins, introduced several innovations in the monarchy of Rome. To symbolize the absolute power of the king, an official called a *lictor* stood in front of the king, holding a *fasces*. The *fasces* consisted of a bundle of elmwood rods bound together around an axe, signifying the power of the king to scourge or behead his subjects. The Etruscans were also responsible for at least two important construction projects: under their rule, the *Cloaca Maxima* ("great sewer") was built to drain the site of the Roman Forum, and a wall was built around the seven hills of Rome. The Etruscans probably also constructed the *Capitoline Jupiter*, a magnificent temple to Jupiter on the Capitoline Hill.

THE REFORMS OF SERVIUS TULLIUS

According to tradition, Servius Tullius, a Roman plebeian, married the daughter of Tarquinius Priscus, and ultimately succeeded his father-in-law as king of Rome. He was credited with making important and lasting reforms in the army and government of early Rome. Some modern scholars believe that Roman historians may have invented the figure of Servius Tullius so that they could attribute certain important developments to a Latin king rather than to the Etruscans. Others believe that Servius was an historical character, arguing that an invented king would have been given a patrician name rather than a plebeian one.

The basis of the reforms attributed to Servius was the need for a larger army. Because of changes in military tactics throughout the Mediterranean world, *hoplites*, heavily armed footsoldiers, came to be considered the most important part of the army. An effective phalanx of infantry therefore became necessary for Rome's security, but the *curiae* were unable to supply sufficient troops.

Servius' first reform was to expand the number of *curiae* so that plebeians and resident foreigners could be included. For this purpose, he took a census of all of the inhabitants of Rome, enumerating the property holdings of each person. He then created 4 new tribes in the city of Rome, and 16 tribes in the surrounding countryside.

Comitia Curiata. The enlarged *Comitia Curiata* continued to function as it had under the monarchy. It was organized by tribes, and its voting procedures were fairly democratic. In private meetings held by each *curia*, the *gentes* were polled by their leaders to determine the majority opinion of the *curia* on any given issue. Each member had an equal vote in this preliminary poll, and the *curia* then delivered its majority opinion in public meetings of the *Comitia Curiata*.

Comitia Centuriata. To determine how the burden of military service should be apportioned, Servius used the results of his census to divide the people of Rome into five classes. The first class consisted of men who could afford to supply a full set of armor and weapons for hoplite fighting: helmet, bronze body armor, shield, sword, and spear. The second class comprised those who could not afford bronze armor; and the third and fourth classes those who lacked other pieces of the equipment. The fifth, and last, class included men who were armed only with slingshots. In addition to the five hoplite classes, the census also defined a class of *equites*, or knights, men who could afford to maintain a horse for the service of the state; and a class of *proletarii*, men who were not armed at all, but acted as servants to the armed men.

Because fully armed men were the most valuable to the state, Servius inducted more wealthy citizens than poorer ones into the army. Altogether, there were 80 *centuries*, or groups of 100 men, in the first two hoplite classes, and 18 *centuries* in the *equite* class. In times of danger, the *Comitia Centuriata*, an assembly of all of the *centuries*, was summoned to the Campus Martius ("Field of Mars"). Each *century* voted as a block, and was called upon to vote in order of rank. Because the wealthier, well equipped *centuries* outnumbered the poorer ones, they were able to decide an issue if they voted as a block. The votes of the poorer citizens of Rome therefore had less weight in the military assembly of the *Comitia Centuriata* than in the *Comitia Curiata*.

In time, the *Comitia Centuriata* took over many of the responsibilities of the *Comitia Curiata*. Servius' reforms thus led to the development of a modified **timocracy**. Many more people were included in the political process, but the poorest people had less influence than the wealthier ones.

RETURN TO ETRUSCAN RULE

According to Roman tradition, Servius Tullius was succeeded by an Etruscan named Tarquinius Superbus (Tarquin the Proud), who became the most repressive king Rome had ever known. In 509 B.C., it was said, the outraged Romans overthrew the Etruscan monarchy and established a republic.

ORGANIZATION OF THE COMITIA CENTURIATA	
Equites (Cavalry)	*18 centuries*
Hoplites - 1st class	*80 centuries*
- 2nd class	*20 centuries*
- 3rd class	*20 centuries*
- 4th class	*20 centuries*
- 5th class	*30 centuries*
Proletarians (support)	*5 centuries*
Total	*193 centuries*

THE ROMAN REPUBLIC After the downfall of the Etruscan monarchy, the word *rex* (king) became a detested symbol of excessive power, and it remained so throughout the long history of Rome. The expulsion of the Etruscans was later celebrated as the foundation of Roman liberty.

DUAL CONSULSHIP

In place of the monarchy, the Romans instituted a system in which two *consuls* were elected by the *Comitia Curiata* for a one-year term. The consuls had *imperium*, or absolute power, during their term of office, and on formal occasions they were preceded by a dozen *lictors* who carried the *fasces*. But although each consul could issue edicts which had the force of law, the other consul could nullify such an edict by exclaiming *Veto!* ("I forbid."). During times of peace, the two consuls alternated in office each month, and during times of war they alternated each day. When a crisis occurred, the Senate and consuls together could appoint a *dictator* who would exercise absolute power for a period of six months. The legend of Cincinnatus relates how one citizen reluctantly agreed to serve Rome as dictator, then happily returned to his farm when the emergency was over.

THE ASSEMBLIES

Under the republican system, the *Comitia Curiata* and the *Comitia Centuriata* continued to play an important part in public affairs. They elected the consuls and other public officials, and also served as a court of appeal for citizens convicted of a capital offense. In day-to-day affairs, however, the Senate had a greater role than the assemblies.

THE SENATE

Because the senators served for life and represented the oldest and most prestigious families of Rome, a consul could not easily disregard their advice. They represented continuity and authority, and, as long as they upheld high standards of conduct, their opinions had the force of law in Rome's republic. In times of war, the Senate influenced the appointment of military commanders and determined how troops would be levied. In times of peace, it controlled the state treasury and collected taxes. The Senate also had an important role in foreign affairs: it received foreign ambassadors, and ratified treaties and alliances with other nations. As Rome acquired more territory, the senators no longer performed all administrative duties themselves, but they appointed many of the officials who governed the provinces.

During the early years of the republic, only *patricians* were eligible to belong to the Senate. In time, however, membership was open to all people who had served in public office, except those excluded for bad conduct. Thus, as plebeians won the right to hold public offices, they also gained representation in the Senate.

CONCILIUM PLEBIS

The plebeians of Rome were soon dissatisfied with the constitution of the republic. In 494 B.C., according to tradition, plebeian soldiers went on strike, stating that they would form an independent city unless they were granted important political rights. Realizing that Rome would be greatly weakened without the plebeians' military services, the Senate granted them the right to form a political assembly of their own. The plebeian assembly became known as the *Concilium Plebis*.

The *Concilium Plebis*, like the *Comitia Curiata*, was organized by tribes into *curiae*. It had the authority to pass *plebecita* ("peoples' decrees"), but these were binding only on plebeians. Thus, Rome had, in effect, one government for the patricians and one for the plebeians.

The Tribunes. The leaders of the plebeians did not have *imperium*, but they were

GOVERNMENT OF THE ROMAN REPUBLIC

CONSULSHIP

Members: Two consuls elected by the *Comitia Centuriata* annually.

Role: Issue laws and decrees—usually, but not necessarily, after submitting decisions to the Senate for a vote. Each consul has the authority to veto a decision of the other.

SENATE

Members: In the early days of the Republic, 100 senators were chosen from the most prominent patrician families of Rome. Later, all who have served in public office are eligible to belong.

Role: Administer the laws and decrees enacted by the consuls; issue resolutions on important matters; receive foreign ambassadors; ratify treaties and alliances with foreign powers.

ASSEMBLIES:

Comitia Curiata

Members: The recognized *curiae* of Rome. (Each *curia* consists of several related *gentes*, or tribes.)

Role: Formally confer *imperium* on newly elected consuls and *praetors*; approve family documents, as for adoptions and wills; vote on legislation presented by the magistrates of Rome.

Comitia Centuriata

Members: The army of Rome, organized into *centuries*, or groups of 100.

Role: Elect *consuls, praetors,* and *censors*; serve as court of appeal for major law court cases; vote on legislation presented by the magistrates of Rome. After 287 B.C., this assembly could enact legislation of its own.

Concilium Plebis

Members: Plebeian *curiae*.

Role: Enact *plebecites*, or people's decrees, which are binding upon all plebeians; elect 10 *tribunes* to defend and represent plebeians in the government of Rome. After 287 B.C., plebecites of the *Concilium Plebis* were binding upon all Romans.

Comitia Tributa Populi

Members: All free citizens of Rome, organized by *curiae*.

Role: Elect *quaestors*; propose legislation; serve as court of appeal for minor law court cases. In 287 B.C., this assembly received the right to enact legislation.

---

accorded several important privileges and powers. In their role as protectors of the plebeians, they were recognized as sacrosanct: anyone who injured a tribune was declared an outlaw, and the house of a tribune was considered an inviolable sanctuary. Thus, a tribune could shield plebeians who had been declared criminals by the consuls or other magistrates. Within a few years, the tribunes also won the right to veto any official act passed by the consuls or the Senate. By 449 B.C., there were 10 tribunes to represent the plebeians.

The power of veto gave the tribunes great importance in the government of Rome, but they had only a negative role: they could prevent the Senate from passing a law, but did not have the authority to substitute laws of their own. During the next century, the plebeians struggled to gain public offices and to make the decisions of their assembly binding upon all Romans. They eventually achieved representation in the highest government offices: a plebeian first achieved office as *quaestor* in 409 B.C.; as consul in 366; as dictator in 356; and as *censor* in 351. (See the descriptions of *quaestor* and *censor* below.) Finally, in 287 B.C., a plebeian dictator passed the *Hortensian law*, making plebiscites of the *Concilium Plebis* binding upon all citizens.

COMITIA TRIBUTA POPULI

Due to the initiative of the plebeians, a public assembly called the *Comitia Tributa Populi* was formed in 447 B.C. This assembly included all free citizens of Rome, and provided a means by which the "will of the people" could be ascertained.

The creation of the Comitia Tributa Populi meant that there were four public assemblies in Rome. None of the three earlier assemblies was abolished, but instead the four assemblies functioned independently, with overlapping functions and membership. In 287 B.C., the *Comitia Tributa*, like the *Concilium Plebis*, received the right to enact laws.

OTHER MAGISTRATES OF THE REPUBLIC

Early in the republic, a number of offices were created to administer the decisions of the consuls and the Senate, and to assist the tribunes. As Rome acquired additional territories, the number of *consuls, tribunes,* and *censors* remained constant, but additional offices of *quaestor, praetor,* and *aedile* were created to handle the increasing burden of administration.

Quaestor. The first consuls of the republic appointed officials known as *quaestors* to serve as their assistants. The *quaestors* were responsible for investigating murder cases and for financial administration. In 447 B.C., as a concession to the plebeians, *quaestors* were elected by the *Comitia Tributa* rather than being appointed by the consuls.

Praetor. In 366 B.C., the office of *praetor* was created. This official assisted the consuls by acting as a judge and had the power of *imperium*, but to a lesser degree than the consuls. He could take charge of the city if the consuls were absent, and could, in an emergency, assume command of the army.

Aedile. The tribunes originally appointed two *aediles* to assist them in administrative matters. In time, two patrician *aediles* were also elected, and the four officers then met as a committee to arrange public games and to supervise the grain supply.

Censor. The important office of *censor* was created in 433. The two censors were responsible for assessing the property holdings of all citizens and assigning them to their *gentes, curiae,* and *centuries.* They also acted as enforcers of public morality. They had the authority to appoint new senators, and to expel from the Senate those whom they considered unworthy to hold office. Although the *censors* did not have *imperium*, their authority to appoint and remove senators gave them great influence. The *censors* were elected by the *Comitia Centuriata* for a term of five years, but they were expected to complete their work within 18 months.

EARLY DEVELOPMENT OF THE CONSTITUTION

Law of the 12 Tablets. Even after the establishment of the *Concilium Plebis* and the guarantee of the tribunes' authority, the plebeians of Rome felt that they needed further protection against the judicial powers of senators and other magistrates. The second major victory won by the plebeians—after the establishment of the Concilium Plebis—was the right of all Roman citizens to be judged equally under the law. In 449 B.C., the traditional laws of Rome were written on 12 wooden tablets which were set up in the Forum for all to see. The Law of the 12 Tab-

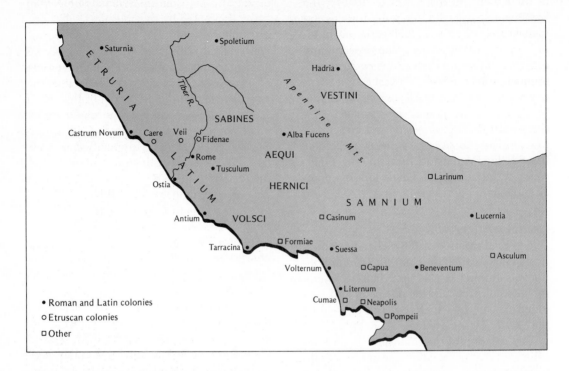

lets, as the code came to be known, was considered to be the source of all civil and criminal law. Every Roman citizen was expected to memorize the laws contained on the tablets.

Canuleian Law. Several years later, in 445 B.C., the plebeians gained another concession: the Canuleian Law, named after Canuleius, the tribune who proposed it, permitted marriages between patricians and plebeians.

EXPANSION IN CENTRAL ITALY

In 493 B.C., Rome and several other Latin city-states created a confederation known as the *Concilium Latinorum*, or Latin League. During the 5th century, the members of the league agreed upon a common foreign policy and, in times of war, elected a dictator to lead their combined armies. The league's forces successfully repelled invasions of the Sabines, the Aequi, the Volsci, and other mountain tribes who were attempting to move into the plain of Latium.

Eventually, the Romans demonstrated that they had enough military power to act independently of the league. In 426, Rome resolved a long-standing dispute with the Etruscans over inland trade routes by conquering the Etruscan city of Fidenae. And in 405, the Romans began to besiege the powerful Etruscan city of Veii. In 395, after a 10-year siege, Veii finally fell to the Romans.

INVASION OF THE GAULS

Shortly after Rome's conquest of Veii, the Gauls, or Celts, warlike Indo-European tribes from the north, began to invade Italy. Because the Etruscan cities to the north had been weakened by their long struggle with Rome, they were unable to stem the force of the invasion, and the members of the Latin

League failed to organize a military force. As a result, Rome was struck particularly hard by the Gauls. In 390 B.C., the Gauls defeated the Roman army and entered Rome. As the Gauls besieged and sacked Rome, many Romans found refuge in the nearby Etruscan city of Veii. For a short time, they even considered relocating to Veii. But they decided that Rome must be rebuilt on its original site because the ground had been blessed by the gods when the city was founded. According to tradition, the Romans paid the Gauls 1000 pounds in gold to leave Rome. The Gauls then withdrew to northern Italy and settled in the area that came to be known as *Cisalpine* ("This side of the Alps") Gaul.

The Romans built aqueducts to bring fresh water to their city from the earliest times. In 272 B.C., an 40-mile-long aqueduct was built between Rome and a spring in the Sabine hills.

One benefit that Rome provided to the members of its confederation was good roads. This is a section of the Appian Way, built in 312 B.C. between Rome and Capua. Eventually, the road extended all the way to Brundisium on the east coast.

THE ROMAN CONFEDERATION

After the Gauls had withdrawn to northern Italy, the Romans gradually rebuilt their city and their army. Most importantly, they began to solve the internal political and economic problems that had arisen by making fundamental changes in their constitution (see page 212). Once their internal affairs were in order, the Romans began a program of territorial expansion. Taking advantage of the disorder that prevailed among the other city-states of Latium, Roman legions swiftly conquered several nearby city-states. The Roman Senate then concluded friendly alliances with the remaining members of the Latin League. By means of treaties and victories in battle, the Romans soon established hegemony throughout central Italy. The Latin League was dissolved, and a new confederation created in which each member was bound by an alliance to Rome.

In dealing with their former allies of the Latin League and other conquered city-states, the Romans created alliances which granted varying degrees of privileges. City-states who had close ties to Rome and had accepted

Rome's domination were granted full Roman citizenship and privileges. Their citizens could vote in Rome's public assemblies and even run for public office in Rome. A second type of alliance governed city-states who were not considered ready to share the responsibilities of Roman citizenship. City-states of this second class were allowed to keep their own independent governments and public assemblies, but were overseen by a Roman praetor, or governor, who encouraged them to follow Roman law and to worship Roman gods. A third class of city-states included those located in outlying areas of Rome's territory. These city-states agreed to defend the borders of Rome's territory against attack by foreign invaders or hostile tribes, and in return were promised Roman aid in the event of such an attack.

The confederation of city-states that Rome created through its alliances was quite different from those that the Greek states had formed. The members of the new Roman confederation were bound only to Rome through alliances; not to each other. Thus, the members could not easily form a coalition against Rome, and Rome was able to arbitrate disputes that arose among the members. The general condition of peace enforced by Roman governors and Roman legions was one of the most important benefits gained by the members of the confederation. Secondly, by holding out the promise of Roman citizenship and by granting trading privileges, the Romans gained the goodwill and cooperation of most of their allies. City-states who were granted Roman citizenship were eligible to share in any spoils that Rome gained through its conquests, and all benefited from the roads that the Romans built to facilitate trade throughout central Italy. Finally, in contrast to the policy of Athens toward members of the Delian League, the Romans did not demand tribute payments to maintain its army. Instead, the troops levied from member city-states were maintained by

Roman taxpayers. By 340 B.C., Rome was the recognized leader of central Italy.

REVISION OF THE CONSTITUTION

In the decades following the Gallic invasion of 390 B.C., the Romans faced a severe economic crisis. The greatest losses were suffered by the plebeians, especially those who owned small farms in the countryside surrounding Rome. In order to finance the rebuilding of their farms, many of these small landholders became deeply indebted to wealthy patricians. Under the laws of the 12 Tablets, debtors were subject to imprisonment or even slavery if they failed to pay back their creditors. Thus a situation arose in which the men who had formed the bulk of Rome's army during the Gallic invasion were forced, by economic conditions, into a position of dependence or even slavery.

In the political struggle that followed, the plebeians pressed for both economic and political reforms, and were eventually accommodated. In 357 B.C., indebted farmers were given some relief by a new regulation that limited the amount of interest a creditor could charge. In addition, small landholders were given the right to colonize territory that Rome had conquered in Italy. These colonies eventually enabled many farmers to free themselves from debt, and at the same time established a Roman presence throughout the conquered areas.

The wealthy plebeians of Rome were more interested in political representation than in economic measures, and they, too, won important concessions. In 367, after a 10-year political struggle, they succeeded in breaking the patrician monopoly of high offices with the enactment of the Licinian law. This law stipulated that one of the two consuls must be a plebeian, and a plebeian was elected as consul the following year.

During Rome's wars against the Samnites (see below), the plebeians demanded and gained additional concessions from the patricians. In 306, a law was enacted which prohibited the imprisonment or enslavement of debtors. And in 287, the Hortensian law made plebescites of the Concilium Plebis binding upon all Romans. This latter law was of great importance, for it meant that Rome at last had a unified government in place of the "state within a state" that had existed since the founding of the Concilium Plebis.

EXPANSION TO THE SOUTH

As Rome expanded its influence in central Italy, it developed several friendly alliances with the Greek city-states of Magna Graecia. Through these alliances, Rome was drawn into a long series of wars against the Samnites, a fierce, well-armed people who inhabited the foothills of the Apennines. The Roman army suffered several devastating defeats at the hands of these tribes, but finally won a decisive victory over them in 306 B.C. A few years after this victory, the Samnites regrouped and united with the Etruscans and Gauls in a final attempt to check the growing power of Rome. The Romans defeated this coalition in 295, and were then recognized as the dominant power in Italy.

THE PYRRHIC WARS

In 281 B.C., Rome became involved in a dispute with Tarentum, the most powerful of the Greek colonies on the southern coast of Italy. The people of Tarentum apparently resented the influence that the Romans wielded in Magna Graecia, and provoked a fight with Rome over the issue of harbor rights. A military force from Tarentum attacked and sank several Roman ships docked in their harbor, and the Tarentines then insulted the Roman ambassador when he arrived to make inquiries. Knowing that the Romans would soon respond to these unprovoked attacks, the people of Tarentum appealed to Pyrrhus, the ruler of Epirus, for military aid.

Pyrrhus, the king of Epirus in Greece, hoped to build an empire by conquering Rome. In their wars with Pyrrhus, the Romans learned how to cope with such tactical elements as charging elephants and the Macedonian phalanx.

Pyrrhus, the ambitious king of Epirus, came to the aid of Tarentum with a force of 25,000 soldiers and 20 elephants. He met the Roman legions at Heraclea. Using the phalanx tactics of Alexander the Great, Pyrrhus managed to defeat the Romans. His victory was so costly, however, that the phrase "Pyrrhic victory" came to mean a victory that is offset by staggering losses. Pyrrhus then moved north, hoping to gain the support of Italian city-states subject to Rome. These cities, however, remained loyal to Rome, and the Roman Senate refused to negotiate peace terms as long as Pyrrhus remained in Italy.

Roman legions again met Pyrrhus' forces in battle at Asculum in 279. Again, Pyrrhus narrowly won victory but left Italy soon afterwards to fight the Carthaginians in Sicily. In 275 Pyrrhus returned, hoping to conquer all of Italy in a final battle with the Romans. The Romans, however, defeated Pyrrhus in this battle. Rome then incorporated many of the cities of Magna Graecia into its confederation through a new series of alliances.

When Pyrrhus left Italy to return to his home in Epirus, he is said to have remarked, "How fair a battlefield I am leaving to the Romans and Carthaginians!" His remark proved to be prophetic. By 265 B.C., Rome was the recognized leader of Italy, and was soon to be drawn into a prolonged war with Carthage, the other great military power of the Mediterranean world.

THE PUNIC WARS It was inevitable that Rome's conquest of southern Italy should bring her into conflict with Carthage, a city founded by the Phoenicians during the 9th century B.C. While Phoenicia itself was successively conquered by Assyria, Egypt, and Persia during the following centuries, Carthage became the center of a rich and powerful maritime empire.

Prior to the Pyrrhic wars, Rome had remained an agricultural society and had not been involved in trade and commerce with the rest of the Mediterranean world. However, Mediterranean trade was of vital concern to the city-states of Magna Graecia who had been incorporated into Rome's confederation after the withdrawal of Pyrrhus. Thus, to maintain its position as the leader of Italy, Rome had to become involved in the ancient struggle between Carthage and the Greek colonies for control of the Mediterranean.

The immediate cause of the conflict between Carthage and Rome was the interest of each in controlling trade with Sicily. In 288 B.C., the Mamertines, a group of Italian mercenary soldiers, had seized the town of Messina in Sicily and established a base for piracy there. In 265 B.C., Hiero II, the king of Syracuse, tried to evict the Mamertines from Sicily. Both Carthage and Rome sent troops to assist the Mamertines, but these two great powers were soon fighting each other. The series of wars that followed came to be known as the Punic Wars from the Latin word *Punicus*, meaning "Phoenician." The Punic Wars lasted for more than a century, and were bitterly fought throughout the western Mediterranean; in Sicily, Italy, Spain, and Africa.

FIRST PUNIC WAR (264-241 B.C.)

In 262 B.C., the Romans captured Agrigentum, but could not take the Carthaginian fortresses on the west side of Sicily, for these strongholds were constantly supplied by the Carthaginian fleet. Realizing that they would have to achieve mastery of the seas in order to defeat Carthage, the Romans captured a Carthaginian ship and used it as a model to build their own fleet of 120 ships. In 260 B.C., the Roman fleet won its first victory over a Carthaginian fleet near Mylae, on the northern coast of Sicily. Following this victory, the Romans seized the island of Corsica, but they still could not manage to expel the Carthaginians from Sicily.

In 256 B.C., the sphere of war shifted to Africa, where the Romans managed to establish a base at Clypea. The next year, however, the Carthaginians turned over the command of their army to a capable Spartan general named Xanthippus. Xanthippus defeated the Roman armies in Africa and forced them to return to Italy.

The Romans next renewed their attacks upon Sicily and achieved some successes there. In 250, the Romans lured a Carthaginian army into battle near the city of Panormus. After capturing Panormus, the Romans besieged the Carthaginian stronghold of Lilybaeum both by land and by sea. This battle ended in a stalemate, for the Romans lost their entire fleet in a storm, while the Carthaginians had to withdraw many of their troops in order to deal with an uprising in Africa.

During the next few years, private Roman citizens made great sacrifices in order to finance and build a new fleet of 200 ships. But due to the brilliant leadership of the Carthaginian general Hamilcar Barca, who had taken charge of operations in Sicily, Roman military forces still could not manage to dislodge the Carthaginians from their strongholds there. Nevertheless, the Roman fleet won a major naval victory over the Carthaginians near the coast of Africa, and in 241 Carthage finally sued for peace. Under the terms of the treaty, Carthage agreed to leave Sicily and the surrounding small islands and to pay an indemnity of 3200 talents.

Although Rome gained control of Sicily, the first Punic War was in fact a "Pyrrhic victory." The cost of the war to Rome is estimated to have been seven times the amount of the indemnity that the Carthaginians paid. And the cost in human life was enormous: the Romans lost about 30,000 of their own citizens as well as 20,000 allied soldiers.

Sicily. In dealing with their new domain of Sicily, the Romans adopted a different policy than the one they had used after earlier conquests. Because the city-states of Sicily did not have a direct interest in Rome's military activities, they were not required to supply troops to Rome. Instead, the farmers of Sicily were asked to pay an annual *tithe*, or 10 percent of their annual harvest, to Rome. A Roman praetor was sent to Sicily to supervise the collection of this tax and to administer the judicial system of the island. Because the Sicilians had been accustomed to paying tribute to Carthage, they made no objection to this system. In this way, Rome established a new type of provincial government; one that would later be utilized to govern vast areas of conquered territory.

SECOND PUNIC WAR (218-201 B.C.)

After the conclusion of the first Punic War, Hamilcar Barca devoted himself to developing and enlarging Carthage's empire in Spain. After his death in 228, his son Hannibal and son-in-law Hasdrubal continued his work. The Romans became concerned about this increasingly powerful Spanish empire, and encouraged the town of Saguntum to resist the Carthaginians. Hannibal complained to Rome about this interference in his affairs, but received no reply. He captured and destroyed Saguntum. After this episode, Rome decided that it had no choice but to declare war on Carthage.

When the second Punic War began, the strategy of the Romans was to hold Hannibal in Spain with their fleet of warships and at the same time mount an attack against Carthage itself. But Hannibal had his own plan for the war. Since he was blockaded by sea, he decided to advance by land into Italy itself. He marched across the Pyrenees Mountains into Gaul with a force of 40,000 soldiers, 37 elephants, and 8000 horses. Five months later, he reached the Alps. The steep descent of the Alps on the Italian side meant dreadful suffering for both men and animals. Livy wrote:

● ● ● *Then came a terrible struggle on the slippery surface, for it afforded them no foothold, while the downward slope made their feet the more quickly slide from under them; so that whether they tried to pull themselves up with their hands, or used their knees, these supports themselves would slip, and down they would come again! Neither were there any stems or roots about, by which a man could pull himself up with foot or hand—only smooth ice and thawing snow, on which they were continually rolling.[3]*

The difficult terrain and hostile Alpine tribes took a great toll on Hannibal's army; only one-half of his men and a few elephants survived the trip. Nevertheless, Hannibal easily won his first major battle with the Romans, which took place in 218 near the town

---

[4]Livy XXI, 36.

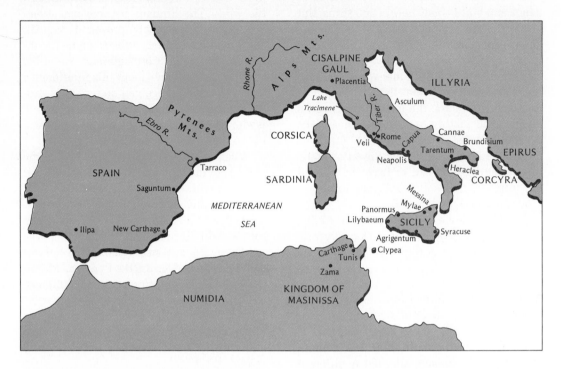

of Placentia in northern Italy. In this battle, Hannibal's superior tactics and well-trained cavalry troops were largely responsible for his overwhelming victory, in which two-thirds of the Roman force was destroyed.

After their defeat in northern Italy, the Romans elected to concentrate upon the defense of central Italy. Two Roman armies, under the commands of the consuls Flaminius and Servilius, took the field to guard the main routes that Hannibal might take to cross the Apennines in the spring. Their plan was to intercept Hannibal close to his point of entry, then unite their armies to fight him. But in May of 217, Hannibal crossed the Apennines and lured Flaminius into following him to Lake Trasimene. There, Hannibal's troops, who had stationed themselves in the hills surrounding the lake, ambushed and killed the consul and two of his legions. Shortly after this disaster, Hannibal's cavalry

encountered and defeated Servilius' advance troops.

The way to Rome now seemed to be open to Hannibal, but before attacking this well-fortified city, he counted on enlisting the support of the Etruscan city-states along the route. Surprisingly, not a single one of these cities opened its gates to him.

In Rome, the *Comitia Centuriata* responded to the emergency by electing a dictator to lead the army against Hannibal. Their choice was Q. Fabius Maximus, a cautious and experienced general. During the next year, Fabius followed a policy of avoiding open battle with Hannibal, using his troops instead to harass the Carthaginians and prevent them from establishing a permanent camp. Although Fabius' delaying tactics successfully avoided any new military disasters, the Roman people became impatient with the situation. When the dictator's term of office expired in 216, they elected in his place two aggressive consuls, Paullus and Varro.

Battle of Cannae. Knowing that the newly elected Roman consuls were eager to give battle, Hannibal carefully chose an advantageous site. He camped near the Roman post at Cannae, in a large, level field where his cavalry troops would be able to maneuver easily. The Roman army led by Paullus and Varro soon arrived.

The Roman army of about 50,000 men far outnumbered Hannibal's army, but Hannibal found a way to turn the Romans' superior strength against them. Before the battle, Hannibal, like the Roman commanders, posted his infantry troops in the center ranks and his cavalry in the wings. But he formed his troops in a crescent rather than a straight line. He then allowed the strong Roman infantry to push back his center ranks, while his cavalry troops engaged the Roman cavalry in the wings. Then, just as the Roman infantry was about to break through his center, Hannibal directed his cavalry troops to turn back and surround the Romans' center and rear. In this way, the Roman advantage in numbers became a liability: massed together and unable to move, the Roman legions were completely encircled by Hannibal's army. The result was an overwhelming defeat: the Romans lost about 25,000 troops, while Hannibal lost only 5700.

The defeat at Cannae was the most devastating that the Romans had ever suffered, and a great effort of will was required even to continue the struggle. The various classes of Rome united as they never had before to contribute to the war effort. Incredibly, they not only managed to raise new forces to defend Italy, but also sent armies to attack the Carthaginians in Spain, Sardinia, Sicily, Africa, and Greece. Although Hannibal continued to make inroads in Italy and established a strong base in the south, the task of meeting the Romans on additional fronts throughout the Mediterranean world prevented him from gathering the strength he needed to besiege the city of Rome.

Spain. Two capable Roman generals, the brothers Publius and Gnaeus Scipio, won the Senate's permission to take a small army and navy to Spain in 218. Because Carthage controlled important bases and valuable silver mines in Spain, the Scipios believed that their attacks would divert Carthaginian troops from the war in Italy.

Soon after his arrival in Spain, Gnaeus captured the important base of Tarraco. He then led his army and navy to the mouth of the Ebro River, where he defeated a much larger Carthaginian fleet. As a result of this battle, the Romans not only gained control of the river, but also asserted Rome's mastery of the sea. This victory provided an important morale boost to Rome and its allies, and helped to offset the loss at Cannae.

In 212, Publius Scipio captured Saguntum, forcing the Carthaginians to divert troops to Spain which had been intended for Hannibal in Italy. But in 211, the reinforced Carthaginian army defeated both Roman armies in Spain. Although the Scipio brothers were killed and their small armies destroyed, they had achieved several important objectives: they had carried the war into the enemy's territory, diverting Carthaginian resources from Hannibal; they had won some allies for Rome north of the Ebro; and they had destroyed Carthage's ability to challenge Rome's navy.

In 210, the Roman Senate yielded to popular demand and placed Publius Scipio's son, also named Publius, in command of a second expedition to Spain. After several years of hard fighting, young Scipio managed to complete the work that his father and uncle had begun. He conquered the important base of New Carthage, and then won an overwhelming victory over the Carthaginians at Ilipa. In 206, Scipio drove the Carthaginians out of Spain entirely.

Sardinia and Sicily. As the agricultural

lands of Italy were destroyed by Hannibal's army, the Romans and their allies increasingly depended upon imports of food from Sicily and Sardinia. Realizing this dependence, the Carthaginians attempted to seize Sardinia in 215. They failed in this effort, but another crisis soon arose in Sicily, the other major supplier of grain to Italy.

In 215, King Hiero II of Syracuse died, and his successors broke the alliance that Hiero had made with Rome. Revolt against Rome then spread to other towns in Sicily, and the Carthaginians gained control of the southern coast of the island. A Roman army and fleet were sent to besiege Syracuse, but for two years they were defeated by the ingenious war machines devised by the mathematician Archimedes (see Chapter 8). Finally, in 212, the Roman general Marcellus succeeded in taking the town. After another year of fighting, the Romans regained all of Sicily.

Greece. The action in Greece did not have a major impact on the outcome of the second Punic War, but it eventually involved Rome in the intricate politics of the Greek peninsula.

After the battle of Cannae, Philip V, the king of Macedonia, allied himself with the Carthaginians. In making this alliance, Philip hoped that Hannibal would help him to seize Illyria and Corcyra, where Rome had recently established bases. Philip attacked Illyria in 214, expecting that he would soon be aided by a Carthaginian fleet. The Carthaginians never appeared, however, and the Roman praetor Laevinus was able to force Philip's departure from the area.

Although Laevinus had successfully dealt with the first emergency, he feared that the Carthaginians might yet come to Philip's aid. He then devised an ingenious solution to the problem: an alliance was arranged between Rome and the Aetolians, stipulating that Rome would enforce the Aetolians' rights over any territory they seized from Philip. Through this alliance, Laevinus managed to enroll the Greeks in the fight against Philip, and conserved the resources that Rome desperately needed to fight Hannibal.

Philip continued to threaten Rome's bases in the eastern Adriatic, but he never received the support of the Carthaginians. In 206, the Aetolians concluded a peace treaty with Philip, for they had not received enough help from Rome to prevent his attacks upon their territory. The next year, Rome, too, made peace with Philip in order to prevent any further distractions in the Aegean area.

Africa. After his successful exploit in Spain, Publius Scipio tried to convince the Senate to let him take the war to Carthage. Although Scipio was recognized as Rome's most capable general, the senators were at first reluctant to send an army to Africa while Hannibal was still in Italy. Finally, however, they yielded to Scipio's enthusiasm. Scipio recruited and trained an army in Sicily and departed for Africa in 204.

Soon after his arrival, Scipio achieved several great victories in Africa. When he captured Tunis, only 15 miles away from Carthage, the Carthaginians began to discuss peace terms and, at the same time, recalled Hannibal to Africa. The conditions of peace could not be resolved, and in 202, Scipio met Hannibal's army at Zama, about 50 miles south of Carthage. The two armies were about equal in strength, each with about 35,000 men, but Scipio had a stronger cavalry division.

From the details that are known of the battle between the two great strategists, Scipio apparently intended to use the enveloping techniques that Hannibal had demonstrated at Cannae. During the battle, however, one of Hannibal's lines remained stationary, and Scipio realized that his plan would not succeed. He then took the unusual step of stopping the battle in midcourse, allowing each commander to regroup his troops. During this interval, Scipio's cavalry troops, who had pursued enemy troops off the field, were given time to rejoin the battle. In the end, Scipio managed to destroy Hannibal's army, while Hannibal himself escaped.

Terms of Peace. The peace treaty that ended the second Punic War allowed the Carthaginians to keep their original territory in Africa, but forbade them from waging any war without Rome's permission. Spain was ceded to Rome, and the Carthaginians also agreed to pay an indemnity of 10,000 talents. Thus, Carthage's term as ruler of a great Mediterranean empire was put to an end, and Rome assumed the responsibility of governing its former possessions.

THIRD PUNIC WAR (149-146 B.C.)

In the years following the second Punic War, Carthage quickly recovered from the devastations it had suffered. Under the able leadership of Hannibal, the Carthaginians enacted measures to help their poorest citizens, revived their agriculture, and developed a thriving international trade. Hannibal's efforts in these areas made him enemies both at home and abroad. His success in creating a more equitable political system inspired the wrath of the powerful oligarchs of Carthage, while the prosperity of Carthage's economy aroused the jealousy of Roman merchants.

In 195, the anti-Carthaginian faction in Rome combined with the oligarchs of Carthage to demand Hannibal's surrender. Hannibal fled to Syria, where he became an adviser to the Seleucid king, Antiochus III. Rome continued to pursue him, and in 183 he took his own life rather than surrender to the Roman delegates sent to extradite him. The Greek historian Polybius paid this tribute to Hannibal's career:

● ● ● *Who can help admiring this man's skillful generalship, his courage, his ability, if he will consider the span of time during which he displayed these qualities? . . . For sixteen years on end he maintained the war*

with Rome in Italy without once releasing his army from service in the field; he kept vast numbers under control like a good pilot, without any sign of dissatisfaction towards himself or friction amongst themselves. And the troops under his command, so far from being of the same tribe, were of many diverse races who had neither laws nor customs nor language in common.[4]

Even after Hannibal's death, the anti-Carthaginian party within Rome continued to press the Senate to take additional action against Carthage. One of the most notable leaders of this faction was Cato the Censor, who concluded every speech he made in the Senate—no matter what the subject of the speech happened to be—with the phrase *Carthago delenda est.* ("Carthage must be destroyed.") Scipio, who had become known as Scipio Africanus after his victory over Hannibal, was one of those who argued that Rome should not take any further reprisals against Carthage.

For 50 years, the Carthaginians carefully obeyed every provision of the treaty they had made with Rome, careful to offer no pretext for their enemies to seize upon. Finally, however, a longstanding territorial dispute between Carthage and Masinissa, the ruler of a large Numidian kingdom, gave Cato and his followers the excuse they needed to declare war against Carthage.

As a young man, Masinissa had provided valuable military aid to Scipio Africanus in the battle at Zama. As a result, the Roman Senate overlooked his repeated aggressions against Carthaginian territory in the decades following the second Punic War. Finally, the Carthaginians became exasperated with the situation and declared war on Masinissa. Because this action was a direct violation of the treaty with Rome, Cato and his followers had the pretext they needed to intervene. In 150,

---

[5]Polybius (trans. Moses Hadas), XI, 19.

a Roman delegation traveled to Carthage and demanded that the Carthaginians surrender all of their arms as well as 30 hostages to them. The Carthaginians complied, only to be told that they must evacuate their city. Realizing that the Romans intended to destroy their city, the Carthaginians then shut themselves within the city walls and began to manufacture weapons with the materials at hand.

The Romans' first efforts to storm the city of Carthage were unsuccessful. In 146, however, the grandson of Scipio Africanus—who became known as Africanus Minor—came to Carthage and set up an effective blockade of the city. When the starving Carthaginians had surrendered, the Romans burned the city to the ground and plowed salt into the soil. Reportedly, Scipio wept as he viewed the burning city, and recited Homer's lines concerning the end of Troy. In fact, the episode marked a new era in Rome's history. To those who had taken pride in Rome's early policy of fairness towards its defeated enemies, the destruction of Carthage was a shameful event. But to others, who foresaw the benefits that Rome could derive from the downfall of Carthage, it signified a new beginning.

EXPANSION TO THE EAST   As we have seen, the Romans did not set out to conquer the world, but gained a Mediterranean empire as the result of a series of defensive wars against Pyrrhus and Hannibal. This pattern of unplanned expansion was to continue. In the years following the second Punic War, Rome was called upon to mediate disputes within the Greek world and to check the growing power of Antiochus III in Syria. As a result of these interventions, Rome acquired the responsibility of administering vast territories in the East.

GREECE AND MACEDONIA

In 205, Rome concluded its first war with Philip of Macedonia and withdrew its troops from Greece. But three years later, Greek in-

dependence was again threatened when Philip invaded Samos, the Cyclades Islands, and Attica. Athens and Rhodes then appealed to the Romans for aid against the Macedonians. Although Roman law prohibited the Senate from declaring war except in defense or on behalf of a close ally, the majority of senators decided that Philip's recent alliance with Antiochus of Syria made him a real danger to Rome. Thus, the Roman people were drawn into a new foreign conflict only four years after the second Punic War had ended.

The Romans declared war on Philip in 200. During the next four years, the Roman army and navy forced Philip to retreat from nearly all of the territory he had conquered in Greece. In 196, after suffering a major defeat, Philip· signed a peace treaty with T. Quinctius Flamininus, the Roman commander who had defeated him. In the treaty, the Romans announced that they intended to restore the full independence of Greece, and would soon withdraw all of their troops from the peninsula. Philip agreed to renounce his claim to the territories he had conquered in Greece and Asia, but was allowed to keep his Macedonian kingdom. The generous terms of Flamininus' treaty outraged the Aetolians, who wanted to invade Macedonia. But the agreement provided several important advantages to Rome. By leaving Philip with enough resources to defend Macedonia, Rome ensured that this strategic region would continue to be an effective buffer zone rather than the object of further conquests by Antiochus or the Gauls. In addition, the lenient terms of peace secured for Rome the friendship of Philip, which would prevent him from aiding Antiochus. In 194, the Roman Senate kept its promise and withdrew all Roman legions from Greece.

ASIA MINOR

As Roman armies were fighting Philip in Greece and Macedonia, Antiochus was completing a wide circle of conquest in Asia Minor. After following the trail that Alexander the Great had taken to India, Antiochus traveled up the Mediterranean coast, conquering the Ionian Greek city-states along his route. In 196, as Rome was concluding its peace treaty with Philip, Antiochus invaded Thrace. He then proposed an alliance with Rome, suggesting that if Rome accepted the status quo, he would not intervene any further in the affairs of the Mediterranean world. But because Antiochus was giving sanctuary to Hannibal, the Roman Senate refused to consider such an alliance. Antiochus proceeded to conquer Thessaly and central Greece, and in 192 the Senate declared war.

The Romans met Antiochus near Thermopylae in central Greece, at the same site where Leonidas and his Spartan army had fought the Persians three centuries earlier (Chapter 6). There, the Romans defeated Antiochus' army and forced him to leave Greece. The Senate then resolved that Antiochus must be pursued to his home territory, for otherwise he might gather another army and conquer Greece again. Accordingly, a Roman army passed through Philip's kingdom and entered Asia in 189. Antiochus gathered an army of 70,000 troops, about two times the strength of the invading Roman army, and met the Romans in Magnesia. In spite of his overwhelming advantage in numbers, Antiochus was defeated and forced to surrender.

Under the terms of the peace treaty negotiated with Rome, Antiochus surrendered all of his conquests and agreed to remain in Syria. Much of the territory he had controlled was given to Rhodes and Pergamum.

ROME'S POLICY IN THE EAST

After its victories in Greece and Asia, Rome did not annex the territories it had conquered, but withdrew its legions as soon as peace had been established. Within a few years, however, Roman policy began to change. Partly in response to continuing disturbances in these areas, Rome began to exert a stern, direct rule in both areas.

Macedonia. When Philip's son Perseus took up arms against Rome and was defeated, the Romans deposed him and divided Macedonia into four independent republics. But many Macedonians longed for the return of their traditional form of government, and by 148 a movement to reinstitute a monarchy had gained momentum. In response, Roman legions landed in Macedonia and quickly defeated the would-be king and his army. Macedonia, Illyria, and Epirus were then declared to be Roman provinces, and a praetor was sent to govern them.

Greece. Even after Rome became the informal protector of Greece, the Achaean League in Greece continued to pursue an aggressive foreign policy for several decades. Among other activities, the league fomented a bitter war against Sparta, and physically attacked Roman senators who had been sent to mediate the dispute. In 146, the same year that Carthage was burned to the ground, the Romans responded to these provocations by dissolving the Achaean League. Then they destroyed Corinth, its leading city. This action demonstrated that Rome was resolved to establish order in Greece at any cost, and marked the end of Greek independence.

Asia. Following the defeat of Antiochus in 189, the Seleucids regained much of their former power and prosperity. Dynastic disputes in Egypt emboldened the Seleucid king Antiochus IV to seize Egyptian territory in Syria-Palestine, and in 168 he invaded Egypt itself. The Roman Senate then sent an ambassador to him, demanding that he immediately evacuate his troops from Egypt and Cyprus. When Antiochus asked for time to consider the request, the ambassador drew a circle around him in the sand and told him that he must give his answer before he stepped out of it. Antiochus then complied with the Senate's request and returned to Syria. Within a few years, the power of the Seleucids was so weakened by their struggle with Egypt and by internal disorders that they no longer presented any cause of concern to Rome.

SUMMARY

Between 750 and 150 B.C., Rome developed from a small village to the capital of an empire. At first, Rome was controlled by a small group of patrician families who claimed a sacred right to govern the city. Eventually, however, military necessity and other factors led to the participation of the plebeians in all aspects of government.

At the same time as Rome's political institutions were being formed, the city was also developing a coherent policy to deal with its neighbors in Italy. Rome's comparatively stable government, respected judicial system, and wise alliances eventually made the city the acknowledged leader of the peninsula.

Beginning in 264 B.C., Rome fought a long series of wars with Carthage. At the end of the Punic Wars, the character of Roman civilization began to change. When Rome inherited Carthage's Mediterranean empire and became the protector of Greece and Asia Minor, it became necessary to create permanent military and bureaucratic establishments to govern these territories. As a result, the progress toward a democratic form of government in Rome was halted, and power was instead monopolized by a small group of ambitious men. In the next chapter, we will examine the effects of these changes.

QUESTIONS

1 According to Roman tradition, what influence did the Etruscan monarchy have upon the development of the Roman republic?
2 Compare the institutions of the early Roman republic to those of Athens' democracy in the 5th century B.C. Which government was probably more efficient? Which allowed a greater degree of participation to poor people?
3 What changes were made in Rome's laws and institutions in response to the demands of the plebeians? What bargaining power did the plebeians have?
4 Compare Athens' leadership of the Delian League and Rome's leadership of its confederation in Italy. How were Rome's policies toward its allies different from those of Athens? What privileges and benefits did Rome's allies receive?
5 What effect did the Punic Wars have on Rome's development? Debate the question: Would Rome have developed a Mediterranean empire if Scipio had fought Hannibal in Italy rather than mounting an expedition to Africa?

BIBLIOGRAPHY

Which books might discuss the influence of the Etruscans on Rome?

BLOCK, RAYMOND. *Ancient Civilization of the Etruscans.* New York: Cowles Book Co., 1969. *A discussion of the archaeological discoveries that have contributed to our understanding of the Etruscans. Conveys the sense of mystery and excitement involved in efforts to reconstruct their society.*

BRADFORD, ERNLE. *Hannibal.* New York: McGraw-Hill, 1981. *A biography of one of the world's most brilliant military strategists. Explores the flexible tactics that led to his incredible victories, and the diplomatic abilities with which he inspired the loyalty and cooperation of troops from many different cultures.*

The Horizon Book of Ancient Rome. Edited by William Harlan Hale. New York: American Heritage Publishing Co. *Follows the progress of Roman civilization from its beginning to the fall of its last outpost, the city of Constantinople. Includes vivid anecdotes of the outstanding personalities involved; beautifully illustrated.*

10

> *Ah, friend, I fear the Ides of March have given us nothing beyond the pleasure and the satisfaction of our hatred and indignation. What news I receive, what sights I see! "Lofty was that deed, aye, but bootless."*
>
> CICERO

The End of the Republic

In the four centuries that followed the founding of its republic, Rome developed, as we have seen, from a city-state to the ruler of a large empire. At the same time, the character of Roman society was also transformed. In the first days of the republic, a small group of wealthy patrician families had controlled the economy and government of Rome. But during the 4th and 3rd centuries B.C., the plebeians, who formed the bulk of the Roman Army, won the right to hold public office and to colonize the *ager publicus*, or public lands, that Rome won through its conquests.

In 287, the struggle of the orders seemingly ended with the enactment of the Hortensian law, which made resolutions of the plebeian assembly binding upon all Romans. Surprisingly, however, this measure did not have the predicted result. The masses of poorer citizens did not participate in political decisions, nor did they benefit from the newly conquered territories. Instead, the government again came to be dominated by a small group of powerful men. Although the republic continued in existence for more than a century, its laws and institutions were gradually undermined. Finally, the republic was replaced by a new form of government which came to be known as the *principate*.

IMPERIAL ROME   Although the constitution of the republic provided a way for its citizens to achieve political and economic equality, the vast majority of plebeians were not able to realize these benefits in the years following the Punic Wars. To a large extent, this failure can be attributed to the changing role of Rome in the Mediterranean world. The development of Rome from city-state to empire had far-reaching consequences in the political and economic affairs of its citizens.

POLITICAL CONSEQUENCES OF THE EMPIRE

During the long years of the Punic Wars, the Senate played the leading role in organizing and directing Rome's military forces. The Senate's success in this endeavor greatly increased its prestige and authority, and demonstrated that it had the qualities necessary to lead the nation in a time of crisis.

As Rome began to consolidate its control over its new empire, the members of the Senate—all of whom were public officials experienced in administration—again took a leading role. The public assemblies did not attempt to challenge the Senate's role in these matters, for most Romans were not interested in the complex problems and day-to-day business of the empire. Thus, by general agreement, the role of administering the Roman Empire fell to the Senate rather than to the public assemblies.

Since public officials received no salary for their service to the state, the administrative offices of the empire tended to be monopolized by a relatively small group of wealthy men. Thus, while the distinctions between patricians and plebeians had been eliminated, new divisions arose within Roman society. Those who served in public office came to be known as the *nobiles* or *Optimates*, and the remainder of Roman citizens, the nonsenatorial class, were known as the *Populares*.

ECONOMIC CONSEQUENCES OF THE EMPIRE

During the second Punic War, small farmers throughout Italy were forced to abandon their homesteads in order to join the fight against Hannibal. After years of service in the army, these men and their families returned home to rebuild their farms. They soon found, however, that their farms would no longer provide a livelihood: due to the new economic conditions that prevailed after the war, small farming had become an impractical venture.

The impoverishment of small landowners throughout Italy had a variety of causes. During the Punic Wars, Sicily and Sardinia had come under the administration of Rome, and continued to pay tribute to the empire in the form of grain after the war ended. The influx of this grain was of benefit to the Roman economy, but also established a market price that small farmers could not match. Moreover, the wars of conquest had brought an abundant supply of slaves to Italy, so that large landowners, by exploiting this free labor, could produce a variety of farm products

much more cheaply than independent farmers. Many small farmers flocked to the cities, but there, too, the easy availability of slave labor made it difficult to find work. As a result, the cities came to be crowded with a large group of unemployed, impoverished people.

THE GRACCHI BROTHERS

Tiberius Gracchus was a grandson of Scipio Africanus, and thus belonged to one of the most prominent *nobiles* families of Rome. As a young man, he distinguished himself during a military campaign in Spain, and earned the gratitude of his fellow soldiers by negotiating a treaty which saved the lives of 20,000 troops. According to the account of his younger brother, it was during his service in the army that he first developed his ideas for agricultural reform.

Traveling through the Italian countryside on his way to Spain, Tiberius noticed that almost no independent farmers remained there—the land was instead being farmed by large gangs of imported slaves. During his service in the army, Tiberius realized that this situation was also having an effect on Rome's military capabilities: the army was desperately short of soldiers, for farmers were no longer eligible to belong to the *Comitia Centuriata* once they had lost their property. Tiberius decided that the solution to this problem was to reinstate the farmers as independent landowners; to help them to again become responsible citizens and soldiers. Instead, Roman officials increasingly overlooked the property qualifications of the *Comitia Centuriata* and began to draft poor citizens into the army. Tiberius spoke about the injustice of this situation:

● ● ● *The savage beasts in Italy have their particular dens, they have their places of repose and refuge; but the men who bear arms, and expose their lives for the safety of their country . . . [have] no houses or settlements of their own, [and] are constrained to wander from place to place*

224

with their wives and children. . . . They fought indeed and were slain, but it was to maintain the luxury and the wealth of other men. They were styled the masters of the world, but had not one foot of ground which they could call their own.[1]

To achieve his plan of distributing land to the poor, Tiberius intended to rely upon an ancient law that limited the amount of land one family could own to 300 acres. This law had been widely disregarded since its enactment in 367 B.C., so that enforcing the legal limit would bring many thousands of acres of land into the public domain. However, a political problem was caused by the fact that many of the most prominent violators of the law were senators. In fact, the Senate was composed almost exclusively of large landowners, for senators were prohibited from engaging in commercial activities.

Although there were many senators who supported Tiberius' ideas in spite of the personal losses they would suffer, Tiberius decided to present his proposal to the *Concilium Plebis*. In taking this step, he ignored the traditional jurisdiction of the Senate over such matters and alienated many of the senators who had supported him.

In 133 B.C., Tiberius was elected tribune, and soon afterwards presented his reform in the plebeian assembly. But the measure was vetoed by Octavius, a tribune who was acting on behalf of the Senate. Angered by this action, Tiberius persuaded the plebeians to depose Octavius from office and to pass his reform.

After his reform had been enacted, Tiberius formed a commission to administer the new law. The commission received little cooperation at first, but Tiberius soon found a way to obtain the funds he needed from the Senate. When Attalus, the ruler of Pergamum in Asia, bequeathed his kingdom to Rome, Tiberius suggested that some of Attalus'

wealth might be used to help Roman settlers colonize the new lands granted to them. The Senate, fearing that Tiberius might become involved in foreign affairs, then gave the commission the funds it needed to operate.

The next year, Tiberius decided to run for a second consecutive term as tribune. Because no tribune had run for reelection in more than 200 years, Tiberius' action was seen by his enemies as an attempt to establish a tyranny. On the day of the elections, a mob of conservative senators attacked and killed Tiberius and 300 of his followers.

After Tiberius' death, a year of civil disturbances and recriminations followed. The Senate established its own court of inquiry, and executed or banished many Gracchus supporters. The Populares were unable to organize an effective opposition to these repressions. Nevertheless, the land reform that Tiberius had initiated continued to be carried out. And when Tiberius' younger brother, Gaius, came of age, he helped to carry forward the program that his brother had begun.

THE REFORMS OF GAIUS GRACCHUS

Following Tiberius' death, the enactment of his reform continued, and thousands of Romans were given grants of land on which to establish farms. Within a few years, however, the lands under direct Roman control had all been distributed, while there remained a sizable group of poor Roman citizens who had not received allotments. The commission then began to apply the rule of 300 acres to the territories of nearby Italian city-states. The Latins and other allies began to protest the grant of their land to Roman citizens, and one Latin colony even rebelled against Rome. The resentment of the allies toward the land distribution program was to become one of the major problems facing Gaius Gracchus as he continued his brother's work.

Gaius Gracchus was known as one of Rome's greatest orators, and soon demonstrated that he was able to organize the Pop-

---

[1]Plutarch, *Lives*, Modern Library ed., p. 999.

ulares into an effective coalition. In 123 B.C., ten years after the death of his brother, he was elected tribune. Gaius then began to challenge the power of the Senate on several fronts. With the support of the public assemblies, he enacted a law that prevented the Senate from setting up its own court of justice, such as the one that had condemned many of Tiberius' followers. He also promoted the interests of the *equites*, the group of wealthy, nonsenatorial families who made their livelihood through trade rather than by owning land, and had been excluded from public office. In one law enacted by Gaius, the equites were assigned the important function of tax collection in the rich province of Asia. A second law provided for equites to serve on the juries in cases where provincial governors were accused of extortion. Through these measures, Gaius greatly reduced the opportunities for senators to abuse their privileges and enabled many members of the equite class to hold important offices in government.

During his two terms as tribune, Gaius took several important measures to alleviate the lot of the poor. He established two colonies in Italy and one near the site of Carthage to provide new opportunities for Roman citizens. He also set up a system whereby the government would buy large quantities of grain and sell it to poor citizens for slightly less than the market price. This system stabilized the price of grain and prevented profiteers from exploiting the poor, but also had an unexpected result: in later years, many people believed that the government had a responsibility to supply grain doles to the poor, and this issue became central to Roman politics.

During his second term as tribune, Gaius tried to solve some of the problems that the land redistribution program had caused for the Rome's allies in Italy. He proposed that all Latin city-states be granted Roman citizenship, and that other Italians be given the modified rights that Latins had held. This proposal cost Gaius much of his support among the Populares, for most Romans were not willing to share the benefits of colonization with other Italians. In 121 B.C., Gaius lost his office as tribune, and his enemies in the Senate moved to cancel his reforms. The Senate declared a state of martial law, and received the full support of the equites. Gaius and his supporters armed themselves to resist the cancellation of their reforms, but they were overpowered and killed. Soon afterwards, 3000 of Gracchus' supporters were arrested and executed without trial.

The Gracchi brothers had devoted their lives to enacting reforms that they believed would benefit their countrymen. After their deaths, many people considered them to be martyrs, for the motive of their actions had been unselfish, while their murderers had acted solely to protect their own interests. In sanctioning political murders and other unscrupulous actions against the Gracchi, the Senate had disregarded the laws and institutions of the republic and permanently destroyed its own reputation for integrity and patriotism. Although the Senate, by these means, triumphed over the coalitions that had challenged its authority, this gain was shortlived. In the long run, the Gracchi affair was to precipitate the end of the republic.

THE JUGURTHIAN WAR After the destruction of Carthage in 146 B.C., much of North Africa was incorporated into the Roman Empire. Because the king of Numidia had helped Scipio Africanus to defeat Hannibal, however, the kingdom of Numidia retained some independence and was regarded as a vassal or client of Rome. In 118 B.C., trouble flared in the area when the king of Numidia died and divided his kingdom among his two sons and his nephew, Jugurtha. Despite the desperate appeals of the royal brothers for Roman support, Jugurtha murdered both of them and seized the entire kingdom for himself.

In Rome, rumors soon began to circulate

that Jugurtha had bribed a number of Roman senators, and that this was the reason the Senate had taken no action against him. The public assemblies of Rome demanded that action be taken against Jugurtha, but the Senate continued to delay, even after Jugurtha's troops killed several hundred Italian merchants in Africa. Finally, the plebeian assembly demanded that Jugurtha be summoned to Rome and forced to disclose the names of the senators and other officials that he had bribed. Jugurtha arrived in Rome in 111 B.C., but apparently bribed a tribune to let the matter drop. He then took the opportunity to murder a relative of his in Italy who had been seen as a possible successor. As he left Rome, Jugurtha was said to have remarked, "Everything in Rome is for sale."

There were several reasons—aside from the possible corruption of its members—for the Senate to avoid a war in Numidia. Little could be gained by such a war except to end the nuisance posed by Jugurtha, and Germanic tribes to the north, meanwhile, might take the opportunity to invade Spain or Gaul. The Roman people, however, refused to consider the legitimacy of such reasons. The Senate's behavior during the Gracchi affair had left a legacy of suspicion and mistrust that could not be overcome.

In 109 B.C., the Senate yielded to pressure from the public assemblies and sent one of its members, Q. Caecilius Metellus, to Africa to wage war against Jugurtha. Metellus belonged to an ancient patrician family, and was regarded as an honest, upright man both in the Senate and in the public assemblies. For the next two years, Metellus commanded the Roman armies in Africa, and achieved some successes. He was unable to capture Jugurtha, however, and so it seemed that the Roman army might be mired in the vast deserts of North Africa indefinitely.

GAIUS MARIUS Gaius Marius was known in Rome as a "new man" because he was the first in his family to be counted among the *nobiles*: none of his ancestors had held public office. Marius married into the ancient noble family of the Caesars, and rose to a high position in the army under Metellus. But Metellus refused to advance his career further, and Marius then returned to Rome to seek higher office on his own. In a speech to the Populares, Marius presented himself as a man who represented the ancient Roman virtues, and complained that the patricians of Rome refused to accept him as an equal:

● ● ● *Compare me, the "new man," my fellow citizens, with those proud nobles. . . . They despise me for an upstart, I despise their worthlessness. . . . My own belief is that men are born equal and alike: nobility is achieved by bravery. . . . If they are right to despise me they should despise their ancestors whose nobility began, like mine, with achievement.*[2]

Marius' political techniques met with success. In 107 B.C., the public assemblies cancelled Metellus' command and appointed Marius as consul in his place. To improve his chances of winning the African war, Marius recruited a large army of impoverished Romans, disregarding the rules that allowed only propertied men to be drafted. He and his quaestor, the patrician Cornelius Sulla, then departed for Africa.

In 105 B.C., after two years of fighting, Marius and Sulla captured Jugurtha and brought the war in Africa to an end. But in the same year, Celtic and Germanic tribes invaded southern Gaul and defeated a Roman army of 60,000 men. In the face of this new disaster, the Roman people again turned to Marius for leadership. He was elected consul in 104, and again the next year, and used these two years to reorganize the Roman army. In 102 and 101, Marius led a campaign against the Germans in Gaul and Spain and finally defeated them.

[2] Sallust, *Jugurtha* (trans. Moses Hadas), 85.

POLITICAL CHANGES

The career of Gaius Marius established a number of precedents that caused lasting changes in the Roman political system. One of these changes was brought about by the methods he used to establish his career. The fact that Marius successfully appealed to the public assemblies for his appointment as general meant that the traditional control of the Senate over such matters of state was overthrown. Later, such leaders as Pompey and Caesar followed the example that Marius had set: rather than advancing their careers in the customary way, these men appealed to the people to let them defend the state against a particular danger. Once they had successfully completed the stated task, they then had the popular and military support they needed to achieve prominence in political life.

REFORM OF THE ARMY

Many of the reforms that Marius introduced concerned the army. By recruiting soldiers from the nonpropertied classes, Marius created an army of professional soldiers—men who did not have homes or farms of their own to return to. Since these men did not have resources of their own, they expected their commander to reward them for the sacrifices they made. Eventually, it became commonplace for military commanders to recruit their own armies and to provide pensions for the veterans. As a result, the primary loyalty of the army was to its commander rather than to the Senate or the state.

During the two years that he was preparing to fight the Germans, Marius introduced several reforms which permanently altered the organization and tactics of the army. Long before the start of battle, he employed soldiers in construction tasks that would facilitate the movement of the army. In addition, Marius had each soldier carry equipment that was used in such construction, so that the army became less dependent upon its baggage train. (As a result, the army became known as "Marius' mules," but this innovation became a permanent feature of Roman military life.) To improve the tactical capabilities of his legions, Marius divided each one into six *cohorts* of six centuries (600 men) each. The army still depended upon the rigid discipline of the legion, but the cohorts allowed the commander more flexibility. Each legion was given its own silver standard, and each cohort, too, carried a flag to serve as a rallying point in battle.

MARIUS AS STATESMAN

In 101 B.C., Marius returned to Rome and received a magnificent triumphal procession in recognition of his defeat of the barbarians. In 100, he was elected to his sixth term as consul. But while Marius enjoyed the popular support needed for a productive career in political life, he proved to be less successful as a statesman than as a general. Instead of using his prestige and authority to reconcile the different political factions of Rome, Marius wavered between one side and the other. In the end, his failures led to the devastating Social War, so-called because the Latin word for allies is "socii."

The most pressing problem facing the republic in 100 B.C. was the need to award benefits to the Roman and Italian troops who had fought under Marius in Africa and in Gaul. To solve this problem, Marius gave his support to two popular leaders, Saturninus and Glaucia, who proposed measures very similar to those the Gracchi brothers had advocated: cheaper grain, colonization projects, and the granting of citizenship to Italians. As in the Gracchi's day, these reforms aroused much opposition—both from Roman plebeians, who did not want to share benefits with other Italians, and from the Senate. In 99, the Senate declared a state of emergency and demanded that Marius abandon his support of Saturninus and Glaucia. Marius complied, and his former allies were killed by an angry mob.

After his betrayal of Saturninus and Glau-

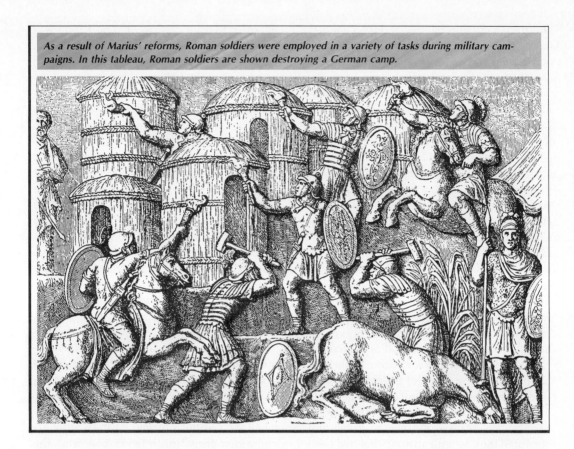

As a result of Marius' reforms, Roman soldiers were employed in a variety of tasks during military campaigns. In this tableau, Roman soldiers are shown destroying a German camp.

cia, Marius lost the support of many members of the Populares faction, and still was not accepted as an equal by the Optimates. Under these circumstances, he departed for Asia for an extended visit as a private citizen.

THE SOCIAL WAR

The failure of the Romans to recognize the contributions of their Italian allies in the Jugurthian and Germanic wars led to a revolt of the allies in 90 B.C. The Social War was waged in central Italy, where the Samnites and other tribes declared independence from Rome and invited other Italian city-states to join them. During the next two years, Roman armies of as many as 60,000 men, commanded by Marius, Sulla, and other generals, descended upon the rebel city-states. Many thousands of Romans and Italians were

killed before the two sides were finally reconciled in 88. In the end, the Romans extended privileges of citizenship to all of their allies in Italy, including the tribes that had rebelled.

MITHRIDATIC WAR AND CIVIL WARS

While the Romans were occupied with the Social War in Italy, a new threat to the Roman Empire arose in the East. Mithridates, the ruler of Pontus in the Black Sea region, began to incite the peoples of Bithyria, Cappadocia, and Ionia to revolt against Roman rule. In 88, Mithridates invaded Asia Minor, and was hailed as a liberator by many of the Ionian Greek city-states. In order to rid the area of Roman presence, Mithridates devised a drastic and terrible solution: he ordered that all Roman and Italian citizens be massacred on a given day. Accordingly, 80,000 civilians—Roman and Italian businessmen and their families —were overtaken and killed.

The Rival Generals. In Italy, Mithridates' massacre of innocent civilians caused a great public outcry, and the leading generals of Rome contended with each other for the honor of leading troops to the East. Cornelius Sulla, a patrician who had served under Marius in the Jugurthian War and had also led a successful campaign during the Social War, emerged as the leading candidate. He was elected consul in 88, and assigned the command of the Asian province.

While Sulla was away from Rome, gathering troops for the coming campaign, Marius illegally transferred the command of Asia to himself. In response, Sulla took an unexpected and unprecedented action: he brought his army to Rome and occupied the city. Marius escaped to Africa, but Sulla took his revenge upon many of his followers.

After asserting his control over Rome, Sulla departed for Greece to fight Mithridates. In his absence, Marius returned to Rome and occupied the city with an army that had been organized for him by Sulla's enemies. He and his followers brutally murdered the patricians who had supported Sulla, then began to kill indiscriminately:

... *In a word, so insatiable a passion for bloodshed seized Marius that, when he had killed most of his enemies and because of excitement could remember no one else he wished to destroy, he passed the word to his soldiers to slay every passer-by, one after another, unless he extended his hand to him. . . . Naturally in the great crowd and confusion . . . many whose deaths he did not in the least desire died needlessly.*[3]

Marius and his ally, the consul Cinna, then outlawed Sulla and his surviving supporters. Their reign of terror was shortlived, how-

ever, for Marius died in 86, and Cinna was killed by mutinous soldiers the following year. Meanwhile, Sulla continued his successful campaign against Mithridates.

VICTORY OVER MITHRIDATES

Sulla landed in Greece in 87 B.C., and began to besiege Athens, which had joined Mithridates' revolt. The city fell to the Romans within a year, and Sulla then met the great army of Mithridates at Chaeronea. Although Mithridates commanded a force that was three times as large as that of the Romans, Sulla overcame this advantage and won the battle. The next year, Sulla was able to arrange a truce with Mithridates. Because of his political problems in Rome, he extended relatively easy terms to the king—Mithridates was allowed to retain his kingdom of Pontus, and was assessed only a moderate indemnity. The cities who had supported the revolt, however, were brought under direct Roman rule and forced to pay ruinous taxes.

CIVIL WAR

In 82 B.C., Sulla returned to Italy with his victorious army and quickly overcame the forces that opposed him. He was elected dictator—an office that had not been held for more than a century—and began a systematic program of terror. Hundreds of people identified as his enemies were killed, and their property distributed to the veterans of his army. In the midst of these reprisals, Plutarch reported, a courageous nobleman asked Sulla to publish a list of his enemies before they were murdered. "We do not ask you," he said, "to pardon any whom you have resolved to destroy, but to free from doubt those whom you are pleased to save."[4] In reply, Sulla began to publish daily lists which came to be known as *proscriptions*. Those on the list were immediately killed and their property was seized. Moreover, the descendants

---

[3]Dio Cassio 30, 102.10.

[4]Plutarch, *Lives*, Modern Library ed., p. 569.

of a proscribed person also forfeited their property and civil rights, and anyone who sheltered a proscribed person was condemned to death. Plutarch described the spread of this process throughout Italy:

● ● ● *Nor did the proscription prevail only at Rome, but throughout all the cities of Italy the effusion of blood was such, that neither sanctuary of the gods, nor hearth of hospitality, nor ancestral home escaped. . . . Those who perished through public animosity or private enmity were nothing in comparison of the numbers of those who suffered for their riches. Even the murderers began to say, that "his fine house killed this man; a garden that; a third, his hot baths."*[5]

GOVERNMENTAL REFORMS OF SULLA

In reforming the institutions of the republic, Sulla's intention was to increase the authority of the Senate and to reduce the role of the public assemblies. Paradoxically, he also acted to prevent others from perpetuating the same abuses that had marked his own career.

In the second year of his dictatorship, Sulla appointed several hundred new senators to replace those that he and Marius had killed. Then, to prevent the public assemblies from enacting legislation of their own, he rescinded the traditional powers of the tribunes. The Senate, rather than the tribunes, became responsible for presenting legislation to the *Concilium Plebis*. Finally, to prevent others from following the example of his career, Sulla decreed that a century-old law concerning the *cursus honorum*, or progression of offices, be respected. Under this system, a young, inexperienced man could not attain high office, for he was required to be elected as quaestor and as praetor before becoming eligible for the consulship. Moreover, the minimum age of a quaestor was 30, and that of a praetor 39. Sulla also decreed that it was a crime, punishable by death, for a commander to lead his troops outside the province to which he was assigned or to declare war without the approval of the Senate.

To the surprise of everyone, Sulla retired voluntarily in 79 B.C., and did not again intervene in public affairs. He died of natural causes a year later.

POMPEY AND CRASSUS

Sulla's work in reforming the institutions of the republic was soon undone, and two of his former lieutenants, Pompey and Crassus, played a prominent part in this process. Like Sulla himself and Marius before him, these two young men rose to the head of government by resolving the military crises that faced the empire.

THE CAREER OF POMPEY

In 78 B.C., civil war again broke out in Rome when Lepidus, a popular leader, was elected consul and began to repeal many of the measures that Sulla had enacted. He reinstituted the sale of cheap grain, which Sulla had cancelled, and proposed that the property of proscribed men be given to their survivors. The next year, Lepidus took control of Gaul and prepared to march upon Rome to enforce his demands for additional reforms. Sulla's followers in Rome chose Pompey to lead an army against Lepidus, even though Pompey met none of the criteria of the *cursus honorum*. Pompey defeated Lepidus within a year, and then forced the surrender of his supporters after a five-year campaign in Spain.

In 73 B.C., Pompey received another chance for military glory when a gladiator named Spartacus organized an army of 70,000 runaway slaves. By the time Pompey returned from Spain, in 72, Spartacus had defeated two Roman armies and had overrun central Italy. Although Crassus was commander-in-chief of the campaign against Spartacus, Pompey was able to capture some retreating slaves and later took much of the credit for suppressing the revolt.

[5]Ibid., p. 570.

POMPEY AND CRASSUS

In 70 B.C., Pompey and Crassus came to a private agreement that each would help the other to be elected as consul. Crassus was one of the wealthiest men in Rome, had served as praetor, and was qualified by age to run for the office. Pompey, on the other hand, was not qualified either by age or experience for the office. To gain public support for their candidacies, Pompey and Crassus promised to restore the powers of the tribunes, and they fulfilled this promise once they were elected. The support of the tribunes later helped both men to achieve the political prominence they craved, and effectively put an end to the *cursus honorum*.

The Pirates. With the support of the tribunes and the plebeian assembly, Pompey received a special commission to clear the Mediterranean of pirates in 67 B.C.. This task was considered so important to the welfare of Rome that Pompey was given an authority superior to that of any other general. Plutarch explained how the pirates had thrived during the years of civil war in Rome:

●●● *Whilst the Romans were embroiled in their civil wars . . . the seas lay waste and unguarded, and by degrees enticed and drew them [the pirates] on not only to seize upon the merchants and ships upon the seas, but also to lay waste the islands and seaport towns. . . . Nor was it merely their being thus formidable that excited indignation; they were even more odious for their ostentation than they were feared for their force. Their ships had gilded masts at their stems; the sails woven of purple, and the oars plated with silver, as if their delight were to glory in their iniquity.*[6]

Pompey cleared the Mediterranean of these audacious pirates in only three months, but his special authority lasted for three years. He then took his armies to the East and

Pompey first won fame by clearing the Mediterranean of pirates, and later reorganized the eastern provinces of the empire.

achieved several resounding victories there. By 62 B.C., he had defeated Mithridates and created an eastern province which extended from the upper Euphrates River to the Arabian Desert, excluding Parthia and Egypt.

JULIUS CAESAR

Caesar was an Optimate by birth, but like Pompey and Crassus, he achieved political power by appealing to the Populares and by winning the loyalty of an army. From the beginning of his career, Caesar emphasized his support for popular causes by subsidizing public works and entertainments. When he had exhausted his own resources, he borrowed vast sums from Crassus to continue this practice. Plutarch described how his methods succeeded:

[6]Ibid., p. 755-6.

••• When he was made surveyor of the Appian Way, he disbursed, besides the public money, a great sum out of his private purse; and when he was aedile, he provided such a number of gladiators, that he entertained the people with 321 single combats, and by his great liberality and magnificence in theatrical shows, in processions, and public feastings, he threw into the shade all the attempts that had been made before him, and gained so much upon the people, that everyone was eager to find out new offices and new honors for him in return for his munificence.[7]

THE FIRST TRIUMVIRATE

In 60 B.C., Caesar returned to Rome after serving as praetor in Spain. Like Crassus and Pompey, Caesar had not received the cooperation he wanted from the Senate, and the three men decided to form an alliance of their own. This coalition, in which each member pledged to support the ambitions of the others, came to be known as the First Triumvirate, and was cemented by Pompey's marriage to Caesar's daughter, Julia.

In joining the triumvirate, Pompey's goal was to achieve ratification of his political arrangements in the East and land settlements for his veterans; Crassus wanted to command a military campaign in Parthia; and Caesar chose a five-year command in Gaul. To accomplish their ends, the triumvirs engineered the election of Caesar as consul in 59 B.C.. As consul, Caesar was so effective in helping his friends—and his co-consul, a man named Bibulus, was so ineffective—that the consulship came to be known as that of "Julius and Caesar."

In 58 B.C., Caesar received a five-year appointment as commander of the armies in Gaul. Within a few years, he had brought a large part of Gaul under Roman rule, an achievement which rivaled the conquests of Pompey. In 55, Caesar met with Crassus and

Julius Caesar in military dress. In addition to his feats as conquerer, administrator, and politician, Caesar became one of the greatest writers of the Latin language.

Pompey in northern Italy to plan the future course of the triumvirate. They agreed that Caesar's command in Gaul would be extended another five years; Crassus would lead a campaign in Parthia; and Pompey would take charge of the armies of Spain and Africa. Within two years, however, the triumvirate collapsed. Crassus' campaign in Parthia ended in disaster, and he himself was killed by the

---

[7]Ibid., p. 857.

Parthians. The death of Julia in 54 dissolved the personal ties between Caesar and Pompey, and their alliance ended soon afterwards.

Cicero. One of the outstanding personalities of the late Roman republic was Marcus Tullius Cicero (106-43 B.C.), a prominent lawyer, orator, and statesman. Like Demosthenes of Athens, Cicero was known as a patriot who tried to uphold the ancient ideals of his country during a period of upheaval and transition. But although he was devoted to the republic, he accommodated himself to the reality of the First Triumvirate. At various times, he was allied to Pompey, Crassus, and Caesar, and defended their interests in Rome while they were away on foreign campaigns.

Many of Cicero's letters and speeches have survived, and provide an invaluable portrait of the personalities and events of the late republic. In Cicero's private letters to his friends, for example, he expressed the hatred that he sometimes felt toward Caesar, and recorded the generous terms of friendship that Caesar always extended to him. During the civil war of 49 B.C. (see below), Cicero chose to ally himself with Pompey despite Caesar's pleas that he stay neutral. After Caesar won the war, one of his first acts was to extend a pardon to Cicero.

In 63 B.C., Cicero was elected consul. One of the most famous incidents of his career took place soon afterwards, when Cataline, a nobleman who had lost the election, plotted to seize the government by force. Cataline had attracted several thousand supporters by promising to cancel all private debts, and was gathering an army in Etruria. Cicero, meanwhile, had heard of these developments, but could not convince the Senate that his information was reliable. Then one evening, the conspirators tried and failed to kill Cicero. Soon after, Cataline appeared at the Senate as if nothing had happened, and Cicero—without any documentary evidence to prove his allegations—had to convince the Senate that Cataline had sponsored the assassination attempt.

The orator Cicero. At a time when Caesar, Pompey, and Mark Anthony wielded absolute power in Rome, Cicero advocated a return to republican principles.

• • • *Review with me then, that night before last; soon you will realize that I am far more keenly on the alert for the safety of the Republic than you are for its ruin. I say that you on that night came to the street of the scythmakers. . . . that in that same place many companions of your mad crime had* come together. *Do you dare to deny it? Why are you silent? I shall prove it, if you deny it, for I see here in the Senate certain men who were there together with you. O ye immortal gods! Where in the world are we? In what kind of city do we live, what sort of Republic do we have? Here, here in our number, Senators, in this most sacred and most important council in the world, are those who plot the death of us all, who plot the ruin of this city and even of the whole world!*[8]

The Senate declared a state of emergency, and, in a poll of its members, voted to execute five of the ringleaders. (Cataline himself had escaped to Etruria.) Without waiting for a court of law to convene, Cicero then carried out the Senate's decision. Most Romans applauded this illegal action, for they believed that it had averted a civil war. Several years later, however, Cicero's political enemies used the incident against him, and he was exiled from the city.[9]

CIVIL WAR In 50 B.C., as Caesar's second term of command in Gaul was about to end, Pompey began to prepare for a confrontation with his former ally. In an attempt to avert a civil war, the Senate passed a resolution asking both Caesar and Pompey to disarm their legions. Caesar indicated that he would comply, but Pompey refused. Instead, Pompey demanded that Caesar disband his army and return to Rome alone. Knowing that he would be at the mercy of his enemies if he did so, Caesar led his army across the Rubicon River, a small stream that marked the boundary between Cisalpine Gaul and Italy.

---

[8]*Greek and Roman Classics in Translation*, compiled by Charles T. Murphy, Kevin Guinagh, and William Jennings Oates (New York: Longmans, Green and Co., 1947), p. 792.

[9]Cicero remained in exile one year. Then, in 57 B.C., Pompey arranged his triumphant return to Rome.

Pompey's Italian legions were no match for the loyal, disciplined legions that Caesar was bringing back from Gaul, and Pompey withdrew to Greece to organize his campaign. Caesar pursued him there, and in 48 B.C., defeated Pompey's army in Thessaly. Pompey then fled to Egypt, but was assassinated when he arrived in that country.

Caesar spent a year in Egypt, consolidating Roman control over the area, and establishing Cleopatra on the throne in place of her younger brother. When he returned to Rome, in 46, Caesar generously extended a pardon to many of those who had supported Pompey's cause, including Cicero. He was elected dictator for a term of ten years, and celebrated elaborate triumphs for his victories in Gaul and over Pompey's forces in Egypt, Africa, and Pontus. Then he departed for Spain, where Pompey's sons had inspired a major revolt.

Caesar's Reforms. After quelling the revolt in Spain, Caesar spent 18 months in Rome administering the economic and political affairs of the empire. With the advice of Greek astronomers in Alexandria, he introduced a new calendar in which the system of months was reconciled with the solar year. The *Julian* calendar, which has only been slightly modified to the present day, had 365 days per year and an extra day every fourth year. Caesar took measures to reduce the debt obligations of poor citizens, and undertook public works such as the building of a new Forum and of roads throughout Italy. He began to draft legislation that would require high qualifications for Roman magistrates, and standardize the system of tax collection throughout the empire.

The Ides of March. Caesar's control of Rome was so absolute that many people feared he would declare himself a king. There was no solid evidence that Caesar actually intended such a step, but several events gave rise to rumors and speculation. In one of these, Caesar's friend, Mark Antony, playfully

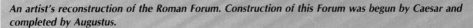

An artist's reconstruction of the Roman Forum. Construction of this Forum was begun by Caesar and completed by Augustus.

placed a crown upon Caesar's head during a public ceremony. Although Caesar brushed the crown aside, it was said he showed no great displeasure.

In reaction to such incidents, a group of 60 conspirators decided that the only way to save the republic was to assassinate Caesar. The leaders of the plot were Cassius, a praetor, and Brutus, an idealistic young man who had been Caesar's friend. Caesar's murder took place on the Ides (15th day) of March in 44 B.C., as Caesar was attending a meeting of the Senate. Plutarch reported that all of the conspirators participated in the murder:

● ● ● *Those who came prepared for the business enclosed him on every side, with their naked daggers in their hands. Which way soever he turned he met with blows, and saw their swords levelled at his face and eyes, and was encompassed like a wild beast in the toils on every side. For it had been agreed they should each of them make a thrust at him. . . . Some say he fought and resisted all the rest, but that when he saw*

Brutus's sword drawn, he covered his face with his robe and submitted, letting himself fall.[10]

ANTONY AND OCTAVIAN

After Caesar's death, a struggle for power developed between the two men who had the best claims to be Caesar's heirs: Mark Antony, who had served as consul with Caesar in 44 B.C., and Octavian, Caesar's 18-year-old adopted son. Antony, the older and more experienced commander, assumed control of the city and arranged a public funeral for Caesar. Plutarch reported that, prior to the funeral, the Romans had listened without emotion as Brutus explained his motives and urged them to rejoice in their liberty. During the funeral, however, the crowd suddenly found a voice when it heard the terms of Caesar's will:

---

[10]Plutarch, *Lives,* Modern Library ed., p. 892-3.

••• But when Caesar's will was opened, and it was discovered that he had left a considerable legacy to each Roman citizen, and when the people saw his body, all disfigured with wounds, being carried through the Forum, they broke through all bounds of discipline and order. They made a great pile of benches, railings and tables from the Forum, and placing his body upon this, burned it there. Then, carrying blazing brands, they ran to set fire to the houses of the murderers.[11]

Soon afterwards, Octavian, who had gathered together an army of Caesar's veterans, marched into the city and demanded that he be named a consul. Antony began to make plans to oppose him with his own army, but his soldiers refused to fight a civil war against their comrades in Octavian's army. Antony and Octavian, together with Lepidus, a proconsul of Spain, then reached an agreement to share control of Italy and to divide the remainder of the empire between them: Antony would command Gaul; Lepidus the province of Spain; and Octavian the provinces of Sicily and Africa. The eastern provinces of the empire were not included in the agreement, for Brutus and Cassius had seized control of them. In 43 B.C., an election was called, and the Second Triumvirate—as the alliance between the three was called—officially won the authority to reorganize the republic.

The following year, Octavian and Antony led an army of 20 legions to Philippi, in northern Greece, to meet the Republican forces led by Brutus and Cassius. They defeated the Republicans in two battles, and Brutus and Cassius committed suicide: Cassius, it was reported, killed himself with the same sword he had used to kill Caesar. Upon their return to Italy, the Triumvirs proscribed their personal enemies and used the property they seized to pay their armies. Ci-

The profile on this coin is probably one of the most realistic portraits of Octavian, who was to become the emperor Augustus. In most later portraits, his features are idealized.

cero, who had often opposed Antony in the Senate, was among the first to die.

As a gesture of unity, Antony married Octavia, the sister of Octavian, and the two triumvirs then combined forces to defeat Lepidus. The empire was divided into two parts, with Octavian controlling the West, and Antony the East. While Octavian began to consolidate his control over the western provinces, Antony retired to Egypt to pursue his celebrated love affair with the Egyptian queen, Cleopatra. In 37 B.C., he divorced Octavia and married Cleopatra.

Antony's action in divorcing Octavian's sister dissolved the alliance between the two triumvirs, and his long stay in Egypt made it appear that he wished to live as an Egyptian pharaoh rather than as a Roman commander. In 32 B.C., Octavian produced confirmation of the damaging rumors that had been circulating about Antony. Antony's will, which he had deposited with the Vestal Virgins in Rome, bequeathed the eastern provinces of the Roman Empire to Cleopatra and her children. When Octavian read this will to the Senate, Antony's supporters in Rome

---

[11]Ibid., pp. 893-4.

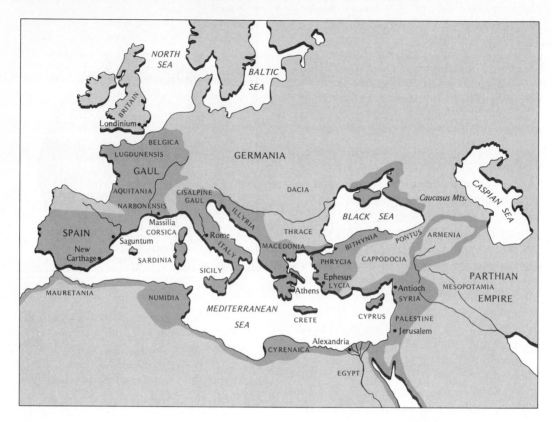

could no longer defend his conduct. There was a great public outcry, and Rome declared war on Cleopatra.

In 31 B.C., Octavian defeated the combined navies of Antony and Cleopatra near Antium, on the coast of western Greece. Antony and Cleopatra then returned to Egypt, and, to avoid being captured by Octavian, committed suicide. Plutarch described how Cleopatra died, shortly after receiving a basket of figs:

••• *The messengers came at full speed, and found the guards apprehensive of nothing; but on opening the doors they [her guards] saw her stone-dead, lying upon a bed of gold, set out in all her royal ornaments. . . . Some relate that an asp was brought in amongst the figs and covered with the leaves*

and that Cleopatra had arranged that it might settle on her before she knew, but when she took away some of the figs and saw it, she said "So here it is," and held out her bare arm to be bitten.[12]

PAX ROMANA After defeating Antony and Cleopatra, Octavian returned to Rome, where he received a magnificent triumph and was hailed as the savior of the republic. In a public ceremony, he closed the doors of the temple of Janus, an act which symbolized the end of the civil wars and peace between Rome and the rest of the world. Later, the grateful citizens of Italy bestowed upon him the title *Augustus*

[12]Ibid., pp. 1151-2.

Evidence of Roman rule can still be seen in sites throughout Europe and the Middle East. At left, the great Roman aqueduct at Nimes, France. Right: Roman ruins in Baalbek, Lebanon.

("Highest one"), and he has been known by this name ever since.

Mindful of what had happened to Caesar when he assumed imperial powers, Augustus was careful to avoid the appearance of supreme authority. He accepted many of the offices and titles granted to him by the Senate, but was careful to put aside certain high offices after a few years. During his long reign, he served as consul, as tribune, as proconsul of his own provinces, and as censor. In each case, the Senate modified the rules of office so that Augustus would not be subjected to the same restrictions as other public officials. When he served as proconsul, for instance, the Senate made his *imperium*, or authority, superior to that of any other proconsul so that Augustus could, if he wished, intervene in the affairs of other provinces. Similarly, when he served as tribune, he was given precedence over others in his power to convene the Senate. Thus, while the rules and institutions of the republic were carefully preserved, Augustus in practice had unlimited authority to carry out his programs.

ORGANIZATION OF THE EMPIRE

In assigning control of the provinces, Augustus carefully arranged the distribution of power so that neither the Senate nor an ambitious general could challenge his authority. The government of stable, settled provinces was assigned to the Senate, while newer territories—those in which Roman legions were stationed—were controlled by Augustus. This arrangement allowed him to retain command of the armies and to prevent other generals from gaining the loyalty of the troops. In border regions, client kings such as King Herod of Judea were allowed to retain their thrones, but were expected to maintain the peace and prevent hostile tribes from invading Roman territory.

Augustus brought about many needed reforms in the administration of the empire. He established a more uniform system of taxation throughout the provinces, and set up an efficient bureaucracy to carry out various functions of government. The provinces under his control were governed by civil servants—often chosen from the equite

In the monuments he built, Augustus emphasized themes such as peace, religion, and family life rather than military exploits. This detail of his Arc of Peace shows members of the imperial family and Roman priests.

class—who were directly responsible to him. Augustus established defensible frontiers wherever possible, and buffer states—usually controlled by client kings—where there were no defensible frontiers. In his old age, Augustus tried to extend the boundary of the empire beyond the Elbe River in Germany, but in 9 A.D., a large Roman army under the command of his protege, Varus, was annihilated by the Germans in the Teutoburg Forest. After this experience, it was reported that Augustus often awakened at night and cried out, "Varus, Varus, bring me back my legions." As a result, Augustus changed his mind about the need for further expansion, and advised his successor to keep the borders as they were.

SOCIAL REFORMS

In the long term, Augustus believed, the success of the Roman Empire depended upon the image that Roman citizens projected to those they ruled. Augustus advocated a return to the simple, basic virtues that had characterized the earliest Romans. To this end, he forbade the use of ostentatious luxuries, and encouraged Romans to devote themselves instead to their family and religious duties. Childless couples were assessed a special tax as a penalty for not producing children, and Augustus often appeared in public in company with his family to illustrate the joys of parenthood. Religious piety was linked to the development of close family ties and also to the success of the an-

Although Augustus did not claim to be a god in Rome, he encouraged the development of an imperial cult in the provinces. This is his temple at Vienne, near Lyons.

Virgil with two muses. His epic poem the Aenead described the heroic origins of Rome.

cient Romans in building their civilization in Italy. To promote a return to traditional religious values, Augustus built and renovated many temples to the ancient gods, and led the observance of religious festivals. In some provinces, Roman subjects were encouraged to worship Augustus himself, in addition to the established pantheon of Roman gods, as an additional measure to promote respect for Roman government and civilization.

Virgil and Livy. As part of his program to encourage patriotism and reverence for the past, Augustus encouraged writers to record the history of Roman civilization. In 29 B.C., Augustus requested that Virgil, a writer known for his poems about rural life, compose an epic poem describing the rise of Roman civilization. The result was the *Aeneid*, a poem which traced the origins of Rome to the Trojan hero, Aeneas. Although Virgil did not live to finish his epic, it was immediately celebrated as a great work of literature and is still so regarded.

Livy devoted his career to the writing of a prose work which traced the history of Rome from its beginnings to his own time (Chapter 9). Although less than a third of Livy's history survives, it has been an invaluable source of information to later historians, for it drew upon many traditions and sources that can no longer be traced. Like Virgil, Livy hoped that his work would inspire Romans with pride in their origins and demonstrate the role of destiny in their achievements.

THE PRINCIPATE

The government that Augustus established blended the institutions of a monarchy with those of the republic. Because he was given the title of *princeps*, many people refer to his government as the *principate*. By the time Augustus died, in 14 A.D., Rome had achieved a level of peace and prosperity unparalleled in her history. To the Romans, it seemed that a golden age had dawned. Today we call the period of history from the beginning of Augustus' reign (29 B.C.) to the death of Marcus Aurelius in 180 A.D. the *Pax Romana*.

SUMMARY

During his long reign, Augustus had carefully preserved the forms of the republic while at the same time creating an imperial administration in which he was the ultimate authority. The trend toward centralization continued under his successors until, in the third century, the emperor was recognized as a dictator.

Many of the emperors who succeeded Augustus were guilty of scandalous behavior, extravagant spending, and mismanagement of governmental affairs. But the administrative bureaucracy and judicial system of the empire continued to function effectively, and the necessity of the imperial office was never questioned. About the year 200, the emperor Septimius Severus made the government a military autocracy. But two centuries later, Rome had become so weak that its army could not defend it from civil uprisings and invasions. While the emperors Diocletian and Constantine stabilized the situation for a few years, the empire ultimately broke into two independent kingdoms. Within a century, the western portion had fallen to the Germans, but the eastern portion survived as the Byzantine Empire until 1453.

QUESTIONS

1 What were the major strengths and weaknesses of the system of government established by Augustus?
2 How did the office of the principate change under Augustus' successors?
3 The reign of Marcus Aurelius is sometimes considered to have marked the beginning of Rome's decline and fall. What special problems did this emperor have to deal with?
4 What measures did Diocletian take to meet the crises that the Roman Empire faced? Was it realistic to believe that his system could continue to function after his retirement?
5 What is a scapegoat? How were the Christians and Jews used as scapegoats during the period of the empire? What were the effects of their persecution and martyrdom?
6 Analyze the causes that have been given for the decline of the Roman Empire. Which do you think were most significant? Could the fall of the empire have been avoided, or was it inevitable?

BIBLIOGRAPHY

Which book might discuss the decline and fall of Rome?

KAHLER, HEINZ. *The Art of Rome and Her Empire.* New York: Greystone Press, 1965. *A survey of Roman art and culture, from the time of Romulus to the fall of Rome. The author stresses the unique quality and character of the Romans' art as seen in their architecture, reliefs, and murals.*

STARK, FREYA. *Rome on the Euphrates.* New York: Harcourt, Brace, 1966. *A discussion of the Roman Empire, ranging from such topics as Hannibal's personality to the character of Roman rule under each group of emperors. Describes how Rome defeated the Seleucids, Parthians, and other peoples and was in turn defeated by the Sassanians.*

STRINGFELLOW, BARR. *The Mask of Jove.* Philadelphia: Lippincott, 1966. *This narrative discussion deals with the character and reputation of the Romans, describing how the culture first defined itself, then learned to convey a positive self-image to others and mask any deficiencies.*

● *While stands the Colosseum, Rome shall stand;*
When falls the Colosseum, Rome shall fall;
And when Rome falls—the world.

BYRON

Rome: Pax Romana and Decline

During his long reign, Augustus respected the Senate and the forms of government established under the republic. Nevertheless, he had more authority than any other leader in Rome's history because of his personal prestige and his skillful diplomacy. Thus, while the institutions of the republic remained in place and were outwardly respected, the government had become dependent upon the strong, centralized leadership of the *princeps*.

During Augustus' reign, the division of authority between the *princeps*, the Senate, and the public assemblies became unclear and confused. There was no thought of re-establishing the republic, however. Although Augustus did not openly proclaim a successor, he copied Caesar's policy of private adoption to designate his intended heir. In the course of his 43-year reign, he adopted as his sons six members of his own or his wife's family, training each to assume the responsibility of public office.

The lack of a clear-cut succession policy and the unsuitability of some candidates were to pose serious problems throughout the period of the empire. At the end of each dynasty's rule, civil wars broke out over the question of succession. The support of the army became the critical factor in determining which candidate would prevail, and emperors were often chosen on the basis of the *donativum*, or gift of money, that they offered to the troops.

JULIO-CLAUDIAN EMPERORS

The four emperors who followed Augustus were known as the Julio-Claudian emperors because each was related by blood or marriage to Augustus, who was the grandnephew and adopted son of Caesar.

TIBERIUS (14-37 A.D.)

Tiberius, a step-son of Augustus, had served as general during several successful campaigns in Germany and was highly regarded by the army. He was described as having a reserved, aloof personality, in marked contrast to the easy manner of Augustus. During his first 10 years as emperor, Tiberius closely followed the policies of Augustus and governed wisely. As Tacitus explained:

● ● ● *Public business and the most important private matters were managed by the Senate:*

the leading men were allowed freedom of discussion, and when they stooped to flattery, the emperor himself checked them. . . . The consul and the praetor retained their prestige; inferior magistrates exercised their authority; the laws too, with the single exception of cases of treason, were properly enforced.[1]

Tiberius demonstrated his respect for the Senate in his administrative reforms. He gave the Senate the task of nominating candidates for public office, and even instructed the senators to nominate only one candidate for each office. Thus, the public assemblies, which had played a real role in nominating and electing public officials under Augustus, were left with only the ceremonial task of ratifying the Senate's choices.

In 23 A.D., Drusus, the only son of Tiberius, died suddenly. Tiberius was deeply affected by this event, and grew increasingly suspicious of those around him. In time, he began to conduct treason trials to prosecute those whom he believed were plotting to kill him. Suetonius, a gossipy biographer who lived two centuries later, gave this account:

●●● *Not a day, however holy, passed without an execution, he even desecrated New Year's Day. Many of his men victims were accused and punished with their children—some actually by their children—and the relatives forbidden to go into mourning. Special awards were voted to the informers who had denounced them and, in certain circumstances, to the witness too. An informer's word was always believed. Every crime became a capital one, even the utterance of a few careless words.*[2]

Suetonius' account, although probably exaggerated, points up a feature of the Roman judicial system that was to cause problems throughout the period of the empire: because there was no public prosecutor,

courts depended upon private citizens for their information about crimes. And, as Suetonius suggests, the court made little effort to investigate the motives of witnesses in cases involving the emperor. Tiberius executed at least 60 people on the basis of witnesses' accounts.

During the last years of his reign, Tiberius entrusted many of his administrative responsibilities to Sejanus, a trusted friend, and he himself retired to the Isle of Capri. In the year 31, Tiberius arranged Sejanus' election to the post of consul. Soon after attaining this high position, Sejanus began to plot to seize the throne for himself. But just as he was about to carry out his plot, Tiberius learned that Sejanus had murdered his son, Drusus, eight years earlier. In a dramatic message to the Senate, Tiberius accused Sejanus of treason. The senators then condemned him, and he was killed in prison.

The events of Tiberius' last years overshadowed his earlier achievements in the minds of his subjects. The common people of Rome disliked him because he managed finances carefully and refused to sponsor lavish gladitorial games. Many senators mistrusted him because of his participation in treason trials. Suetonius wrote the following account of his death:

●●● *The first news of his death caused such joy at Rome that people ran about yelling: "To the Tiber with Tiberius!" and others offered prayers to Mother Earth and the Infernal Gods to give him no home below except among the damned.*[3]

CALIGULA (37-41)

Tiberius was succeeded by his popular grandnephew, Gaius. As a child, Gaius had been nicknamed *Caligula* (Little Boots) by soldiers who served under his father. He is still best known by this name.

---

[1]Tacitus, *Annals* VI, 6.
[2]Suetonius, *The Twelve Caesars* III, 61.

[3]Ibid., III, 75.

Caligula's rule began with promise: he pardoned political offenders, abolished certain taxes, and put an end to treason trials. Then, shortly after recovering from a serious illness, he suddenly became mentally unbalanced. He began to use the treasury that Tiberius had accumulated to carry out lavish building projects which had little or no practical purpose. More seriously, he abused his powers and insulted public officials: on one occasion he demonstrated his contempt for the elected consuls by breaking their *fasces*. Many stories about his outrageous behavior were circulated. Suetonius reported one of the most famous anecdotes:

• • • *To prevent Incitatus, his favorite horse, from being disturbed he always picketed the neighborhood with troops on the day before the races, ordering them to enforce absolute silence. Incitatus owned a marble stable, an ivory stall, purple blankets, and a jewelled collar; also a house, a team of slaves, and furniture — to provide suitable entertainment for guests whom Gaius invited in his name. It is even said that he planned to award Incitatus a consulship.*[4]

When Caligula had exhausted the treasury, he revived the practice of conducting treason trials in order to force wealthy families to give him their money.

In the fourth year of his reign, Caligula was assassinated by members of the Praetorian Guard. While the Senate was pondering the question of succession, some soldiers of the Praetorian Guard discovered Caligula's uncle, Claudius, hiding behind a curtain in the emperor's palace. Claudius, not knowing whether he was to be murdered or made emperor, promised each member of the Guard a *donativum*, or reward, if he became emperor. With the Senate's agreement, Claudius was then proclaimed as Caligula's successor.

---

[4]Ibid., IV, 55.

CLAUDIUS (41-54)

Claudius had several physical handicaps; he walked with a tottering gait, slobbered, and spoke in a manner that was difficult to understand. Probably because of these eccentricities, Augustus and Tiberius had kept him in the background, and had not appointed him to public office. For most of his life, Claudius had occupied himself in writing about Roman history, with special emphasis on the careers of Julius Caesar and Augustus. After his accession, many of his reforms reflected his admiration of these two men.

Claudius proved to be an able and energetic ruler. He respected the Senate and dealt with it on easy terms, but, like Augustus, he served a term as censor so that he could expel senators he believed to be unworthy. Following Caesar's example, he began to finance and construct major public works, including two aqueducts, three new roads, and an improvement of the harbor at Ostia. In the second year of his reign, he personally participated in the conquest of Britain, thus completing a campaign that Caesar had begun in 54 B.C.

One of Claudius' major concerns was the issue of granting Roman citizenship to provincial peoples. He granted full citizenship to several "Romanized" provinces, those which had lived under Roman rule for a long time and had adopted Roman culture and values. He also insisted upon the right of Gallic chieftains to be seated in the Senate. In a speech to the Senate concerning these issues, he remarked that one of the sources of Rome's greatness had been its ability to absorb foreign peoples into its citizen body.

In the second half of his reign, Claudius increasingly fell under the influence of his wives and close associates. Late in his life, he married Caligula's sister, Agrippina, who persuaded him to name her son, Nero, as his successor. Once the succession was established, Agrippina determined to murder Claudius. Tacitus related how this deed was accomplished:

•••The poison was infused into some mushrooms, a favorite delicacy, and its effect not at the instant perceived, from the emperor's lethargic, or intoxicated, condition. . . . Agrippina was thoroughly dismayed. Fearing the worst, and defying the immediate obloquy [bad repute] of the deed, she availed herself of the complicity of the physician. . . . Under pretence of helping the emperor's efforts to vomit, this man, it is supposed, introduced into his throat a feather smeared with some rapid poison; for he knew that the greatest crimes are perilous in their inception, but well rewarded for their consummation.[5]

Although Claudius' last years were marred by his willingness to promote the selfish interests of his friends and family, the many achievements of his early reign were not forgotten. After his death, the Senate conducted a ceremony of deification, an honor that had not been accorded to an emperor since the death of Augustus.

NERO (54-68)

Agrippina probably expected to act as the power behind the throne, for Nero was only 16 years old when he became emperor. The new emperor, however, turned to other advisers. Under the guidance of his tutor, the philosopher Seneca, Nero administered the empire well during his first few years in office. He prosecuted governors who extorted money from their subjects, forbade gladiatorial fights to the death, and refused to engage in wars except for defense.

In the second year of his reign, Nero became increasingly resentful of his mother's attempts to dominate him, and began to plot her death. To develop a justification for this act, he first sent several officials to her house to accuse her of treason. Agrippina, however, persuasively argued her innocence, and the officials could not think of any way to prove her guilty. Nero then arranged for her to take

---

[5]Tacitus, *Annals* XII, 67.

These three coins show Nero as a teenager, as a young man in his 20s, and shortly before his death at 30. In the first coin, he is pictured with his mother, Agrippina, who wished to be considered co-emperor.

a journey in a collapsible boat. But although the boat sank as planned, Agrippina managed to swim ashore. Finally, in desperation, Nero hired some sailors to kill her, without any court sanction.

After his mother's death, Nero showed no restraint in pursuing his desires. He murdered his wife so that he could marry his mistress, neglected the daily business of the empire, and devoted himself to music and poetry. Suetonius reported that he forced people to attend concerts in which he played the harp, sang, or recited his own poetry.

• • • *No one was allowed to leave the theater during his recitals, however pressing the reasons. We read of women in the audience giving birth, and of men being so bored with listening and applauding that they furtively dropped down from the wall at the rear, since the gates were kept barred, or shammed dead and were carried away for burial.*[6]

The beginning of the end for Nero came in 64, when a devastating fire ravaged the city of Rome. The fire rendered thousands of Romans destitute and homeless, and destroyed several sacred buildings associated with the legendary kings of early Rome. Rumors immediately began to circulate that Nero had set the fire, even though he probably had been in Antium, about 50 miles away, at the time. Suetonius recorded the colorful account of Nero's actions which was current a few years later. Nero, he said, had set the blaze for his own entertainment:

• • • *Nero watched the conflagration from the Tower of Maecenas, enraptured by what he called "the beauty of the flames;" then put on his tragedian's costume and sang "the fall of Ilium" from beginning to end. He offered to remove corpses and rubble free of charge, but allowed nobody to search among the ruins even of his own mansion; he wanted to collect as much loot as possible himself.*

Then he opened a Fire Relief Fund and insisted on contributions, which bled the provincials white and practically beggared all private citizens.[7]

To deflect criticism from himself, Nero blamed the Christians for the fire, and carried out the first recorded persecution of this sect (see Chapter 12). Many hundreds of Christians—including, reportedly, the apostles Peter and Paul—lost their lives.

The next year, many of the most prominent citizens of Rome took part in a conspiracy to murder Nero and replace him with another emperor. Nero discovered the plot, and ruthlessly crushed anyone whom he suspected of having taken part in it. Many citizens, including Seneca, were killed or forced to commit suicide during this period. Tacitus reported the last speech of one of the conspirators:

• • • *Questioned by Nero as to the motives which had led him on to forget his oath of allegiance, "I hated you," he replied; "yet not a soldier was more loyal to you while you deserved to be loved. I began to hate you when you became the murderer of your mother and your wife, a charioteer, an actor, and an incendiary."*[8]

Throughout the empire, rebellions broke out in response to Nero's administrative actions. In Germany, Roman soldiers became rebellious after Nero murdered their commanders. The citizens of Palestine revolted when the emperor demanded that they worship him in the Temple at Jerusalem. Roman army commanders in Spain, Gaul, and Africa began to make preparations to seize control of the government. Faced by these mounting insurrections, Nero fled from Rome and was condemned to death by the Senate in his absence. As he took his own life, he reportedly exclaimed, "Oh what a great artist the world is losing."[9]

---

[6]Suetonius, *The Twelve Caesars* VI, 23.

[7]Ibid., VI, 38.

[8]Tacitus, *Annals* XV, 67.

[9]Suetonius, *The Twelve Caesars* VI, 49.

FLAVIAN EMPERORS (69-96)

The death of Nero marked the end of the Julio-Claudian dynasty. After a year of civil war in which four military commanders claimed the title of emperor, Flavian Vespasian won the upper hand. In December of 69, he arrived in Rome with his legions to begin his principate. Although he was not related to the Julio-Claudians, Vespasian assumed the title of "Caesar" when he entered office.

Vespasian had a successful record in military service, and commanded 15 legions, or about half of the Roman armed force, at the time of his accession. Like Claudius, he made a practice of extending citizenship to the Romanized colonies, but exerted stern control over newly conquered and rebellious territories. He suppressed revolts in Gaul, and ordered his son Titus to put down a revolt in Judea (see Chapter 12). There, Roman forces sacked Jerusalem, destroyed the Temple, and forced most inhabitants to flee.

TITUS (79-81)

Titus succeeded his father as emperor and followed his father's practice of treating the Senate with respect while retaining the power of government firmly in his own hands. His rule, which lasted only two years, spanned a plague, another great fire in Rome, and the major eruption of Mount Vesuvius which buried the cities of Pompeii and Herculaneum in 79.

> *Pompeii was buried under 30 feet of volcanic ash which perfectly preserved the conditions that existed at the moment the volcano erupted. When the city was excavated during the 18th century, mosaics, paintings, furniture, food items, and other artifacts of everyday life were found— just as the inhabitants had left them.*

DOMITIAN (81-96)

Domitian was the least popular ruler of the Flavian dynasty. He made little attempt to cooperate with the Senate, and insisted that he be called "Master and Lord." His ineffective military leadership led to defeats and to the payment of large bribes to rebellious tribes. These and other expenses led to tremendous financial deficits. Domitian made Christians and Jews the scapegoats for his empire's problems, and severely persecuted them. In 96, Domitian was murdered by palace conspirators, and the Flavian dynasty came to an end.

THE GOOD EMPERORS (96-180)

After Domitian's death, the Senate prevailed upon the Praetorian Guard and the army to establish one of its members as emperor. Nerva, an elderly senator, served as emperor for only two years, but managed to accomplish a great deal. He restored power to the Senate, adopted a frugal budget, and distributed land to the poor. Most importantly, he selected and trained a competent successor, just as Augustus had done after establishing the principate. The four emperors who succeeded Nerva also followed this important precedent, for none of them had sons of their own: they each chose a well-qualified successor and adopted him as a son.

TRAJAN (98-117)

Nerva chose Trajan, a Spaniard who had served as military commander in Germany, as his successor. Trajan was the first Roman emperor who was not of Italian origin.

As emperor, Trajan immediately became popular with the army because of his extensive military campaigns. He was also well-liked by the senators, for he sent them reports of his campaigns and waited for their approval before concluding any treaties.

In order to divide and weaken the hostile Germanic tribes who presented a constant

Trajan was the first Roman emperor of provincial birth. His military conquests extended the Roman Empire to the western boundary of Parthia.

HADRIAN (117-138)

In view of the revolts that threatened Rome upon his accession, Hadrian decided to reverse Trajan's policy of conquest. He renounced the annexation of Mesopotamia by withdrawing Roman troops from that region. In other parts of the empire, too, he elected to establish defensible borders rather than conquering new territory. He built a wall 73 miles in length across Britain to protect Roman settlements from the Picts and other fierce tribes of Scotland, and another wall in Gaul to protect the Rhine frontier from invading Germanic tribes.

During his term as emperor, Hadrian spent much of his time traveling in the provinces. His primary goal was to make sure that the army remained in a state of readiness, but he also took the opportunity to study and correct any other problems he noticed. He improved Roman administration in Italy and the provinces by ordering a complete modernization of the code of laws, which came to be known as the Permanent Edict.

threat to the western portion of the empire, Trajan led his armies across the Danube into Dacia (present Rumania). After conquering this territory, he relocated thousands of Dacians to areas south of the Danube, while colonists from eastern provinces were moved into Dacia. To reduce the threat posed by the Parthians in the East, Trajan annexed Armenia and northern Mesopotamia.

During Trajan's reign, the boundaries of the empire reached their greatest territorial extent, reaching from the Atlantic Ocean to the Caspian Sea, and from Britain to Egypt. But although these conquests brought many benefits, the lengthening of the frontiers was to cause severe problems for his successors. Trajan died in the East while on a campaign to suppress major revolts in Asia Minor, Mesopotamia, Cyprus, and Egypt. On his deathbed, Trajan chose Hadrian, another native of Spain, to be his successor.

The emperor Hadrian. During his 20-year reign, Hadrian concentrated upon the defense of the empire and supervised the construction of large-scale building projects.

THE ROMAN EMPIRE AT ITS GREATEST EXTENT, 117 A.D.
Why did Hadrian decide to pull back from some of the boundaries that Trajan had established?

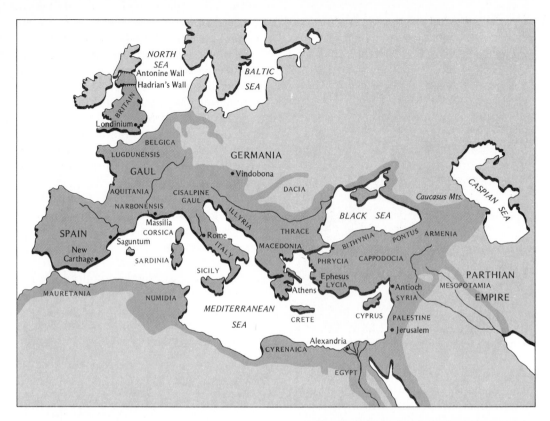

Hadrian's particular interest in Greek culture led him to spend six months in Athens, where he completed the temple of Olympian Zeus and built a magnificent library. Hadrian also planned the rebuilding of the Pantheon in Rome, and designed a beautiful villa, called Tivoli, in a suburb of the city. His tomb, on the bank of the Tiber River in Rome, was so large that it was used as a fortress during the Middle Ages. It is known today as the Castel Sant' Angelo.

Although no major military campaigns were conducted during Hadrian's rule, his decision to build a new city on the site of Jerusalem—which had been destroyed by civil disturbances at the end of Trajan's reign—precipitated a revolt of Judea. After three years, Hadrian's forces crushed the re-

One of Hadrian's most notable boundary fortifications was the 73-mile wall that protected the Roman province of Britain from the fierce tribes of Scotland.

volt and forbade the Jews to worship in their sacred city.

ANTONINUS PIUS (138-161)

Hadrian chose as his successor a wealthy senator from Gaul named Antoninus Pius. Antoninus' reign marked the climax of the era known as the Pax Romana.

Antoninus maintained excellent relations with the Senate, and presided over the great festivities that celebrated the 900th anniversary of Rome's founding. Although there were rebellions in all parts of the empire, Antoninus remained in Rome and did not mount any military campaigns. On his coins, he used such terms as "peace," "tranquillity," and "happiness" to describe his reign.

MARCUS AURELIUS (161-180)

Marcus Aurelius, whom Hadrian had designated an emperor candidate in childhood, succeeded Antoninus. A scholar and Stoic philosopher, Aurelius would have preferred a quiet life of contemplation and study. But his *Meditations*, written while he was engaged in a military campaign, indicate his determination to be a good emperor.

Unfortunately, Aurelius' immediate duties upon becoming emperor included the waging of difficult wars both in Dacia and Parthia. And while Roman troops were gathered in the East, German tribes began to threaten the western borders. In 166, a plague that had started among soldiers fighting in Parthia swept across the empire, killing at

One of the greatest architectural monuments of Hadrian's reign is the Pantheon in Rome, a temple in honor of the ancient Roman gods.

ROMAN EMPERORS	
Julio-Claudian Emperors	
27 B.C.-14	*Augustus*
14-37	*Tiberius*
37-41	*Caligula*
41-54	*Claudius*
54-68	*Nero*
68-69	Civil Wars
Flavian Emperors	
69-79	*Vespasian*
79-81	*Titus*
81-96	*Domitian*
"Good Emperors"	
96-98	*Nerva*
98-117	*Trajan*
117-138	*Hadrian*
138-161	*Antonius Pius*
161-180	*Marcus Aurelius*
180-192	Commodus
192-193	Civil Wars

Marcus Aurelius was the last of the "good" emperors. A Stoic philosopher by vocation, he spent most of his reign on campaign.

least one-fourth of the population. This loss of life made it difficult to recruit soldiers for the army, to collect taxes to maintain the government, or to grow crops to feed the population. Aurelius himself was stricken by the plague while campaigning in Vindobona (present-day Vienna) and died there.

THE CHAOTIC THIRD CENTURY Marcus Aurelius did not follow the custom of adopting a qualified successor. Instead, he chose his son Commodus to succeed him, perhaps fearing that a civil war would result if he made another choice. Like Nero and Domitian before him, Commodus came to be so detested that his reign brought about the fall of his dynasty.

COMMODUS (180-192)

Soon after his accession, Commodus began to show signs of mental instability. He developed the characteristics of a megalomaniac, and demanded that the Senate recognize him as a reincarnation of the hero Hercules as well as emperor. He devoted most of his time to chariot races, lion baiting, and persecution of his political enemies. In 192, he was assassinated, and the Senate marked the ignominious end of his dynasty by expunging all mentions of his reign from its records.

THE SEVERI After Commodus' death, a civil war broke out over the question of succession, and three emperors were proclaimed within a few months. The second of these emperors, a wealthy ex-consul, actually bought the imperial office from the Praetorian guard, who had offered it to the highest bidder. Meanwhile, the armies of Syria, Britain, and the Danube each attempted to proclaim their leaders as emperor. Septimius Severus, the commander of the army of the Danube, finally prevailed.

SEPTIMIUS SEVERUS (193-211)

Severus' reign was a military **autocracy** based on the power and interests of his troops. He

Commodus was not satisfied merely to be honored as emperor, but demanded to be recognized as a reincarnation of Hercules.

inces, where he used Greek phalanx tactics to fight the enemy. He also issued an important decree which continued the work of his father: in Caracalla's decree, Roman citizenship was extended to all of the various peoples of the Roman Empire.

CARACALLA'S SUCCESSORS

Caracalla was murdered by one of his chosen officials. His two successors, Elagabulus and Alexander, were unable to provide the leadership so desperately needed to stem the invasions and revolutions that then threatened the empire. After the death of Alexander Severus, in 235, there followed 50 years of chaos in which 26 emperors were proclaimed, only one of whom died a natural death.

Taking advantage of the weakness of Rome, the Goths and Vandals from the eastern German provinces marched south and threatened the provinces of Greece and the Black Sea. In 267, they plundered Athens.

During this period, Rome was threatened by an internal weakening of its economy as

rarely consulted the Senate, and once advised his sons to "enrich soldiers and scorn all other men." An African by birth, Severus also made a policy of promoting the interests of provincials at the expense of Italians. He opened membership in the Praetorian Guard to men from the provinces, and dismissed the Italian guards. He accepted tribesmen from outlying territories into the army, and even enabled them to rise to the highest offices in the government. Finally, he withdrew the special tax exemptions that Augustus had granted to Italians, making them liable to the same taxes as provincials.

CARACALLA (211-217)

Severus named his eldest son, Caracalla, as his successor, and appointed his younger son, Geta, assistant emperor. Soon after Severus died, Caracalla murdered his younger brother and became sole emperor.

Caracalla fancied himself to be another Alexander the Great, and devoted most of his short reign to expensive wars in the prov-

Caracalla devoted his short reign to military campaigns, and extended Roman citizenship to all peoples of the empire.

well as by external factors. Pirates preyed upon shipping in the Mediterranean and disrupted the import of food to Italy. Inflation spiraled to the point where people stopped using Roman coinage and instead bartered goods and services. Still another plague struck Rome, and the deaths of 5000 people every day created further havoc in the economy. By the year 300, prices were 200 times greater than they had been a century before.

The chaos of the third century brought an end to the powers of the Senate, just as the civil wars of the first century put an end to the republic. After 300, the emperor ruled Rome as a despot.

DIOCLETIAN AND CONSTANTINE The total collapse of the empire was delayed through the efforts of two strong rulers, Diocletian and Constantine. Both of these leaders believed that the only way to save the empire was to impose harsh controls over every aspect of their subjects' lives.

DIOCLETIAN (285-305)

Diocletian was born in Illyria into a poor family. But due to the measures enacted by Septimius Severus at the beginning of the century, Diocletian's provincial origins could not prevent him from rising to the highest offices in the Roman army and government.

In 285, at a time when many areas of the empire were in revolt, Diocletian's troops declared him to be emperor. He immediately assumed all powers of government without seeking the advice or consent of the Senate. By adopting the robes and court etiquette of Oriental kings, he made it clear that he intended his rule to be an autocracy.

As emperor, Diocletian led a successful campaign against the Franks and Burgundians, who were leading raids across the Rhine, but was unable to suppress revolts in Britain and Gaul. In 293, he decided that the empire had become too extensive to be ruled by one man, so he divided it into two parts.

He assigned the title of *Augustus* to himself as ruler of the eastern provinces and also to Maximian, whom he assigned to rule the western provinces. He then assigned the lesser title of *Caesar* to Galerius, whom he chose to be his assistant in the East, and to Constantius, whom Maximian chose as his assistant in the West. Diocletian announced that he and Maximian (the *Augusti*) would reign for 20 years, and would then step down in favor of the Caesars. All laws were to be issued jointly in the names of the Augusti and Caesars, and were to be uniformly enforced throughout the empire.

Diocletian decided that small units of government would be easier to administer than large ones, and would prevent lesser officials from gathering too much power. Therefore, he divided each of the four *prefectures* into 12 *dioceses* and appointed a ruler (*vicarius*) for each. Diocletian ruled the entire eastern area from his capital in Nicodemia, in Asia Minor, while Maximian ruled the western area from Milan, in Italy. Thus, Rome ceased to be the capital of the empire, and the Senate became the equivalent of a city council for the city of Rome.

Events soon demonstrated the wisdom of Diocletian's new administration in the military sphere. Constantius managed to reconquer Britain, as Diocletian had not been able to do as sole ruler. Maximian suppressed an uprising in the African provinces, while Diocletian himself overcame a pretender in Egypt, and Galerius defended Armenia from the Persians.

In civil matters, Diocletian's administration was not as successful. One of his most notable policies was the attempt to unify the empire by imposing one religion upon all of its peoples. To this end, he issued regulations which forced Christians to worship the gods of the state upon pain of death (see Chapter 12). The martyrdom of thousands of Christians did not have the effect of promoting Roman religion, however, nor did Diocletian's Caesars enforce the edicts uni-

After ruling the eastern half of the Roman Empire for 20 years, Diocletian retired to Split. This is a temple that he built in that city.

formly. In other edicts, he attempted to impose uniform taxes and to prevent merchants from "profiteering," but these regulations could not be effectively enforced.

In 305, Diocletian and Maximian abdicated their positions as Augusti, just as they had promised they would 20 years before. Diocletian retired to an estate in Split, in modern Yugoslavia, which was close to medicinal sulphur springs where he could receive treatment for the ailments of old age.

CONSTANTINE (312-37)

Constantius and Galerius advanced to the positions of Augusti, and selected two new men to serve as Caesars. When Constantius died shortly after his promotion, in 306, the armies of Britain and Gaul acclaimed his son, Constantine, as his successor. Constantine then became involved in a civil war as he struggled to assert his claim against six other candidates. In 312, he brought his army to Italy, and emerged as the victor of a great battle fought at the Milvian Bridge near Rome. Constantine then reached an agreement with Licinius, who had been appointed an Augustus, to share control of the empire.

After becoming Augustus, Constantine announced his conversion to Christianity. In 313, he and Licinius issued the Edict of Milan. This edict annulled the anti-Christian measures enacted by Diocletian and extended toleration to all religions—especially Christianity. When Licinius later renounced the decree and began to persecute Christians, Constantine defeated him in battle and became sole emperor.

In 330, Constantine built a new eastern capital on the site of Byzantium, in present-day Turkey, and renamed the town Constantinople. This city eventually became the capital of the eastern portion of the empire and the center of the Byzantine Christian civilization (Chapter 13).

CONSTANTINE'S SUCCESSORS

After Constantine's death, his empire was divided among his sons, Constantine II, Constantius, and Constans. The three emperors soon began to fight each other, and in 340, Constantine II was killed and the empire redivided between the surviving two brothers. Ten years later, the great armies of Gaul and the Danube were nearly destroyed in a battle between Constantius and a usurper. In this and later dynastic struggles, the military resources of the empire were strained to their limit, and few troops could be spared to defend the borders. Taking advantage of this weakness, the Sassanian Persians in the East and the Goths in the West began to conduct frequent raids in Roman territory.

Julian, the army commander who succeeded Constantius as emperor, tried to unify the empire by instituting paganism in place of Christianity as the state religion. This program did not receive great popular support, however, and Julian lost his life while trying to defend the eastern borders of the empire against the Persians. All of the emperors who succeeded him, both in the eastern and western portions of the empire, were Christians.

THE 5TH-CENTURY INVASIONS

While the Roman emperors were preoccupied with dynastic struggles and religious controversies, the Huns, a fierce nomadic people from Asia, began to invade western Europe. Because they fought on horseback, the Huns were easily able to overcome the German tribes they encountered. In 376, the Romans allowed a large group of Visigoths (western Germans) to seek refuge from the Huns in Thrace, within the borders of the Roman empire. Within a short time, however, the Visigoths began to voice bitter complaints about the way that Roman bureaucratic

The conquest of Rome by the Visigoths, in 410, was one of the dramatic episodes that marked the fall of Rome. In 455, the city was again sacked by the Vandals.

officials were treating them. When no action was taken in response, the Goths rose up in arms. In 378, they defeated an imperial army led by the emperor Valens at Adrianople.

The battle between the Romans and Visigoths at Adrianople was followed by a century of invasions that finally brought an end to the Roman Empire in the West. In 406, the Vandals, a primitive Germanic tribe, invaded Gaul and Spain, then proceeded to northern Africa, where they set up a powerful seafaring kingdom. From their base in Africa, they were able to disrupt the supply of grain to Rome and prevent communications between the eastern and western portions of the empire. Britain fell to the Angles and Saxons, and the Franks and Alemanni moved into Gaul. In 410, the Visigoths entered and sacked Rome.

The sack of Rome by the Visigoths effectively marked the end of the Roman Empire in the West. Although emperors continued to be proclaimed in Rome, they were, in effect, the puppets of powerful Germanic leaders who were struggling for control of Europe. In 476, the German chieftain Odoacer deposed Romulus Augustulus, the last Roman emperor in the West, and proclaimed himself king. The eastern portion of the Roman Empire survived as what we call the Byzantine Empire until 1453.

DECLINE AND FALL OF ROME

Ever since the capture of Rome by the Visigoths in 410, people have debated the causes of the empire's collapse. The early Christians were particularly troubled by this question, for they had believed that the period between Jesus' resurrection and the Last Judgment would be marked by an orderly progress of civilization. In response to their concerns, Saint Augustine, one of the early Church fathers (see Chapter 12), wrote the first major analysis of Rome's fall in *The City of God*. In this work, he argued that the decline of Rome was due to the character of the Romans themselves, not to the fact that the last emperors had promoted Christianity as the religion of the empire.

Since Augustine, many other writers have identified reasons to explain Rome's decline. It is now generally recognized that no one issue can be singled out as the most important; rather, a great number of different, often overlapping, causes were involved.

ECONOMIC AND SOCIAL CONDITIONS

During the 2nd and 3rd centuries, many regions of the empire suffered a prolonged economic crisis. This economic stagnation has been identified as a major factor in the decline of the empire, for it affected the emperors' ability to pay for the soldiers needed to defend Roman borders. The citizens of the empire, in turn, afflicted both by ruinous taxation and by the threat of foreign invasions, began to perceive that the emperors could no longer provide the conditions of peace and prosperity that had once justified their autocratic powers.

One major cause of economic instability throughout the Roman world was the institution of slavery. The Romans' widespread use of slave labor discouraged the invention and use of new technology which would have led to the development of more varied and sophisticated products. Instead, pottery, textiles, and other products tended to be manufactured in as simple and uniform a manner as possible, especially in the western portion of the empire. As a result, there was little variety in the goods produced in different provinces, and little incentive for trade and commerce. Although wealthy people continued to import finely crafted luxury goods from the East, there was no corresponding demand for western products. Frequent civil wars and repeated attacks by the barbarians accelerated the breakdown of trade and communication. By the middle of the 3rd century, the great trade route that had once linked London and Byzantium was nearly impassable.

Between 250 and 270, a plague decimated the population of Europe, causing further economic decline. In order to find the resources necessary to maintain the empire, successive emperors resorted to increasingly severe methods of taxation. The emperor Diocletian (285-305) was so desperate for funds that he imposed strict control upon all aspects of the economy: middle-class families were heavily taxed, and sons were obligated to follow the same trades as their fathers so that they could continue to pay at the same rate. In the long run, such measures bankrupted and alienated many citizens. In addition, the autocratic form of government imposed by Diocletian allowed little scope for the senatorial class to participate in the affairs of the empire. Rather than entering political life, many prominent families withdrew to the countryside and concentrated upon developing self-sufficient manor farms.

SUCCESSION PROBLEMS

The civil wars that accompanied each disputed succession played a major role in weakening the empire. These wars not only consumed valuable troops and resources in themselves, but often gave an opportunity for the Persians, Germans, and other hostile tribes to invade and plunder Roman territory.

Although disputed successions had been a problem throughout the period of the empire, the choice of Trajan, a professional soldier from Spain, as emperor (98-117) further complicated the question. Once it was established that emperors no longer had to be of Roman or Italian extraction, the number of possible candidates was greatly increased. As a result of the heightened competition, Rome gained some of the best rulers in its history, and citizens of outlying provinces gained a sense of citizenship in the empire. But it also meant that many more people became involved in disputes over succession. Armies in such faraway provinces as Syria, Africa, and Britain began to advance their generals as emperor candidates, and the resulting civil wars were fought on battlefields throughout the Roman world.

In an attempt to put an end to such internal struggles, Diocletian established a system whereby the emperor, or *Augustus*, chose a successor based on merit rather than blood relationship. The designated heir was then appointed to the office of *Caesar* so that he became known to the public well ahead of time, and at the same time gained valuable administrative experience before his accession. Even during Diocletian's lifetime, however, Roman armies continued to demonstrate their loyalty to certain leaders by honoring their sons or other relatives. In 306, for instance, the armies of Britain and Gaul acclaimed Constantine, the son of an Augustus, as his father's heir rather than accepting the designated ruler.

THE BARBARIANS AND THE PERSIANS

Although the invasions of the Germanic tribes were the immediate cause of Rome's downfall, there were also, as we have seen, internal economic and political problems within the empire which contributed to the success of the invaders. Another factor in Rome's inability to defend its western borders was the threat of invasion from the East.

From the time of Crassus' disastrous campaign in Parthia in 53 B.C., the Parthian Empire had occupied the attention of the Romans. The Parthians, an Iranian people, controlled much of the ancient Persian Empire, and their territories extended to the Euphrates River, the eastern boundary of Roman Syria. Although they were not strong enough to conquer the Roman Empire, they did pose a constant threat to Rome's rule of its eastern territories.

Trajan attempted to weaken the Parthians by conquering Armenia and Mesopotamia, thereby preventing them from using the resources of these territories. But Hadrian, his successor, decided that direct Roman rule over these territories was impractical. He reverted instead to the policy of creating a buffer zone, and installed vassal kings in Mesopotamia and Armenia. During the reigns of Marcus Aurelius and Septimius Severus, the Romans successfully repelled Parthian attempts to invade these kingdoms. But in 241, the threat from the East was unexpectedly revived when a new dynasty, the Sassanians, replaced the Parthians as rulers of Iran and Persia. Following the example of Cyrus the Great, the Sassanian rulers improved the political administration of their territories, and extended religious freedom to Jews, Christians, and other sects. They thus won the sympathy of peoples who had been persecuted under the Romans, and achieved several victories over Roman troops in Syria-Palestine, Cappodocia, and Mesopotamia.

SUMMARY

During the span of history we have discussed, the institutions of the Roman Republic were undermined by a series of conflicts between the various factions of Roman society. Instead of trying to solve the underlying social and economic problems of the republic, the Roman Senate attempted to maintain its authority by forcibly suppressing its opponents.

After it sanctioned the murders of the Gracchi brothers and other reformers, the Senate lost much of the prestige and authority that had enabled it to govern. Many people came to regard the Senate as a group of men more concerned with their own interests than with the welfare of the republic, and began to question even its decisions about foreign policy. The public assemblies were not able to organize an effective resistance to the Senate, but they did promote the rise of military commanders who achieved dictatorial powers. The civil wars inspired by rivalries among these commanders brought an end to the republic and paved the way for the modified dictatorship of Augustus.

QUESTIONS

1 What pressing problems faced the republic in 133 B.C.? What specific reforms did the Gracchi brothers propose?
2 To what extent did the reforms of the Gracchi brothers succeed or fail? Why did their actions mark the beginning of the end for the republic?
3 Trace the rise to power of Caesar, Pompey, and Crassus. What common bonds between them led to the formation of the First Triumvirate? Why and when was the triumvirate dissolved?
4 Compare Caesar's treatment of his political enemies to the methods that Marius and Sulla used. Which method would be more likely to prolong a civil war?
5 What major problems faced Octavian when he returned to Rome in 29 B.C. What means did he use to restore order and consolidate control over Rome and its empire?

BIBLIOGRAPHY

Which books might discuss the government established by Augustus?

EARL, DONALD. *The Age of Augustus.* New York: Exeter Books, 1980. *Describes the personality and achievements of the man who established lasting peace and political stability in the Roman world during his long reign as emperor. Outstanding illustrations of the mosaics, architecture, and pottery of the imperial period.*

GRANT, MICHAEL. *The World of Rome.* Cleveland: World Publishing Co., 1968. *A survey of Roman civilization from 133 B.C. to 217 A.D., with emphasis on the commerce, architecture, and military activities of this period. Introduces the writings of Cicero, Tacitus, Seneca, and others, and emphasizes our heritage from ancient Rome.*

HUZAR, ELEANOR GOLTZ. *Mark Antony, a Biography.* University of Minnesota Press, 1978. *Recounts the events of Mark Antony's career, and describes the nature of Roman politics in his time; the alliances, feuds, and ambitions of rival generals. The author concludes that the empire required a dictatorship, but that Antony would have introduced this form of government in a more deliberate, less revolutionary way than did Octavian.*

CHINA

3000 B.C.–220 A.D.

At the height of the Roman Empire, richly laden caravans traveled to markets in the Middle East, bearing exotic goods from the East. Fine silks from China were among the luxuries for which wealthy Romans were willing to pay dearly. By the 1st century A.D., however, when these contacts between China and the West were taking place, China already had a long history stretching back over 3000 years.

In China, as in Mesopotamia and Egypt, the earliest civilization grew up in a fertile river valley—the Huang Ho, or Yellow River, valley of northern China. Other rivers of importance to the early development of ancient China were the Yangtze, the Huai, and the Si rivers. Each river provided the fertile soil and the annual flooding that was crucial to the success of ancient agricultural societies. But the flooding of the Huang Ho was not regular and predictable as was that of the Nile River in Egypt. Instead, it often caused great devastation, and because of this the river became known as "China's Sorrow."

According to Chinese legend, the first cities were founded along the Huang Ho by the Hsia dynasty about 3000 B.C., but as yet, little evidence has been found to verify the existence of this ancient dynasty. China emerges onto the stage of history with the Shang dynasty (c. 1766–1027 B.C.). Archaeologists have found the remains of *Anyang*, the oldest known Chinese city and a Shang capital that dates to about 1300 B.C. The Anyang archaeological finds indicate that the Shang Chinese used wheeled chariots; had developed sophisticated methods of working with bronze; planted wheat, millet, and rice; and domesticated fowls, pigs, dogs, and elephants.

In addition, artifacts from the Shang period include oracle bones with pictographic writing, which were used by Shang priests to foretell the future. The pictograms that they carved on bones posed certain questions to the gods or to their ancestors, whom the Chinese revered. The bones were heated and the resulting cracks were interpreted as the answers to the questions. Although this pictogram writing developed later in China than in Mesopotamia or Egypt, it endured far longer. The 2000 or more Shang characters became the basis for the Chinese language that has survived, with modifications, to the present day.

CHOU DYNASTY

About 1027 B.C., the Shang capital of Anyang fell to rebels who founded the Chou dynasty

Oracle bones were used by priests of the Shang period in their search for supernatural advice. Once the characters were carved, heat was applied to the bone and the patterns of the cracks were interpreted for answers.

flooding was severe, famine occurred, invasions threatened, or the dynasty was unable to maintain law and order.

During the Chou dynasty, China moved ahead on many fronts. Metal coins were used as a money economy developed. Iron was introduced and was used in the making of tools and weapons. New farming methods, such as the ox-drawn plow, helped peasants increase food production. Work on major irrigation and transportation systems including the Grand Canal was begun, and Chinese scholars made great achievements in astronomy.

During the early Chou period, Chinese rulers expanded the boundaries of the kingdom both westward and southward to include the Yangtze River basin. As a result, the kingdom was four to five times larger than it had been under the Shang. To govern this large territory, the Chou rulers instituted a feudal system. That is, powerful nobles were given fiefs, or land to administer in return for their loyalty and obedience to the emperor. In addition to maintaining law and order in their fiefs, these local lords pledged to protect and fight for the em-

(1027–221 B.C.). The Chou justified their seizure of power by claiming that they had been granted the Mandate of Heaven—the approval or legitimation of Heaven. This concept became a central premise of Chinese government. According to the mandate, as long as a ruler governed well he enjoyed the approval or legitimation of Heaven. Conversely, a ruler lost the mandate when he governed badly, and Heaven transferred the mandate to other ruling families based upon their performance. The Chinese saw their rulers as humans but believed that they had been chosen by Heaven to carry out its divine purpose. Historically, Chinese dynasties were said to have "lost" the Mandate of Heaven when irrigation systems failed,

The art of casting bronze was perfected during the Shang and Chou dynasties. Fine vessels such as this were used for ceremonial purposes, to present offerings to ancestors.

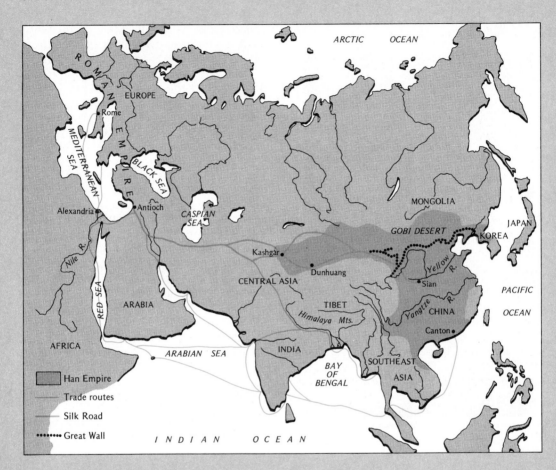

peror. In so doing, they became vassals of the emperor. In time, many local lords became powerful enough to challenge the authority of the emperor and also fought each other. Eventually, as the Chou dynasty disintegrated, it lost control over its vassals, and China endured a prolonged period of feudal warfare lasting from about 771 to 221 B.C.

During this period of instability and uncertainty, people looked around for reasons to explain the collapse of the social order. Many philosophers offered advice to rulers. Among the schools of philosophy that emerged in this period were three that had a profound impact on China: Taoism, Confucianism, and Legalism.

Unlike the religions of Hinduism and Buddhism that focused on the ultimate goal of freeing the individual soul from the cycle of rebirth, these traditional Chinese philosophies were concerned with the practicalities of everyday life—getting along with family, friends, acquaintances, and leaders. They were not concerned with sacred texts or revelations from a deity or supernatural being. They taught no "holy" commandments or rituals that must be observed. Instead, these Chinese philosophies were concerned with relationships—the establishment of harmonious social and political interactions.

Taoism. Lao-tse (born about 604 B.C.), the

"Old Philosopher," is traditionally considered the founder of Taoism. The earliest Taoist teachings are contained in the *Tao Te Ching*, or *The Way of Virtue*. Lao-tse believed that, whatever their basic nature was, people were corrupted by civilization. He urged people to follow the *tao*, or the way, which could only be felt and could not be explained. Taoists tended to shun the world and retire as hermits to a contemplative life. They looked on government as an unavoidable evil but believed the least government was the best.

In time, Taoism became both a religion and a philosophy. Taoist priests used charms and magical prayers to influence the spirits that they believed inhabited the world. From their studies of nature and the planets, Taoists are also credited with making advances in science and astronomy.

Confucianism. The great Chinese philosopher and teacher Confucius (551–479 B.C.) was descended from the Shang kings. To his students, he was known as Kung Tzu, or the Master Kung. When the first Christian missionaries reached China, they Latinized this name to Confucius. It is interesting to note that Confucius lived at a time of intellectual ferment around the world. In Persia, the teachings of Zoroaster were taking root; in Greece, the age of Socrates was dawning; and in India, the Buddha was trying to reform and revitalize the Hindu religion.

Confucius believed that people were by nature good, and he was concerned with ways to organize a stable and just society. He emphasized the virtues of loyalty, respect for elders, and hard work. Confucius propounded a code of ethical conduct that he believed would ensure a return to the peaceful order that had existed in the past. He set out five basic relationships that defined an individual's place in society. These were the relationships between ruler and subject; parent and child; husband and wife; older brother and younger brother; and friend and friend. In each relationship, individuals had duties and responsibilities toward each other. Only when people accepted these responsibilities, Confucius said, would an orderly society be possible.

Confucius, the great Chinese teacher, attracted many followers. The philosophy constructed from his sayings has influenced Chinese thought even to the present.

The teachings of Confucius were collected by his followers in a work known as the *Analects*. Besides defining the role of the individual in society, Confucius also emphasized the importance of education and *filial piety*, respect for one's elders. He believed the best government officials were those who were well educated, and urged the rulers of China's warring feudal states to turn to such men. Although in his lifetime Confucius was unable to find any ruler who would accept his philosophy, his teachings had profound impact on later Chinese civilization.

Legalism. A third school of thought to develop in the late Chou period was Legalism. Among its chief proponents was Han Fei Tzu (died 233 B.C.), who rejected the Confucian emphasis on ethical conduct in favor of an authoritarian view of society. Legalists thought that people by nature were dishonest and lazy, and insisted that only strict laws and harsh punishments would ensure an orderly society.

CH'IN EMPIRE

In the 3rd century B.C., at the same time as Rome was expanding its power in Italy, the Chou dynasty collapsed after a prolonged period of civil war. Out of the chaos, a local feudal lord, the ruler of the Ch'in kingdom, led a successful attempt to unite and unify China. In so doing, he established the short-lived Ch'in dynasty (221–206 B.C.). Some scholars think that it is from the Ch'in dynasty that China derives its name. After subduing the other powerful feudal lords, the Ch'in ruler also successfully defended northern China from attacks by the Huns.

After crushing all opposition, the Ch'in ruler took the title Shih Huang-ti, meaning the "First Emperor," and he permitted his new subjects to call him the "Son of Heaven." Shih Huang-ti was determined to destroy the power of the feudal lords, and his reign was marked by cruelty and harshness. To destroy feudalism, he reclaimed all the land of China in the name of the emperor, confiscated and melted down the weapons of his enemies, and issued orders that only his own soldiers could possess weapons. To ensure obedience to his commands, the emperor maintained a strong, fully trained army. He improved existing roads and built new ones in order to facilitate the movement of his armies throughout the empire.

Further, Shih Huang-ti began the vast task of unifying, joining, and improving the scat-

These terracotta soldiers and horses guarded the tomb of Shih Huang-ti, founder of the Ch'in dynasty. The discovery of the tomb in 1974 focused much attention on this era of China's history.

tered earth walls that various local lords had built to keep out invaders from Central Asia. Using forced labor, the rebuilding process, completed under the succeeding Han dynasty, resulted in the construction of the massive Great Wall of China, which is 22 feet high, 20 feet wide, and approximately 1400 miles long. The emperor reorganized the government and adopted the Legalist philosophy. He divided China into 36 regions, appointing officials responsible to him to rule in each region. With rigid rules and harsh punishment, he sought to impose unity on all China.

Unlike the chaotic years of the late Chou dynasty, when intellectual freedom was permitted and encouraged, the Ch'in ruler decreed that all books, writings, and literature related to non-Legalist philosophies were to be confiscated and burned. However, as part of his plan to unify the empire, Shih Huang-ti also decreed that there should be a single form of writing throughout the empire, and he commanded his officials to institute such a system. By standardizing the writing of Chinese characters, people from different parts of China could communicate with each other through written documents even though they spoke different dialects. In addition to the standardization of the written language, Shih Huang-ti set up a uniform system of weights and measures, including a standard gauge for all wheel axles.

Although the Ch'in Empire collapsed a few years after the death of its founder in 210 B.C., the "First Emperor" had laid the foundations for a unified state. Two hundred years before the Roman emperor Augustus, Shih Huang-ti had issued coins that were used throughout his empire and had built an efficient road system, with lines radiating from his capital at Changan to the furthest outposts of the empire.

HAN EMPIRE

Out of the chaos that followed the collapse of the Ch'in dynasty, a peasant leader named Liu Pang rose to power at the head of a powerful army. In 202 B.C., Liu Pang became emperor by right of conquest and founded the Han dynasty (202 B.C.–220 A.D.). Under this dynasty, China enjoyed a golden age similar to that of the early Roman Empire. The first Han emperor restored peace and instituted programs to erase the harsh measures of Shih Huang-ti. In place of Legalist principles, he adopted Confucian ideas of government, and he restored intellectual freedom to writers and artists.

The Han dynasty reached its peak under the emperor Wu Ti (141–87 B.C.). Continuing the Han tradition of implementing Confucian ideas, Wu Ti created a system of civil service examination to find the best qualified individuals to administer the government. As a result, literacy became the means for government advancement. Confucian ideals were stressed, since the examinations were based on the Confucian classics as well as on knowledge of the law. This examination system provided China with some of its most gifted government officials and contributed to stability and order even when dynasties fell. In fact, this civil service system continued in China until 1912—nearly 2000 years.

A pottery model of a house unearthed from a tomb of the Han era. The 400 years of the Han dynasty were marked by many artistic and technological advances.

Wu Ti incorporated Korea and Southeast Asia into the Chinese empire and extended part of the western boundary to the Caspian Sea. In the process of expansion, he established commercial contact with Rome, India, and Southwest Asia. In creating the largest and wealthiest empire of that time, Wu Ti is also credited with establishing the *Pax Sinica* ("Chinese Peace")—a period of commercial and social stability that lasted for almost 200 years.

Commercial contact with Rome, Greece, and the Middle East necessitated the creation, maintenance, and protection of a trade route through the western territories of the empire. Along this route, camel caravans carried silk, jade, and lacquerware westward to exchange for glass, amber, asbestos, and

265

Silk, an important commodity in the East-West trade that began in the 1st century, was usually manufactured by Chinese women. In this painting, women are shown pounding the newly woven fabric to tighten its weave.

linen. Because silk was the mainstay of this trade, the route became known as the Silk Road. Although silk was commonplace in China (where it was issued as pay to the soldiers), it was a marvel to the people of the Mediterranean world.

During the Han dynasty, the Chinese made many technological and scientific advances. By the 2nd century B.C. the Chinese were using the foot stirrup, a thousand years before it reached the West. About 100 A.D., the Chinese invented paper. They developed other practical devices such as the wheelbarrow, water mill, and harness. In science, Chinese scholars emphasized observation, as the Greeks had done, and used their observations to discover natural laws of the universe. In addition, the Chinese invented the sundial and water clock, and developed a highly accurate calendar.

Increased trade and contact with the West brought new products and ideas to China.

During the Han dynasty, Buddhist missionaries made their way into China. At first, the Chinese found little appeal in the new religion, although they saw elements of Taoism in its rejection of worldly pursuits. As the Han dynasty weakened, however, Buddhism gained in popularity, offering hope to those who felt that life was full of suffering and sorrow.

By the 3rd century A.D., the Han dynasty was unable to defend itself from internal and external threats. Like the Roman Empire in the West, weak Han rulers were unable to maintain their power. China's traditional enemies, the Huns, again threatened in the north. In 220 A.D. the Han dynasty collapsed, and contacts between China and the Mediterranean world declined. In the next centuries, China experienced a period of anarchy with a succession of ruling houses attempting to restore order. It was during this "Period of Six Dynasties" (220 A.D.–589 A.D.) that

Buddhism took root in China and adapted itself to the traditional Chinese philosophies of Confucianism and Taoism.

The teachings of Confucius pointed the way to happiness through correct behavior. A skillful teacher, much like the Buddha, Confucius considered himself not an innovator but a transmitter of the values that had ensured harmony in the past. Central to Confucian thought is the idea of *jen*—perfect virtue—which brings to society the cooperative behavior of individuals, and to the individual a sense of moral right.

Basic to Confucianism is the belief that individuals are innately good. Taoism, in contrast, accepts people the way they are with no moral judgment made about their innate character. According to legend, Lao-tse could never understand why Confucius worried so much about changing people and ordering their lives. He is said to have confronted Confucius, criticizing his attempt to change people with the comment that "the swan is white without a daily bath, and the raven is black without daily coloring itself." Lao-tse believed that people should not desire anything, not even goodness. For Lao-tse, hatred, greed, pride, and ambition were all a waste of time. Instead, he directed people to copy nature, saying that a tree does not want things or struggle to control other trees, it just grows. Taoism encouraged people to lead simple lives, while proclaiming love of nature and harmony with nature as goals for living.

Taoism is a philosophy based on harmony rather than on assertiveness. It views humankind as an integral part of nature rather than as a controller of nature. To attain harmony with nature and with all the forces of the universe, Taoists believed that people must utilize the principles of *yin* and *yang*. According to Chinese philosophy, the yin and the yang are the two primary principles, or forces, of the universe. These forces are said to be eternally interacting, and eternally opposed to one another.

The yin principle is equated with brightness, heat, activity, masculinity, Heaven, sun, south, above, roundness, and odd numbers, while the yang principle is equated with darkness, cold, inactivity, femininity, Earth, moon, north, below, squareness, and even numbers. The yin and the yang are said to work in conjunction with five elements: wood, fire, earth, metal, and water. According to Taoist philosophy, a person should not strive for the dominance of one set of principles over another. Instead, the goal of life is the attainment of harmony—the perfect balance between opposing principles.

DOCUMENT 1   CONFUCIUS ON FILIAL PIETY

The master [Confucius] said: "filial piety is the force that continues the purposes and completes the affairs of our forefathers. . . . To gather in the same place where they earlier have gathered; to perform the same ceremonies which they earlier have performed; to play the same music which they earlier did; to pay respect to those whom they honored; to love those who were dear to them; in fact, to serve those now dead as if they were living, and those now departed as if they were with us still. This is the highest achievement of filial piety."

SOURCE: Confucius, *Chung Yung*, Chapter XIX, as found in *The Sacred Books of Confucius and other Confucian Classics*, pp. 11–12.

How does the Confucian ideal of filial piety ensure social order?

245.   The Master said: "One who governs by virtue is comparable to the polar star, which remains in its place while all the stars turn towards it."

246.   The Master said: "Govern the people by laws and regulate them by penalties, and the people will try to do no wrong, but they will lose the sense of shame. Govern the people by virtue and restrain them by rules of propriety, and the people will have a sense of shame and be reformed of themselves."

247.   Duke Ai asked: "What should I do to secure the submission of the people?" "Promote the upright and banish the crooked," said the Master; "then the people will be submissive. Promote the crooked and banish the upright; then the people will not be submissive."

248.   Chi Kang Tzu asked: "What should be done to make the people respectful and be encouraged to cultivate virtues?" "Approach the people with dignity," said the Master, "and they will be respectful. Show filial piety and kindness, and they will be loyal. Promote those who are worthy, and train those who are incompetent; and they will be encouraged to cultivate virtues."

255.   Tzu Kung asked about good government, and the Master said: "The essentials [of good government] are sufficient food, sufficient arms, and the confidence of the people." "But," asked Tzu Kung, "if you have to part with one of the three, which would you give up?" "Arms," said the Master. "But suppose," said Tzu Kung, "one of the remaining two has to be relinquished, which would it be?" "Food," said the Master. "From time immemorial death has been the lot of all men, but a people without confidence is lost indeed."

270.   The Master said: "If a prince has rendered himself upright, he will have no difficulty in governing the people. But if he cannot rectify himself, how can he hope to rectify the people?"

SOURCE: Confucius, *The Confucian Analects*, Lu Version, as found in *The Sacred Books of Confucius and other Confucian Classics.*

What does Confucius think is the best way of maintaining order? Why do you think the rulers with whom he tried to share his ideas rejected these teachings?

Although Lao-Tse, the supposed founder of Taoism, may only be a figure of legend, a number of works are credited to him. Typically, Taoists speak in paradoxes that often are seemingly contradictory and emphasize harmony with nature.

As the soft yield of water cleaves obstinate stone,
So to yield with life solves the insoluble:
To yield, I have learned, is to come back again.
But this unworded lesson,
This easy example,
Is lost upon men.

SOURCE: Arthur Cottrell and David Morgan, *China's Civilization* (New York: Praeger Publishers, 1975), p. 35.

Banish wisdom, discard knowledge,
And the people will be benefited a hundredfold.
Banish human kindness, discard morality,
And the people will be dutiful and compassionate.
Banish skill, discard profit,
And thieves and robbers will disappear. . . .
The more prohibitions there are, the more ritual
   avoidances,
The poorer the people will be.
The more "sharp weapons" there are,
The more pernicious contrivances will be invented.
The more laws are promulgated,
The more thieves and bandits there will be.
Therefore a sage has said:
So long as I "do nothing" the people will of themselves
   be transformed.
So long as I love quietude, the people will of
   themselves go straight.
So long as I act only by inactivity the people will of
   themselves become prosperous.
So long as I have no wants the people will of
   themselves return to the "state of the Uncarved
   Block."

SOURCE: Arthur Waley (ed.), *The Way and Its Power, A Study of the Tao Te Ching and Its Place in Chinese Thought* (Boston: Houghton Mifflin, 1935).

Compare Taoist ideas of government as reflected in these sayings to those of Confucius in Document 2.

Legalist principles were adopted during the brief Ch'in dynasty. All succeeding dynasties enthroned Confucian ideas over the harsh measures proposed by Han Fei Tzu. The selection below summarizes the beliefs of the Legalists.

When the sage rules the state, he does not count on people doing good of themselves, but employs such measures as will keep them from doing any evil. If he counts on people doing good of themselves, there will not be enough such people to be numbered by the tens in the whole country. But if he employs such measures as will keep them from doing evil, then the entire state can be brought up to a uniform standard. . . .

. . .when the Confucianists of the present day counsel the rulers they do not discuss the way to bring about order now, but exalt the achievement of good order in the past. They neither study affairs pertaining to law and government nor observe the realities of vice and wickedness, but all exalt the reputed glories of remote antiquity and the achievements of the ancient kings. . . . The intelligent ruler upholds solid facts and discards useless frills. He does not speak about deeds of humanity and righteousness, and he does not listen to the words of learned men.

Those who are ignorant about government insistently say: "Win the hearts of the people." . . . For all that the ruler would need to do would be just to listen to the people. Actually, the intelligence of the people is not to be relied upon any more than the mind of a baby. . . .

Now, the sovereign urges the tillage of land and the cultivation of pastures for the purpose of increasing production for the people, but they think the sovereign is cruel. The sovereign regulates penalties and increases punishments for the purpose of repressing the wicked, but the people think the sovereign is severe. Again, he levies taxes in cash and in grain to fill up the granaries and treasuries in order to relieve famine and provide for the army, but they think the sovereign is greedy. Finally, he insists upon universal military training without personal favoritism, and urges his forces to fight hard in order to take the enemy captive, but the people think the sovereign is violent. These four measures are methods for attaining order and maintaining peace, but the people are too ignorant to appreciate them.

SOURCE: Wm. Theodore de Bary, Wing-tsit Chan, and Burton Watson, *Sources of Chinese Tradition* (New York: Columbia University Press, 1964), Vol. I.

Why did Legalists reject the Confucian view of good government?

TIME LINE FOR CHINA AND THE WEST

CHINA		THE WEST	
		3100 B.C.	Narmer unites Upper and Lower Egypt; Sumerian city-states flourish in Mesopotamia
3000 B.C.	Legendary Hsia dynasty rules villages of Huang Ho valley	2600 B.C.	Pyramid of Khufu built
1766 B.C.	Shang dynasty; development of pictographic writing	1100 B.C.	Mycenaean civilization collapses
1027 B.C.	Chou dynasty wins Mandate of Heaven; begins to expand China's borders		
771–221 B.C.	Stability of Chou government undermined by feudal warfare	750 B.C.	Assyrians conquer Syria-Palestine
		600 B.C.	Zoroaster founds new religion in Persia
551–479 B.C.	Lifetime of Confucius	509 B.C.	Roman Republic founded
		500 B.C.	Cleisthenes reforms Athens' democracy
		479 B.C.	Persian Wars end; Pericles assumes leadership of Athens
		469–399 B.C.	Lifetime of Socrates
221 B.C.	Ch'in dynasty overthrows Chou government; imposes unity on China	246 B.C.	Punic Wars begin
206 B.C.	Han dynasty; era of prosperity and expansion		
141 B.C.	Reign of Wu Ti; era of Pax Sinica	146 B.C.	Punic Wars end; Rome rules Carthaginian empire
		27 B.C.–180 A.D.	Pax Romana; trade and commerce established between China and the West
220 A.D.	Collapse of Han Empire; period of Six Dynasties begins		
		476 A.D.	Collapse of Roman Empire in the West
589 A.D.	Buddhism takes hold in China		

WHEN DOES HISTORY HAPPEN?

Barbara Tuchman's Practicing History, *from which the following excerpt was taken, is a compilation of essays on the difficulties a scholar faces when trying to write a history book. Select an important current event, and prepare two written explanations of it, first subjectively and then objectively.*

Who are [historians]: contemporaries of the event or those who come after? The answer is obviously both. Among contemporaries, first and indispensable are the more-or-less unconscious sources: letters, diaries, memoirs, autobiographies, newspapers and periodicals, business and government documents. These are historical raw material, . . . but that does not make [the writers] historians. . . .

At a slightly different level are the I-was-there recorders, usually journalists, whose accounts often contain golden nuggets of information buried in a mass of daily travelogue which the passage of time has reduced to trivia. . . . Daily journalism, however, even when collected in book form, is, like letters and the rest, essentially source material rather than history.

Still contemporary but dispensable are the Compilers who hurriedly assemble a book from clippings and interviews in order to capitalize on public interest when it is high. . . . The Compilers, in their treatment, supply no extra understanding and as historians are negligible.

All these varieties being disposed of, there remains a pure vein of conscious historians of whom among contemporaries, there are two kinds. First, the On-lookers, who deliberately set out to chronicle an episode of their own age—a war or depression or strike or social revolution or whatever it may be—and shape it into a historical narrative with character and validity of its own. Thucydides' *Peloponnesian War* . . . [is an] . . . example.

Second are the Active Participants or Axe-Grinders, who attempt a genuine history of events they have known, but whose accounts are inevitably weighted, sometimes subtly and imperceptibly, sometimes crudely, by the requirements of the role in which they wish themselves to appear. Josephus' *The Jewish War,* . . . [is in] this category.

The contemporary has no perspective; everything is in the foreground and appears the same size. Little matters loom big, and great matters are sometimes missed because their outlines cannot be seen. . . .

The contemporary, especially if he is a participant, is inside his events, which is not an entirely unmixed advantage. What he gains in intimacy through personal acquaintance—which we can never achieve—he sacrifices in detachment. He cannot see or judge fairly both sides of a quarrel. . . .

SOURCE: Barbara W. Tuchman, *Practicing History* (New York: Knopf, 1981), pp. 27-8.

1. *Into what categories does Ms. Tuchman divide historians?*
2. *What is Ms. Tuchman's concept of the relationship between "current events" and history?*
3. *How can the political and/or religious beliefs of a historian affect what is written as "history"?*

THE LITTER OF THE PAST

Richard Leakey is the son of Mary and the late Louis Leakey, who uncovered the fossil remains of "Zinjanthropus" at Olduvai Gorge in Kenya in 1959. Like his parents, Richard is interested in studying human beginnings and behavior. During the late 1960s, Richard excavated at Lake Rudolph, in northern Kenya, where he found an almost complete skull, which he named "1470."

People have always dropped litter. We see evidence of this all around us, in our city streets and rubbish dumps. Our museums display objects salvaged from the litter of past eras: Roman coins, Egyptian pottery, Ming china, Inca textiles. The list is endless, and each item tells us the same general story: that humans make things, use them, and then dispose of them, either casually as rubbish or occasionally as part of a ceremony such as the burial of an important person.

Litter of the past is the basis of archeology. The coins, the pottery, the textiles and the buildings of bygone eras offer us clues as to how our predecessors behaved, how they ran their economy, what they believed in and what was important to them. What archeologists retrieve from their excavations are images of past lives, but these images are not ready made from the ground: they are pieced together slowly and painstakingly from the information contained in the objects found. Archeology is a detective story in which the principal characters are absent and only a few broken fragments of their possessions remain. Nevertheless it has been possible, in many cases, to fill out the details of the story. We know, for instance, how the Incas operated their highly structured welfare/feudal economy and how the Romans organized their sprawling empire.

Although the detective work involved in reconstructing such civilizations can be difficult, those of us who are concerned with the very early stages of human evolution look with envy at the abundant evidence about these recent periods. One of the outstanding features of human history is the steady increase in the production of objects, such as tools, clothing and artificial shelters. As we search back through time, towards our origins, we find an ever-thinning archeological record. Somewhere between two and three million years ago, human artifacts disappear from the fossil record entirely. The task of discovering what our ancestors did in their daily lives therefore becomes more and more difficult the farther we search into the past.

SOURCE: Richard L. Leakey, *The Making of Mankind* (New York: E. P. Dutton, 1981), p. 76.

1. What characteristics must discarded items have in order to be useful to an archaeologist 100 years from now?
2. What is meant by the statement: "As we search back through time ... we find an ever-thinning archaeological record"?

THE BUILDING OF THE PYRAMID

Herodotus was born at Halicarnassus, a Greek colony in Asia Minor, early in the 5th century B.C. He had an inquiring mind and the ability to write, and set out to record as much as he could about the world in which he lived. Herodotus traveled to Egypt to learn about the marvels of that land, and reported on the pyramids— particularly the one built by Cheops about 2600 B.C.

The pyramid was built in steps, battlement-wise, as it is called, or, according to others, altar-wise. After laying the stones for the base, they raised the remaining stones to their places by means of machines formed of short wooden planks. The first machine raised them from the ground to the top of the first step. On this there was another machine, which received the stone on its arrival, and conveyed it to the second step, whence a third machine advanced it still higher. Either they had as many machines as there were steps in the pyramid, or possibly they had but a single machine, which, being easily moved, was transferred from tier to tier as the stone rose—both accounts are given, and, therefore, I mention both. The upper portion of the pyramid was finished first, then the middle, and finally the part which was lowest and nearest the ground. There is an inscription in Egyptian characters on the pyramid which records the quantity of radishes, onions, and garlic consumed by the labourers who constructed it; and I perfectly well remember that the interpreter who read the writing to me said that the money expended in this way was 1600 talents of silver. If this then is a true record, what a vast sum must have been spent on the iron tools used in the work, and on the feeding and clothing of the labourers, considering the length of time the work lasted, which has already been stated, and the additional time— no small space, I imagine—which must have been occupied by quarrying of the stones, their conveyance, and the cutting of the underground canal.

SOURCE: Herodotus II, 125. In *The Greek Historians*, ed. M. I. Finley (New York: Viking Press, 1960), p. 80.

1. *What do we call the "machines formed of short wooden planks"?*
2. *What technique does Herodotus use to describe the achievement of the pyramid builders? Are his deductions reasonable, given the evidence he cites?*

SONG OF ATON

Akhenaton, a pharaoh of Egypt during the 14th century B.C., instituted a new religion based on worship of the sun, Aton-Re, as the only god. The masses of Egyptian people were opposed to the concept of monotheism. But the Hebrews—who were captives in Egypt at this time—were apparently more receptive to Akhenaton's ideas.

Thou appearest beautifully on the horizon of heaven,
Thou living Aton, the beginning of life!
When thou art risen on the eastern horizon,
Thou hast filled every land with thy beauty.
Thou art gracious, great, glistening, and high over every land;
Thy rays encompass the lands to the limit of all that thou hast made:
As thou art Re, thou reachest to the end of them;
(Thou) subduest them (for) thy beloved son.
Though thou art far away, thy rays are on earth;
Though thou art in their faces, no one knows thy going.

When thou settest in the western horizon,
The land is in darkness, in the manner of death.
They sleep in a room, with heads wrapped up,
Nor sees one eye the other.
All their goods which are under their heads might be stolen,
(But) they would not perceive (it).
Every lion is come forth from his den;
All creeping things, they sting.
Darkness is a *shroud*, and the earth is in stillness,
For he who made them rests in his horizon.

At daybreak, when thou arisest on the horizon,
When thou shinest as the Aton by day,
Thou drivest away the darkness and givest thy rays.
The Two Lands are in festivity every day,
Awake and standing upon (their) feet,
For thou hast raised them up.
Washing their bodies, taking (their) clothing
Their arms are *raised* in praise of thy appearance.
All the world, they do their work. . . .

SOURCE: James B. Pritchard, *Ancient Near Eastern Texts Relating to the Old Testament* (Princeton University Press, 1969), p. 70.

1. *Why has the sun been an object of worship in so many cultures?*
2. *What can you deduce from the line, "All their goods which are under their heads might be stolen"?*
3. *Compare the* Song of Aton *to Psalm 104 in the Bible.*

SOLON ON HAPPINESS

During his travels abroad, the Athenian philosopher Solon was reportedly entertained by Croesus, the king of Lydia in Asia Minor. After showing off his vast treasures, Croesus asked Solon to name the happiest man in the world. In reply, Solon cited the names of several Athenians who had lived modestly and died glorious deaths. Angered by this answer, Croesus asked Solon to explain his reasoning.

Later, Croesus lost his kingdom to the Persians and was taken prisoner by Cyrus. In light of these circumstances, Solon's answer to Croesus acquired new meaning and was widely cited as an example of his wisdom.

"O Croesus," cried [Solon], "you asked a question concerning the condition of man, of one who knows that the god is full of jealousy, and fond of troubling our lot. A long life gives one to witness much, and experience much oneself, that one would not choose. Seventy years I regard as the limit of the life of man. . . . The whole number of days contained in the seventy years will . . . be 26,250, whereof not one but will produce events unlike the rest. Hence man is wholly accident. For yourself, O Croesus, I see that you are wonderfully rich, and are king over many men; but with respect to that on which you questioned me, I have no answer to give, until I hear that you have closed your life happily. For assuredly he who possesses great stores of riches is no nearer happiness than he who has what suffices for his daily needs, unless it so hap that luck attend upon him, and so he continue in the enjoyment of all his good things to the end of life. For many of the wealthiest men have been unfavored of fortune, and many whose means were moderate have had excellent luck. Men of the former class excel those of the latter but in two respects; those last excel in many. The wealthy man is better able to content his desires, and to bear up against a sudden buffet of calamity. The other has less ability to withstand these evils (from which, however, his good luck keeps him clear), but he enjoys all the following blessings: he is whole of limb, a stranger to disease, free from misfortune, happy in his children, and comely to look upon. If, in addition to all this, he ends his life well, he is of a truth the man of whom you are in search, the man who may rightly be termed happy. Call him, however, until he die, not happy but fortunate. Scarcely, indeed, can any man unite all these advantages; as there is no country which contains within it all that it needs, but each, while it posesses some things, lacks others, and the best country is that which contains the most; so no single human being is complete in every respect—something is always lacking. He who unites the greatest number of advantages, and, retaining them to the day of his death, then dies peaceably, that man alone, sire, is, in my judgment, entitled to bear the name of 'happy.' But in every matter it behooves us to mark well the end; for oftentimes the god gives men a gleam of happiness, and then plunges them into ruin."

SOURCE: Herodotus I, 32. In *The Greek Historians*, ed. M. I. Finley (New York: Viking Press, 1960), pp. 42-4.

1. *Why does Solon withhold his judgment of Croesus' life?*
2. *According to Solon, what role does wealth play in determining the quality of a person's life?*

THE WOLVES AND THE SHEEP

The identity of the ancient writer known as Aesop is still a mystery. Herodotus, writing in the 5th century B.C., thought that Aesop had been a slave and had lived in the 6th century B.C. In the 1st century, Petrarch identified the poet as an adviser to Croesus. Most likely, the collection of animal fables known as "Aesop's Tales" were composed by a variety of anonymous authors. "The Wolves and the Sheep" may have been written in the 5th century B.C. as a commentary on the wars that had devastated the Greek world.

After a thousand years of war declared,
The sheep and wolves on peace agreed,
Of which it seems both parties stood in need;
For if the wolves no fleecy wanderer spared,
The angry shepherds hunted them the more,
And skins of wolves for coats in triumph wore.
No freedom either knew,
The harmless sheep or bloody crew;
Trembling they ate, or from their food were driven,
Till peace was made, and hostages were given.
The sheep gave up their dogs, the wolves their young.
Exchange was made, and signed and sealed
By commissaries on the field.
Our little wolves soon after getting strong,
Nay, wolves complete, and longing now to kill,
The shepherd's absence watched with care.
One day, when all within the fold was still,
They worried half the lambs, the fattest there,
And in their teeth into the forest bore.
Their tribes they slyly had informed before.
The dogs, who thought the treaty sure,
Were worried as they slept secure;
So quick that none had time to wail,
For none escaped to tell the tale.

From hence we may conclude—
That war with villains never ought to end.
Peace in itself, I grant, is good,
But what is peace with savages so rude,
Who scoff at faith and stab a peaceful friend?

SOURCE: Aesop, "The Wolves and the Sheep." In *Five Centuries of Illustrated Fables*, selected by J.J. McKendry (Greenwich, Conn.: New York Graphic Society), p. 58.

1. A common element of all "Aesop's fables" is the use of animal characters. What reasons might the author(s) have had to tell their stories through animals?

FUNERAL ORATION OF PERICLES

In 431-430 B.C., Pericles was invited to give a eulogy for the Athenians who had died during the first year of the Peloponnesian War. In his speech, Pericles outlined the unique institutions and character of Athenian democracy, and presented his view of the city's role in the Greek world.

Our constitution does not copy the laws of neighbouring states; we are rather a pattern to others than imitators ourselves. Its administration favours the many instead of the few; this is why it is called a democracy. If we look to the laws, they afford equal justice to all in their private differences; if to social standing, advancement in public life falls to reputation for capacity, class considerations not being allowed to interfere with merit; nor again does poverty bar the way, if a man is able to serve the state, he is not hindered by the obscurity of his condition. . . .

If we turn to our military policy, there also we differ from our antagonists. We throw open our city to the world, and never by alien acts exclude foreigners from any opportunity of learning or observing, although the eyes of an enemy may occasionally profit from our liberality . . . while in education, where our rivals from their very cradles by a painful discipline seek after manliness, at Athens we live exactly as we please, and yet are just as ready to encounter every legitimate danger. . . .

We cultivate refinement without extravagance and knowledge without effeminacy; wealth we employ more for use than for show, and place the real disgrace of poverty not in owning to the fact but in declining the struggle against it. Our public men have, besides politics, their private affairs to attend to, and our ordinary citizens, though occupied with the pursuits of industry, are still fair judges of public matters; for, unlike any other nation, regarding him who takes no part in these duties not as unambitious but as useless.

In short, I say that as a city we are the school of Hellas; while I doubt that the world can produce a man, who where he has only himself to depend upon, is equal to so many emergencies, and graced by so happy a versatility as the Athenian. . . . For Athens alone of her contemporaries is found when tested to be greater than her reputation, and alone gives no occasion for her assailants to blush at the antagonist by whom they have been worsted, or to her subjects to question her title by merit to rule.

SOURCE: Thucydides II, 37-41. In *The Complete Writings of Thucydides*, the unabridged Crawley translation, with introduction by John H. Finley, Jr. (New York: Modern Library), pp. 104-6.

1. *How does Pericles describe the difference between "public" and "private" men in Athenian society?*
2. *How does the Athenian democracy of Pericles' time compare to present-day democratic governments?*
3. *How does Pericles characterize Athens' role in the Greek world?*

DIALOG BETWEEN ATHENS AND MELOS

During the Peloponnesian War (431-404 B.C.), Athens' hegemony over its allies in the Delian League became critical to its war strategy, and the measures that should be taken to control reluctant allies were a subject of much debate.

In 416 B.C., the 16th year of the war, the Athenians decided that they could not allow any of the Greek island states to remain neutral in the war—especially Melos, which had been founded as a Spartan colony. The dialog excerpted below took place as the Melians struggled to maintain their neutrality.

Melians: Your military preparations are too far advanced to agree with what you say, as we see you are come to be judges in your own cause, and that all we can reasonably expect from this negotiation is war, if we prove to have right on our side and refuse to submit, and in the contrary case, slavery. . . .

Athenians: For ourselves, we shall not trouble you with specious pretenses—either of how we have a right to our empire because we overthrew the Mede, or are now attacking you because of wrong you have done us—and make a long speech which would not be believed; in return we hope that you . . . will aim at what is feasible, holding in view the real sentiments of us both; since you know as well as we do that right, as the world goes, is only in question between equals in power, while the strong do what they can and the weak suffer what they must. . . .

Melians: So that you would not consent to our being neutral, friends instead of enemies, but allies of neither side.

Athenians: No; for your hostility cannot so much hurt us as your friendship will be an argument to our subjects of our weakness, and your enmity of our power. . . . As far as right goes, they [our subjects] think one has as much of it as the other, and that if any maintain their independence it is because they are strong, and that if we do not molest them it is because we are afraid . . . the fact that you are islanders and weaker than others rendering it all the more important that you should not succeed in baffling the masters of the sea. . . .

Melians: You may be sure that we are as well aware as you of the difficulty of contending against your power and fortune, unless the terms be equal. But we trust that the gods may grant us fortune as good as yours, since we are just men fighting against unjust. . . .

Athenians: When you speak of the favor of the gods, we may as fairly hope for that as yourselves; neither our pretensions nor our conduct being in any way contrary to what men believe of the gods, or practice among themselves. Of the gods we believe, and of men we know, that by a necessary law of their nature they rule wherever they can. . . .

SOURCE: Thucydides XVII, 86-105. In *The Complete Writings of Thucydides*, the unabridged Crawley edition, with introduction by John H. Finley, Jr. (New York: Modern Library), pp. 330-7.

1. *Do the Athenians cite moral or religious principles to support their demands? On what principle is their argument based?*
2. *What do the Athenians say about the behavior of the gods? How do they characterize the nature of man in comparison?*

THE CAVE

Plato wrote The Republic *to present his concepts of an ideal state. The work is written in the form of a dialog between Socrates, who makes the long comments, and a person named Glaucon, who makes brief responses. In the extract given below, Socrates uses the image of a cave to describe the state of ignorance or partial knowledge in which most people live.*

And now, I said, let me show you in a figure how far our nature is enlightened or unenlightened:—Behold! human beings living in an underground den, which has a mouth open towards the light and reaching all along the den; here they have been from their childhood, and have their legs and necks chained so that they cannot move, and can only see before them, being prevented by the chains from turning round their heads. Above and behind them a fire is blazing at a distance, and between the fire and the prisoners there is a raised way; and you will see, if you look, a low wall built along the way, like the screen which marionette players have in front of them over which they show the puppets.

I see.

And do you see, I said, men passing along the wall carrying all sorts of vessels, and statues and figures of animals made of wood and stone and various materials, which appear over the wall? Some of them are talking, others silent. . . .

Yes, he said.

And if they were able to converse with one another, would they not suppose that they were naming what was actually before them?

Very true.

And suppose further that the prison had an echo which came from the other side, would they not be sure to fancy when one of the passersby spoke that the voice which they heard came from the passing shadow?

No question, he replied.

To them, I said, the truth would be literally nothing but the shadows of the images.

That is certain.

And now look again, and see what will naturally follow if the prisoners are released and disabused of their error. At first, when any of them is liberated and compelled suddenly to stand up and turn his neck around and walk and look towards the light, he will suffer sharp pains; the glare will distress him, and he will be unable to see the realities of which in his former state he had seen the shadows; and then conceive some one saying to him, that what he saw before was an illusion, but that now, when he is approaching nearer to being and his eye is turned toward more real existence, he has a clearer vision,—what will be his reply? And you may further imagine that his instructor is pointing to the objects as they pass and requiring him to name them,—will he not be perplexed? Will he not fancy that the shadows which he formerly saw are truer than the objects as which are shown to him?

Far truer.

And if he is compelled to look straight at the light, will he not have a pain in his eyes which will make him turn away to take refuge in the objects of vision which he can see, and which he will conceive to be in reality clearer than the things which are now being shown to him?

True, he said.

And suppose once more, that he is reluctantly dragged up a steep and rugged ascent, and held fast until he is forced into the presence of the sun himself, is he not likely to be pained and irritated? When he approaches the light his eyes will be dazzled, and he will not be able to see anything at all of what are now called realities.

Not all in a moment, he said.

He will require to grow accustomed to the sight of the upper world. And first he will see the shadows best, next the reflections of men and other objects in the water, and then the objects themselves; then he will gaze upon the light of the moon and the stars and the spangled heaven; and he will see the sky by night better than the sun or the light of the sun by day?

Certainly.

Last of all he will be able to see the sun, and not mere reflections of him in the water, but he will see him in his own proper place, and not in another; and he will contemplate him as he is.

Certainly.

> *Socrates and Glaucon then speculate about a meeting between the cave-dwellers and a person from the outside world: the cave-dwellers would likely despise the newcomer, for his sunblindness would render him unable to see the shadows in the cave. The "newcomer," of course, is comparable to a philosopher, who has a superior vision of reality and truth. Socrates then goes on to describe the role of the philosopher in an ideal state.*

Observe, Glaucon, that there will be no injustice in compelling our philosophers to have a care and providence of others; we shall explain to them that in other States, men of their class are not obliged to share in the toils of politics; and this is reasonable, for they grow up at their own sweet will, and the government would rather not have them. Being self-taught, they cannot be expected to show any gratitude for a culture which they have never received. But we have brought you into the world to be rulers of the hive, kings of yourselves and of the other citizens, and have educated you far better and more perfectly than they have been educated, and you are better able to share in the double duty. Wherefore, each of you, when his turn comes, must go down to the general underground abode, and get the habit of seeing in the dark. When you have acquired the habit, you will see ten thousand times better than the inhabitants of the den, and you will know what the several images are, and what they represent, because you have seen the beautiful and just and good in their truth. And thus our State, which is also yours, will be a reality, and not a dream only, and will be administered in a spirit unlike that of other States, in which men fight with one another about shadows only and are distracted in the struggle for power, which in their eyes is a great good. Whereas the truth is that the State in which the rulers are most reluctant to govern is always the best and most quietly governed, and the State in which they are most eager, the worst.

SOURCE: Plato, *The Republic* (trans. Benjamin Jowett), VII, 514-20. In *Greek Literature in Translation*, ed. George Howe and Gustave Harrer (New York: Harper & Row, 1924), pp. 608-11.

1. *Why do people within the cave look away from the sun and from the objects outside? How do they perceive the real world when they are led outdoors?*
2. *In Plato's ideal state, what role do philosophers play? How does Plato characterize their attitude toward their responsibilities?*

THE THIRD PHILIPPIC

Demosthenes (384-322 B.C.) delivered his first oration against Philip in 351 B.C., just five years after Philip had become king of Macedonia. By the time he delivered his third "Philippic," in 341 B.C., Philip had gained control of much of northern Greece, and was preparing to seize Byzantium, the gateway to the Black Sea area.

Heavens! is there any man in his right mind who would judge of peace or war by words, and not by actions? Surely, no man. To examine then the actions of Philip. . . . The peace he had ratified by the most solemn oaths. And let it not be asked, of what moment is all this? . . .

But farther: when he sends his forces into the Chersonesus, which the king, which every state of Greece acknowledged to be ours; when he confessedly assists our enemies, and braves us with such letters, what are his intentions? for they say that he is not at war with us. For my own part, so far am I from acknowledging such conduct to be consistent with his treaty, that I declare that . . . by his constant recourse to the power of arms, in all his transactions, he has violated the treaty, and is at war with you; unless you will affirm that he who prepares to invest a city is still at peace until the walls be actually assaulted. You cannot, surely, affirm it! He whose designs, whose whole conduct, tends to reduce me to subjection, that man is at war with me, though not a blow hath yet been given, not one weapon drawn. . . .

That Philip, from a mean and inconsiderable origin, hath advanced to greatness; that suspicion and faction divide all the Greeks; that it is more to be admired that he should become so powerful from what he was, than that now, after such accessions of strength, he should accomplish all his ambitious schemes; these and other like points which might be dwelt upon, I choose to pass over. But there is one concession, which, by the influence of your example, all men have made to him, which hath heretofore been the cause of all the Grecian wars. And what is this? an absolute power to act as he pleases, thus to harass and plunder every state of Greece successively. . . .

All Greece, all the barbarian world, is too narrow for this man's ambition. And though we Greeks see and hear all of this, we send no embassies to each other, we express no resentment: but into such wretchedness are we sunk (blocked up within our several cities) that even to this day we have not been able to perform the least part of that which our interest or our duty demanded; to engage in any associations, or to form any confederacies; but look with unconcern upon this man's growing power, each fondly imagining (as far as I can judge) that the time in which another is destroyed is gained to him, without ever consulting or acting for the cause of Greece; although no man can be ignorant, that, like the regular periodic return of a fever, or other disorder, he is coming upon those who think themselves most remote from danger.

SOURCE: Demosthenes, *The Third Philippic*, trans. Thomas Leland (New York: Colonial Press, 1900), pp. 134-7.

1. *In your own words, summarize Demosthenes' opinion of Philip.*
2. *What did Demosthenes think the Greeks should do about the threat of Philip?*

FIRST ORATION AGAINST CATILINE

During the 1st century B.C., the Roman Republic was beset by a series of political crises. One of these crises occurred in 63 B.C., when Catiline, a young Roman nobleman, ran for the office of consul. His campaign promise to cancel all private debts made him popular with poor Romans and also with nobles who, like himself, had squandered their fortunes. After losing the election to Cicero, Catiline plotted to seize the government by force.

In the speech below, Cicero urged Roman senators (the "Conscript Fathers") to take action against Catiline.

And now . . . Conscript Fathers, . . . listen carefully, I pray you, to what I shall say and store it deep in your hearts and minds. For if our country, which is much dearer to me than my life, if all Italy, if all the state should speak to me thus: "Marcus Tullius, what are you doing? This man is a public enemy as you have discovered; he will be the leader of the war, as you see; men are waiting for him to take command in the enemies' camp, as you know: author of crime, head of a conspiracy, recruiter of slaves and criminals—and you will let him go, in such a way that he will seem to be not cast out of the city by you but let loose against the city! Will you not command him to be cast into chains, to be hauled to death, to be punished with the greatest severity? What, pray, hinders you? The custom of our ancestors? But often even private citizens in this state have punished with death dangerous men. Is it the laws which have been enacted regarding the punishment of Roman citizens? But never in this city have those who revolted against the state enjoyed the rights of citizens. Or do you fear the odium of posterity? A fine return you must be making to the Roman people who have raised you, a man distinguished only by your own deeds, and by no achievements of your ancestors . . . if because of the fear of unpopularity or any danger whatever you neglect the safety of your fellow-citizens!

But if that did seriously threaten me, still I have always believed that unpopularity won by uprightness was glory and not unpopularity. And yet there are some in this body who either do not see the disasters which threaten us or pretend that they do not see them; these have fostered the hopes of Catiline by mild measures and they have strengthened the growing conspiracy by not believing in its existence; under their influence many ignorant men as well as villains would be saying that I acted cruelly and tyrannically if I punished Catiline. Now I know that if he arrives in Manlius' camp whither he is now making his way, no one will be so stupid as not to see that a conspiracy has been formed, no one will be so depraved as to deny it. But if this man alone is executed, I know that this disease in the state can be checked for a little time, but it cannot be completely crushed. But if he shall take himself off, if he shall lead out his friends with him and gather together in the same place other derelicts now collected from all sources, not only this plague rampant in the state but even the roots and seeds of all evil will be obliterated and destroyed.

SOURCE: Cicero, *First Oration Against Catiline*, trans. L.E. Lord. In *Portable Roman Reader*, ed. Basil Davenport (New York: Viking Press, 1951), pp. 239–41.

1. *Explain Cicero's ideas about "unpopularity."*
2. *What plan does Cicero suggest to the "Conscript Fathers" for dealing with Catiline?*
3. *Compare Cicero's oration against Catiline to Demosthenes' oration against Philip.*

CICERO'S LETTERS TO ATTICUS

Cicero's letters to his friend Atticus provide much insight into the social and political life of Rome during the last years of the Republic. The letters excerpted below were written during the political crisis of 50-49 B.C., as it appeared increasingly likely that Caesar and Pompey would dissolve their alliance. Like other prominent Romans, Cicero had to decide which man he would support in the event of a civil war.

The final break between Caesar and Pompey came when Caesar led his army across the Rubicon on January 11, 49 B.C. Cicero chose to follow Pompey to the East, but later returned to Rome and received Caesar's pardon.

Formiae, December 17, 50 B.C.

My fears as to the political situation are great. And so far I have found hardly a man who would not yield to Caesar's demand [that both he and Pompey simultaneously give up command of their armies] sooner than fight. That demand is shameless, it is true, but stronger in its appeal than we thought. But why should we choose this occasion to begin resisting? . . . You will say, "What then will your view be?" My view will be not what I shall say; for my view will be that every step should be taken to avoid a conflict, but I shall say the same as Pompey.

Formiae, December 25 or 26, 50 B.C.

Your guess that I should meet Pompey before coming to Rome has come true. On the 25th he overtook me near the Lavernium. We reached Formiae together, and were closeted together from two o'clock until evening. As to your query whether there is any hope of a peaceful settlement, so far as I could tell from Pompey's full and detailed discourse, he does not even wish it. He thinks that the constitution will be subverted if Caesar is elected consul even after disbanding his army; and he reckons that when Caesar hears of the energetic preparations against him, he will give up the idea of the consulship this year and prefer to keep his army and his province. Still, if Caesar should play the fool, Pompey has an utter contempt for him and firm confidence in his own and the state's resources. Well, although the "uncertainty of war" came constantly to my mind, I was relieved of anxiety as I listened to a soldier, a strategist, and a man of the greatest influence discoursing in a statesmanlike manner on the risks of a hollow peace. We had before us a speech of Antony made on December 21, which attacked Pompey's entire life, complained about the condemnation of certain people, and threatened war. Pompey's comment was, "What do you suppose Caesar will do, if he becomes master of the state, when a wretched, insignificant subordinate dares to talk like that?" In a word, Pompey appeared not only not to seek peace, but even to fear it. But I fancy the idea of leaving the city shakes his resolution. What annoys me most is that I have to pay up to Caesar. . . . It is bad form to owe money to a political opponent.

Menturnae, January 22, 49 B.C.

It is a civil war, though it has not sprung from division among our citizens but from the daring of one abandoned citizen. He is strong in military forces, he attracts adherents by hopes and promises, he covets the whole universe. Rome is delivered to him stripped of defenders, stocked with supplies: one may fear anything from one who regards her temples and her homes not as his native land but as his loot. What he will do, and how he will do it, in the absence of senate and magistrates, I do not know. He will be unable even to pretend constitutional methods. But where can our party raise its head, or when? . . . We depend entirely upon two legions that were kept here by a trick and are practically disloyal. For so far the levy has found unwilling recruits, disinclined to fight. But the time of compromise is past. The future is obscure. We, or our leaders, have brought things to such a pass that, having put to sea without a rudder, we must trust to the mercy of the storm.

Formiae, February 8 or 9, 49 B.C.

I see there is not a foot of ground in Italy which is not in Caesar's power. I have no news of Pompey, and I imagine he will be captured unless he has taken to the sea. . . . What can I do? In what land or on what sea can I follow a man when I don't know where he is? In fact, on land, how can I follow, and by sea whither? Shall I then surrender to Caesar? Suppose I could surrender with safety, as many advise, could I do so with honor? By no means. I will ask your advice as usual. The problem is insoluble.

Formiae, March 1, 49 B.C.

I depend entirely on news from Brundisium. If Caesar has caught up with our friend Pompey, there is some slight hope of peace: but if Pompey has crossed the sea, we must look for war and massacre. Do you see the kind of man into whose hands the state has fallen? What foresight, what energy, what readiness! Upon my word, if he refrain from murder and rapine he will be the darling of those who dreaded him most. The people of the country towns and the farmers talk to me a great deal. They care for nothing at all but their lands, their little homesteads, and their tiny fortunes. And see how public opinion has changed: they fear the man they once trusted and adore the man they once dreaded. It pains me to think of the mistakes and wrongs of ours that are responsible for this reaction.

SOURCE: Cicero, *Letters to Atticus* VII, 6, 8, 13, 22; VIII, 13. Loeb Classical Library ed., trans. E.O. Winstedt (Cambridge, Mass. and London: Harvard University Press and William Heinemann Ltd., 1913), Vol. 2, pp. 37, 45-6, 62-3, 89, 161-2.

1. *What is Cicero's attitude toward Caesar? Does his attitude change as Caesar's success appears more certain?*

2. *In Cicero's opinion, who is to be blamed for the crisis?*

Caesar's work **De Bello Gallico** (On the Gallic War) *was essentially a political pamphlet, written for the purpose of advancing Caesar's reputation and political career in Rome. Nevertheless, it provides much valuable information about the early societies of the Gauls and the Germans as well as about the military tactics of the Roman army. Moreover, the book earned Caesar a reputation as one of the greatest writers of the Latin language. In an essay entitled* **Brutus,** *Cicero described Caesar's language as "pure and uncorrupted," and praised his style in these words: "His aim was to furnish others with material for writing history . . . but men of sound judgment he has deterred from writing, since in history there is nothing more pleasing than brevity clear and correct."*

On the Gauls

Throughout Gaul only two classes of men are of any real consequence—the Druids and the baronage. The common people are treated as little better than slaves: they never venture to act on their own initiative, and have no voice in public affairs. Most of them, burdened with debt, crushed by heavy taxation, or groaning under the hand of more powerful men, enter the service of the privileged classes, who exercise over them the rights enjoyed by a master over his slaves.

The Druids are a priestly caste. They regulate public and private sacrifices and decide religious questions. The people hold them in great respect, for they are the judges of practically all inter-tribal as well as personal disputes. They decide all criminal cases, including murder, and all disputes relating to boundaries or inheritance, awarding damages and passing sentence. Any individual or tribe refusing to abide by their decision is banned from taking part in public sacrifices—the heaviest of all their punishments. . . .

The druidical doctrine is commonly supposed to have reached Gaul from its original home in Britain, and it is a fact that to this day men going on for higher studies usually cross to Britain for the purpose. The Druids are exempt from military service and do not pay the same taxes as the rest of the people. Such privileges attract a crowd of students. . . . It is said that these young men have to memorize endless verses, and that some of them spend as long as 20 years at their books; for although the Druids employ Greek characters for most of their secular business . . . they consider it irreverent to commit their lore to writing. I suspect, however, that a double motive underlies this practice—unwillingness to publicize their teaching, and a desire to prevent students relying upon the written word at the expense of memory training; for recourse to text-books almost invariably tends to discourage learning by heart and to dull the powers of memory.

Their central dogma is the immortality and transmigration of the soul, a doctrine which they regard as the finest incentive to courage since it inspires contempt of death. But they also hold frequent discussions on astronomy, physics, and theology, in all which subjects their pupils receive instruction.

The whole baronage takes the field in the event of war—and indeed before my time these outbreaks (aggressive or defensive) might have been described as annual occurrences. Every nobleman is accompanied by his servants and armed retainers, whose greater or less number is an indication of his wealth and rank, and in fact the only recognized criterion of position and authority.

On the Germans
The German institutions are entirely different. They have no Druids to organize religious observances and rarely indulge in sacrifice. They recognize as gods only those visible objects from which they derive obvious benefits—the Sun, for instance, the Moon, and Fire—they have never so much as heard of any others. They spend all their lives in war and the chase, and inure themselves from their earliest years to toil and hardship. Those who retain their chastity longest are held in highest honour by their fellow men; for continence, so they believe, makes a man taller, hardier, more muscular. . . .

The Germans are not agriculturalists: their principal diet is milk, cheese, and meat. They have no landed estates with definite boundaries, but the magistrates and local chiefs make an annual assignment of holdings to clans, groups of kinsmen, and other corporate bodies. . . .

Every German state takes the utmost pride in devastating an area adjacent to its frontier and thereby surrounding itself with the widest possible belt of uninhabited territory. To drive one's neighbor from his land and make it too dangerous for others to settle in the vicinity is considered the essence of greatness as well as a precaution against surprise attack. On the declaration of war a high command is set up and invested with powers of life and death; but in peacetime there is no central government. Justice is administered and disputes settled by various local chiefs. . . .

The Germans have never risen above their ancient standards of poverty and privation; they have never so much as improved their diet and clothing. The Gauls, on the contrary, live close to the Roman Province: they have experience of sea-borne trade, and are plentifully supplied with luxuries in addition to their daily requirements. Yet these same Gauls have become gradually so used to their inferiority, after numerous disasters on the field of battle, that they no longer pretend to rival the martial eminence of Germany.

SOURCE: Caesar, *The Gallic War*, VI. In *Caesar's War Commentaries*, Everyman's Library ed., trans. John Warrington (London: J.M. Dent & Sons Ltd., 1953), pp. 103-7.

1. Based on Caesar's descriptions, how did the religion and political system of the Germans differ from those of the Gauls?
2. In the last paragraph on the Gauls cited above, Caesar makes a reference to himself. How does he describe his impact upon Gaul?

In the first century A.D., the historian Tacitus wrote an account of the Germans which, together with Caesar's commentary, is the most important source of information we have concerning the early history of these peoples. Like Caesar, Tacitus noted that the Germans had a relatively democratic political system in which all of the armed men of the tribe participated. He also described the battle tactics that had made the Germans such formidable adversaries.

They choose their kings by birth, their generals for merit. These kings have not unlimited or arbitrary power, and the generals do more by example than by authority. If they are energetic, if they are conspicuous, if they fight in the front, they lead because they are admired. . . . And what most stimulates their courage is, that their squadrons or battalions, instead of being formed by chance or by a fortuitous gathering, are composed of families and clans. Close by them, too, are those dearest to them, so that they hear the shrieks of women, the cries of infants. They are to every man the most sacred witnesses of his bravery—they are his most generous applauders. The soldier brings his wounds to mother and wife, who shrink not from counting or even demanding them and who administer both food and encouragement to the combatants. . . .

About minor matters the chiefs deliberate, about the more important the whole tribe. Yet even when the final decision rests with the people, the affair is always thoroughly discussed by the chiefs. They assemble, except in the case of a sudden emergency, on certain fixed days, either at new or at full moon; for this they consider the most auspicious season for the transaction of business. . . . Their freedom has this disadvantage, that they do not meet simultaneously or as they are bidden, but two or three days are wasted in the delays of assembling. When the multitude think proper, they sit down armed. Silence is proclaimed by the priests, who have on these occasions the right of keeping order. Then the king or the chief, according to age, birth, distinction in war, or eloquence, is heard, more because he has influence to persuade than because he has power to command. If his sentiments displease them, they reject them with murmurs; if they are satisfied, they brandish their spears. The most complimentary form of assent is to express approbation with their weapons. . . .

When they go into battle, it is a disgrace for the chief to be surpassed in valour, a disgrace for his followers not to equal the valour of the chief. And it is an infamy and a reproach for life to have survived the chief, and returned from the field. To defend, to protect him, to ascribe one's own brave deeds to his renown, is the height of loyalty. The chief fights for victory: his vassals fight for their chief. . . .

It is well known that the nation tribes of Germany have no cities, and that they do not even tolerate closely contiguous dwellings. They live scattered and apart, just as a spring, a meadow, or a wood has attracted them. Their villages they do not arrange in our fashion, with the buildings connected and joined together, but every person surrounds his dwelling with an open space, either as a precaution against the disasters of fire, or because they do not know how to build.

SOURCE: Tacitus, *Germany and Its Tribes*, 7, 11, 14, 16. In *The Complete Works of Tacitus*, Modern Library ed., trans. Alfred Church and William Brodribb (New York: Random House, 1942), pp. 712, 714, 715-7.

1. *How did the assemblies of the Germanic tribes function?*
2. *In Tacitus' time, the role of hereditary kings in German societies was becoming less important, while military chiefs were gaining authority and prestige. Eventually, the new alignment of loyalties led to the system known as feudalism that predominated in the Middle Ages. How does Tacitus characterize the relationship between chiefs and vassals?*

CARACALLA AND THE GERMANS

The emperor Augustus originally planned to safeguard the northern boundaries of the Roman Empire by conquering and resettling Germanic territories as far east as the Black Sea area. This campaign failed, however, and the presence of hostile Germanic tribes remained a problem for all of Augustus' successors.

The historian Dio Cassius described the behavior of the Germanic tribes that the emperor Caracalla encountered. Like other emperors, Caracalla attempted to bribe the Germans when military tactics failed.

Caracalla waged war also against the Cenni, a Germanic tribe. These warriors are said to have assailed the Romans with the utmost fierceness, even using their teeth to pull from their flesh the missiles with which the Osroëni wounded them, so that they might have their hands free for slaying their foes without interruption. Nevertheless, even they accepted a defeat in name in return for a large sum of money. . . .

Many also of the people living close to the ocean itself near the mouths of the Albis sent envoys to him asking for his friendship, though their real purpose was to get money. This was made clear by the fact that, when he had done as they desired, many attacked him, threatening to make war, and yet he came to terms with all of them. . . . The gold that he gave them was of course genuine, whereas the silver and the gold currency that he furnished to the Romans was debased. . . .

SOURCE: Dio Cassius, *Roman History* LXXVIII, 14. Loeb Classical Library ed., Vol. 9, trans. Earnest Cary (Cambridge, Mass. and London: Harvard University Press and William Heinemann Ltd., 1927), pp. 313, 315.

1. *What disadvantages arose from the Roman policy of bribing Germanic tribes to accept peace settlements?*

THOUGHTS

Marcus Aurelius, emperor of Rome from 161 to 180 A.D., adopted the principles of Stoicism when he was a young man. Because of his strong convictions, he became known as the "philosopher-king" of Roman emperors, but was forced to spend most of his time in military campaigns. While leading Roman troops along the Danube, he wrote a series of philosophical statements which were later published under the title Meditations: *the quotation below is one of these statements.*

Begin the morning by saying to thyself, I shall meet with the busybody, the ungrateful, arrogant, deceitful, envious, unsocial. These are so by the reason of their ignorance of what is good and evil. But I who have seen the nature of the good, that it is beautiful, and of the bad, that it is ugly, and the nature of him who does wrong, that he is akin to me, not only of the same blood and origin, but that he participates in the same intelligence and the same portion of divinity, I can neither be injured by any of those I meet, for no one can fix on me what is ugly, nor can I be angry with my kinsman, nor hate him. For we are made for cooperation, like feet, like hands, like eyelids, like the rows of the upper and lower teeth. To act against one another then is contrary to nature; and it is acting against one another to be vexed and to turn away. . . .

If thou workest at that which is before thee, following right reason seriously, vigorously, calmly, without allowing anything else to distract thee, but keeping thy divine part pure, as if thou shouldst be bound to give it back immediately; if thou holdest to this, expecting nothing, fearing nothing, but satisfied with the present activity according to nature, and with heroic truth in every word and sound which thou utterest, thou wilt live happy. And there is no man who is able to prevent this.

SOURCE: Marcus Aurelius, *Thoughts.* In *Readings in European History*, vol. 1, ed. J.H. Robinson (New York: Ginn and Co., 1904), p. 17.

1. *What is Aurelius' attitude toward those who "do wrong"?*
2. *Why does he consider himself to be impervious to injury or bad fortune?*

OF GOD'S GOVERNMENT

In the 5th century, as Rome fell prey to Germanic invaders, many Romans debated why their proud and ancient civilization was unable to withstand the onslaught. Some blamed Rome's weakness on Christianity. Others, like Salvian, a Christian priest, believed that God was punishing Romans for their evil ways. In his work Of God's Government, *written about 440, he argued that Roman citizens had become morally inferior to the Germanic peoples who were attacking them.*

In what respects can our customs be preferred to those of the Goths and Vandals, or even compared with them? And first, to speak of affection and mutual charity (which our Lord teaches is the chief, saying, "By this shall all men know that ye are my disciples, if ye have love one for another"), almost all the barbarians, at least those who are of one race and kin, love each other, while the Romans persecute each other. For what citizen does not envy his fellow-citizen? What citizen shows to his neighbor full charity? . . .

Even those in a position to protest against the iniquity which they see about them dare not speak lest they make matters worse than before. So the poor are despoiled, the widows sigh, the orphans are oppressed, until many of them, born of families not obscure, and liberally educated, flee to our enemies that they may no longer suffer the oppression of public persecution. They doubtless seek Roman humanity among the barbarians, because they cannot bear barbarian inhumanity among the Romans. And although they differ from the people to whom they flee in manner and in language; although they are unlike as regards the fetid odor of the barbarians' bodies and garments, yet they would rather endure a foreign civilization among the barbarians than cruel injustice among the Romans.

So they migrate to the Goths, or to the Bagaudes or to some other tribe of the barbarians who are ruling everywhere, and do not regret their exile. For they would rather live *free* under an appearance of slavery than live as captives under an appearance of liberty. The name of Roman citizen, once so highly esteemed and so dearly bought, is now a thing that men repudiate and flee from . . . .

SOURCE: Salvian, *Of God's Government*. In *Readings in European History*, Vol. 1, ed. J.H. Robinson (New York: Ginn, 1904), pp. 28-9.

1. *In Salvian's opinion, why were Roman citizens moving to the regions controlled by Germanic tribes?*
2. *What types of conduct is Salvian referring to in the phrases "Roman humanity" and "barbarian inhumanity"?*

Index